The Spirit of the Age

DAVID SELBOURNE

THE SPIRIT OF THE AGE

SINCLAIR-STEVENSON

First published in Great Britain by Sinclair-Stevenson Limited
An imprint of Reed Consumer Books Limited
Michelin House, 81 Fulham Road, London SW3 6RB
and Auckland, Singapore and Toronto

Index by Frank Dunn

A CIP catalogue record for this book
is available from the British Library.
ISBN 1 85619 204 0

Typeset by CentraCet, Cambridge

Printed in Great Britain by
St Edmundsbury Press Limited
Bury St Edmunds, Suffolk

For ARNOLD GOODMAN

CONTENTS

Di doman non c'è certezza

Lorenzo de' Medici

AUTHOR'S NOTE

This is an alternative, Jewish history of our
times. I have written it because I have not found
in other accounts what I was myself seeking.
These will also be years in which, for better and
worse, nation, ethnicity and religion will play a
larger part. If Muslims and Christians increasingly stake their intellectual claims to a deeper
(or superior) understanding of the age, then so
must the Jew, whether he wishes to or not.
Such compulsions have always existed, and with
temerity I have responded to them.

D. S.

ONE

In the Air

The world's population is rising towards 6 billion at the rate of some 250,000 or more a day – or three new lives per second. It is a rate to give pause to any true humanist, save one who believed blindly that contraception was wicked. Mankind might have been bidden in Genesis to 'increase and multiply', but God too can be wrong. Not even Judaic scruple, which recoils by moral intuition both from abortion and euthanasia, can stand in the way of the thought that it is not contraception but teeming prodigality in human reproduction which is *contra naturam*.

Our myriads have grown six-fold in two hundred years; but they have grown by almost 50 per cent, from 4 million, in the last twenty. It is a rate of acceleration far beyond most earlier projections. Epidemic disease and other catastrophe allowing, there could be a total of 10 billion people on the planet within the lifetimes of today's children, or 'by 2050', according to a joint statement issued in February 1992 by the US Natural Academy of Sciences and the Royal Society of London. A minority of demographers even believes this figure could be reached earlier, yet it is not long since '10 billion' was a projected population total for the end of the twenty-second century. In the next ten years alone, there could be one new China (which counted no fewer than 1.158 billion citizens in 1991) to feed. By this time, the urban populations of the 'developing' countries will have reached twice the total of the urban populations of the 'developed'. One quarter of all Mexicans already live in Mexico City, which emits over 4 million tons of pollutants over itself per annum; in the next quarter century, the population of Africa, disease permitting, is expected to double. By the century's end, Bangladesh, which is roughly the size of England, could have a population of 150 million, and Nigeria – its oil exhausted – 160 million or more.

According to the United Nations, armed conflicts since 1945, of which there have been about one hundred, have claimed an estimated 20 million lives, or an average of 30,000–40,000 per month. It is a mere bagatelle against such exponential population increases. They already make it difficult or impossible for many Third World countries to feed themselves, while the 'developed' nations consume annually 80 per cent of the world's available food and other resources. There are more than one billion people in the world without access to safe water; to be without water at all (and to be dependent for food on imports, including basic cereals) will be another matter. In forty years, water consumption in the world has doubled. It will double again in the next decade.

As for the suffering of humanity from disease, poor health and malnutrition – which affects 'over 1 billion people', or one in five of the world population – from 'destitution' ('over 1 billion'), and from illiteracy ('890 million', or more), the orders of magnitude, even if they were wrong by a factor of two, are so large as to cripple judgment; each year, according to the WHO, nearly 13 million children in the developing countries die before they reach the age of five. To absorb such matters intellectually is impossible. Moreover, there will always be the healthy sceptic, as well as the indecent cynic, who disbelieves all such statistics and projections; even a decent man could be forgiven for wondering whether they were magnified by anxiety or the desire for sensation. Nevertheless, the enormities which these statistics contain are real. They are not in the category of Methuselah's 'nine hundred and sixty nine years', which, like resurrection from the dead, is beyond all possibility of rational belief. They are, rather, the data, however imperfectly recorded, of the truly human; the mark of man, creator and destroyer, architect of wonders and skilled life-taker, cunningly prescient yet fecund with barely a thought for the morrow.

To assert a determined lack of purpose and foresight in much of the action of *homo sapiens* is a vulgar commonplace. But it has never been on such a scale. The population of Greater Tokyo is over 30 million. Nearly 60 per cent of New Yorkers, so surveys have suggested, want to leave their city, the site of over 2,000 murders a year. On the one hand, the tribal, the nomadic, and the peasant ways of life are assailed and eroded; on the other, the teeming metropolis, centre of the world's sophistications and magnet for the impoverished, turns increasingly to nightmare. The inner city was once the hub of the civic culture, place of the forum, meeting place and market. At its best, its civic architecture matched its civic functions, and helped induce a sense, even, of civic splendour and virtue. Now, in some societies, the city's very heart has become a wasteland. In others, where it has not, the forshadowings are often evident, the indices telling. Historically, violence is a constant of city life, as is dereliction and re-foundation, and even feral gangs of predators are nothing new; conurbation and conflict, market and mayhem, are everywhere inscribed in the human record. Satiety with the city, and a longing for the countryside – the desire for an idyllic refuge – are common poetic themes, including among the ancient Greeks and Romans.

But the madding crowd (from which the madding crowd itself attempts to flee) now totals over 5 billion. Some Third World cities, with their vast shanty-town peripheries, are swelling towards 15, 20 and 30 million inhabitants each; the mass urban environment of the 'developed' world is becoming impoverished in complex ways beyond the capacity of any latter-day Gustave Doré to picture. The foul Victorian 'rookeries' of London, as in St Giles, were dirty, overcrowded, disease-ridden, and done away with. But the birds have not flown. In denser clusters than ever, they, or we, have merely re-grouped elsewhere (or in the same place), darkening the sky with our numbers as never before.

Into the city, as always, presses the throng of workers, pleasure-seekers, hopeful job-hunters, criminals and – not only in the Third World – the poor, the hungry and homeless. Out of it again, struggle the suburban home-goers, the weary, the increasingly scared (or neurasthenic), the rich, and the defeated or disillusioned. In this maelstrom there is increasing pressure and increasing depression. The very mood of the buildings of many of our cities reflects the sense of over-use, anonymity, exhaustion. From the days of post-war austerity and slum clearance, East and West, millions of citizens have been left a legacy, greyly egalitarian, of mean ideas, a pinched vision and poor materials, a legacy which stands drab guard over the spirit; it colours, or fails to colour, the daily coming-and-going of huge numbers of individuals. Workers were resettled and rehoused, East and West, from Liverpool to Leipzig, in the same kinds of drear proletarian setting: welfare made concrete. High-rise bunkers for a short while elevated the hopes of those who lived in them. But they swiftly became, and remain, for the most part prisons. Nor is it only their inhabitants who suffer. Those who merely pass them by, day by day, experience their own sinking and mortification of spirit, a sinking which cannot be measured. But who can doubt that millions, and tens of millions, howl against what they see, in silence?

The mass moving away, or flight, including the end-of-day flight, from the saturated cities of the First World, and the equally mass moving towards them in the Third, are only part of the restless ebb-and-flow of human motion of the age. But the fixities of endeavour in this vortex are also plain. The aspiration which underlies much of the *perpetuum mobile* – the will to self-improvement or the pursuit of self-interest – is precisely that which Adam Smith celebrated. Even on a dung-heap or at the Day of Judgment man's eyes, like the ant's jaws, would be set to the task before him. So it is that prodigious effort to rebuild and revive the worn-out and ransacked places of human habitation continues, in a fashion fit for Judaic awe. Against the natural processes of vacation-by-decay, economic failure or shifts of population, against damage by war, civil insurrection, vandalism or natural disaster, *homo faber*, indefatigable and with his will intact, returns heroically to the scene of dereliction armed with the instruments of reconstruction. Even an entire ant-hill, crushed underfoot as at Hiroshima or Nagasaki, will be remade; the pock-marks of lesser war are quickly hidden, the craters filled, the dead interred.

But destruction cannot always be made good; Pompeii's overwhelming was too great to be repaired. Dresden, once the 'Florence of the Elbe', barely survived – aesthetically or civically – the combined effects of Allied bombing and communist reconstruction. It is as difficult to envisage the reconstitution of the ravaged slums of New York into a flourishing citizen-order, as to imagine Calcutta, with its patches and sores, turned into a new Jerusalem shining beside the Hooghly. Some cities, against the odds, sustain themselves and the spirits of those who live in them despite every depredation; but no megalopolis can maintain the civic order which once dwelt in them. Yet, many East European cities, thought to have been reduced forever to lassitude and silence under the weight of communism's collective depression, have seemingly sprung to life on the rebound, casting aside their grave-clouts as if they had never worn them.

Such resilience is more obvious still in certain parts of rural Eastern Europe, where village life – the life of the domestic hearth, family farm-work and community worship – has survived the worst that could be done to it. There, it is as if the collectivist tornado, which sought to grub up the elements of a truly social existence, had never passed across the landscape. The ambition of the *Communist Manifesto* to 'combine agriculture with manufacturing', and 'gradually to abolish the distinction between town and country', was purest hubris. In many countries it did its worst (before nemesis overtook it), placing satanic mills in green and pleasant land from Poland to Bulgaria. Now, these proletarian totems of 'progress' stand like marooned juggernauts, or rusting Leviathans, in their polluted rural settings. As in the West's weariest cities, their very presence reduces the most Job-like of spirits. They provoke a recoil from that which human instinct knows to be an outrage against man and nature; they set off in the soul both the desire for flight and an unnameable feeling of anger. Like much else (and much worse) done in the name of socialism and the 'interests of the people', the desire to 'vanquish' Nature was beyond forgiveness. Jews, like the ancient Greeks, know that in some circumstances forgiveness is not strength but cowardice and moral weakness.

Yet, rural spoliation by socially and economically destructive forms of industrial development and urbanisation, the dislocation of community, and the disruption of settled ways of productive life are not the hallmarks of failed socialist intentions alone. Since the turn of the century, the discomfiture, uprooting and urbanisation – later suburban-isation – of rural communities in the United States have advanced rapidly. In 1950, 44 per cent of Americans lived on farms and in small towns. Four decades later, the figure had almost halved to around 23 per cent, and the process continues; some areas of Iowa, at the rural heart of the United States, registered a 17 per cent fall in population during the 1980s.

The abandonment of small farms, the disappearance of peasantries, the turning over of agricultural land to building, the growth of big-farm agglomerations, the arrival of nature-seeking second-home owners and the conversion of once-working rural villages into dormitory towns and even into suburbs of cities, are the features of a common pattern. But they are also part of the flow and counter-flow, greater in scale with each year that passes, of human migration. In the First World it has produced vast suburban accretions of population, bidding fair to do the *Communist Manifesto*'s work for it. In the Third it has produced pullulating *bustees*, shanty-towns and *favelas*, crowded now with tens of millions of the uprooted. In both cases, the core of the city – whether in good physical order or in breakdown – becomes a civic failure, either too big or too depressed for community, or overwhelmed by the impermanence of an asocial population. The outer or suburban ring becomes a displacement camp for migrants, both rich and poor, from the countryside or the city.

This aspect of the accelerating movement of peoples may be regarded

as largely involuntary, being propelled by pressure of economic circumstance, by dispersal of community and family, even (as in the case of
New York and certain other cities) by centrifugal responses to the fear
of urban violence. Somewhat different in nature, but similar in many of
its consequences, is the lemming-like hypermobility – sometimes merely
pleasure-seeking – of an increasingly large part of the world's population, mainly but not exclusively in the 'advanced' industrial countries.
Unlike those historic forms of human movement to which a fully
rational purpose can be ascribed – movement driven by the desire for
conquest, the fear of neighbours, the duty of pilgrimage, the quest for a
market, the search for instruction – this century has witnessed a
prodigious increase in what appears to be the habit of motion for its
own sake, motion in ever widening circles, motion at ever increasing
speeds.

In 1914, H. G. Wells, in his *An Englishman Looks at the World*, saw
clearly that the 'speeding up and cheapening of travel, and the increase
in its swiftness and comfort' would 'go on steadily, widening experience'. This was prophecy but, not being Jewish, was both too bland and
over-optimistic. What Wells could not see, or preferred as a socialist
not to see, was that the increasingly universal desire to escape the
'masses' and 'get away from it all' on an increasingly overcrowded
planet would lead merely to confrontation with them – our own *alter
ego*s – elsewhere; only the most privileged on their private islands can
(temporarily) refute John Donne's admonition. Nor could Wells know
or say that the widening of experience to which he referred would
derive for millions from an increasingly aerial-borne, but still leaden-
footed or bison-like, movement along certain, increasingly dusty, global
pathways. To say that such tracks were 'well-beaten' would no longer
describe the matter.

Annually, some 300 to 400 million 'tourists' now travel 'abroad' in
the world – before the Second War there were only about one million –
with at least another 'four or five' times as many travelling in their own
countries. A total of 2 billion people or more are thus in transit in the
world each year; in the next two decades this already huge figure may
double. (Moreover, such estimates cannot take into full account the
billions of miles logged each year by the globe's half a billion car
owners; 25,000 miles per car-owner per annum is an average figure in
many Western industrial countries). By 2000, tourism is expected to be
by turnover the world's largest industry, exceeding in value every kind
of manufacture. Today, more money is already made from tourism than

from the world trade in raw materials, iron, steel, ores and minerals. In Australia, for example, tourism has replaced wool as the country's main revenue-earner; in Britain it is worth £15 to £20 billion a year. Entire national economies – including such European economies as those of Spain and Italy – are greatly dependent upon it. Given the projected volumes of 'tourism' to come, the dependency must grow still greater.

In certain countries the impact is already overwhelming. On average, 108 visitors enter Notre Dame cathedral in Paris for each minute it is open: an unholy 11 million a year. (A mere 2 million visitors a year invade the Tower of London.) 51 million tourists visited Czechoslovakia in the first year of its political freedom, more than three times the total of its population. The Mediterranean littoral, home to 130 million people, is assailed each year by 100 million tourists. By the year 2025, at present rates of increase, this figure may have arisen to a now unimaginable 700 millions per annum. 'Tomorrow,' God warned Pharoah, 'will I bring the locusts into thy coast.' On the Mediterranean coast, too, a biblical plague of tourists will 'cover the face of the earth', 'filling every house' and eating the fruit of 'every tree which groweth'.

Because of damage by visitors from attrition, access to the Parthenon is already restricted, the prehistoric caves at Lascaux have been closed (and a replica with fake frescoes constructed nearby), and the solitary Pennine Way, tramped much of the year into a black ooze, is now 50 yards wide in places. Venice, with its population reduced to less than 80,000, is each year besieged by from 6 to 8 million tourists. Choking on the size of the influx, it has on at least one occasion shut its gates entirely. So, too, did parts of the English Lake District in June 1989 and of the New Forest in June 1992 when they seized up with traffic. On an average August day in Benidorm, once a small Costa Brava fishing village of lemon and olive groves, there are to be found tens of thousands of tourists, the majority of them British. Elsewhere on the Costa Brava, in Tenerife, Majorca, Ibiza, Corfu and other Greek islands – and in The Gambia, in Mauritius, in the Seychelles, and in remoter tropic places still – nothing could now restore the household gods. In the 'high season', the *genius loci* of the Piazza della Signoria, the Taj Mahal and Pompeii, Stonehenge, St Mark's Square and the Alhambra, hides its head. The European Parliament has even been driven to appeal for the curtailment of skiing in the Alps, to which over 50 million people have recourse each year. Without such curtailment the Alps, where there are now no fewer than 14,000 ski lifts and 40,000 ski runs, risk being 'trodden to death'.

The flow of people arrives at, and leaves from, this or that point of mass embarkation and holiday return, encroaching upon and receding from place as do the tides upon the shore. As millions briefly flee their own cities – paradigm of that permanent flight to which so many citizens aspire – so other millions briefly flock to them. New York alone receives from 17 to 20 million visitors a year. The search for a change of air or scene, for respite and repose, has now attained the scale of an organic and all-consuming force. Like other volumes (of population, of indigence, of mouths-to-feed), the statistics of it are satiating and beyond full intellectual grasp. The innocent 'seaside' visits of our childhoods, unharmed and unharming, seem to have occurred on some other planet. The hapless spoiling of the very resources the visitor has come to see; the moving-on from that which is despoiled to the 'still unspoiled' and more exotic; the local pressures not to disclose the degree of spoliation for fear of deterring others from continuing the spoil – all make up a now irreversible folly.

'The sole cause of man's unhappiness,' wrote Pascal, 'is that he does not know how to stay quietly in his room.' But in man's search today for a last resort there is much that is dangerous too. In swift and random mass itineration – no travels of Ulysses these – lies disillusion (and even anger) at the bliss unfound in distant places, as well as nearer home. When Western detritus bestrews even the Himalayas, now visited each year by half a million tourists, what then of Wells' 'widened experience'? The logic of our disappointment is to find repose in Pascal's room, or Voltaire's garden. Instead, the gyrations of one man are a goad to the next. The already beaten path is the path most commonly followed; teeming exodus and swarming influx – a perpetual going out and coming in – are the marks of times which have been maddened into continuous motion. From vivid days of childhood reading, when a favourite book was full of wonders, I recall illustrations from the ('racist') tale of *Little Black Sambo*. They showed tigers circling a tree, running round it ever faster until they turned first to a mere blur of yellow and then into a pool of melted butter.

Yet, such motion – there are 30 million visits 'abroad' by Britons every year – has many aspects. There is more to it than merely the transformed (and often reduced) quality of local inhabitants' lives, or, say, the urbanisation of coastlines, and other forms of environmental depression; more than merely the corruption of human relations when, at its plebeian worst, 'tourism' brings with it a propensity to brawling and violence. Over a century and a half ago, De Tocqueville had already found in democratic America what he called an 'all-pervading and restless activity'; in the 1830s 'everything' was already 'in constant motion'. Some eighty years later, Wells remarked on that motion's 'increasing swiftness'. Some eighty years later again, hundreds of millions are each year in the air. New and improved means of transportation – which, with new means of communication, are the most revolutionary of all changes in human affairs – have torn men from their moorings, turned travel into a giant 'industry', and created in much of mankind an urge to 'save time' by getting everywhere, or anywhere, faster. Like Puck in *A Midsummer Night's Dream*, Everyman may now circle the globe in (relatively speaking) the twinkling of an eyelid.

The consequences are even larger than they seem. Such headlong itineration has brought with it a diminishing sense of movement. It has paradoxically reduced awareness of cultural difference; it launches and lands millions in circumstances with which their minds and bodies cannot deal, or hardly. It also takes the insouciant, the well-fed and the long-lived in their hundreds of thousands, and even millions, to places of poverty and hardship, where the waiter's expectation of life (as in The Gambia) may be thirty years less than the diner's. The language of 'tourism' has also helped to corrupt perception. Holidays are now 'sold' by the million; tourists themselves are a market; and travel is a 'product' which the customer is induced to 'buy'. This is not only the language of 'industry' and driven by an industrial logic, but an industry which bids to be the world's largest. Moreover its 'product', like any other and more than most, is subject to the whirling dictates of fashion. The brochures are full each year of 'new' destinations. From year to year, Turkey or Tuscany or Thailand are in, or not in, vogue. Indeed, the citizen is no longer even on holiday. He is instead consuming an industry's latest product.

All this, however, is only part of the ever grosser restlessness of an overpopulated planet. If the movements of its inhabitants were to be analysed, plotted, turned into 'flow charts', it would be shown to be more akin to a mass swarming. From east to west, from south to north, come the peoples by the millions: Hispanics (perhaps 10 million in the last decade) into the United States, Maghreb Arabs into Western Europe, Central Europeans moving westwards, Africans moving northwards, Jews moving to Israel, and so on. There have been mass movements of peoples throughout history, migrations of millions out of need, out of fear, out of compulsion. Migrant labour, indentured labour, transported slave labour, have helped build empires, including the British Empire, from the times of the Pharaohs. The United States' economy was founded upon the labour of the slave, just as in our own times much of the wealth of the oil-rich Arab countries is being created by foreign, migrant and indentured labour. From Italy, from Ireland, from the Pale of Settlement – flowing from east to west – the poor moved to seek their fortunes. From north to south and east, in more intrepid times than these, the colonising British set out to tame and loot the 'savage'. From west to east, Hitler and his myrmidons moved for 'living space'; from Rome and Athens, Tartary and Constantinople, conquerors and their armies ranged their various worlds to every point of the compass.

But there has never been such movement as now. The compulsive daily stirrings of hundreds of millions of car-owners, the journeyings to and fro of commuters, the mass wanderings of tourists make past ages immobile by contrast. 'Homegoing' brings ethnic Germans from the former Soviet Union, Poland and Romania to the Federal Republic, 'homegoing' carries Jews to Israel. 'Asylum-seeking' – from the Horn of Africa, Iran, Iraq, Turkey, Sri Lanka and many other countries – brings waves of flight from Third World despotism, political upheaval and internecine violence. Expulsion of minorities, as of the Asians from Uganda or the Turks from Bulgaria, sets other hundreds of thousands in motion; pressure of African famine, poverty and unemployment, the collapse of socialist economies, or the lure of universal television, bring millions and tens of millions to leave their native lands. On television, as the Albanian Ismail Kadare has written, 'the nomad in the desert can see green fields, the starving can see cattle, the oppressed liberty'.

Here, the gradual dissolution of a whole country, as in the case of the former Yugoslavia, can propel the flow of peoples; there, the refusal or unwillingness of indigenous populations to do their own work – as in the United Kingdom in the 1960s, or in the Gulf sheikhdoms from the 1930s – brings immigrants to do it for them, as permanent settlers or 'guest workers'. Here, the displaced seek shelter; there, the victim is (or is not) given refuge. Turks in Germany, Algerians in France, Moroccans in Belgium, Pakistanis in Britain, Vietnamese in Hong Kong and Malaysia, Cambodians in Thailand, Cubans in Florida, Palestinians in Detroit, Bangladeshis in London speak, in their different tongues, to the turmoils and pressures of the planet. Seven million Afghans, two million Angolans and Mozambicans, one million Vietnamese, a third of a million Cambodians fled their various wars. The stranger at the gate has become a host.

No pressure, demographic and moral, is greater than that of swelling populations staring, as in Central America or North Africa, through the ring-fence of a nearby well-being. The population of Africa stands at around 650 million, and is accelerating; the population of Europe, excluding Russia, is some 500 million, and is static, or declining. (In 1950, Africa had half the population of Europe.) By the year 2020, epidemic disease permitting – an unlikely grace – the population of Africa could be as high as 1.5 billion. The purchasing power of the 'average citizen' of the European Community is already estimated to be seven or eight times that of the 'average' African. But by the year 2000 there will be some 300 million Africans – well over half the total projected population of Europe at the century's end – aged between fifteen and twenty-four, the commonest age of migration; and perhaps as many as 100 million, one-fifth of the entire population of Europe, unemployed in North Africa alone, where some two-thirds of the under twenty-fives are already estimated to be jobless.

There is a clear (and natural) correlation between population growth and those countries which are 'migrant exporting'; this term of art is as much an industrial analogue as the new vocabulary of mass tourism. Algeria, Egypt, Nigeria, Mexico, Haiti, Indonesia and India, all of whose populations are expected (by some demographers) to rise by a huge 50 per cent in the next twenty years, can be expected to reach their migratory bursting-points together. More than three-quarters of Algeria's population is under the age of thirty; one thousand Central Americans, most of them Mexicans crossing the Rio Grande, already enter the United States every day.

Again the totals tire and the prospects bewilder. If, for example, the force of Islamic fundamentalism were to continue to make ground in the Maghreb – to go no further – then a greater flight of refugees from its rigours into France, Spain, Italy and beyond could be expected, adding to every existing pressure. Yet it is apt, too, to judge those same migratory forces (product of restlessness, of need, of anxiety) as irresistible, part of the tide in human affairs which, at the last, no human effort can govern. In Eastern Europe, the desire for migration had so mounted in the very heart of the communist order that no counter-force on earth could in the end have baulked it. When Hungary opened its borders with Austria in September 1989, effectively raising the Iron Curtain, men, women and children appeared almost on the instant; and, as if charmed by a continent-wide Pied Piper, flowed wherever there was passage. Dammed-up migratory pressures (and the desire to travel) had helped bring down an empire. The attempt to prevent citizens leaving the land where they had 'chanced to be born' was *ab initio* foolish. Such prohibition merely spoke for their rulers' own perception: that 'this country is bad, and so poorly governed, that we forbid any man to leave it, for fear lest everyone should leave it,' as Voltaire mordantly put it in his own times. No such prohibition, then or now, can succeed. The pressure to move, when it becomes strong enough, cannot be stayed.

During and since the fall of communism, new (and old) migrations have continued from the former Soviet Union and Eastern Europe to Western Europe and beyond, including to Australia, Canada, Israel, South Africa and the United States. In these migrations – less in spate than some feared – there was movement from east to west within a reconstructed Germany; egress, and attempted egress, from Albania, Bulgaria and Romania into neighbouring central European and West European countries, including Austria, Greece, Italy and Yugoslavia; flights, under pressure of civil war, from Yugoslavia into Hungary, Italy, Germany, Sweden, Austria and other countries. During the failed Moscow coup of August 1991, Russians even sought refuge in Poland; Polish gypsies fled harassment into Sweden; clandestine immigration brought Bulgarians, Romanians, gypsies and others across all Germany's borders.

Among the most publicised of these migrations was the rapid exodus of hundreds of thousands of Soviet Jews to Israel, after the relaxation of restrictions on their emigration in 1989. (Estimates of the total Jewish population in the Soviet Union at the fall ranged from 1.5 to 3.5 million.) This exodus, which saw the number of arrivals in Israel sometimes running at 700 a day, recalled that from 1881 to 1905, when one million Jews left Russia and Poland with greater, but not dissimilar, fears. In addition, some 15,000 Ethiopian Jews were flown to Israel; thousands of other Jews left the Soviet Union for other destinations, including the United States and Germany. Today, these 'wandering Jews' no longer stand out for special scorn, when so many individuals are on the move. Rather, it is as if much of the world, the Palestinians included, had become Jews and was searching for its quietus.

But such quietus is harder to find, the scale of the need prodigious, the instinct for human generosity outrun by the strains put upon it. Hostility to the stranger – too loosely termed 'racism' – is in the air. The flux of peoples has become daunting; local anxiety, confusion and disorder accompany them as they go. In New York over one in three of its citizens, or ostensible citizens, is foreign-born, and approaching one half are 'non-white'. By the year 2000, the city is expected to be 60 per cent black, Asian and Hispanic. The influx into the United States during the last decade, the biggest since the first years of the century, has been so great that one-third of America's recent national population growth is attributable to migrants. In parts of major conurbations in some states, such as Florida or California – where only 58 per cent of the population is white – English has become a minority language.

The population of Washington is now over 70 per cent black. In two generations 'white Americans' could well be in a minority in the United States. This would be a second great historical reversal: a nation of white settlers which had put much of its original indigenous population to the sword, and founded its economy upon the labour of the black slave, would have been itself ethnically overtaken. There would be a species of Hebraic justice in such reversal, even if it is no more than part of the great rolling tide of human upheaval. But it also represents a dangerous sea-change whose outcome is likely to be increasingly violent. The scale of such demographic flux is much less in Europe, but its effects are growing. Ten million of the French population (of some 58 million) is classed as of 'recent French origin', a figure which includes the French-born children of immigrants. One in four Viennese school-children is now non-Austrian; more than one in three in the London borough of Brent is from an 'ethnic minority'; one in four of the population of Brussels is said to be 'foreign'. There are unknown numbers, certainly several millions, of illegal immigrants, mainly from the Maghreb, in Western Europe; it is estimated (by some) that there are 'a quarter of a million' illegal immigrants living in the Paris area alone.

There are also said to be 14 million legal immigrants in Western Europe, and large annual increases in those seeking asylum: to around 400,000 a year in the case of Germany, and up fifteen-fold in the last decade in Britain. These immigrations represent small proportions, between 4.5 and 7 per cent, of the indigenous white, or 'non-ethnic', populations. But with differences in birth-rate they are proportions which are rising. Turks and Yugoslavs in Germany, Algerians, Moroc-cans and Tunisians in France, and Indians, Pakistanis and West Indians in Britain are among the most notable of the settler populations.

Xenophobia magnifies their numbers, but timidity – often an inverted racism – hides them. At the same time, seemingly tough-minded egalitarians, who at heart may be no less xenophobic, pretend to race- and colour-blindness, rolling up their sleeves to the business of securing 'equal opportunities' and fighting racial discrimination. At their elbows, as in any morality tale, stand the figures of Forbearance, Understanding and round-the-clock Toleration. But, despite the efforts of the most benign, this is now a battlefield of competing emotions. Upon this battlefield, moralities go to the wall under the pressure of numbers; the melting pot boils over; the fomenting of discord is compounded by the follies of the well-intentioned.

Arguments about 'loss of national identity', or the obligations of immigrants to 'adapt', collide with 'multi-culturalist' endeavour. Political agitation to 'stem the flow' clashes with traditions of asylum or with objections to family break-up. The preconditions for citizenship and its entitlements – the right to vote, the right to state benefits and so on – are hotly disputed; hearts (and heads) are broken over access to jobs and housing; attempts at expulsion or deportation are challenged in the streets and before courts and tribunals; desperate migrants and refugees are smuggled across borders, or equipped with false passports in return for payment. Ghettos are created, including, in certain countries, of immigrant squatters reduced to vagrancy and permanent unemployment. Extremist political groups prowl for new pickings, amid old fears and hatreds.

In the interstices of the social order the successful immigrant of the past might find his way to prosperity, and in some cases prowess, by dint of hard work and application. Such a progress, most often an anonymous pilgrim's progress, continues. But today the 'huddled masses' – of the hosts as well as of the incoming population – increasingly stew in their own juices. The climb to security, often under conditions of social and educational breakdown (in which indigenous fears of being 'swamped' become acuter), is harder than ever. The Czechs, Poles and Scandinavians fear being one day 'swamped' by Russians; the Germans fear being 'swamped' by hordes of Slavs and Third World asylum-seekers; the Provençal and the Yorkshireman fear being 'swamped' by their respective incomers. At the same time, and unlike in the past, new immigrant populations, careless of local resentments, grow increasingly belligerent and demanding. Equally thick-headed counter-belligerence, quick to sense (or imagine) favouritism to the stranger, fingers its weapons. At the worst, excessive identity checks, police harassment, violent incursions into immigrant homes, assault and even murder can provoke inter-racial riot, arson, looting and even counter-killing. A relative commonplace in the United States, such events have also struck Belgium, France, Germany, Italy and Britain. Germans have fought Turks, French and Belgians have fought North Africans, and the British have fought Pakistanis, just as Peking Chinese have fought student Africans, New York blacks have fought Jews, and Jews (Soviet and Falasha) have even fought each other. In the latter case, white Soviet migrants to Israel demanded to be segregated from their black Jewish fellow-migrants. And in a final irony, demands were heard during the collapse of communism for the erection of a new Iron Curtain, in order to deter the feared onrush of refugees from the former Soviet Union and its satellites into neighbouring countries.

Likewise, Western Europe, especially the Mediterranean littoral states alarmed at the prospect of increasing North African migration, has begun to try to pull up its drawbridges – or to erect a 'strong perimeter fence' against non-Europeans – while simultaneously moving towards the abolition of internal border controls between member countries of the European Community. But Italy, for example, has 3,000 miles of largely un-policed coastline and tens (or hundreds) of thousands of itinerant migrants from the Maghreb without documents, but also without protection from local abuse and exploitation. Migration has even become a political weapon; the former Soviet Union attempted to use the West's fear of a mass exodus in order to exert increased pressure for Western aid.

Many kinds of misery, most of it invisible and humdrum, stalk the economic migrant. They include insecurity, physical hardship and chronic unemployment; nearly 30 per cent of Algerians in France, and at least twice that proportion of young Caribbeans in Britain, are jobless. Skills taken from a poor country are unused or unusable in a rich one; harsh bureaucracies are bent upon using the denial of benefit and support in the (generally vain) hope of driving migrants homewards. Germany and Britain have 'tightened up' their asylum regulations; France has sought to penalise employers who give work to illegal immigrants, while politicians have called for the right to citizenship by birth on French soil to be ended. 'We must not be wide open to all-comers simply because Paris, Rome or London seem more attractive than Bombay or Algiers,' declared the British Prime Minister, John Major, to accusations of 'racism'. In Hong Kong, where more than 60,000 Vietnamese boat-people had taken refuge, administrators – before beginning a programme of 'phased deportation' – threatened to 'tow the Vietnamese back out to sea'.

At unification, Germany similarly began sending home tens of thousands of Vietnamese, Mozambicans and Angolans who had been guest-workers in the eastern part of the country. The Italians in the summer of 1991 tricked their turbulent Albanian immigrants by first dispersing them around the country as if for resettlement, and then, once pacified, expelling them by the plane-load. This grappling with migration and the migrant, most of it unavailing, was as old as migratory man – that is, merely another chapter in the ancient history of itinerant mankind, its pogrom whiffs included. The number of foreigners in France, declared Jacques Chirac in June 1991, was an 'overdose'; and, well knowing its appeal to the sensibilities of the eternal proletarian, added that 'the French worker' was 'going mad' with the 'noise and smell' of the newcomer. (Enoch Powell, the British member of parliament, had passed this way before him.) And while strenuous French egalitarianism introduced 'emergency measures' to 'disperse' immigrant ghettos – including by trying to force rich 'immigrant-free' towns to construct low-rent immigrant housing – the National Front called itself 'the Party of Resistance against the immigrant invasion'. Even in Denmark, 'Denmark for the Danes' was heard from gangs of skinheads.

These are words. The pointing of fingers and jeering at the stranger – the fearsome black, the hook-nosed Jew, the thieving gipsy of some Grimm fable – are one thing; sticks, stones, knives another. 'Racially motivated' attacks, including (at the worst) gang attacks and killings, are on the increase in Europe. They have been reported from every country with significant racial-minority populations, and have been accelerating in number, especially since the late 1980s and most notably in France, Germany and Britain.

In Britain, there is great disparity in the assessments of their scale. They range, for example, from official figures of over 6,000 racially motivated attacks per annum – a bad enough statistic – to unofficial estimates that as many as 90 per cent of such attacks go unreported and that there are perhaps some 70,000 a year. But it is clear that racially inspired acts of hostility and violence in Britain have become more common. It is also clear that some of these attacks are organised; that they are mainly committed by white working-class males; and that Asians have borne the brunt of them. They have included persistent harassment – sometimes directed for months, and even years, at a single family – violent threats, vandalism, arson, physical assault and murder. It is also plain that the police tend to discount allegations of a racial motivation in most such incidents. There has been some (small-scale) counter-violence by groups of Asian vigilantes. Whether there are 6,000 or 70,000 attacks, few of the malefactors have been arrested, charged and brought to trial. That some council tenancy agreements have made conviction for racial harassment a ground for eviction therefore remains largely a dead letter. Much of the violence, whatever its scale, can be said to be carried on with relative impunity.

The nature, or type, of the violence observable in those cases which have been publicised – because of their notoriety, or because arrests followed, or both – is an index of the stress, fear and hatred which lie beneath the civic, or ostensibly civic, surface. In September 1986, a white boy aged thirteen plunged a knife into the stomach of a thirteen-year-old Pakistani boy on a Manchester school playground; 'Do you want it again, Paki?' he shouted at the dying victim. In September 1987, a skinhead gang in Bristol attacked a disabled Sikh boy, also aged thirteen, kicked and punched him, tore off his turban and with a knife hacked off his hair. In Newport in May 1990, a man armed with a 'makeshift flamethrower' stopped a twelve-year-old Pakistani boy to ask directions. As the latter answered, the former fired the device into his face, causing severe burns.

In June 1990, Manchester Crown Court heard how a group of laughing youths, one of them armed with an air-rifle, shot from a passing car at two Asian brothers, the elder aged fourteen, the younger a handicapped child of eight; the elder was shot in the eye, and died. As the car sped away, the assailant, who received a life sentence, was reported to have said, 'I shot the black bastard;' when informed of his death he was said to have declared, 'He was only a Paki.' Similarly, two Wolverhampton youths, aged eighteen and nineteen and armed with a 'pneumatic rivet-firing gun', made a series of 'sorties' in a van, firing at Asian passers-by. One Asian was blinded in the eye during these 'sorties'; the assailant was sentenced in August 1990 at Wolverhampton Crown Court to nine months' youth custody for unlawful wounding.

In the United States, race violence has been on the increase since the late 1980s, and has reached its highest levels since the Ku Klux Klan beatings and lynchings of the 1950s. (Most American violence is, however, not inter-racial; for example, 95 per cent of homicides by blacks are committed on other blacks.) In race violence, gang-attack predominates. Gangs of white American skinheads are said to be involved in two-thirds of race attacks in the United States, using firearms – unlike in Britain – knives, baseball bats, steel-toed boots and

other weapons. There are equally violent black gang-attacks on whites
and Asians. When a squad of club-wielding, knuckleduster-wearing
French paratroopers attacked a North African immigrant district in
Carcassonne in the South of France in July 1991, they were cashiered,
modestly fined and received suspended prison sentences. The case
attracted passing attention. In the rest of Europe it barely rated mention.

Such relative unconcern is one of the most disturbing historic features
of the collective response to racial violence against ethnic minorities. In
the 1930s, German anti-semitic violence went under-reported and
(seemingly) under-noticed. It is as if such violence – whether against the
Berlin Jew or the Bosnian Muslim – is seen as part of the natural order of
things; and, in certain dire respects, it is. It also evokes for Everyman, the
Jew included, his own bad self. It is therefore natural enough not to wish
to be reminded of it. Moreover, except for the victim, the actual incidents
of racial offence are readily displaced (in some) by compensatory
responses, or reflexes, which possess their own rationale and ethic. These
responses help certain individuals to allay the complex emotions which
such offence arouses by transferring attention to analysis of causes and
passive consideration of 'solutions.' Most common of all is a moral ardour
for inaction. Such inaction presents itself in many guises, including
'understanding', vague hand-wringing, 'prayer' and so on. Against mod-
ulated (or repressed) responses of this kind, grief and anger – or, worse,
the desire for racial revenge – will be seen, especially in the Anglo-Saxon
tradition, as unseemly and the matter, together with the victim's hurts,
will be quickly buried.

To a Jew, such responses are inadequate. Indeed, they are themselves
moral defects, particularly in a (Judaeo-Christian) culture at the basis
of which stands an ostensible belief in the possibility of, and need for,
human redemption. But, as I shall show in a later chapter, the scale and
type of violence in general which some citizens are now almost routinely
capable of inflicting upon others, sometimes with gratuitous brutality
and not uncommon sadism, disturbs the moral order much less than it
might. When the moral order is itself increasingly anaesthetised, it
suffers diminishing pain. When serial killings, or beatings to death, or
dismemberments, barely ripple the surface of public concern, a racial
assault counts for little or nothing. Even when the victims of racial
violence are counted in millions, as the Jews know, grief and anger may
still be regarded (by some) as unseemly.

Today, in a new complication, it is also as if it had come to be taken
for granted that in the seething metropolis and louring suburb, anxiety

will increasingly take out its fears and frustrations on family members, neighbours or the passing stranger. The dead and the assaulted, the raped and the robbed, are seen as the casualties of urban warfare; the arrested are the prisoners taken. As the statistics of crime soar and the prisons grow larger or more crowded, the forms of everyday violence become little by little more brutal. At the same time, the law-abiding citizen becomes increasingly habituated to it, and even sated. The older may shift uneasily over the rapine and bloodshed; to the younger, it is more easily assimilated in their daily diet. Civic violence, too, is in the air, with thresholds of tolerance for what was once thought intolerable raised to meet it. Yet, paradoxically, it is a reduction in the level of tolerance of certain others – of their colour, their behaviour, their words, even the look in their eyes – which sets off much violent emotion itself, especially among the young. This suggests that in some circumstances we are less able to tolerate the presence of others than we are to tolerate the violence which may be committed against them. This, too, the Jews have cause to understand.

Indeed, a setting of overt and repressed violence, of anxiety about the future and of disappointment with the present, and (above all) of dulled moral perception, has always been unpromising civic ground. In such a context the crash of the socialist utopia – resounding through an over-populated and needy world – requires new consideration. Utopian illusion, as I wrote in *Against Socialist Illusion* in 1985, 'is both a menace and a consolation', and this was as true of socialist illusion as any other. Moreover, insofar as such illusion promises hope of redemption on earth or in heaven, it exerts a 'powerful attraction upon citizens tired in one way or another with the given'. But when the given – that is, the daily actuality around which anxieties gather – triumphs so wholly over the illusion, what then?

Like every loss of faith in secular societies, it plainly portends a moral crisis whose consequences will unfold in due time. Nor is it necessary to have been a socialist or communist to perceive (in good faith) how large a hole has been made in the political and ethical ozone layer by socialism's failure; like the real ozone hole, socialism was the size of a continent in some men's thoughts and aspirations. It is not only the natural world, but the political world too, which abhors a vacuum. But that socialist ethics aborted themselves so spectacularly in both a moral and a practical collapse sheds light upon the nature of the illusions which nurtured them. Such collapse does not, because it cannot, dethrone political (and other) illusion itself from its eternal aerial function as Job's comforter, as solace. Moreover, the more disappointing, oppressive or frightening the present and actual, the greater the need (in those not sunk into moral catalepsy or mere indifference) for the compensations which illusion, especially utopian illusion, can offer.

But are there new utopias which have not already been tried and tested to destruction? Certainly, some of the old ones – the utopia of ethnic purity, the utopia of 'complete national independence', the utopia of this or that Zion's rebirth – are being resuscitated and refurbished. They, too, are in the air. And in Europe, there is the dream of 'Europe'. Like the dictatorship of the proletariat or the Thousand-year Reich, it stands on the political horizon as a laboratory specimen of illusion. The very language of it – the utopian language of panacea for a continent's problems – should have put the sceptical citizen on his guard long before it did. When already-European nations spoke of 'joining Europe', of 'getting into' or 'going into' Europe, or, in the case of the Baltic states, of 'going back to' Europe – as well as of being 'kept out of' or 'isolated from' Europe – it was plain that something was out of rational kilter; or, rather, that 'entry' into 'Europe' had (for some) become, in old utopian fancy, something akin to passage into Eden.

It is true, although only in a certain metaphorical sense, that the 'Iron Curtain divided the continent'. It is similarly true that Eastern Europe found itself in a 'socialist limbo', economically disadvantaged and with sense of nation and national culture damaged, though (as is also evident) not irreparably so. It is true, too, although the truth is again largely metaphorical, that communism 'turned' the satellite countries of what was once called Central Europe 'Eastwards', and that with the fall of communism many of them have now 'turned back' towards the West. But illusion also lurks in all these 'movements' of states 'into' or 'towards' 'Europe'. (It is not states, but peoples, that are on the move, in their millions.) Moreover, the characteristic metaphorical images of utopian thinking – from which the 'classless society' and the 'kingdom of heaven' both derive – have at every stage accompanied the debate about the 'new Europe'.

At the head of them is the 'common European home', with its 'rooms' (in the more elaborate versions) occupied by the various nations and others 'knocking at the European door'. This dolls' house view of the European continent – a sentimental utopia to displace the 'fortresses' which the proletariats on the one side, and the super-race on the other, once thought they were building – has about it once more the aura of hallucination. It is also no less the complex product of anxiety, and the natural desire for its alleviation, than have been other political utopias; it must, like them, be at best a temporary political arrangement. Nevertheless, a currency union, a forum for debate, and a network of market deals have been wildly aggrandised by wishful thinking, again in classic utopian fashion. A trading bloc – the 'single European market' – has been made to masquerade as a 'new European power'. This market is even presented in the old distorting mirror of fancy as the re-embodiment of the 'values of European civilisation'. These values are real. They possess, despite the depth of their betrayal in the Holocaust, political and cultural substance, a substance which requires to be defended. However, to discover such values in the lucubrations of a round-table of market-managing politicians and administrators is to be led by delusion.

The dangers of it are already clear enough. Among them, is the ease with which the political mountebank can (without much cost) proclaim sympathy for such fancies, knowing them to contain more hot air than real meaning. Thus, in June 1990, President Ilie Iliescu of Romania, in his inaugural speech, professed 'full adherence' to the 'values of European civilisation' only a week after summoning miners, armed with crowbars and pickaxe handles, to attack Bucharest's democratic protes-tors. It is no less dangerous – more, perhaps – that political virtue should be duped by wishful thinking, as that political cynicism should have a field day with other men's benign illusions. When President Havel declared, on behalf of a then still-united Czechoslovakia, that the countries of Eastern Europe could become a 'zone of chaos and hopelessness' if they did not 'integrate with the rest of Europe', the vices of this particular utopian fancy were again disclosed: of the 'entry' into Europe as into a paradise garden, of the dichotomies of political light and dark – hell here, and heaven yonder – and of unreal hopes of redemption raised only to be dashed hereafter.

When a nation's spokesmen cast off a sense of their own nation's virtues under the stress of bogus discourse, matters become more tragic still. In this moral helter-skelter, often the product of a cowardly stooping to passing intellectual fashion, the British citizen has been told that his country now 'has little sense of its own artifice and fragility. It behaves as if its status as a nation were inherent and inviolable, the legitimacy of its government were rooted in the mists of Arthurian antiquity, its island geography were a statement of divine political content' (Richard Cottrell, *Independent*, 1 December 1988). Intended as a lampoon, this Aunt Sally speaks more truth than the ventriloquist on whose knee she perches. Moreover, 'nation', 'national sovereignty' – or the right to rule without challenge within one's own national boundaries – and 'national tradition' have plainly not become entirely nugatory concepts in Europe, as distinct from 'Europe'. The evidence of a rearing nationalism is everywhere, especially in the former territories of the Soviet Union and Eastern Europe. The vortex of peoples in movement, gradually acting to dissolve 'national identity', is another matter, but it too is not ground for national self-deprecation.

'It is as well,' wrote Hazlitt, 'to be a citizen of the world, to fall in, as nearly as we can, with the ways of feelings of others, and make one's self at home wherever one comes.' (There were not, however, five billions on the planet at the time of his writing.) These were the sentiments of a generous and open-minded spirit; what Hazlitt had to say has a healthy cheerfulness and reason about it which now seems entirely remote. Today, a hard-pressed administrative prose, itself a function of harassment and unreason, strenuously rolls up its verbal sleeves to the 'construction of Europe'. The 'best place for Britain', it is urged, is 'right at the heart of the community' – the fantasy of a fixed geographical location transposing itself across the map is implicit – or 'in the mainstream of European history'. But if there is a 'mainstream' at all, Britain has always been 'in it'. Now, nation (apparently) competes with nation to be the more 'European-minded', or the more 'committed to European integration'; a 'union' of twelve, fifteen or even twenty-four and more distinct nations takes on as mystical a form as that of the Holy Trinity itself, and is similarly comprehensible only to believers.

Each man's 'Europe', as is standard in utopias both secular and religious, is different, and is often no more than the projection of the individual's own ideal virtues. To Laurent Fabius, the former French prime minister, for example, 'Europe' will be 'democratic, secular, tolerant, social, respectful of nature and the environment, peace-loving and dynamic': a self-portrait of Laurent Fabius. Much of this 'Euro-peanism', as in the case of other utopian political idealisms which preceded it, is rhetorical only; again, in the air. It is also as if there were an anxious desire in some nations – Germany and Italy, for example – to lose themselves, and their tarnished recent histories, in a 'new' Europe where the ghosts of their pasts might be exorcised and memory cancelled by utopian expectations of the future. Failure is inscribed in such fancies; and only renewed nationalisms, more jealous than ever of their histories and traditions, are to be expected from it.

It is equally clear that the larger the number of nations which climbs aboard – or thinks that it is climbing aboard – the metaphorical, or metaphysical, 'European' vessel, the quicker it will keel over. A putative 'community' of 400 million and more 'citizens' embracing the whole of Western Europe, most of Eastern Europe, and stretching from the Arctic to the Bosphorus and the Bug to the Ebro, cannot (except to a utopian) be a true community, nor its 'citizens' members of a common civic body. Even on its present scale it could not for long, or at all, harmonise its member-nations' economic interests, to go no further.

Twenty or more separate nations, and 400 million (or more) increasingly heterogeneous individuals – from Surrey stockbrokers to Sardinian shepherds, and immigrant Pakistani imams to Parisian models – cannot be constituted into a univocal 'political actor' on the 'world stage', except under conditions created in utopian fantasy. Rule of law states cannot be composed into a true political union with, say, the lawless Italy of the Mafia and Camorra, nor ancient parliamentary democracies with recently dictatorial one-party regimes, let alone in a 'single European super-state' under a 'European government'. (To compound the illusion, there is no national government in 'Europe', or presently suing to 'enter' it, which would permit such an outcome.) Indeed, the political cultures and traditions of such nations cannot be, and should not be attempted to be, reconciled. The Jews, who carry much of what remains of Western culture about with them, know as well as any that no nation can be expected simply to flow indistinguishably into a common stream with others. To insist otherwise, and to 'reconstruct Europe' on the basis of such insistence, is to succumb resistlessly to a new phantasmagoria of the times. It is as if the sheer turbulent scale of things, and their continuous inflation, were again carrying even the wisest, the very sages of the day, out of their heads and into the air, to escape anxiety in new realms of fancy.

In Jewish folklore, the *Luftmensch*, the insubstantial and unworldly dreamer, also walks-and-lives-on-air; as well he might, today, when there are more than five billions on the ground beneath him.

TWO

Jubilee

The ground shifted, the statues fell and the old Soviet Union vanished. East and West, even left and right, shed, sloughed off, much of their meaning. The money-changers – some of them Jewish – now occupied the Marxist temple; the Warsaw stock exchange was installed in the former Party headquarters and opened for business to the clink of champagne glasses. Even in Mongolia, where half the population herds sheep, goats, horses, yaks and camels for a living, capitalism – now known as the 'market economy' to the squeamish – was re-established. The new commodities exchange in Moscow was blessed by an Orthodox priest, bearded as any rabbi and in full regalia. Bell, book and candle chased away the hammer and sickle. A chorus from Glinka's *A Life for the Tsar* became Russia's national anthem.

There were strippers and roulette players now in the basement of Warsaw's Palace of Culture, the Enver Hoxha shrine and museum in Tirana was converted into a disco, part of the Bulgarian Party's central office became a cinema – the first film it screened was *Sex, Lies and Videotape* – and the Leipzig Stasi headquarters was turned into an unemployment benefit centre. A swim-suited Miss Albania was crowned to acclamation, an elected president of Russia referred to the Gospels as the 'foundation of human morality', and in the Saxon village of Weissig East Germany's first post-communist brothel opened. The mummy of Georgi Dimitrov was extracted from its mausoleum in Sofia and cremated, and Frederick the Great was brought back in pomp to Potsdam and reburied. Egon Krenz, the last general secretary of the East German Communist Party, found employment with a West Berlin business tycoon, and Mieczyslaw Jagielski, who in 1980 had led the negotiations with Solidarity on behalf of the Communist government, became a beekeeper.

Now, there was a Macdonald's in Moscow and Kentucky Fried Chicken in Peking; and even Vietnam, in its Lewis Carroll-like currency reform, floated the *dong*. The bells of St Basil's Cathedral, opposite the Kremlin, pealed for the first time since 1922, Lourdes had record numbers of extra pilgrims from Eastern Europe, the collapsing 'Soviet Union' was paid 12 billion dollars by Saudi Arabia for its support in the Gulf War, Aeroflot began regular flights to Miami, and a memorial to the victims of the Stalinist purges was unveiled opposite the Lubyanka. The Red Proletariat works in Moscow printed Solzhenitsyn's *Gulag Archipelago*, *Mein Kampf* was serialised in Moscow's official *Military Historical Journal*, popular with the military elite, and a Greek millionaire bought *Pravda*. In Uzbekistan, statues of Tamerlane replaced those of Lenin, and even Genghiz Khan was rehabilitated in Mongolia.

The world over, the old names, emblems and programmes of communist and socialist parties disappeared. The Union of Soviet Socialist Republics became the Commonwealth of Independent States; the Italian Communist Party became the Party of Democratic Socialism and chose an oak-tree as its symbol; the Bulgarian Communist Party became the Bulgarian Socialist Party, dropped its red star and chose a rose, as did the British Labour Party; even the People's Revolutionary Party of Kampuchea opted for a market economy and a multi-party system. In November 1991, on the eve of the seventy-fourth anniversary of the Bolshevik Revolution, Boris Yeltsin issued a decree 'abolishing' the Communist Party entirely; an Association in Defence of the Rights of Communists complained of 'persecution' and began meeting 'underground'. The star and hammer on the national flag of Laos was replaced by a dome-shaped Buddhist stupa; Leningrad was St Petersburg again, and Karl-Marx-Stadt once more Chemnitz. Red became a taboo colour, the term 'comrade' fell under an anathema, and communism – even socialism – became a dirty word. 'Words about brotherhood, equality, and the future communist paradise are now no more than jokes in our society,' declared Victor Yakovlev, the Siberian miners' leader in May 1990. When the red flag of the Polish United Workers' Party was carried ceremonially off stage at its eleventh and final party congress in January 1990 there was complete silence.

In this silence at the end of the party there was cause for both relief and fear, old Jewish fear included. Marx, the Jewish apostate, had sought with the apostate's ardour – strengthened by Lenin's admixtures – to turn the world upside down. Now Marxism-Leninism's ground, turned by *soi-disant* Marxists into a Golgotha, had been retaken. 'Down With The Red Fascist Empire!', 'Seventy Years Of Shit On The People!' and even 'Socialism? No Thanks!' had appeared as slogans, before the fall, in the streets of Moscow; 'Red Filth, Get Your Hands Off Our Yeltsin!' also. ('Mongolian brothers and sisters, to your horses!' shouted the more benign Ulan Bator demonstrators.) When turmoil is in prospect, including turmoil in which they may themselves have had a hand, whether directly or at a great remove, the anxiety of most Jews increases. But in the complex moral dilemmas inherent in the collapse of the communist utopia, there was reason for more general confusion.

As the process deepened, Albania was being brought to endorse the rights of man – including the right to own a car – Mongolia to introduce the separation of powers, the former Soviet Union to 'dismantle' the KGB and join the IMF, and the Cambodia once ruled by Pol Pot to restore Buddhism as the state religion. But communist collapse also brought Kazakhstan to sell off its housing stock, took gangs of low-wage Russian labourers to Finland to work on road-construction projects, created a Club of Young Millionaires in Moscow, and led Boris Yeltsin to declare 'Take what you want!' in a speech to potential American investors. China even made an offer to Sweden of cheap labour from its jails in return for investment, and was fastidiously refused. The rejection of the notion of 'class struggle' was one thing; the return of the phenomena which would restore it, another. Here, the 'progressive' Jewish intellectual – whose brother, the Jewish capitalist, has his own fish to fry and in his own fashion – was as ever torn. 'Fraternity', always less and usually worse than it seemed, offered or appeared to offer some earnest of socialist good intentions. The term was of sound Judaeo-Christian provenance; it at least suggested, even if it did not mean, that under the skin all men are brothers. At a certain level (but never too deeply) the Jews saw and still see in such profession of brotherhood a lifting of burden and danger, that of particularity and difference. It is what made many Jews, Marx included, socialists and 'internationalists' in the first place.

The dissolution, permanent or temporary, of this fraternal ideal contained a threat within it: that of the enforced return to particularity, the return of each to a condition of being defined by his own difference, whether of race, religion or nation. Even the Jew proudest of his Judaic identity would hesitate to see this as an unmixed blessing; the assimilated Jew, especially if embarrassed by his provenance, looks on it with foreboding. Moreover, most Jewish intellectuals, whether or not 'on the left', find it difficult, both by tradition and intuition, to take part with enthusiasm in the destructive overthrow, as distinct from the criticism, of intellectual ideas. They are even less attracted by the dumping of books on rubbish tips, as was to occur throughout Eastern Europe with texts of Marxist-Leninist holy writ; and least of all by book-burning. In Judaism there is an ancient and powerful taboo against the casting away of bread, even stale and inedible bread, into the fire.

However subversive of established wisdom the Jewish intellectual may be, that same intellectual is equally unlikely to be an entire iconoclast. In biblical times, the Jewish worship of Baal (and the Golden Calf) survived for a considerable period the Mosaic enthronement of Yahweh as the divinity of Jewish monotheism; and Marx was rooted in Hegel. Consequently, if a swift show of hands or a quick pressure on an electronic button – in one post-communist parliament after another – was imagined (by some) to be sufficient to discard the thought of a century and longer, any Jewish intellectual worth his salt would be the first to demur. Overnight conversion and sudden revelation are not part of the Jewish tradition, religious or lay. The sceptical Jew requires proof; miracles must be repeated. In the Bulgarian parliament in November 1989, immediately after the deposition of Todor Zhivkov, deputy after deputy, all of them until a moment before loyal to a granite-seeming orthodoxy, pronounced themselves on the instant converted from it. One such, ending his feverish denunciation of a regime to which he had to the last hour given unwavering obedience, even shouted 'I vote for Todor Zhivkov!'; his old reflexes were too strong for the new position.

In the face of this degree of hysteria, intellectual scruple reasserts itself, and in so doing doubles its dilemmas. Moreover, the Jew to whom 'Arise, citizens!' – a slogan of the Chinese democratic movement of 1989 – stirs echoes of the Napoleonic opening of the ghettos is instinctively on the side of civic freedom. But the Jew, the same Jew, to whom 'Seventy-three Years on the Road to Nowhere' suggests Russian despair at wasted decades of life and effort, fears for the civic angers which might claim him as an early victim, and flees them. And when the populist in the street shouts 'All Power to the People!', even the most democratic of Jews thinks instinctively of taking cover.

'We have been cheated, we have been used like idiots!' and 'Down with Fascism!' read the Tienanmen slogans, before the tanks crushed them in June 1989. With even the police applauding, tens and hundreds of thousands had marched: students, journalists, trade unionists, soldiers of the People's Liberation Army on furlough, magistrates in their court uniforms, hotel bell-boys, staffs of the foreign ministry and the ministry of aeronautics, and Mao-suited cadres. In such upsurges of hope for a freer and juster order, every pulse – some in anxiety, others in exhilaration – has always quickened. Even socialists (or, perhaps, especially socialists) whose instincts were, and are, to side with every upsurge of the 'masses', were drawn towards the revolutionary spectacle. That this same spectacle portended the downfall of their beliefs provoked in all socialists that confusion and discomfort with which all Jews are familiar: the discomfort of being simultaneously with, and not with, or even against, 'the people'.

For, at the last, a Jew – socialist or not, democrat or not, religious or not – is a Jew, and not only because others insist upon it. Indeed, there is a limit to which most Jews can identify wholly or without reservation with the actions of non-Jews, even if this limit is not one which many Jews would acknowledge either to themselves or to others; the chronically dissenting Jew – an archetype – can identify wholly and without reservation with no one at all. This is more true still in relation to the actions of the hydra-headed 'masses', of the 'plebs', or of the 'proletariat'. To a Jew, *vox populi*, even of five billions, is not *vox dei*; only *vox dei* is *vox dei*. (In this, the Jew reveals himself to be what he is: the very model of a Judaeo-Christian.) Both populism and the unpredictable mass suggest a potentiality for unreason. The Jew, as capable of unreason as any – though not capable of organising a holocaust in any circumstances whatever – fears most of all the unreason of the crowd. Marxist and communist Jews paid lip-service to, sometimes led, and (when workers themselves) were part of the proletariat. But mass-man and the Jew were, and are, alien to one another. The 'working class' and even more the 'peasant masses' – doubtless from long atavistic memory – always aroused complex and contradictory emotions in the ostensibly socialist Jew, just as they did in many socialist non-Jews, especially socialists of the middle class. In such contradictory emotions were to be found fastidious antipathy as well as 'compassion', contempt as well as human fellow-feeling, condescension as well as egalitarian impulse; it was the play of such complex emotions which coloured and determined the behaviour of many communist apparatchiks towards 'the people'. Indeed, the fact that antipathy and condescension generally predominated in this behaviour contributed to communism's fall. I believe that Jewish Marxists embodied more acutely than most these dichotomies of feeling towards 'working people'; it is arguable that they can now understand better than most how a notional egalitarianism could turn to actual party tyranny over the proletariat, and the communist ethic fail.

But it was more than the ethic which failed. The edifices which communism erected, those great monoliths of 'state power' and of 'mass party', were armed to the teeth and ostensibly secure in their bunkers. Yet, they seemed to vanish into thin air, proving as insubstantial as the morning dew. At first sight it appeared some miracle of levitation. On closer inspection, mountains of rubble – of lives, landscapes and dreams ruined – reached to heaven; bad faith had lain waste whole nations. But almost at the first trump the walls of Jericho had fallen, and the defenders had fled, most often without a single shot being fired. Not even the restorationist plotters against Gorbachev made the least mention in their statements of 'socialism', let alone 'communism', among the values which they claimed to be defending. Party member-ships, previously legions-strong, melted away before the eyes. At the end, the East German Communist Party, one of the most powerful, lost 90 per cent of its members in eighteen months; *Pravda*'s readership had fallen from 13 million to under a million by 1992 and was barely able to maintain publication. An opinion poll in the Russian Republic in April 1991 found not a single respondent who still wanted to see a communist society established. 'We smell death,' shouted young heck-lers at a Bulgarian communist rally in Sofia in November 1990.

Communism vanished so fast in Poland that the subsequent political difficulties of the successor Solidarity-led regime were attributed by some to its 'not having had time to work out the transition to democracy in detail'. In Bulgaria, the Academy of Sciences had to be called in to settle a controversy over the correct Bulgarian word for 'democratic'. (Was it, the professors were solemnly asked, *'democratichen'*, or *'demo-craticheski'*?) Almost overnight, the Party's omniscience and omnipotence turned to helplessness, hands spread before its accusers; and the accusers, many of them recent turncoats, were soon fitting themselves out in new coats-of-many-colours, the colours of the political rainbow. In January 1990, Petar Mladenov, Zhivkov's newly-liberal (but old-time communist) successor, was swiftly to be heard describing his prede-cessor as 'an egotistical maniac', no less. A mere matter of weeks before, his chieftain had been the embodiment of socialist virtue, 'dialectical' wisdom made flesh.

It turned out that fidelity of socialist belief, sworn for decades on the Marxist bible, was itself of no substance. The working class was not, after all, the instrument of a messianic deliverance from capitalist thraldom. Capitalism was not even thraldom. It had all been an error. The struggle of the classes was not the law of the world; socialism was not the 'dialectical' supersession of the 'anarchy of the market'. 'Surplus value', 'wage slavery' and other terms of art from the socialist lexicon were, it seemed, now declared null and void. There was also not to be a New Socialist Testament; not even a communist Lamentation of Jeremiah. The good book was closed, the failure of socialism its last chapter.

This degree of apostasy – the Ark of the Covenant abandoned, the scriptures left to flutter in the wind – had no parallel in the history of faith. Who could explain it? No one but a Jewish Marxist, or ex-Marxist. For Marxism is, or was, Revelation. To any unbeliever the Truth, secular or divine, which has been revealed to the faithful is no truth at all, but hocus-pocus; its acolytes seem mere dupes of organised superstition. Marxism, especially in its messianic belief in the proletariat, appeared thus to most non-Marxists. But Revelation, being Revelation, and unsusceptible to scientific verification, is dependent upon faith. In Marxism's case this dependency was its undoing. Faith may move (and climb) mountains, but faithlessness is quick to turn its back on them. Moreover, Marxism's foothills were relatively accessible; its peaks, both of insight and rank misperception, were unscaleable by the ordinary mortal. The average servant of the communist apparatus, a mere technician of a system of power, knew little (and cared less) of the Jewish philosopher's immense confection; the average Christian or Jewish worshipper knows as little of the arcana of biblical exegesis or rabbinics. But, worse, the Party card-holder had no deep faith either, and in most cases no faith at all. His self-interested obeisances to the totems of Marxism-Leninism were merely formal; ritual without belief, thought, or meaning. Thus, when the high priests, the very Aarons of the communist temple, abandoned their altars, their congregations, barring those few who had taken the dumb-show more seriously than the high priests had intended, vanished with them.

The issue here arises as to whether the high priests – the ideology chiefs of the communist parties' various central committee secretariats – took counsel together before breaking their holy staffs and burying their bibles. Was there a 'nerve centre', or shadowy international committee of Marxist-Leninist leaders as in the time of the Comintern, which, from the early 1980s onwards and long pre-dating Gorbachev's perestroika, orchestrated the strategy of the gradual democratisation of communism's totalitarian institutions? Did it dictate the choice of 'the market', the jettisoning of the hammer-and-sickle, the transformation of one communist party after another into 'democratic socialist' parties?

The questions are reasonable ones: these things followed a clear pattern, even down to the clauses and sub-clauses of the separate acts of legislation which in each country abolished the hegemony of the communist parties, restored civil freedoms, permitted private property, and so on.

Other questions follow. How, for example, could so many legislatures, at the time overwhelmingly dominated by communists, opt – as did the Hungarian national assembly in January 1989 – for a plural electoral system and the restoration of civic liberties, when such reforms were plainly a death-warrant for the communist system? And how could one central committee after another, including that of the then Soviet Union, vote itself (without bloodshed) into oblivion? Though it is tempting to believe it, I do not think that there was a master plan to abandon the communist system. Why? Because the words '*mene, mene, tekel upharsin*', or 'thou hast been weighed in the balance and found wanting' – the Babylonian writing on the communist wall – had been legible in Eastern Europe and in the Soviet Union for at least a decade. Indeed, after his resignation in December 1991, Gorbachev claimed that 'the signs that the system was dying' were clear to him in 1978. Many countries, Bulgaria, for instance, had fitfully introduced make-believe political-and-economic reforms (to 'liberalise' the market, to permit multi-candidate but still single-party elections, and so forth) long before the real cascade began in earnest.

Once under way, fear of popular revenge concentrated minds as economic collapse beckoned. Led by Hungary and Poland, reform became a landslide, with each country's communist leaders looking to the others to see how they might save their skins, and manage the final bail-out. I recall Kalman Kulcsar, the non-communist minister of justice in the 1989 Hungarian government, laughing in puzzlement over whether the communist deputies in parliament 'really knew' what they were doing, as they voted near-unanimously for the restoration of a multi-party system. It was a step which could only eviscerate the communist order. Marian Orzechowski, Poland's ideology chief, appeared to me to be entirely unruffled as the system foundered. Moreover, although there were exceptions – Tienanmen Square and Ceausescu's Romania the most obvious – in country after country, including in the former Soviet Union, police and army stood idly by, more unwilling than unable to intervene, as the numbers attending 'illegal' protest rallies mounted.

Some, of course, continued to believe that by recourse to dramatic measures, including 'capitalist' and parliamentary measures, they would still be able to 'save the system'. Others persisted in the illusion that in a system of free choice, communists would still be chosen. But most of the 'reform communists' had little or no faith in the Revelation whose ministers they were supposed to be. Weary of the ideological burden they had carried for decades, they were relieved to be ridding themselves of it. The high priests had no more energy to raise their hosannas. As the crowds massed at their sanctuaries' gates, they resignedly divested themselves of the last trappings of their hieratic power; though there were isolated suicides, men of little faith do not commit *hara-kiri*. The objects of their devotion – Class, the Plan, the Party – had long become in their own eyes objects without substance. It was as if the Holy Scroll, or the Host, were to be seen by rabbi or bishop as tainted and evanescent. To a Jewish intellectual, loss of belief on this scale is no light matter; any belief, especially a coherent system of belief, might seem better than none.

As communism collapsed, to hold left beliefs at all, and anywhere, was to be seen as an ideological loser. Thus, when the split between 'left' and 'right' in Polish Solidarity widened during 1990, a spokesman for the 'right-wing', pro-Walesa faction of the movement declared that its opponents, grouped around the Jewish Adam Michnik, feared being 'pushed into the left-wing corner, because there you have to lose'. Did the left fear to be thought left? It seems so. 'If I am a member of the lay left or a crypto-communist, then you, dear antagonists, are just swine,' Michnik robustly replied. It was not merely that the Temple had been vacated; its very articles of faith had become taboos. Equally abruptly, societies which once seemed to the West to represent a sinister threat to the 'free world' – and to which it had responded with such little self-confidence – became, almost overnight, benign. Inversions of belief on this scale are historically unprecedented. Revolution even seems the wrong word for it. Rather, perception on all sides appeared to become bewitched, as if a *dybbuk* or goblin were at work in socialism's ruins. The 'American dream', canvassed openly by an American president in Moscow in July 1991, was being dreamed aloud as the Soviet Union fell apart, while communism, seemingly made of imperishable stone, swiftly became as tenuous as a wraith to those who bemusedly tried to recall it. 'God knows what communism is,' declared Albania's communist deputy prime minister, as the regime fell asunder. 'There is nothing left of communism except a ghost,' announced *Komsomolskaya Pravda* (no less) in March 1991. 'What is socialism?' asked a woman delegate to a writers' conference in Hanoi, of all places, in October 1989. 'It is a ghost,' she answered. 'No one can see its real form,' she added.

A dream of capitalism had displaced communism's ghost. It was the stuff of fiction, or of a fantasy acted out by 'rude mechanicals' before an audience of sceptical Western bankers. At the fall of communism, in the real world of the Soviet Union, some 80 million (of a population of 286 million) had been reduced to a state of bare subsistence on one-sixth of the planet's land surface. In response, mass-man's new leaders, ditching socialism, had thrown themselves headlong, as from the Tarpeian rock, upon the mercies of 'the market' and of Western aid and investment. In a welter of shortages, falling living standards, falling production, rising unemployment, a largely worthless currency, a huge budget deficit, an outdated industry and infrastructure, loss of central control over the economy, a widening system of demonetised barter, inadequate distribution, a grossly polluted environment and long-ingrained habits of industrial pillage, civic non-cooperation and mutual suspicion, a new Jerusalem was expected to be built anew, stone by stone. ('Everything you name, it is a disaster,' announced Leonid Abalkin, a deputy Soviet prime minister, in April 1990.) And while communism's survivors were constructing – in their heads – their new market utopia, similar fantasy was elsewhere busy with the 'new world order', the 'new Europe', and the 'new era'.

A new era, or jubilee, has been man's fond hope in all ages, but the concept is essentially Hebraic. Marx's belief that the triumph of socialism would end man's 'pre-history' and start the clock of history proper was a particularly Jewish illusion. The word 'jubilee' – a word which subsequently passed into Greek, Latin, French and English – is Hebrew in origin. It is derived from the word for a ram, and (by association) for the ram's horn, used as a trumpet to proclaim a year of emancipation every fifty years according to Jewish tradition. During the revolutionary year, slaves were to be set free, lands which had been sold under duress during the previous half-century were to revert to their previous owners or their heirs, and the fields were to be left untilled. A jubilee was a year both of release and reformation, or revolution.

In the calendar of communism, derived from Marx's witting or unwitting ancestral vision, 1917 was as eagerly anticipated in the revolutionary scriptures as the coming of the Messiah. When the revolution came, and for decades thereafter until the vision waned, it was seen exactly as a year of jubilee: a year of release of the wage-slave and of reformation in production. In its elaborated modern version, the vision dictated that productive forces would be raised to levels as yet undreamed-of in capitalism by means of classless socialist co-operation. A 'new socialist man', or *golem*, his capacities developed to unprecedented levels by the free tapping of the 'springs of co-operative wealth', would be created. But the springs died, or were not there to start with. The biblical dreams withered on the vine. No 'new man' was created. There was only the old Adam.

The Jewish Marx, with prodigies of intellectual effort, had tried to understand, among other things, the laws which governed the money-madness of capitalism, and had largely succeeded. Lenin and his successors tried politically, and with huge violence, to create an alternative political order which after seventy years had catastrophically failed. The judgment, which all socialists have shared to large degree, that the market was so imperfect and random in its operations that it required to be replaced, in whole or in part, by the state's ownership and management of society's resources had also turned to ashes. So, too, more obviously, had the notion that the use of such resources was a matter to be determined neither by producers nor consumers but by party apparatchiks and planners. Indeed, the conviction that the satisfaction of human wants was a political issue, to be governed by socialist priorities and socialist theory, was at the heart of communism's political failure. It was a costly failure: the application of these ideas had left the Soviet Union unable to feed itself and in an abyss of stagnation.

As for 'keeping up' with, let alone 'overtaking', the West, it had ceased even to be a desert mirage. 'Marxism,' said Hu Yao Bang, the general-secretary of the Chinese Communist Party in the early 1980s – later to lose his job for his 'reformism' – 'does not embrace all truths in the unending course of history.' Marxism, said a bolder Cambodian government official in January 1990, beating a much firmer retreat, 'has nothing to do with Cambodia'. How far this communist retreat had gone in Europe was most clearly measurable in Bonn in April 1990, at the inaugural Conference on Security and Cooperation in Europe. Its concluding document, signed by all European nations including the then Soviet Union and by every East European nation except Albania, categorically declared that 'economic well-being was best achieved by market forces'.

In the history of ideas there has, again, been no intellectual capitulation to match the scale of this one, nor one so uncontested. Both Galilean revolutions – that of the Jewish preacher and the Italian astronomer alike – were at least fiercely resisted in their times. The surrender of the principles upon which the activities of hundreds of millions had rested for decades was a vast volte-face. Yet, it also lacked the intellectual and spiritual passion worthy of it; and since there was no battlefield surrender, there was neither conquering hero in shining armour nor captive foe to be marched away into oblivion. A Marxist (or ex-Marxist) alone could grasp the moral significance of a general secretary of the Communist Party of the Soviet Union declaring, as did Gorbachev for the first time in specific terms in October 1990, that 'only the market can ensure the satisfaction of people's needs'. Friederich von Hayek could not have put it more baldly.

At the same time, the edge was taken off this ideological drama by the obviousness – as seen in retrospect – of communism's fall. 'Any social State,' wrote H. G. Wells in 1913, four years before the Bolshevik Revolution, 'not affording a general contentment, a general freedom, and a general and increasing fullness of life must sooner or later collapse and disintegrate again, and revert more or less completely to the normal social life.' In his essay prophetically entitled 'The Great State', he tells us what he means by the 'normal social life'. It is a 'traditional economy, with individually owned property, family life, customary law and religious belief at its centre'. Conversely, the 'more rigid and complete' the 'superimposed social order' the 'more thorough will be its ultimate failure. . . . Even the illiterate peasant,' Wells added, 'will only endure lifelong toil with the stimulus of private ownership and the consolations of religion.'

That 'civilisation' as well as 'normality' lay just across the horizon, and that the socialist system had been cut off for too long from such 'civilisation', were recurring themes of communism's moment of historic failure. 'We should abandon everything which led to the isolation of socialist countries from the mainstream of world civilisation,' said Gorbachev (in a fashion reminiscent of the debate about 'Europe'). What this revaluation meant for socialist theory was wholly drastic. The West's ideas and institutions, albeit capitalist and market-based, were of a universal validity; the particularist, or specialised, ideas of socialism, virtuous in intention as they might have been, had not only failed but had kept those who had espoused them out of the world's 'mainstream'.

Typical was the assertion in London in February 1990 by Vadim Medvedev, last ideology chief of the Soviet Communist Party, that the Party had 'realised that ideas thought fallacious because "bourgeois" were the property of all civilisation'. Interestingly, the same kind of revaluation of 'civilisation' was being made in China before the curtain was (temporarily) brought down on such heresy in June 1989. 'Bourgeois law and democracy' had 'transcended the limits of time and space', announced the *Guangming Daily* in February 1987; the 'rule of law', stated the *Nanfang Daily* in September 1987, was 'of great value to humanity's spiritual civilisation'; the 'modern capitalist system' was a 'great creation of human civilisation', declared Xu Jia Tun, Peking's ambassador to Hong Kong, in June 1988. He was later expelled from the Chinese Communist Party.

Such judgments, when they were made in his own day, were scoffed at by Marx as the mere vapourings of sentimentalists. Now, it was being conceded not only that there was a world of 'human values' beyond the ghetto-like confines of the socialist system, but that such values were both 'normal' and *transcendent*. The ultimate heresy for a hard-headed 'scientific materialist', this was a notion which once would have stuck in the craw of every Marxist.

In other words, capitalism, hitherto seen as a mere way-station on the high road (or forced march) to socialism, was now a 'normal' expression of human endeavour. It was even, for some, its *summum bonum*. Alexander Yakovlev, Gorbachev's adviser and one of the principal (Jewish) architects of perestroika, declared in June 1990 that the 'convergence of the capitalist and socialist systems' was an 'objective process' – an old Marxist formula – and that it would 'gain momentum'. The concept of an unchanging and unchangeable 'human nature', hitherto perceived by 'scientific socialists' as a bourgeois deceit to legitimise exploitation and ethical inertia, was being re-perceived as a universally valid descriptive term for that which is most human and, again, 'normal'. Neither 'civilisation' nor 'society' now required a class label – 'feudal', 'bourgeois' and so on – to give them meaning; civilisation was civilisation, and society society, *tout court*. And like the people of other countries, the former Soviet people now aspired to the first, and sought to create a 'normal, healthy, just and prosperous' version of the second.

In this Hebraic jubilee more than status tumbled. On all hands, the fondest socialist expectations were demolished. It was 'the workers', from Solidarity's shipyard hands to Siberian miners – the vary vanguard of the industrial proletariat, in whose name the Party had claimed to rule – who led the way against the communist system. 'The [Polish] working class,' declared Prime Minister Jan Bielecki in May 1991, rubbing it in, 'fought against communism and won.' And when, of all workers, Soviet miners began to demand the privatisation of their mines with the aid of Western capital, the pit-roof fell in upon socialist assumptions. On the wall of the strike committee room at the Oktyabrskaya mine in Donetsk in the Ukraine, where they called the communist system 'fascist', a cartoon hung in May 1991, showing a manacled and chained worker, the links composed of the word for the Party. 'We Have Nothing To Lose But Our Chains' read the caption. In Bulgaria and Albania – militant Serbia too – communists survived their first exposure to democratic elections only by mobilising the peasant vote against the industrial proletariat and the urban intelligentsia. In Marxist terms, 'social backwardness' was at the last being called to the aid of the Party, as it foundered. This was class struggle with a difference.

The essence of it was the re-emergence from the thraldom of theory, especially of class theory, of live actors with their own notions of where their actual, or practical, interests lay. For the first time in decades, such interests were expressing themselves freely and making choices which owed nothing either to socialist prescription or to the restraints of socialist taboo. More striking still, as the burden of having to subscribe to falsehood began to be lifted from their shoulders, even communist leaders seemed relieved to be able to tell the truth. Thus, in June 1988, Deng Xiao Ping (a year before taking fright at the democratic upsurge) was reported to have told President Chissano of Mozambique that 'judging by China's experience, I advise you not to adopt socialism.' His then prime minister, Zhao Ziyang – who was to become the scapegoat of a hardline restoration – added, on the same occasion, that Chissano should 'concentrate on private enterprise'. Behind the smoke-screen of decades of ideological pretence, truth had been sedulously veiled. When the veil was raised, even the Chinese emperor could be observed admitting (for a moment) that he had no clothes.

Those who prescribed Marxist doctrine to others seem to have been among the least believing; it was as if the most devout of Talmudic or Koranic scholars were secret pork-eaters. Vyacheslav Shostakovsky, rector of the Moscow Higher Party Academy and one of the keepers of the Ark, turned out, at the twenty-eighth and last Soviet Party Congress in July 1990, to hold no brief for communism at all. He not only categorically 'rejected its ideals' but wanted nothing to do with the word 'socialism' either, let alone with the 'class struggle', which was now merely the 'politics of confrontation'. A Pope of Marxism had declared the promised resurrection – of the working class – a hoax; a Chief Rabbi had cast out the Ten Commandments and abandoned his congregation.

'Now I must admit,' said even Todor Zhivkov, for thirty-five years absolute master of Bulgaria, 'that we started from the wrong basis. The socialist foundation was wrong. If I had had my time over again,' he continued in November 1990, 'I would not have been a communist, and neither, if he had been alive today, would Lenin.' There was heaven-darkening tragedy in this as well as the basest farce: of lives taken, lost, and wasted in pursuit of a will o' the wisp, many of whose Oberons themselves turned out to have no faith. Their various admissions, once the game was over, pointed (at the mildest) to long-standing doubt, not only as to whether they had taken the right path but also as to whether the destination to which they were leading the 'masses' even existed. Moses led the Children of Israel into the wilderness (though only, in their case, for forty years); he showed them the way out of it too, bringing them to the borders of a promised land whose existence was real. The socialist journey of the masses was not geographical but ideological. That is, it was largely in the head, rather than through time and place: much of Tolstoy's Russia is also today's Russia. Ideology, not territory, was its principal terrain; the cerebral world of consciousness – 'class' consciousness, 'true' consciousness, 'false' consciousness – was its imaginary *terra firma*. True 'socialist man' was expected to prize above all things the quality of his (class) perceptions rather than the quality of his possessions, the base metal of human existence. 'Progress' was to be moral as well as material; moral rather than material, even.

When material development failed to deliver the basic necessities of life, the belief that at least the socialist order was morally superior to others was, for some, sustaining. Indeed, moral aspiration, behind the web of economic analysis, stands at the heart of Marx's Judaic dream. But so, also, does a moral zeal which is beyond the reach of ordinary, or 'normal', mortals. A dogmatic ideology, much of it bogus, sought to make good by endless repetition the flagging sense of purpose of those – the vast majority – who lacked both the Hebraic vision of a socialist deliverance and the discipline of the Jew's intellectual ambition. In the case of socialism, such dogma, as in all faiths, disturbed the sense of self, the sense of others, and the sense of the world which surrounded and seemed to threaten the socialist system. The return to the 'normal' was a return through this Alice's mirror.

Whatever else it represented, this was a defeat for Judaic thought, as well as for the everyday aspects of socialist planning and its command system. All systems of belief seek to impose a schema upon the real world, and all religious systems of belief are utopian. Moreover, in their fundamentalist versions all religious systems of belief tend to have vicious effects on 'normal' human relations. But Judaic thought, being simultaneously more cerebral, more imaginative and more energetic than most, has a propensity to seek to sweep all before it by force of argument, the creative use of words and (a term I have already employed) intellectual ambition. Marx's Marxism is of this kind. But the unstoppable force of such thinking had met the immoveable object not merely of 'human nature' in the abstract, but of actual human recalcitrance, human weariness, and human preference for the 'normal', the most decisive preference of all. Yet, only upon the point of escaping from a failed utopian endeavour did many exhausted citizens in the Soviet Union and Eastern Europe look about them, realising for the first time that what they wanted, particularly of material goods, would never be provided by the system they had built and inhabited for so long. But many intellectuals – this was essentially an intellectual revolution – had seen it, and said it, long before. They were the first not only to recover their senses, but to demand what a system created in the head could not give: intellectual freedom.

These 'dissidents' were individuals who had escaped the prevailing orthodoxy into their own internal worlds. It was called, justly, an 'internal migration' and had been going on, in one form or another, for decades. Each band of active dissenters – with relatively little cross-border contact between them until the mid-1980s – constituted in their own countries a species of conventicle of non-believers; that is, non-believers in Marxism. A minority of them, of different size in each country but larger in the formerly Catholic countries, such as Poland and Slovakia, than in the Protestant or Orthodox, were active Christians, sustained and aided by a counter-faith. A smaller but significant number (especially in Hungary, Poland and Romania) were Jews, or of Jewish descent. The majority were not so much 'on the right' – and few were in favour of the 'free market' as an article of faith – as anti-totalitarian, with contempt for the communist system and its servants. They wanted, above all things, freedom of thought, worship and movement.

Together, the leaders of the dissent essentially composed a small middle-class intelligentsia, hidden in internal exile and many of them descended from the 'bourgeois intelligentsia' and professional classes of the pre-communist order: survivors. Among them there were relatively few proletarians, including in Poland and despite the pre-eminence there of Lech Walesa and his Solidarity trade union movement. They were preponderantly teachers, writers, scientists, philosophers, actors, artists and other members of the liberal professions. Observed in their tabernacles – 'underground' seminars, secret meetings, church gatherings – their demeanour and often their appearance were familiar. They could have been, and in some respects they were, the West's left utopians of the late 1960s; and were destined, like the latter, for only a passing role.

In their hands, though many in the benighted East Europe of the mid-1980s still did not know it, they held a Pandora's box. It contained not only the spirit of the intellectual freedom they desired but also the promise of a capitalist restoration then wanted by a minority only. (It was an irony that Marxists were among the few who knew, from 'first principles', that one would be likely to lead to the other, at a time when most 'ordinary' people and many dissenters had no clear idea of what a market economy and market freedoms might entail.) Ranged around, and against, the intellectual dissenters were communists – among them, often, the dissenters' own family members in senior party positions – who, affected by the growth of dissent and themselves disillusioned, nevertheless hoped that the existing system could be made more effective by reform, and thus be saved. The transformation of communism into an out-and-out capitalism of the free market few on either side contemplated, whether as dream or nightmare.

It was salvation – salvation from communism, salvation for communism – which was the object of the rival ardours of the mid to late 1980s. The first salvation was to be achieved by Freedom, the second by Reform; some, like Gorbachev himself, lurched unsteadily back and forth between the camps, uncertain which they belonged to. ('Why do we need to rescue socialism by restoring private property?' Yegor Ligachev, the 'Kremlin hardliner', mordantly asked in July 1990.) But when it became plain that Reform, however radical, would not succeed in redeeming communism from itself and its apparatus, the Party of Freedom swiftly carried all before it. It had been discovered, as crisis deepened and the black market spread, that the collapsing productive system of socialism could not be modernised or 'marketised', as some reformers still hoped, under a socialist aegis. It also became plain that democratic aspirations could not be satisfied without a democratic system; and that neither process – of marketisation and democratisation –

could be resisted without violence, once they had begun in earnest. The last straw for communism and for communists, and a source of alarm to many dissenters, was the dawning awareness that there was no 'third way'. It was not possible to have a 'developed and successful market order' without it being capitalist also.

For a while, 'reform communists', by feats of prestidigitation, tried to square the circle. They balanced on the ends of their noses the 'regulated market economy'; in their heads crossed a high wire linking the Party-state and 'free initiative'; looked in their silk handkerchiefs for democratisation without democracy, and marketisation without a genuine market. Only the Chinese, being more acrobatic than the rest, managed both to set out on the Long March Towards Capitalism and to remain 'rock solid' in their socialist commitment. But the central dilemmas of communism – and socialism too – had been found out. The first dilemma was that a bureaucratically managed productive system had been an economic disaster. The second dilemma was that it was not possible to 'liberalise' such an economy without, on the one hand, casting aside socialist goals and on the other arousing irresistible pressure for greater individual freedoms. Violence to prevent the latter could only be a stop-gap measure. The third dilemma, bitter for the left the world over, followed from the first and second: no 'shaking up', or 'updating', of socialist theory and practice was available which did not make wholesale concessions to the laws and values of the capitalist market system.

For those who had already suffered enough from the failures of faith there was nothing to be done except to bring obeisance to its rule to an end, and to move on. In the end, the very heart of the *Communist Manifesto*'s predictions had been broken. The proletariat had not turned out to be capitalism's 'gravediggers'. Worse still, the communists – the proletariat's vicars on earth – had not only dug their own graves but, at the last, had handed over their very shovels to the returning entrepreneurs and private investors. Nevertheless, there remained in the heads of some members of the communist apparatuses, including those who were supervising the last stages of this debacle, the belief that it might be possible to have the best of both worlds, a communist-run and manipulated free market; that is, a capitalism over which communists still presided, either directly or covertly through surrogates and frontmen.

From October 1991, secret internal memoranda of the defunct central committee of the expiring Soviet Communist Party began to be

brought to light. They disclosed extravagant plans to 'penetrate independent commercial structures' being set up in the disintegrating Soviet
Union, to create an 'invisible party economy' – *inter alia*, through joint
stock companies part-owned by the Party – and to 'establish control in
key spheres of the market economy at home and abroad', including by
the investment overseas of the (collapsing) Party's billions of roubles. A
Triad-style or mafia capitalism, in which communists and ex-communists sat in the free market's back-rooms, was Soviet communism's last
and most desperate project. It would, so it dreamed, mastermind the
very deals which were being struck to 'open up the economy'; have the
accompanying socialist satisfaction of promoting the well-being of the
'masses', but now through Western-funded investment in the capitalist
development of the productive system; and, thereafter, (presumably)
fan into life the renewed 'class struggle' against the exploitative foreign
owner and investor. Meanwhile, crypto-communists, masquerading as
agents of the market order but with the flame of their utopian socialist
faith still burning, would be secretly building the new Jerusalem in their
heads once more, until the moment was 'ripe' for a socialist restoration.

Whether it was a merely fanciful delusion time will tell. But one of
the first reflexes of communism-in-retreat, when it was still unsure
where it was ultimately heading, had been to cut a deal with the market.
The idea of a 'state-controlled market economy' was dreamed up more
or less simultaneously by most communist apparatuses. Another feint
was to set up 'cooperatives', a half-way house between, or hybrid of,
socialist and capitalist impulses; the leasing for life rather than the
selling of property was another. Gradually, under the duress of gathering economic failure, the floodgates of market reform opened. But,
throughout, the hope remained that a market economy might not be
wholly synonymous with capitalism – or could be prevented from being
so by rearguard action – and could still be governed by socialist
prescription. After all, do not 'democratic socialists' and 'social democrats' in the West believe exactly this?

Such hope on the left, a utopian Hebraic hope, plainly springs
eternal. Its conditioned reflex, as communism collapsed, was that the
market, once shunned as a taboo and forbidden by doctrine, could yet
be made to 'serve' socialism, and even Marxism. (The Chinese clearly
believe something like this.) For a communist or socialist to accept a
new-fangled 'market Marxism' is not as difficult as may appear,
provided that policy dictates it and that there is a chance, however
remote, that the socialist brand might still be plucked from the capitalist

fire. A Chinese rationalisation about the meaning of the new Shanghai stock exchange was worthy of Fu Man-chu: the use of stocks and bonds as a means of financing business, one of their ideological magi declared, was 'not peculiar to capitalism'. In other words, the concept of a 'socialist capitalism', or at least an instrumental socialist use of the capitalist market, had made its embryonic appearance. It was but a short further step from here to the argument that the market economy could be made the basis of a socialist productive system and of 'socialist renewal'. Whether it would have staying power as a new layer of Marxist doctrine is open to question; that it had made an appearance at all was a sign, or cock-crow, of a possible intellectual Resurrection. There have been other signs of it too, not least in the claim from the Chinese that what they were engaged in was *not* a surrender to 'bourgeois liberalism' but the 'complete industrialisation and commercialisation' of the Chinese economy, a process of reform which would be 'firmly maintained for a hundred years'.

The implications of this were that the 'commercial' and the 'capitalist' are distinct, and could be kept so; that trade, including international trade, might be overseen by communist mandarins as well as any, without final subordination to the capitalist world economy; and that entrepreneurism, whether in private or state hands, was compatible with socialist ends, or could be made so. 'If it leads to improving people's well being, there is no contradiction with socialism,' Gorbachev had himself said of the market in May 1990. In Romania, a 'post-communist' National Salvation Front government had long been prepared for; the revolution of December 1990 was, at least at its outset, more apparent than real. Here, part of the Securitate, the praetorian guard of the communist dictatorship, had as early as 1988 been making its dispositions for Ceausescu's fall. Its agents had gone to the lengths of befriending, and even protecting, certain dissidents who might become the nation's post-communist leaders. 'You'll thank me one day,' one such agent genially told a cabinet-minister-to-be, Andrei Plesu, two years before the 'revolution'; and reappeared in Plesu's ministerial office, two days after the 'revolution', to shake him by the hand and to take up his duties as the new minister's security adviser. Such calculation, as the entire communist imperium began its fall, was worthy of the pen of a Tacitus, or Josephus. But then no communist, or socialist, has ever been, nor ever can be, wholly reconciled to failure. In every socialist the ideal survives the actual; and in every left intellectual, theory and theory-making survive practice and its failures. As for the men-of-the-apparatus, generally 'principled' in their own estimation but time-serving and venal in the estimation of others, they were on the whole far readier to give ground and to serve new masters than could easily have been credited.

All of it, including full-scale capitalist restoration in the former Soviet Union, could be clad (by some socialists) in the utopian left's Judaic cloth-of-gold. It could be seen – or dreamed of – as no more than a necessary 'detour' in the socialist 'liberation' of pullulating mankind from its universal 'alienation' and 'exploitation'. But before the pilgrim could attain this insight, building a new extension to Jacob's ladder of theory in order to reach it, he had the daunting failure of 'real socialism' to deal with. His task was, and is, made easier by the knowledge that this failure, and the Hebraic jubilee which brought it, had not been a subject for entire jubilation. Civic order itself, above all in the advanced world, was under increasing pressure; the demise of the only doctrine apart from fascism which had succeeded, at least in part, in mastering the turbulent wills of entire populations was not an unmixed blessing.

The desire for a 'return to the normal' was also a desire on the part of new hundreds of millions to join the market of hedonistic consumption and political freedom. The world, however, needs not only plenty and liberty – the first less attainable by all than ever, the second a relative, not absolute, matter – but also such order, civic, social, economic and moral, as human ingenuity can devise. Marxism was, above all, ingenious. Its true failure, a Jewish intellectual's failure, was to have been not ingenious enough.

THREE

St George and the Dragon

In Bolshevik iconography, St George was an heroic red revolutionary on a charger, the spirit of top-hatted capitalism a speared dragon, with Mother Russia in its relaxing coils. But now St George has lost both horse and halo, the dragon has become a milch-cow and Mother Russia has shaken off her fraternal saviour. The seven decades of socialism and Stalinism now seem an interregnum; the four decades of it in the socialist penumbra of Eastern Europe not even a life sentence.

Compared with the Ottoman, Austro-Hungarian or British empires, the Soviet empire – with all its might – was a relatively brief episode in the history of continents and nations. The ancient constellation of Great Russia with the Ukraine and White Russia, or the old fifteenth- and sixteenth-century Hanseatic league, had greater staying power. The magnetic force of Catholicism, the hold of Islam, and the 'Jewish Question' have all easily outlived the communist utopia, and its failed experiments in political and economic organization. Even the old fault-line across Croatia, which for 300 years marked the boundary of Ottoman rule in Europe, has reappeared. The 'upsurge' of Russian, Ukrainian, or Armenian nationalisms has been less an aberration than an attempted resumption of historical existences interrupted by the handful of decades of Soviet power. From the time of Pope Gregory VIII to that of Marshal Pilsudski or Semyon Petlura, there is a record to be recovered and re-learned. It is a history of faiths, peoples and nations to dwarf the deeds of Marxist-Leninism, deeds both base and heroic. Even the great war against Nazism, the brunt of which was borne by the Soviet Union, may turn out to have been pyrrhic.

The Soviet socialist imperium was hardly the first empire to have come down in ruins, merely one of the shortest-lived. Incredulity accompanied its steep decline; but Herodotus and Gibbon would not have had difficulty in tracing and understanding the causes of it. Grand parallels are just: the fall of Moscow, which neither Napoleon nor

Hitler could achieve by force of arms, has had consequences as great in their reach as any past imperial fall. In its wake, a united Germany began swiftly to establish its suzerainty in the old Austro-Hungary, and Islamic Central Asia to recover its ancient identity. The 'non-aligned' movement collapsed, and Catholic dominion began to be reasserted in Central Europe. Old Balkan confusions revived; Yugoslavia disintegrated into civil war. In Teheran, Bonn and Paris, in Rome, Ankara and Athens, and even in Stockholm, Vienna and Karachi, ambitions awakened and stirred to the prospects of hegemony and influence over individual countries of the former Soviet empire. India lost its patrons in Moscow, and China its position of leverage between the United States and the Soviet Union; English replaced Russian as the second language of education in Central Europe; and the past's old voices could be uncannily heard once more.

In Sofia, the historic complaint was resumed that Ottoman rule had denied Bulgaria 'the Renaissance, the Reformation and the Age of Enlightenment'. At the castle of Visegrad, where once the kings of Poland, Bohemia and Hungary had forged a compact against the Habsburgs, the representatives of the new Poland, Czechoslovakia and Hungary met to agree on common policy and joint action towards 'Europe'. In Croatia, the Serbs were seen as barbarous (as well as communist) legatees of Orthodoxy's ancient hostility to the Church of Rome; in Bosnia, Serbs, Croats, and Muslims took up arms against one another. In Tirana, representatives of an old Balkan confederacy – Albania, Bulgaria, Greece, Romania, Turkey and Yugoslavia – gathered for the first time since the second war; Russia, Ukraine, Moldova, Azerbaijan, Armenia and Georgia came together, as independent nations, to form a Black Sea 'economic cooperation zone' with Romania and Turkey; and in Poland, Hungary, Slovakia and the Baltics, Christendom was reinvoked as the 'true bond' of European nations. It was as if communism had never existed.

Annexations were undone, independences proclaimed from the confines of Scandinavia to the remotest reaches of the Transcaucasus and Central Asia – 'shall a nation be born at once?' inquired the prophet Isaiah – and armed conflict was joined, for the first time since 1945, in Europe. The Balkans, ruled for more than four decades (as to the manner born) by a variety of 'communist' autocrats – Zhivkov, Ceausescu, Hoxha, Tito – resumed their pre-communist paths, threatening themselves, their minorities and their neighbours with age-old troubles. Hungarians in Romania and Slovakia grew insecure, Czechs and

Slovaks drew apart, Serbs set upon their neighbours and were set upon in turn. Everywhere, the criss-crossing mismatch between national borders and the distribution of ethnic groups promised violence and insecurity, and the break-up of states into ethnic enclaves. Russians and Ukrainians made their mutual antipathies plain, Armenians slew Azeris, Tatars refused to join the new Russian Federation and Cossack mercenaries came to the aid of ethnic Russians in Moldova. Suppressed by 'socialist internationalism' and the supposed transcendence of race by class (and class by classlessness), both class and race made their comeback. This, too, was a 'return to normal'.

A new intellectual agenda, as well as a new political and economic agenda, was being set by such changes. The boulder of communism having been rolled back from the cave-mouth, hitherto half-employed intellectuals were pressed into service once more: to open the archives, to raise the dead, and to re-write the history of Central Europe, again. Now we were to know how many Polish officers were killed by the Red Army at Katyn; with what unsavoury enthusiasm indigenous populations – in Poland, in Slovakia, in the Ukraine, in the Baltic States – assisted the Nazis in their extermination of the Jews; how few in number were the communists in Estonia, Latvia and Lithuania during the 'popular' Soviet takeover in 1940.

While nations were being dismantled or restored, and even monarchs waited in the wings for a summons, baseness was everywhere exhumed into daylight. Parties-for-the-Swift-Reburial-of-the-Dead, especially the Jewish dead, crowded to the newly opened gravesides, shaking their fists or seeking forgiveness, or commonly both together. Standing again in the shadows of unrequited crime, both Stalinist and Hitlerian, many preferred to forget. For others, the wounds were too deep. Past wrongs committed by Hungarians against Romanians, Croats against Serbs – and Serbs against Croats – against Poles by Ukrainians, or against Armenians by Azeris, claimed prior attention. One man's family lost in Auschwitz was another's Karelia or Bukovina, the first lost by Finland to the Soviet Union in 1940, the second by Romania to the Ukraine. For others again, resentment at Serbia's royal mastery over Croatia from 1918 to 1939, or the plight, under communist rule, of the Black Madonna of Czestochowa, counted as much as, or even more than, the slaying of peoples. Moreover, memory of past deaths by the million, and (in the case of Stalin's victims) by the tens of millions, swiftly gave way – for many – to the pressures of present economic and political need. The threat of hunger in Russia or Albania, the struggle with the tasks of economic reform in Hungary or Poland, the suing to join the organisations of Western Europe, and, in some places, mere fighting, occupied the foreground of attention.

Indeed, the speed at which the institutions of the Soviet empire dissolved and vanished – Comecon in June 1991, the Warsaw Pact in July 1991, the Soviet Union itself in December 1991 – barely left time for reflection. The Potsdam agreement and the Yalta settlement of 1945 were undone in a matter of moments, historically speaking. The 350,000 strong Red Army presence began swiftly to steal away from most of Eastern Europe; German reunification occurred in a trice. The issue of how to 'bridge East and West' after the fall of communism itself fell suddenly on Western Europe with the tonnages of the Berlin Wall and the Iron Curtain, first breached in November 1989. The neutrality, followed in a twinkling by the friendship, of formerly hostile nations – Hungary on the instant applied to join Nato – caught the whole of the West by surprise, so quick was the process of transformation. In the Soviet Union, the generals were shocked at the 'loss of Eastern Europe'; in the West, no less so.

Equally or more unsettling was the prospect, made lurid by the first overwrought predictions, of hordes of Soviet and other migrants fleeing across the 'Mexican border between East and West', as the (Jewish) *éminence grise* of the Romanian revolution, Silviu Brucan, described it. Unpredictable, too, were the possible rapprochements, new ententes and old hostilities among the former constituent republics and satellite nations of the Soviet Union, as well as between them and their neighbours in Europe and Asia. Some in the West feared a 'geo-political vacuum' in this or that region of the former Soviet empire; others the disappearance of 'traditional buffer states'; others, again, drew dark comparisons with the aftermath of the collapse in 1918 of the Habsburg empire. In the former satrapies of the Soviet Union, the quickest off the mark – such as the Czechs – attempted to use the West's sudden anxiety and confusion to their own ends, without ado seeking admission to its institutions. Both Vaclav Havel and Gorbachev before his fall hinted that the Soviet Union's collapse threatened not only Central Europe but Western Europe also; Boris Yeltsin warned of 'fascist dictatorship' in Russia if the West did not come to his economic aid. Havel's was a prophecy almost biblical in its forebodings. If 'the West' did not extend its borders to the Dnieper and the Urals, he implied, the former communist nations might soon be 'furiously warring together'. At the same time, the dependency of Eastern Europe upon a Soviet economy in collapse – dependency upon its raw material supplies, especially oil, and as a captive market for the former's shoddy manufactures – had left the satellites in a condition which the West could not make good quickly, or make good at all.

That Germany in late 1989 and early 1990 chose the moment of greatest European insecurity, as the communist world collapsed, to equivocate in fearsome fashion about the Oder-Neisse line – even arguing in full view that the German Reich continued to exist within its 1937 borders, which had included present-day swathes of Poland and of the dissolving Soviet Union – briefly terrified many, both Jew and non-Jew. That Germany, from the outset of communism's fall, had poured billions of marks eastwards (until, saddled with the East German *Länder*, economic difficulties began to threaten their ambition) served only to remind historians of an old truth. There has never been room in Central Europe for two great powers: if not Germany then Russia, if not Russia then Germany. The Tsar and the Kaiser, in one historical incarnation or another, have been (in alternation) the rulers of the marches of Central Europe. A 'return to normal', once the Soviet tsars had lost their dominion, also involved a return to a latter-day Kaiser's protection of Central Europe. Indeed, as early as 1988, the Federal Republic, toying with 'neutrality', was already scaring its European partners by its 'unreliability' as it pushed its thinking eastwards in anticipation of the collapse of the Soviet empire. But if not Germany (with Austria's and Hungary's traditional support), who ultimately might be Central Europe's new gendarme? Who otherwise could tame the Serbs and the Croats, the Hungarians and the Romanians, the Czechs and the Slovaks, when the need arose? The envoys of Brussels? The Elysée Palace? The State Department? The United Nations? The Pope and his bishops?

Jews, who have thought so much of the thought of Europe, also know a great deal about the continent's periodic bouts of turmoil. They have had experiences of their own not only of the unchained Teuton but of the peasantries – and ex-peasant proletarians – of Great Russia and its immediate neighbours, from Poland to Romania, and the Black Sea to the Baltic, from Vilnius and Bialystok to Kishenev and Odessa. But the undoing of European agreements and treaties, from the 1815 settlement of Vienna to the 1919 settlement of Versailles, together with the withdrawal (and arrival) of armies, has historically threatened not only minority peoples but the stability of entire states, seemingly secure

within their borders. Detente has always spelled peace for some and
war for others. Today, the nations 'betrayed by Yalta' look to the 'unity
of Europe'. But the unity of Europe is itself a pipe-dream. Once an
integral part of the 'international socialist movement', semi-fictitious
and oppressive as it may have been, ex-communist Eastern Europe and
the territories of the former Soviet Union are now full of loose cannon.
Worse, some of these countries, including many of which the Jews have
the worst memories, are destined to permanent second-class membership of a 'poor man's club' of nations. At the same time, in this vortex
of pressures, the fear in prosperous Western Europe of being 'dragged
backwards' by the plight of the ex-communist countries has been
balanced by the shift eastwards (as in the phased transfer of Germany's
capital from Bonn to Berlin) of Europe's centre of gravity. It is the
former Czechoslovakia and Hungary, Germany and Austria, Slovenia
and Croatia, which stand at the heart of yet another 'Europe'. From
this Europe, Britain – which now has its smallest army since 1830 – is
far away. But Italy, for example, which formed a pentagonal alliance for
'regional cooperation' with Austria, Hungary, and the then Yugoslavia
and Czechoslovakia, is near.

The 'political void', or vacuum, left by the collapse of communism
was not as most commentators suggested. It was communism which
had stepped into outer darkness, the darkness of Gehenna, leaving
Europe, East and West, to most of its old devices. Moreover, it became
clearer than ever that, far from transcending Europe's past in a new
utopia, the practice of communism – and the struggle against it – had
accorded with universal patterns of human behaviour, from the noblest
to the vilest. The Donetsk factory worker, on strike in April 1991, who
declared that 'we have nothing to lose, we have already wasted our lives
in this country' was not the inhabitant of a new order, but of an old one.
The 'masses' who were convinced that nothing could be 'put right'
under the communist system were the 'masses' of any system *in extremis*.
Stalin's labour camps, together with the huge numbers of his servants
who manned them, were not under communist patent, even if their
scale staggers the imagination. As for the dreams of another way of
living, the pressures to emigration, the wild casting about for panaceas,
the conspiratorial melodrama of the attempted and failed Moscow coup
of 1991, with the suicides which followed, they were more Russian than
communist or anti-communist.

So, too, were the dark undertones of passionate torment which
attended Soviet communism's downfall. When Alexander Prohanov in

Literaturnaya Rossiya – the journal of the Russian Writers' Union – described the Soviet Union in January 1990 as an 'exploding galaxy with a black hole in its centre', the sentiment owned nothing to seven decades of dialectical materialism, and everything to the nature of Russian literary expression. 'The world will watch our bleeding land with horror,' he went on, 'as it vomits forth a nuclear and chemical miasma into the sea and air.' In this hysteria there were mock-heroics, but also a violence of emotion which Jews, often thinking similarly themselves, long ago learned to fear; their new exodus was largely prompted by it. In the anxieties about (and even wild hopes of) civil war, with innocence perceiving itself to be pitted against conspiracy and crypto-communists hiding in every wainscot, a Russian 'normality' was also restored. 'Clouds of terror', declared Boris Yeltsin, were 'gathering', as the Soviet Union – which he, more than any, had hurried towards disintegration – tried to ride the blows of the 1991 'putschists'. 'Despair' (in some) greeted Gorbachev's first brief ouster, as well as sycophantic deference to the coup's short-lived leaders. No dialectic could account for mood-swings such as these.

In Belgrade, another fevered Slav – Vuk Draskovic, the Serbian opposition leader – had described the Yugoslav communist victory in the December 1990 elections as a vote for 'bondage, Bolshevism, the past, disgrace and darkness', rather than for 'democracy, the future, light, salvation and honour'. This old rhetoric of depression and elation had for decades been sublimated in the vocabulary of 'struggle' against the sinister machinations of the 'class enemy' and the 'imperialist powers'; it was in the language of heroic endeavour to conquer nature and to raise production to undreamed-of levels, as well as in the rhetorical anticipation of the triumph of every socialist ambition. Such excess came from a lexicon (of words and emotions) which was at once strenuous and paranoid, bracing and violent, forceful and empty. At the same time it spoke to, even if it did not address, the spirits of 'the future, light, salvation and honour', and against 'bondage, disgrace and darkness'. In the communist period, the promise of communism represented the former, the pre-communist and the anti-communist the latter.

Now, it was the turn of communism to be trodden underfoot, and in a similar manner. 'Communist worms', warned a prominent slogan at one of Yeltsin's vast anti-communist rallies in July 1990, 'this body won't feed you any more'. And from the rally platform a speaker asserted, to thunderous applause, that 'neither the Tatars, nor the

Tsars, nor even the Nazis brought as much misery and poverty on the
people as the Communist Party of the Soviet Union'. (At such feverish
moments in Russian history, it is a sensible precaution for a Jew to pack
his bags.) In December 1990, even Gorbachev referred in Dostoevskyan
colours to the 'raging of dark forces' beneath the Soviet surface; a
luridness of vision which long predated Lenin.

Solzhenitsyn's essay, 'How We Must Rebuild Russia', published in
Komsomolskaya Pravda in September 1990 – an essay which Gorbachev,
while disagreeing with much of its content, described as a 'great and
deep work' – also depicted Russia in apocalyptic terms. 'We must try to
save ourselves', he declared, 'from being crushed by the rubble of
crashing Communism.' The latter's deeds, destined to be destroyed in
turn, had been work of destruction, work of unmitigated evil. 'We have
destroyed the peasants as a class, with their villages. We have polluted
our earth and water;' Russia itself had been 'destroyed' by its Empire.
On the Day of Atonement the Jews also beat their chests thus. This
world of foreboding and catastrophe was a world which for centuries
the Russians and the Jews had inhabited together, brooding – between
pogroms – in like fashion.

A desperate counter-rhetoric of communist self-defence also rent the
air. In Russia it employed a familiar, almost Judaic, vocabulary of
prophecy and lamentation. 'A huge, unprecedented disaster has taken
place,' announced *Rossiya Gazeta* in July 1991 on behalf of communist
restorationists, bewailing the nation's 'misfortunes'. 'The Motherland,
which was passed to us for preservation by history, nature and our
glorious ancestors,' it continued, 'is dying, coming apart, and sinking
into darkness.' Also to be heard were the accents of classical Marxism,
those of Marx himself in the *Eighteenth Brumaire of Louis Napoleon*. 'By
proclaiming anti-communism as their ideology,' Ivan Polozkov, then
leader of the Russian Communist Party, declared, 'they [the reformers]
assemble . . . the heirs of the overthrown classes, nationalists, dealers in
the shadow economy, and all those in whose way Soviet power stood,
and continues to stand.' This might be a dead language, as dead (for
most) as Latin. But it was still, in its own dark way, phosphorescent.

The layer of the years of Stalinism was merely another geological
stratum; the sub-stratum was eras deep. 'You have not lived through
totalitarianism, with a single ideology for seventy years', Boris Yeltsin
told Euro-MPs in April 1991; 'we are escaping from the burdens of the
past, and only after we have done that will we be ready to integrate with
Europe.' This was true, half-true and false. The burden of the Russian

past, older than a mere seven decades, was not so easily 'escaped', and 'integration with Europe' the illusion which cannot come to pass. The legacy of the seven communist decades did not 'accustom Soviet citizens to authoritarianism and the concentration of power', as one commentator put it. They had long been accustomed to it. In December 1991, Yeltsin, simultaneously president, prime minister and defence minister of the 'new' Russia, with emergency powers to rule by decree, compared himself in an address to the Byelorussian parliament with the seventeenth-century Tsar Alexei. Autocracy and the desire for a saviour are a matching Russian pair. So, too, are deference to authority, about which Russian Jews came to know a great deal, and abuse of power.

Indeed, the Russian 'soul' is first cousin to the 'Jewish soul', even if today's Russian anti-semites would move heaven and earth to disown it. Ancient premonitory doubt, in both, shadows every promise. Revolution and counter-revolution, tyranny and freedom – from the Tsarist emancipation of the serfs to its latter-day equivalent in perestroika-and-glasnost – have equally been the objects of fear and hope, unease and celebration. Of reforms, as of new princes (or party leaders), the Russian (and Jewish) reflex has always been to ask, 'How long will they last?' To doubt the permanence, the will, and the good faith of the 'reformer', a figure who has made almost as regular an appearance in Russian history as the tyrant, is Russian (and Jewish). To be sceptical as to the real limits of a new 'freedom', and even to fear such freedom, is Russian and Jewish; to agonise, usually without rebellion, over the morality of rulers and the wisdom or folly of their ukases is Russian and Jewish; to be troubled even by well-being, and to harbour near-paranoid suspicions of the motives of others, including the well-intentioned, are Russian and particularly Jewish. To deepen every Russian depression – and most of the former are depressive symptoms – was Marxism-Leninism's signal achievement. The latter also blended socialism's plebeian jealousy of merit and its 'egalitarian' contempt for the 'bourgeois' (both of them demotivations of effort which helped to sink the 'socialist project') with existing, fathoms-deep, forms of Russian inertia of spirit; the energies of minorities, such as the Jews, had always been required to help move the Russian leviathan from its slumbers. And, at the moment of its release, the native proletariat characteristically wanted to have (and to consume) more than it could afford (and could produce), while remaining envious, in a fashion dangerous for the newly-rich and energetic, of those few who quickly achieved what all were seeking.

But the survivors of the Soviet experiment cannot be considered a different species from those who have been spared the experience by geography and fortune. If it was clearly necessary for the individual under communism to 'foster some attributes and repress others' – including initiative, sense of responsibility and conscience – in order to 'come through', such self-repressions are the stigmata of every totalitarianism's survivors. Moreover, the Soviet party-state was merely a contemporary variant, if a highly elaborate and organised one, of autocratic Russian rule. In addition, the plebeianising effects of 'modern' socialism's policies and ethics have proved universal, even in Western liberal democracies where a socialist party's rule can at most be intermittent. Furthermore, despite the decades of specialised socialist taboo and the moral legacy it left behind it, old entrepreneurism, old xenophobia, old criminality, old hedonism, old religion, and old forms of literary and artistic expression sprang into reinvigorated life almost on the instant.

How so? Because Rip van Winkle had been asleep, not dead, and his sleep, historically speaking, had lasted only moments. The younger generation of (ex-) Soviet citizens also woke, usually long before its elders, disturbed by the sound of 'Western culture' and the appeal of its world-view; the last to leave their communist parties tended to be the old. A Western-sponsored poll of eighteen- to twenty-five-year-olds, conducted in November 1990 by the Soviet Institute of Sociology in six regions of the Russian Republic, found no fewer than 85 per cent in favour of the private ownership of land, thought to be the taboo of taboos in the Soviet Union. Marx, in his fulminating essay 'On The Jewish Question', had excoriated the Jews of capitalism for 'Judaising' the world with their ethics. Now, it seemed as if all Adam's Marxist offspring, or nearly all, would have invested even in the Garden of Eden. By 1990, China had 20 million registered private entrepreneurs, and boasted 452 millionaires.

There were many other resumptions, benign and malign, in which not only were the political reins of the pre-communist past taken up but also some of the precise party dispositions which had gone with them. In Hungary, for example, the structure of the election results in the first free elections since the communist takeover almost exactly reproduced the party rankings of 1945. 'After decades of dictatorship,' the new prime minister, Josef Antall, commented, 'the political reflexes of the Hungarian people have not changed.' A similar phenomenon was noted in the former German Democratic Republic, where regional voting patterns replicated those of the pre-communist and pre-Hitlerian era. The countries of Eastern Europe had, of course, experienced twenty-five years less of socialism-and-Stalinism than had the Soviet Union, the difference of an entire generation. In some of these former Soviet dependencies memories of parliamentary democracy and of economic well-being were real and still vivid; in a minority, including Poland, significant private ownership, including private ownership of land, had continued.

Nevertheless, in nearly all these countries – and most obviously in the former Soviet Union – responsibility for the transition to democracy was placed in the hands of those who had no working knowledge of democratic institutions. In the cases of Walesa, Gorbachev and Yeltsin, for instance, they had no reliable democratic instincts either. Still more dubious in quality of purpose, ex-communists lately steeped in an authoritarianism (and worse) of their own making became latter-day evangels of a democratic order. Dyed-in-the-wool proletarians professed to see virtue in meritocracy, and recent egalitarians adjusted themselves, in rapid order, to the survival of the fittest. But no wonder; the political turncoat, like the political Johnny-come-lately, is a universal figure. There was nothing here peculiar to the morality of ex-Marxists, or foreign to the mentality of those ready to serve any master. The failed Soviet conspirators who hurried in August 1991 to Gorbachev's Crimean dacha, in order to sue for mercy from the man against whom, perhaps with his foreknowledge, they had plotted – contributing to his downfall, but themselves returning to disgrace, suicide and prison – could all have stepped from the pages of a Russian novel. 'We can't give in to illusions any more,' they had told Gorbachev; a glimpse, before the gaol door closed on them, and the suicide's pistol shot rang out, of ordinary mortals, or familiars, caught struggling in the coils of circumstance from which nothing could extricate them.

Indeed, the revolutions had proceeded so quickly that many of their protagonists, Gorbachev included, fell by the wayside, unable to keep up with their momentum. The Hungarian Imre Pozsgay, the radical cynosure of all eyes until 1989, was a lost figure of the past a mere one year later. There were many like him in every former socialist country. In some cases, those tainted with any communist affiliation or sympathy whatever were held unfit to continue in the ranks of the reformists. In others, camouflaged as born-again democrats, they led a charmed life until a more rigorous anti-communism disqualified them from the political process. In rare but prominent instances, as with Boris Yeltsin in Russia and Leonid Kravchuk in the Ukraine, former communist authoritarians became the popularly elected heroes of the democratic hour.

In all countries, the earlier struggles for power between reformists and conservatives were complicated, and then overtaken, by bitter rivalries, personal and intellectual, between 'moderate' and 'radical' reformists. At the last, in almost every country, each political group was pursuing, or appeared to be pursuing, the end of the socialist order, but at confusingly different speeds or according to different political and economic prescriptions. In the collapsing Soviet Union, the restoration-ists tried to make hay, although their days were numbered, as the reformists fought each other. The cry to 'launch the battle against counter-revolution' could be heard in the background, as fur flew and teeth were gnashed over one economic grand plan and another for the transition to the market. While rival politicians blamed each other for the confusion, and the growing distinction between the Party and the state drove the former towards extinction, simultaneous revolutions – from totalitarianism towards democracy, from a socialist command economy toward capitalism, and from political centralism towards the independence of constituent nations – swiftly undermined the old orders. In the Soviet Union, monopolies of power in every area of political, economic and cultural life began to dissolve in the hands of those who wielded them, while the 'rock in which they trusted', the Party, no longer provided a footing. 'Preserving the Union', a great mosaic of peoples, languages, territories, histories and religions, was beyond the efforts of individuals or committees. Decrees, laws, pleas, threats, fell on deaf ears. The urge to independence in the Baltics, to conflict in Yugoslavia, and to the establishment of sovereign states in the former Soviet Union, were stronger than all countervailing forces.

In almost every socialist country, but most dramatically in the Soviet Union, capital markets and currency values, as well as systems of production and distribution, staggered towards collapse at the same time as the ideological hold of decades of Marxist-Leninist orthodoxy weakened and was extinguished. Apathy, anxiety and a drawing-back from violence between them provided (in most cases) a barrier of orderly inertia to a Hobbesian war of all against all. Despite suffering years of subordination to the interests of Party, state apparatus, and security police, the tenuous rule of law in general held, while streams of new law – much of it unread and unenforced – flowed from new organs of executive power both democratic and undemocratic. Enabling legislation, sweeping in scope but generally lacking in substance, was agreed upon in principle yet with no clear notion of how it might be turned into practice. Late converts to democracy persisted – as did Gorbachev, Walesa, Yeltsin and many other leaders – in believing that democracy could be introduced on impulse, or by fiat. Those unreconciled, and even flatly opposed, to democratic innovation found themselves swept along by the democratic tide.

In the bringing of an entire political system to confusion and breakdown there was an overwhelming sense, too, of justice being done; of decades of transgression of human rights and dignities at last beginning to be corrected. In the former East Germany, site of a half-century of political evil-doing, organisation came almost to a standstill. Administrators, judges and teachers, steeped in decades of the conscienceless issuing and obeying of diktats, were held by the West Germans to be unfit to the tasks of taking democratic decisions, of understanding Western legal practice, or of thinking freely. (But if they knew no better, they would also quickly show themselves willing to jump to new orders). In the Soviet Union, as the exodus from the once 20 million-strong Party turned it into an empty vessel, the very heart of the Party's system of power – its control over army, police, secret police, judiciary and education system – was being broken. Remaining Party members, some still professing loyalty to their faith, abandoned their last hopes after the failed 1991 coup. Clutching crumpled Party cards, or talismans which had lost their magic, the vanguard of the revolution found itself in outer darkness. Indeed, darkness seemed to cover the earth; the decades of 'socialist construction' had come to nothing. To Party members, disconsolately drifting away into the shadows, 'false consciousness' – and worse – had utterly triumphed.

The sense of having been abandoned to their fates was also a strong one. The Party was, after all, both God and Father in the Leninist heaven. Thus, Todor Zhivkov in February 1991 accused Gorbachev of 'having abandoned all the socialist countries, each country to itself'. Eduard Shevardnadze, the then Soviet foreign minister, was denounced by Party hardliners not merely for having 'abandoned' Eastern Europe, but for having 'brought down the whole structure of the socialist commonwealth'. The Party had been led like lambs to the slaughter by its own trusted shepherds; or so the Party, recently seen as red in tooth and claw by others, saw itself in its final travails. In expressing this sense of abandonment and betrayal by the 'Judases' of the reform process, the Party's last spokesmen disclosed the very essence of what it meant to 'belong' to the Party. To 'belong' signifies not only being part of or being connected with something, but also being in the latter's rightful possession. Membership of the Party was to be *possessed* by the Party. The flock of members was at the Party's disposal as well as in its safe-keeping. To the Psalmist, salvation 'belonged' to the Lord. In the communist faith, a general political salvation and the particular interests of the Party member rested together in the dove-like hands of the Party's leaders.

The ducking-and-weaving by Marxism-Leninism's avatars on the road to the capitalist market was of all things the most disconcerting and disorientating to the Party faithful. Here, betrayal of 'principle', or ideological treason – more commonly termed 'selling out' – was allied to unprecedented failure to rationalise such betrayal in terms familiar to the Party member. Indeed, the early vacillation, and even paralysis of will, of those who found themselves at the head of the column moving towards a capitalist restoration was a symptom of guilt and confusion at the sense of having 'betrayed' a cause. In China, each staggering step towards the market was ethically compensated for by self-lacerating Maoist injunctions to 'self-reliance', 'hard struggle', 'plain living' and so forth; each 'easing' of restriction, such as it was, was generally followed by invocations to the 'universal truth of Marxism' and so on. This was too simply interpreted as evidence of Chinese 'in-fighting', 'party splits' and 'faction', when moral ambivalence about the 'betrayal' of socialism was dividing many individuals from themselves throughout the socialist system. In the toils of the ethical, as well as practical, dilemmas posed by socialist failure, a Statue of Liberty erected in Peking's Tienanmen Square became, for the popes of Chinese Marxism, a goad to violence. In the Soviet Union, scruple was set aside in a different fashion, and socialism itself abandoned.

But what had to be overcome in every socialist country was the puritan aspect of the socialist ethic: the sense of sin inhering in capitalism's 'extreme individualism' and 'worship of money'. Both were assailed in July 1988 by Jiang Zemin, the general secretary of the Chinese Communist Party, typically cancelling Deng Xiao Ping's early *pronunciamento* that 'to get rich is glorious'. Indeed, slogans of austerity, discipline and self-command, however hypocritical, always came more easily to the lips of communism's lay clergy than pagan injunctions to eat, drink and be merry. And for every Soviet Party functionary lamenting the 'break-up of the Union' and the chaotic struggle for republican and even regional autarchy, there were doubtless at least two rank-and-file Party members for whom 'privatisation' suggested not emancipation but moral regression. Apparatus Stalinists, straining every nerve to sabotage the reform process, hated more the loss of their political monopoly or 'leading role', the transfer of their local powers to elected bodies, the haemorrhage of their numbers, the growth of organised factions within the Party, the ban upon their cells in workplaces, and the final seizing of their funds and sealing of their offices. The floundering opportunist suddenly found himself without his life's bandwagon; disappointed idealism was a different matter.

In decree and counter-decree, manoeuvre and counter-manoeuvre, the battle for power between the putative new tsars of the post-communist worlds which were being established on the territory of the former Soviet Union added to every confusion, practical and moral. Thus, in the 'war of laws' between Gorbachev and Yeltsin during 1990 and the first half of 1991, the decrees of Gorbachev's Soviet parliament were cancelled by Yeltsin's Russian parliament, and on occasions the cancellations were themselves cancelled; a similar farce was played out in April 1992 between Russia and the Ukraine over the possession of the Black Sea fleet. The three-day-long Emergency Coup Committee of August 1991 likewise cancelled the Russian parliament's decrees, and in turn had its own (four) decrees cancelled. Even ambition for reform and the making good of a suffering social order were lost from sight in a wrestling for position. Catching and holding a political rival in an arm-lock took precedence, as economic failure deepened, over every other purpose, that of establishing a market economy included. It was as if the very energies for reform were being exhausted by the struggle for pre-eminence itself. At the same time, plan and counter-plan for political and economic change were dragged down together, not only by rivalry and faction but also by the dead-weight of cumbersome new legislative processes; beyond extrication by decree, they remained mired in that Russian mud of ages which had halted a Napoleon. Not even the attempted coup of 1991, which sceptics declared to have been fixed, served to concentrate effort. On the contrary, it set in train only a more headlong collapse of central power, in which no tsar's writ any longer ran throughout what had once been the Soviet Union.

One tsar, Yeltsin, had been the Soviet Communist Party's Moscow secretary until the late autumn of 1987, yet spoke – or seemed to speak – for headlong pluralism and market reform. The other, Gorbachev, general secretary of the Party until the summer of 1991, seemed (eventually) to speak for much the same, but in dilute and contradictory fashion. In common, they had the authoritarian instincts of the communist and offered the democratic professions of the reformer; Gorbachev's greater ambivalence, wrongly perceived as simple indecision, and Yeltsin's greater brashness, wrongly perceived as democratic ardour, separated them. The first set in train, with his perestroika, political and other consequences from which he then recoiled; the second, driven by lust for power, was impelled to outbid his rival in radical pretension. Neither, at the outset, had wanted the drastic outcomes – a capitalist restoration, a political disintegration – which were to engulf them. Both had had in mind, as erstwhile 'good communists', a greater or lesser degree of liberalisation in order to preserve the viability of the system; both came to preside, at loggerheads, over a gathering political stampede and a growing economic chaos. The difference between them was that Gorbachev swung back and forth like a pendulum, and was undone; Yeltsin, head lowered, charged full pelt into the turmoil.

A sample eight weeks – from March to May 1990 – taken at random from the history of Gorbachev's uncertainties reveals the nature of his own, and his society's, moral upheaval. In March 1990, in his reformist persona, he declared forthrightly, 'We must get down to creating a full-blooded domestic market'. A month later, his compensatory socialist persona restored, he was himself denouncing Party reformists for wanting to 'restore capitalism'. A mere month after that, moral confusion further compounded, he was blaming others – in this case, 'the people' – for the slow progress of reforms while simultaneously confessing that 'everywhere we are being hindered by complexes.' That his own 'complexes' were included among them he did not, and could not, admit. The consequences of this ambivalence had already been six years of largely meaningless economic plans, without significant action to implement them. But mockery of the Abalkin Plan, the Ryzhkov Plan, the Shatalin Plan, the Second Ryzhkov Plan, the Abanegyan Plan, the Pavlov Plan, the Yavlinsky Plan, the Yeltsin Plan and so on, did not get to the heart of the matter. Merely to point with scorn or disbelief at the tragic printing of money, the bare shelves, the juggling with prices, the desperate barter deals and the rest was to underestimate the role of that paralysis of the will, as I have called it, which afflicts every backslider from orthodoxy. 'I am a Communist,' the Byelorussian Alexander Zhuravlyov told the Congress of People's Deputies in Moscow as late as September 1991, 'a convinced Communist, because I believe that the Communist idea is a state form of Christianity.' For many, there is no greater fear than that of transgressing such orthodoxy's outer limits.

The apostate, lay or religious, is a wracked figure; the pains of apostasy may include crucifixion of one kind or another. Some forms of this crucifixion may come to be invested with a sublimity all their own, but most will never earn a posthumous celebration, or even notice. The socialist apostate, like any other, must live with his conscience, always provided that he has one. Here, the equable contemplation of an open market in men's fates, as well as in mere goods and chattels, was as beyond most Marxists, communists and socialists (or even most ex-Marxists, ex-communists and ex-socialists) as it is beyond most Christians. The Western banker and entrepreneur, pushing and pressing for the legalisation in the former socialist countries of every form of private economic initiative, for the entire decontrol of prices, for the transfer of most – or even all – productive economic activity into private hands, for the tax-free repatriation of foreign investors' profits and so forth, entered upon the ravaged socialist scene as the money-changer intruded into the Temple. But the desecration of any Ark is the worse if the faithful believe, or bring themselves to believe, that they are in some way to blame for it. Guilt is the other face of ritual observance.

Its consequences in the Soviet Union, where the taboos were strongest, stalled reform *in medias res*. Ambivalence sought to preserve state and public property, while ostensibly promoting privatisation. It baulked at currency reform and let loose a promiscuous variety of roubles, dollars, coupons and vouchers; it prodigally allowed Nature's resources to run to waste while the moral dithering and political infighting – closely connected – continued. The 'impatience' of a Yeltsin fastened upon, and made political use of, every equivocation; equivocation, in turn, justified and concealed itself as 'practical difficulty', as 'defence of principle', as the 'people's interest'. Warnings of violent revolution, if reforms were not pushed to their limits, served to hustle some of the hesitant onwards; the momentum of events swept others before it. For a time at least, reformers (of different kinds) and conservatives (of different kinds) were united in pursuing the fantasy of Soviet society's 'rebirth' – by reconstruction in the one case, by closer adherence to holy writ in the other. Yet, even the drive towards capitalism was, for most, a means to a moral end rather than the end itself. Anti-socialism, socialism's *alter ego*, could no more free itself from a utopian ethic than God and Satan could be divorced in Milton's epic.

Indeed, if socialism could not redeem society, many socialists in their quandaries had concluded, then capitalism or the 'market economy' must be invested with the task instead, as I have shown. For a while it was wishfully believed, by some, that socialism's moral ends – 'equality' and 'social justice' chief among them – could be made compatible, somehow, with 'democratic choice' and market freedoms. When the illusion faded, the anxiety of some communists and socialists became intenser, while others jettisoned their scruples as if they had never had them. For some, the black marketeer remained a black marketeer, or turned into a 'Jew', a 'Pole', a 'gipsy' or a 'Romanian'. For others, gritting their teeth, he became at best the free-booting embodiment of the new 'market spirit', or at worst a 'negative aspect' of society's 'renewal'.

From the service of the gods of party and proletariat to service of Mammon's unrighteousness was a harsh transition; the old transition 'from feudalism to capitalism' in the Marxist rubric was as nothing compared with it. Western commentators concentrated on the technical difficulty of moving quickly, or at all, from a command to a market economy, but the moral transition went largely unconsidered. This was in part because it was so widely held in the West to be self-evident that private property (for example) was a good-in-itself; in part because so many believed the Soviet system, and even socialism itself, to be immoral. Almost any change of economic order, so the hidden argument ran, would be ethically for the better. But for those, East and West, who thought that socialism's ethic was a universal one, even if it had in practice proved fallible or been 'betrayed', reconciliation with 'private' business, 'private' employment and 'private' ownership was a different matter. Socialist recoil from them in the former Soviet Union and Eastern Europe was most often expressed indirectly. Indeed, outright moral opposition to the market everywhere grew more difficult as the 'real socialist economy' collapsed at the feet of the market economy's critics. It was argued, instead, that 'the people' were 'not ready' for the freeing of prices or a steep rise in unemployment; or that the social consequences of the reform would create 'unrest' and even 'destroy the social fabric'; or that a 'full scale' property market would fall into the hands of 'speculators' – a coded term in the old Stalinist vocabulary for Jews – and so on.

Reform gradualists, throughout the disintegrating socialist world, fought with 'sudden-shock' reformers over what appeared to be purely practical economic considerations. But it was inhibitions over the break-up of state monopolies, or over the contents of privatisation legislation, which constituted the actual agenda of contention, much of it guilt-ridden and most of it hidden. It was to salve consciences, and not only from motives of obstructiveness, that some sought (uselessly) to combine 'the plan' with 'the market'; and it was not only 'lack of experience' but simple unwillingness which prevented the speedy creation of the legal framework for enterprise, as well as the 'investment environment' upon which Western capital was insisting. Even in Hungary, on paper the most market-orientated of all the post-socialist countries, the govern-ment – a government of the centre-right – tried to keep control over much of the economy. In Poland, as state firms collapsed, subsidies and centralised decision-making began to be reintroduced to save them; the market, it was now being held, could not be the economy's 'sole regulator'. The state, declared a spokesman, with desperation increas-ing, 'must take part in the construction of the conditions for a market economy'. Indeed, in many ostensible post-socialist economies, the Party-state's old placemen, transmuted into the (unwilling) agents of the new market order, continued to manage, or mismanage, the national economy in the manner to which they were accustomed. Particularly in Yeltsin's Russia, this was business as usual. And if the Chinese condemned capitalism while continuing to seek capitalism's assistance, or tried to confine the market's 'excesses' to 'special economic zones', they were merely riding the moral tiger in their own fashion. The desperate spread of barter (exchanging natural gas for potatoes, or meat for oil) had as much to do with a subconscious desire to postpone the evil day of an entirely free market as with the lack of hard currency, or the collapse in value of the rouble.

When some Soviet peasants began applying, in 1990, to collective farm chairmen for the long leases which were being newly allowed them – in lieu of fully private land ownership – they were frequently allocated the worst land, and denied equipment and resources. When Bonn transferred billions of marks to its new Eastern provinces for investment in infrastructure and job creation, they looked hard for, but had difficulty in finding, economic 'lift off'. Millions of people, after decades of collectivisation and state ownership, did not want the responsibility of owning their own land or of becoming entrepreneurs. Despair and anxiety, not the galvanisation of effort, characterised many responses to the dawning of political and economic freedom. In many East European countries, most notably in the former German Democratic Republic, an avalanche of claims for the return of, or compensation for, property and land confiscated by communist (and Nazi) regimes also greeted the new dawn. 'It seems as if the whole country is up for grabs', declared a Berlin official at the end of 1990, as West Germans swarmed into what had been East Germany like gold prospectors. At the same time, especially in the collapsing Soviet Union, confusion and hesitation over the very principle of private ownership rights bedevilled reform. In particular, the idea of a 'market in land', despite the reported readiness for it among younger Russians, aroused powerful aversion.

Such a market, Boris Yeltsin himself declared in 1990, 'might come later', but only when 'the people' were 'psychologically ready to accept it'. In Czechoslovakia, for instance, farmers resisted the dismantling of cooperatives, forcing the government to back down from some of its reform proposals. In the former Soviet Union, a characteristic vacillation, rooted in reasons to which Yeltsin had pointed, afflicted even dilute land reform measures. Officially, there were 'no land registers', land valuation was a 'slow process', and so on. Unofficially, taboo impeded change. Even in Russia under the seemingly headlong Yeltsin, the private ownership of land was to be confined to 'plots used for the growing of farm products'. And though the sale of land was to be permitted, against bitter opposition, such right would not be able to be exercised until the lapse of ten years, and then only in a re-sale to the state, in the shape of the local council.

Collectivisation had cost hundreds of thousands, even millions, of peasant lives in the 1930s. Decollectivisation was now being (partially) introduced over the politically dead bodies of its 'hardline' opponents. 'Our country is special,' Gorbachev had declared; reforming property relations was 'very painful'. Quite apart from the historic memory of the old Russian communal village, the *obshchina*, and the unwillingness to own land privately at all, it was as if the collectives, whose birth was in bloodshed, had established their own landmarks; or as if the old biblical taboo against moving them, after only seven decades, was stronger than any reform measure. Even the most liberal of Russian reformers, such as Vadim Bakatin, repeated Yeltsin's assertion that the Russians were 'not ready psychologically' for the 'selling of land'. It was not only the conservative Yegor Ligachev who was opposed to property in land with his 'whole soul'. 'People here,' declared Yeltsin in December 1990, 'do not understand the concept of buying and selling land. The land is like a mother. You do not sell your mother.' This was more animism than Leninism, but not to understand it, Yeltsin added, was not to understand the 'Russian soul'. Twelve months later, in December 1991,

Yeltsin reversed his position, issuing a decree legalising the private ownership of land. But the language of his explanation of the resistance to it, old as the hills, put the false premises of the Western investment consultant (say) at a planetary distance. The soul is not the coin of the banker.

It was not that cultivable land had been entirely kept from private hands in the former Soviet Union. Indeed, a mere 3 per cent of it, privately owned even under communism, had produced a staggering 25 per cent of the total value of Soviet agricultural output. Statistics, however, could not touch the heart of the problem of understanding Gorbachev's 'special country'. Thus, that the 'Soviet Union' was always 'Mother Russia' in communist disguise was comprehensible, if comprehensible at all, only to the most cosmopolitan (or Jewish) of Western imaginations. Moreover, seven tormented decades of 'scientific socialism' had added a further dense layer – particularly impenetrable for the non-Marxist – to the already many-layered life of the 'Russian soul', a life which had also been carried away from Russia in the thoughts and memories of hundreds of thousands of Jewish migrants. This 'soul' now inhabited a world pre-communist, communist, non-communist, anti-communist and post-communist; Occidental, non-Occidental and anti-Occidental; pagan, Christian, Muslim, Jewish; religious, non-believing and strongly atheistic; rational, and steeped in darkest superstition; peasant, proletarian, nascently bourgeois and plebeian. Yet the 'Russian soul' remained, despite everything, predominantly peasant and mainly Christian. At the same time, it was never fully represented by the Christian ethic, just as it had never been fully bent to the purposes of Marxism; and was neither redeemed nor suffocated by the decades of socialist construction.

In the system's prolonged crisis, sentiments which had always lain close below the surface of the thin veneer of Bolshevik orthodoxy provided a common basis of mutual understanding among many of the opponents of the communist order. Religious restorationists, monarchists, slavophil nationalists, anti-semites and even conservative communists appealed in their various ways – and sometimes in the same way – to the 'Russian soul'. The neo-Stalinist Yegor Ligachev's 'soul', recoiling from private property, was kin to the 'soul' of Solzhenitsyn, bleeding for Mother Russia. To Ligachev, the restoration of private property was a 'step backwards towards exploitation'; to Solzhenitsyn, a step forward towards Russia's reconstitution. Each, from opposite standpoints, was seeking a return to fundamental principle as a means to the salvation of an ideal Russia. Likewise, the Russian anti-semite might be equally communist or anti-communist; the nationalist could as well be a dyed-in-the-wool Party loyalist, or ex-loyalist, as he could be a former inmate of the gulag. Warnings against the 'exploitation of man by man' in the market, and fear of the revival of old class divisions, came equally from religious conservatives as from Stalinists; the emergence of a 'new bourgeoisie' was as much the object of anticipatory envy and hostility among ex-Party proletarians as among the reappearing bigots for a restored (and 'purified') Old Russia.

Hence, to have for so long reduced the fierce agonisings about the former Soviet Union's future direction to a narrow Western focus upon the mechanics of privatisation or the foibles of its competing leaders was a *reductio ad absurdum*. Similarly, if conservative communists objected to 'hired work and hired employment', the objection spoke to more than mere Marxist dogma; if the shops emptied and citizens fought for a loaf of bread, the memories and feelings it aroused afflicted 'Russian souls' as well as bodies; and when the voice of the anti-semite was once more heard in the land the Jews rightly fled.

Indeed, throughout the collapsing socialist system, the loss of value of currencies, the opening of the stock exchanges, the reappearance of the foreign investor, the public auctions of state property and the swarming everywhere of the street hustler – 70 per cent of Poland's new tax-paying entrepreneurs in 1990 were street-traders – stirred historic emotion, much of it of unease and ill-feeling. While Western politicians debated among themselves about whether to 'give money to a man with holes in his pockets' (or wait until he had bought himself a new pair of trousers), the deepening distress became increasingly complex and dire. There were potentially dangerous hiatuses, everywhere in Eastern Europe, as plans to 'sell off the state sector' stumbled over lack of buyers, both domestic and foreign. Unworkable voucher schemes, free share distributions, loans, and systems of payment by instalments were dreamed up to assist citizens to purchase 'stakes' in industries which were beyond rescue. At the same time, the moody crowd saw asset-stripping, financial scams, tax evasion, and the acquisition of sudden riches going on before their very noses, as prices rose, supplies failed, and tens of millions stood on the bread-line.

Whether governments meant business (in every sense) or wavered in their courses, advancing and stalling, living standards generally fell, unemployment rose, and – in relation to the scale of need and expectation – there was little foreign investment. The dragon of communist oppression had been slain, but at the price of slump, inflation, rising personal debt, and the collapse of markets. Poland, for example, struggled successfully to bring its inflation under control, but at the familiar (capitalist) cost of accelerating bankruptcies and unemployment. Russia's attempted transition to a market economy brought the ending of price controls, huge increases in living costs and millions of jobless. In place of command systems able to produce goods which the consumer did not want, or with a choice would not have chosen, came free markets in more desirable goods which few without access to black money could afford to buy; public opinion surveys in ex-communist countries pointed to growing disillusion with many of the consequences of the economic upheaval.

It was to the widening of social inequalities and other old class grumbles in the East that the Western left, such as it was, pricked up its ears and paid most attention. Its hope of a renewal of 'class struggle' springs eternal, and not without reason. It had been the proletariat which had borne the brunt of 'socialist construction'; now, its old duress was ending in the deepening prospect of unemployment and exclusion from the very choices the gaining of which had been a principal object of the upheavals. (No one would choose to be a Jew in such a setting.) At the same time, domestic output and productivity fell throughout the former socialist countries. As the old factories began to close and the new shops to open, exhausted and cynical working people, far from being spurred to new effort, recoiled from their labours; many folded their arms and looked on; some ripened into an ancient resentment.

It was not surprising. Most of the *nouveaux riches* of the dissolving Soviet Union and the other former socialist countries were less interested in self-denying productive investment, which had helped set American capitalism in motion, than in conspicuous consumption. After decades of scarcity and the repression of hedonism, access to new consumer goods became the hope of all. But especially for the industrial working class, many of whose defunct plants were closing down rather than being transformed into the shining joint stock companies of a new market utopia, a Dickensian world seemed to beckon. In it, the noses of the poor remain for ever pressed to the tantalising windows of the rich man's emporia. Moreover, if an individual's 'class position' has always been measured by his or her distance from doing the dirty work of production – the nearer to it, the 'more working class', the further, the less – how was the employed post-socialist proletarian to escape

Marx's class stereotypes in new market economies which were too impoverished to provide 'opportunities for all'?

'Barracks socialism' may have been formally brought to an end but not the 'class interests' it thought it was promoting. Furthermore, those who were most attracted by the blandishments of the market economy were everywhere those who stood most to gain from its freedoms: in particular, those who had youth, marketable skill, energy, ability, education, professional qualification, or (best placed of all) those who had already found prosperous niches in the illegal shadow economies of the communist period. Now it was they, not the proletarian, who emerged into such daylight as there was; they who largely formed the metropolitan crowds which rallied in August 1991 to the defence of the democratic revolution in the crumbling Soviet Union; they who constituted the new (and old) political class which came to the forefront of the post-communist orders.

As ever, the 'ordinary man' at his proverbial – and provincial – lathe, had no place in, and no realistic chance of joining, the quickly-forming circles of power-and-pelf seekers under the new dispensation. A Donbass miner, or his son, now had as little (and as much) hope of becoming a Moscow commodity exchange broker as a nineteenth-century Parisian *grisette* had of finding her way into the *Almanach de Gotha*. Instead, the embryo and new capitalists were often those who had already become accustomed to supplying the (black) market for gain. Their number included the managers of state enterprises, and ministry or Party officials. Through their networks of contacts they were particularly well-placed to profit from the liberalisation of foreign trade and from the development of joint ventures. But nimble-witted street-trade, too, was an alien world to the average stolid proletarian, habituated to the torpid work-rhythms of the 'socialist system of production'. The truth was soon plain. Tens, even hundreds, of millions of workers and others in the old socialist imperium – above all, the elderly, the uneducated, the unskilled and those whose skills were unadaptable or outmoded – would be entirely unable to 'compete' in the new, or putative, market systems. In addition, most, including the long-standing anti-communists, had had their habits and even their emotions shaped by a 'socialist culture'. Many would therefore feel an instinctive satisfaction when their fellows failed to 'get on' in the market, should they try.

At the root of all this was, as ever, class and 'class feeling'. The latter could quickly turn ugly. Anti-Walesa Solidarity trade union activists were complaining by May 1991 that their old hero, recently installed as president, had 'sold Poland out to the bankers', a claim whose sub-text could read, and in Poland would be read, as 'sold to the Jews'. 'Smugglers', announced a burly Solidarity representative from Bydgoszcz, 'rule in this country'. In Romania, in June 1991, an angry factory striker could be heard shouting, 'We don't need boutiques and shops in this country, we need work'. 'Market Economy, Yes; Unemployment, No', read a slogan at Moscow's 1990 May Day Parade, as one utopian fantasy replaced another. Tens of thousands vainly marched and rallied in the former East Germany against the closure of state firms and its effect on employment; many knew, here and elsewhere in the old socialist system, that they were unlikely to work again. Indeed, there seemed to be little or no work for millions, despite the huge and evident tasks of reconstruction needing to be fulfilled. Not surprisingly, the 'contradictions of capitalism' (or the problems of life in a free market) were being quickly perceived as no more than a 'big swindle'. 'Herr Kohl, do you want to make a poor-house out of Thuringia?', inquired a demonstrator's placard at a 30,000-strong Berlin protest-rally called by the German metalworkers' union.

The restoration of capitalism and of civic liberty in the former socialist societies was having a predictable consequence: the return of a class-inspired trade unionism, employing the slogans and methods of the Western industrial class-struggle in its heyday. During the upheavals in the socialist system from 1988 onwards, including in China, there were under-regarded and under-reported general strikes, warning strikes, sympathy strikes, hunger-strikes and sit-in strikes, including underground protests by Albanian miners. Coal-miners everywhere, iron-ore miners in Romania, zinc, lead and copper miners in Poland, gold-miners in Siberia and even uranium miners in Mongolia entered the fray, sometimes in unpredictable fashion, as economies and political systems decomposed around them. 'Let us roll up our sleeves and show our fists like the miners,' Boris Yeltsin bellowed demagogically to a vast opposition rally in Moscow in March 1991. Romanian coalminers attacked the democratic movement with clubs and pickaxe handles, shouting, 'We will not sell our country.' Others, like the Siberian miners, demanded the right to 'earn our bread independently', struck for the free market, and threatened, in April 1991, to flood their mines if Gorbachev did not resign. Port workers at Novorossiisk on the Black Sea even struck, in January 1992, over demands that they be paid not in roubles but in dollars.

As socialism went under, there were strikes which were principled and strikes which were opportunistic; strikes for more food and strikes for better equipment; strikes for higher wages – or 'market wages in a market economy' – and strikes for lower prices; strikes for better working conditions and social protection; strikes against the threat of unemployment and strikes against the victimisation of strikers; strikes, especially in the evaporating Soviet Union, for the restructuring of firms, the removal of communist managements and the ousting of Party cells in workplaces; strikes demanding the resignation of governments and the holding of free elections. In the Albanian, Bulgarian, Czech and Polish democratic revolutions strikes played a major role in finally bringing down the communist regimes. ('Thanks to strikes,' declared President Walesa, 'I am where I am.') In Ulan Bator, there was even a strike of seven TV repair-men in protest against privatisation in Mongolia. But, in the longer term, it was the strikes which occurred after the socialist fall which were most telling, however inchoate and sporadic. They revealed opposition to the selling-off of state firms, opposition to the ending of subsidies, opposition to the introduction of new taxes, opposition to the limitation of wage demands and to wage freezes, and opposition (as in the former East Germany) to policies of the 'survival of the fittest'. In Poland, there were strikes and factory occupations demanding the 'protection of the Polish economy' and the 'defence of workers' interests'.

All these strikes made plain, like it or not, that class goes to the heart of the social order. But in collapsing communist societies there had been a difference: militant class action had expressed itself in favour of capitalist restoration, as well as against it in an older, reflex class-reaction. Proletarian protagonists took up the cudgels both for the socialist St George and the capitalist dragon. Yet, it should have been plain from the history of the Nazi period – for example – that there was never a *necessary* connection between roused working-class emotions and socialist aspiration. This the Jews, at least, have always known, and have carried the knowledge with them from decade to decade, and nation to nation.

The industrial working class had been the brawn, not the vanguard, of the Bolshevik Revolution. At its demise, the Soviet trade union movement had some 140 million members. The expectation that, having borne the socialist burden for seventy years, they would now without demur bear the social cost of the escape from socialism was a forlorn one. Nor did these millions constitute a 'reservoir' of pliant, cheap, skilled and hard-working 'labour' which could simply be placed at the disposal of the thrusting entrepreneurial spirit. Moreover, class despondencies and angers are not satisfied by the toppling of statues; without a party – though not the Party – to espouse their interests, working-class fears must find some other outlet.

Such interests and fears are real, and rooted in the experience of ages. In March 1990, a bill was being debated in the doomed Soviet parliament to restore the legitimacy of private property, including in the (Marxist) 'means of production'. A 'conservative' or 'hardline' amendment to the bill – an amendment believed by its supporters to accord with the dictates of the 'Russian soul' – sought, in terms, to forbid the 'exploitation of man by man'. The amendment was hotly opposed by 'progressives'. 'Those who propose this amendment,' declared Yuri Boldyrev, a young radical deputy from Leningrad, 'are unable to explain what is meant by exploitation.' There was an angry interjection. 'I, as a potential victim of exploitation,' shouted another deputy, who announced himself to the assembly as a 'worker', 'understand very well what it is.' Such class feeling was unlikely to recede, despite the countervailing pressures to unity in conditions of shared hardship. Indeed, class was inscribed from the first in trade union resistance to the 'shock therapy' approach to market reform; fear of class reaction could readily be detected in the hesitations of the reformer. A preparedness to resist class angers also made an appearance in the attempts – such as those of Gorbachev in April 1991 – to curb strikes in the public sector, ban political protests in working hours and make illegal the impeding by pickets of others seeking to reach their places of employment. 'Those who act illegally to prevent people working,' announced Valentin Pavlov, the then Soviet prime minister and one of the 1991 coup plotters, 'should know they will be punished.'

As the prospect grew of permanent disinheritance (and the old toil) for many, and of new plenty for some, so too did the risk increase of a resumption of the antagonism of classes and of its traditional forms of expression. In March 1992, Gorbachev – in his new post-communist and even anti-communist persona – had warned that communism could 'come back to life'; it was 'like the Hydra of Greek myth', he unappealingly declared, 'whose heads grew back after they had been cut off'. Within a month, in April 1992, a new United Communist Party of Russia was being set up at a 'secret' meeting in Jeleznodorojnyi, near Moscow; a week later, the communist youth movement, the

Komsomol, which had broken up after the failed 1991 coup, also announced its re-formation; in July 1992, the rump of the banned Soviet Communist Party furtively held its 'twenty-ninth congress' at Pushkino, outside Moscow.

Less rational forces also stirred. When, in April 1990, the delegates to a 'United Workers' Front' meeting in Moscow were revealed to include 'military officers, war veterans, party functionaries and supporters of the ultra-patriotic Fatherland Association', the 'workers' cause' took on (in embryo) a familiar dimension; such *amis du peuple* had gathered before. By 1992, old guard communists and extreme Russian nationalists were joining forces – including in mass street protests – to denounce Boris Yeltsin as a 'traitor', while calling for the restoration of the Soviet Union and an end to the 'sell-out of the Fatherland'. In such protests, groups like the Socialist Party of Workers and the Moscow Labour Movement could be found shoulder-to-shoulder with the far right, variously demanding workers' control, the revival of faith and an army seizure of power. Many landmarks of 'left' and 'right' were being uprooted, as they had been in the 1930s. When President Iliescu of Romania, an old-guard communist to the bone, called on miners in June 1990 to protect Bucharest – with boots and iron-tipped bludgeons – from democratic protesters, he too invoked the 'interests of workers'. 'Dear miners,' Iliescu smilingly told them after they had cracked heads and ransacked houses, 'we know that we can rely on you.' But he was wrong. Fifteen months later, in September 1991, in further Bucharest riots over deteriorating economic conditions, the same miners were demanding that he be set to work in the pits.

Now, without 'socialism' as a catch-all proletarian cause, on what breed of horse might a new St George be mounted, and who the dragon?

FOUR

The Return to Normal

'An unknown,' said Eduard Shevardnadze in May 1991, 'could suddenly appear on the political stage with a law-and-order programme. Another Hitler could rise up here.' 'I am not sure,' said Boris Yeltsin, 'that we can achieve reform without violence.' Yet, though a Ceausescu might be executed (with some 1,000 other Romanian deaths in December 1989), the Soviet Home Ministry's 'Black Berets' vengefully kill Lithuanian border-guards, Armenians and Azeris fight, civil war break out in Yugoslavia, Georgians take up arms, or Romanians and Albanians riot, the relative lack of violence in the first phases of the anti-communist convulsion was everywhere noted. This seemed to be a latter-day French Revolution without a Terror; a victory for a Resistance without the shaving of the heads of the collaborators. 'Civil war,' declared Valentin Pavlov, four months before taking part in the attempted coup against Gorbachev, 'is impossible in the Soviet Union.'

Although Lech Walesa bitterly referred to the 'evil period of communism' when being sworn in as his country's president, there was said to be, despite the acute economic hardship, 'calm in the air' in Poland. Mass political rallies in Moscow drew hundreds of thousands, but there was no violence. Fierce denunciations of the nomenklatura and fulminating demagoguery provoked no lynch mobs; reformers who were not reformist enough were displaced without recourse to Jacobin measures. This was a revolution which dealt unkindly with those who hesitated, but it did not devour them. Even a Russian coup attempt, with tanks on the streets of Moscow and a president arrested, produced only three dead. Except where nationalist passions intruded and the (relative) serenity of the revolutionary process was disturbed, it was as if the retreat from collectivism's impositions, falsehoods, and continuous political violence was being greeted by an echoing sigh of collective relief. Multiplied tens of millions of times, and in general without recourse to arms, it seemed that this sigh alone had blown communism away. This had been, so all the commentators gratefully pointed out, a peaceful revolution, using peaceful means to a peaceful, democratic end. It was a revolution, they said, against an idea whose time was over and whose own exponents knew so, better than any; a revolution which, in immediate retrospect, appeared as 'natural' and as 'obvious' as that day should follow night. There was, in any case, so everyone said, no alternative. Communism was finished.

As to 'the people's' general mood, however, there was puzzlement. Was it 'patience' that the commentators were observing in the crumbling Soviet Union and elsewhere, or 'resignation'? Was this seeming quiescence 'apathy' or a deep, unspoken 'satisfaction'? Was violence being so generally avoided out of a sense of public responsibility, or from some deep despair for which no one had a name? Here and there – when Boris Pugo, the Soviet interior minister, shot himself in the mouth, or Nikolai Kruchina, the Party's business manager, threw himself from a seventh-floor window – some other kind of passion seemed to stir. But the shuffling silence, the silence of the early morning food queues, was uncanny, or so it appeared. Even in savage Romania, after the privations and lunacies of the 'Ceausescu era' and its brutal dénouement, the grey dust settled. Intermittent riot there might be, but afterwards the miners – or *sans culottes* – returned to their pits. Angels of mercy attended to the orphans, the new government took over part of Ceausescu's grandiose palace, and the people went about their new, and old, business as if nothing much had happened. Here and there, it is true, tempers flared. Old communists in the former Soviet Union accused anti-communists of having used the 'dirtiest gimmicks' to 'destroy our moral traditions and mode of life'; the beaten-up democratic opposition in Romania was described by an aide to the prime minister as 'social garbage'. But within hours of the ugly fracas in the streets of Bucharest in June 1990, President Iliescu was himself again: genial and mild-mannered, and pledging himself to Western democratic values.

A worm-eaten timber crumbles – or is said to crumble – to dust at the first touch. In the same way, the seemingly solid political edifice of the socialist order in country after country had not even required clenched fists for it to be brought to ruin. Violence in its defence, as in Czechoslovakia, had had as little staying power. The offices of the liberal *Moscow News* might be fire-bombed and gutted (in February 1990) and the premises of Democratic Russia, the embryo opposition party, shattered by a bomb (in May 1991), but these were the vain actions of desperadoes. Even the plotters of coups could be laughed to scorn. The former East German Communist Party – renamed, like many of the others, the Party of Democratic Socialism – had promised in December 1990 to 'punish Kohl [the West German chancellor] for his ruthless takeover' of East Germany. Having made its threat, it effectively disappeared into thin air. Communist hecklers at Polish public meetings might, here and there, be set upon with cries of 'sons of bitches' and 'seed of the devil', but passivity prevailed. Zviad Gamsakhurdia, the dictatorial but democratically elected president of Georgia, might arrest his leading opponent in September 1991, calling his foes 'scum' and 'enemies of the people' in the old Stalinist fashion. But such things, it was felt, were exceptions or aberrations. The new norm was the avoidance of excess and trouble; Gamsakhurdia, who appeared to court both, was chased from office for it.

Gone, so it seemed, were the times when 192 people could be killed (between 1961 and 1989) trying to cross the Berlin Wall; gone the days when Polish Catholic priests were murdered, one of them, Father Stefan Niedzielak, by a karate blow. Past, if not long past, were the times when a Solidarity journalist investigating the activities of the secret police could have his flat set on fire (in April 1990), and his wife die jumping from a window to escape the flames. Surely it was an exception, too, that Detlev Rohwedder, head of the German trust agency responsible for privatising formerly state-owned East German firms, could be assassinated in Düsseldorf (in April 1991) by the Red Army Fraction; its statement calling for the intensification of 'struggle' against the 'imperialist beast' and the 'reactionary Greater German plan to suppress and exploit the people' was doubtless mere political recidivism, a last left reflex or spasm. After his peremptory sacking, Romania's tourism minister, the liberal Mihai Lupoi, sought political asylum in Switzerland in July 1990, claiming to fear for his life; he was soon forgotten. Three months later, the finance officer at Romania's London embassy was also said to be 'concerned for his safety'. When an emigré critic of Romania's new regime was shot dead in a lavatory at the University of Chicago, in May 1991, it was barely noticed. Chicago is a violent city.

True, Serbia's attacks on Croatia and Bosnia, spearheaded by the Yugoslav federal army, could have been interpreted as a vengeful blow struck on behalf of one of communism's surviving *anciens régimes* against its tormentors. But it was surely a last, or at least, a late one. And when weeping relatives of Marshal Akhromyeyev, the Soviet army chief of staff – who hanged himself after the failed Moscow coup – attributed his death to 'liberal fascists', they were clearly beside themselves with grief. He went to war at eighteen, they sobbed, in order to 'fight against fascism', and he had died, as he had lived, 'in the fight against fascism at home'. What on earth were they talking about? Had not a vast army, numbering hundreds of thousands of men, been pulling out of Eastern Europe in good order, bands playing? This was, surely, the true martial art of our times, and one to be celebrated, not lamented.

Vengefulness, it could be said too, was restricted. This was essentially – was it not? – a Christian, not a Jewish, revolution. The scenes of retribution at the end of the Second World War had not been repeated. Indeed, Czech intellectuals (for example) pronounced themselves opposed to 'looking for revenge', bitterly criticising in October 1991 a law banning hundreds of thousands of former communist and secret police officials from holding public office. It amounted, they declared with dismay, to the imposing of 'collective guilt' on an entire cohort of people. In Hungary, pressure to prosecute those responsible for thousands of political trials and executions in the communist period, going back to 1944, was criticised in November 1991 by the Hungarian president himself as undemocratic; other critics retreated from the prospect of a 'witch-hunt'. In Poland, in June 1992, the government of Jan Olszewski fell after attempting to use files on former communist collaborators against its opponents. When the Red Army began to withdraw from its former fiefdoms in Eastern Europe, a few jeers and graffiti – and the odd punch thrown – were the worst it had to suffer. 'I oppose the principle of collective guilt,' declared President Havel; 'everybody should have a chance.'

This revolution was to be a generally polite one: good manners, after the proletarian decades, were being resumed. 'I told the plotters I had no connection with them,' Anatoly Lukyanov pleaded modestly, two days before his arrest for involvement in the August 1991 Soviet coup attempt, 'and that I would not sign any of their documents.' Even communist conspirators tried to be on their best behaviour; contempt greeted their efforts, once the first shock was over, not popular anger. ('Everyone makes a sorry figure in the pillory,' said Hazlitt, wisely.) Little valour was required to defeat them. There was no real trial of arms; despite the best efforts of the foreign press, the low-key prevailed over an excess of passion. There were few in high places righteous or bold enough – Gorbachev included – ostentatiously to cast the first stone, while the 'man-in-the-street', when the brief crisis had passed, seemed to shrug his shoulders as over a minor domestic drama. Even the industrial working class of Russia, quick to respond in other ways, barely heeded Boris Yeltsin's call for a general strike in defence of the democratic revolution. Apart from a scattering of miners' protests (once again) at the attempted Moscow coup, most workers continued working, fearful for their jobs and the coming winter.

On the surface of things, the settling of scores for past miseries and hardships was rejected. The offices and funds of communist parties in the old East Germany and elsewhere might be sealed and seized, some homes raided, or the Party itself banned – in Czechoslovakia the promotion of communism was made an offence – but no apparatchiks, however loathed by their local populaces, would hang from the lamp-posts. Indeed, communist party officials often had enough leeway, as their worlds collapsed, to transfer party assets to accounts in Western banks, and to launder other huge sums through last-minute currency transactions and foreign investments. In Bonn, the government struggled to frame charges against, and bring to trial, new fellow-citizens for offences such as espionage committed against the Federal Republic, or for crimes which East Germans had committed against each other, as when border guards shot down would-be escapees to the West. In these contentious cases, an attempt was being made to hold the malefactors retroactively responsible under West German law for acts which were not only not punishable under East German law but which had once – *autres temps, autres mœurs* – made them heroes.

Communist emblems, flags and trophies, dismantled and destroyed at the first possible moment, often seemed to arouse more odium than those who had raised or borne them. Once removed, much of the desire for amends appeared to evaporate and vanish. Parks became necropolises; keeled over on the grass, the statues of fallen dictators and their servants became merely the objects of idle citizen curiosity, while children played innocently around them. The Federal Office for the Protection of the German Constitution placed members of the former East German Communist Party under surveillance. Passing disputes over the preservation of, and access to, communist secret police archives (the East German Stasi had amassed files on six million people) broke out throughout the post-communist world. One after another, as their links – usually in the role of informers – with the old police regimes were disclosed, politicians of the new democracy, churchmen and other public figures, especially in the former East Germany, stepped down, usually quietly, or were sacked from their positions; even the Rector of East Berlin's Humboldt University was alleged to have been a secret police informant, as were more than 20,000 of East Germany's 180,000 teachers. Most of communism's former leaders melted away into pensioned obscurity, and suicides were few. Old age and infirmity saved others from the law's rigours. Erich Honecker for seven months sought refuge in the Chilean embassy in Moscow, protesting (in familiar fashion) that Germany had no right to prosecute a former head of state for activities carried out in the execution of his office; the border guards who had shot down fleeing citizens had done 'nothing other than carry out their duty'. But there were no Nuremberg-style trials – even if in Romania Ceausescu's henchmen were factitiously tried for 'complicity to commit genocide' – and there was generally no desire for them.

When vengeful voices were raised they were as quickly stilled; even in Afghanistan, *mojahedin* reprisal against the overthrown communist regime was relatively modest. 'Apologising for forty years of failed policies is not good enough,' declared Joachim Nowack, a leading member of the right-wing conservative German Social Union; 'if it were, Goebbels could have apologised three times over and then everything would have been forgotten.' Nowack's sentiments were themselves forgotten. Groups of people had jeered the fallen Honecker, shouting in the street outside the house in Berlin where he had first gone into hiding; to cries of 'communist swine' a few policemen and other servants of the collapsed East German regime were set upon in December 1989. But, a mere stone's throw from Hitler's last bunker, as in most of Eastern Europe, it seemed as if the darkest emotions had been vanquished, or suffocated by communism's repressions. In Romania, there were uglier moods. On the day of his arrest, Nicu Ceausescu, son of the dictator, was stabbed in the liver. 'I would like to hang him by the tongue and watch him die,' declared the mother of the gymnast Nadia Comaneci, whom he was accused of sexually abusing. And a mere eight weeks after the trial and execution of Nicolae Ceausescu, General Gica Popa, the chairman of the military tribunal – or kangaroo court – which had sentenced him to death, himself 'committed suicide' in his office in the justice ministry; he was found with a bullet in the head. For their part, communists, as their worlds foundered, took out their private frustrations on erstwhile 'comrades' in their own ways. Almost everywhere, and to the very last, communist parties were investigating and expelling their floundering leaders for 'grave political error', 'abuse of power' and so on, as the parties themselves stood on the verge of extinction.

Yet, not all was as it seemed. There was neither discreet mercy for all, nor much rest for certain of the wicked. Hans Modrow, East Germany's last communist prime minister, was accused of 'electoral fraud'; Andrei Lukanov, last communist prime minister of Bulgaria, where the desire for revenge was relatively strong, was charged with embezzling state funds; Enver Hoxha was exhumed from his hero's tomb and his wife was accused of corruption. With arrests, and often mere threats of arrest, of former communists for alleged thefts of state property and fraud came standard tales of numbered Swiss bank accounts, and of Ali Baba-like 'hoards' of valuables and 'heaps of gold' which the men of the apparatus were said to have accumulated: 'sixty-five kilos' of gold in the case of Miroslav Milewski, Poland's former head of espionage.

Indeed, communist parties throughout the fallen socialist world had amassed real-estate empires worth billions. They owned buildings galore, including office complexes, educational institutions, holiday centres, hotels – including hotels in foreign countries – publishing houses, and fleets of limousines for their officials. Erich Honecker was said, with a strange relish, to have 'personally owned an island in the Baltic'; Harry Tisch, the former East German trade union leader, to have had a 'multi-million-mark hunting lodge' in the forests of Mecklenburg 'with marble floors, a solarium, a sauna and [even] an artificial waterfall'. (Attempts to convict him on corruption charges failed.) Todor Zhivkov, the Bulgarian dictator, was similarly accused of having had 'thirty' residences, of diverting '£400 million' to his own and other people's uses, of having distributed '100' houses – always round figures – as bribes and kick-backs to his supporters, and of 'selling government limousines to relatives at bargain prices'. Indeed, his private yacht was purchased by a Finnish businessman for a cool million. The day before his fall, Zhivkov had been fawned upon by an entire nation as 'Tatko' or 'Daddy'. The day after, he was Bulgaria's Attila or Ghengiz Khan. 'Why am I being prosecuted?' he himself asked at his trial. 'We were members of a generation, some of whom died with "Long Live Stalin!" on their lips. But it was Roosevelt and Churchill who handed us all over at Yalta.'

Jerzy Urban, the hated former spokesman of the Polish Communist Party, was even charged with 'publishing pornography' in a new weekly. (The pornography was a photograph from *Penthouse*.) Yet, at the same time, former Stasi chiefs were given amnesties by Bonn in return for silence on the involvements with them, including in financial corruption, of leading West German politicians and public figures. But thousands of rank-and-file Stasi servants – 7,000 teachers in Saxony alone – were summarily fired. These might not have been the Romanian executions at Trgoviste, where the demented Nicolae had walked to his death with tears streaming, and his wife had struggled and screamed in panic. But these sackings, too, were an unseemly and swift dispatch, made no juster for having been carried out on the grounds that an amnesty might 'fuel discontent among the East Germans'. Worse, these were the East German regime's minor functionaries; most of the larger fry, throughout Eastern Europe, went free.

To reclaim the rule of law and establish a 'legal state', in fond hope of justice, had been among the main purposes (for many) of the dethronement of the communist dictators. At the same time, the moral scruple to avoid revenge, or a Stalinist-style 'purge' – perhaps strongest in the then Czechoslovakia, under Vaclav Havel's influence – brought its own moral dilemmas. The setting of new ethical standards and the rejection of retribution were placed above the need, felt by millions who had suffered from communism's depredations, to distribute a just blame for the past decades. It was to make restoration of respect for law still harder. In Czechoslovakia, unsubstantiated accusations of past collaboration with the secret police also threw the desire for justice into confusion; in Bulgaria, a non-communist administration was divided over the issue of a 'purge' of former communists from the state structure; in Romania, so many had been implicated with Ceausescu's Securitate that there was resistance from all sides to disclosures of secret police files. Matters grew worse when seized lists of secret police informants were suppressed and even destroyed, and not always by the secret police themselves; in some countries they had been found to contain hundreds of thousands of names. It was reminiscent of immediate post-war France, where millions of individuals were embarrassingly disclosed to have made reports, many of them in writing, to the Gestapo. In Poland, military counter-intelligence alone had 180,000 informers; the East German Stasi had 'over one million' in a population of only 16 million, some of whom were revealed to have spied on their closest friends and even their spouses; the Czech StB had '140,000 agents and collaborators'. Scepticism, founded upon an inherited paranoia, about the newness of the 'new' orders was everywhere quick to surface. It was strong enough to find deceit in the new moralities and old fraud in the new economic dispensation.

Indeed, the new post-socialist economic order was not always the 'opening to the market' which it made itself out to be. In Poland, as in other East European countries, former members of the communist apparatus, using their privileged positions and corruptly-acquired wealth, acted swiftly to establish '*nomenklatura* companies'. Such individuals, typically, would first set up private companies within state trading organisations, and then, as the old order disintegrated, take over and use buildings, property, and existing employees for their own profit. In other countries, existing cooperative movements were similarly exploited by their officials, who would then strike, or try to strike, their own deals with incoming foreign investors and purchasers, pocketing part of the proceeds. The agility of many state and party officials, including in the most complex of market manoeuvres, was aided by a financial expertise acquired in long years of corruption. Old habits of readiness to break the law for personal gain also proved useful. Those who were amoral by instinct found no ethical difficulty in acquiring for themselves parts of the hitherto state-owned properties and businesses which they had helped to manage. While the former (Jewish) financier of the East German regime, and Stasi colonel, Alexander Schalck-Golodkowski, was settling into comfortable exile in Southern Bavaria – protected by the German authorities as a quid pro quo for his silence about former Stasi agents in the West – far-away workers at Uralmash, a vast Soviet machine-building enterprise in the Urals, were on strike in an unavailing effort to 'stop the Party and its senior officials engaging in business activities'. In the Gdansk shipyards, too, workers struck (in January 1991) in protest at the takeover of the docks and its services by sixty-nine separate private firms, most of them run by former communist officials.

Vaclav Klaus, the Czech finance minister, confronted by the phenomenon of senior communist functionaries turning overnight into energetic or seemingly energetic new entrepreneurs, was unconcerned. 'The main consideration', he declared in April 1991, 'is to get a private sector started'. In pointing the finger of moral reproach at the new capitalist dispensation, some ex-communists, winded by larger defeat, hoped for political advantage, even to the extent of reviving their defeated cause. A left (and far right) puritanism stirred, seeking to reap what benefit it could from the emerging disillusion. Other ex-communists, landing on their feet and profiting from every confusion, now felt free to act without conscience. In Poland's 1990 municipal elections, cynical ex-members of the apparatus and other former loyalists even formed themselves into a 'Citizens' Democratic Forum' the better to confuse the electors. 'The political forces responsible for leading Poland to crisis,' declared the prime minister Jan Bielecki in exasperation, in October 1991, 'are now cloaking themselves as defenders of the people, calculating that all of us have lost our memories.' In Albania, disappointed local apparatchiks were reported in September 1991 to have turned to vandalistic revenge, wrecking and stripping public buildings, including hospitals and schools, in blind frustration at the defeat of their cause. Others, trained to contempt for both capitalism and democratic ethics, preferred to make a fast buck and gain any advantage by whatever method, with the devil taking the hindmost. More often still, they remained quietly in their old jobs, acting as before for their new, and sometimes their old, masters in the new political and economic market.

Many state farm managers and their workers joined in the mayhem in their own fashion, setting up black markets and rings in the scarce commodities they produced or handled. Some trade unions, in particular in the collapsing Soviet Union, began to function openly – instead of covertly, as before – as mafia-like distribution organisations, providing only their own members with otherwise unobtainable goods, often pilfered, and delivered directly to their places of employment. In Rostov-on-Don forgers did a roaring trade in fake ration coupons; counterfeit Western products, falsely labelled, flooded East European and Russian markets; Albanian warehouses packed with emergency food and other aid, including Red Cross supplies, were pillaged. Even Tirana's main hospital became a target for looters. Dog was eating dog in immemorial fashion. But now the dogs were, or felt themselves to be, licensed as never before.

In the food queues, the foreign observer might still find patience or resignation. But in the spirits of the queuers the bitter images of past corruption – such as that of Harry Tisch's waterfall, with its cool cascade – and of the prompt onrush of ex-communists into the market, played a different and a larger part. In the old East Germany it was believed, in the streets, that former communists and Stasi officers were still 'running the country'; in Romania, that former communists and the Securitate were still in charge. In Czechoslovakia, it was thought that the 'velvet revolution' had left the old centres of hidden influence intact. In the new St Petersburg, the liberal mayor Anatoly Sobchak even appointed former KGB officers as area bosses of the city; one of them had headed a section responsible for monitoring 'ideological diversity' and persecuting dissenters. Everywhere popular opinion saw, or thought it saw, charmed circles of ex-communist 'opportunists' in power. In addition, some of those who had risked all in opposition to the old regimes found themselves excluded from, and beginning to oppose, the new. Most galling for former dissidents was to find themselves elbowed aside in the struggle for position by battle-hardened former party loyalists turned overnight-reformists. There was a growing army of the outwitted and defeated in the new conditions: disappointed intellectuals, workers unemployed or drudging in the same old fashion, functionaries left behind in the stampede to market, disbanded officers whose units had vanished, and everywhere individuals with a sense of grievance that colleagues, relatives or neighbours were prospering and 'advancing', while they remained in the rut of the old order. Some turned such grievances into demands for compensation for the harms – imprisonment for political crime, loss of job, eviction – which had been inflicted upon them. Others suffered, and seethed, in silence.

Beneath the outward patience of the passer-by, disappointment and its neuroses was deepening every existing tendency to depression and paranoia. It was confidently asserted that the bulk of former secret police forces, formally disbanded and refashioned, had been re-recruited to their positions. The Stasi in East Germany, the Statni Bezpecnost in Czechoslovakia, the Sluzba Bezpieczentswal in Poland, the Allambiztonsagi Szolgalat in Hungary, the Darzhaven Sigurnost in Bulgaria, the Sigurimi in Albania, the Securitate in Romania and the KGB in the former Soviet Union were alleged – despite the weeding out of a minority of officers and the replacing of one acronym by another under new direction – to be essentially intact. They, after all, were the professionals, the 'experts', and every nation requires (does it not?) to defend itself from subversion. Thus, the Polish secret police became the State Protection Office; the Romanian Securitate, 'abolished' in January 1990, was renamed the Romanian Information Service in August 1991, two thirds of its former 15,000 officers were rehired, and its budget was more than doubled by the 'new' regime. They might now be tackling crime and drug trafficking, but not many, and especially not the disillusioned and demoralised, believed it. Stanislaw Tyminski, the 'Polish-Canadian millionaire' candidate in the 1990 Polish presidential elections – who had called his party 'Party X' – stood on a platform of opposition to the 'cancer of corruption', an equitable tax system, support for peasant farmers, a nuclear-armed Polish army and the defence of Poland's 'economic and territorial sovereignty'. But it was also pointed out that on his personal election staff he had a communist secret police colonel; other 'former' secret police officers, it was said, helped to run his campaign in the country.

In Polish Silesia, secret policemen were similarly alleged to be 'running a chain of private gunshops'. In the former East Germany, paranoia was not allayed by the disclosure, made by a former high-ranking Stasi officer, that the 'storming' in January 1990 of the Stasi headquarters in East Berlin by 'the crowd' had in fact been staged by the Stasi itself, in order to permit it to carry off and destroy certain compromising files. In Poland, a team of cadets at the military police training centre at Minsk Mazowiecki was said with awe to have burned 'twenty to thirty sacks a day' of counter-intelligence files almost continuously for eight months; three tons of other secret files were shredded. In Bulgaria, the file on Georgi Markov, believed to have been killed with a poisoned dart fired from an umbrella by agents of the Darzhavan Sigurnost in London, was admitted in March 1991 to have been destroyed, under the noses of the supposedly new democratic system, by 'top interior ministry officials': one of them, General Stoyan Savov, was found dead forty-eight hours before he was due to stand trial in January 1992, charged with removing the file from state security archives. In almost every East European country, new regimes threatened to arrest and try those responsible for such destruction. Nothing came of it. Instead, in country after country, including in Hungary, it was revealed that the secret police services had continued to spy on post-fall leaders – on Mazowiecki in Poland, for example, and on members of Iliescu's government in Romania. After a brief flurry of anxiety, no more would be heard of it.

Communism had, over decades, induced disbelief: disbelief in words and actions, disbelief in meanings and motives. It had prompted doubt about, and fear of, self, others, events and even places. In the absence of secure sources of truth, the line between the real and the imagined was less certain even than in the West. From the outset of the upheavals, moreover, a deep foreboding about the post-socialist future had darkened many brows in the giant slums which passed for Eastern Europe's and the former Soviet Union's industrial centres. Into this miasma, in which neither 'privatisation' nor 'the market' had been adequately explained let alone fully understood, came immediate evidence, both real and imagined, of unheard-of levels of new crookery and corruption. Aroused hope – for instance in Chancellor Kohl as an all-German redeemer – was swiftly dashed. In early 1990 he was greeted in East Germany's grim cities as a saviour; before the year's end, in Leipzig, there were roars of 'pig' from a crowd of 60,000 whenever his name was mentioned. Order, programmed and monitored, had disappeared;

'democracy', thought to be the harbinger of plenty as well as of freedom, had come in its place, but (for many) empty-handed. Pessimism, larded – often for good reason – with suspicion, succeeded the first brief euphoria. By July 1992, three in four Poles were said to be both 'bored with life' and to believe that there had been 'too many changes'. 'It reminds me,' said Vaclav Havel, 'of prison. We learned to use the limited space, we knew where to go and where not to. And suddenly we are free, and start to panic.'

But anxiety about the unknown, fear of inadequate social provision, suspicion and jealousy of neighbour, feelings of helplessness, and other anxieties and grievances too obscure to be named amounted to something deeper than 'panic'. It was precisely panic which was not observable; better, perhaps, had there been panic than the darker, unexpressed emotions. 'Our people are not used to bankruptcy and failure,' said Dr Wicslaw Rozlucki, the new head of the Warsaw stock exchange, casting about for fit words in the awkward silence. Children's voices could be more telling. 'In social studies our teacher says the opposite of what she stated last year,' declared a young pupil of an *Oberschule* in Grünau, in the former East Germany. 'How is she able to do that when she is the same person?' the innocent voice inquired. 'We don't have any faith in that type of teacher. That's why we've become more unruly,' the child added.

Ominous, too, were the first strident political judgments, including from the only partially-interred left. The new governments had 'rushed into a savage capitalism', 'the people' had been 'lied to', lifelong convictions had been surrendered for a mess of market pottage. As social inequality – poverty and homelessness, also – became more visible, losing the camouflage of socialism's public provision, the reforms themselves began (for many, and in many places) to lose their first lustre, such as it was. The shadows of the night had not flown, even if Solomon's new day had broken. While a minority of optimists quickly found new ways to prosper, envy and self-pity, noxious separately but more noxious together, quickly set to work on many working class hopes and illusions, such as they were. The vague post-communist injunction to 'seize the initiative', or, worse, to 'fend for oneself', generally fell on the stony ground of decades of reliance upon others. Consumption of bananas, rare as hen's teeth in the old Eastern Europe, soared; but voter turn-outs in the newly-free electoral systems fell in most countries, once the first flush of enthusiasm for the democratic process had faded. In East Germany, there had been a 93 per cent

turn-out in the March 1990 election; in Czechoslovakia, a huge 96 per
cent of the electorate voted in the June 1990 election; in Bulgaria, also
in June 1990, 91 per cent voted; in Albania, in April 1991, 95 per cent
voted in the first free elections since the 1920s. (It had been '99.95 per
cent' under the rules of the old order.) In Poland in June 1989, and in
Hungary, where twenty-eight separate parties contested the March
1990 election, the first turn-outs were around two-thirds. In Mongolia,
with its few cars, few roads, and large population of nomads, 91.9 per
cent of the electorate appeared at the polling booths in its first free
elections.

Within months, and especially in municipal and regional elections, a
spreading disillusion or 'resignation' had led almost everywhere to the
abstention of tens of millions from the electoral process. (Bulgaria was
an exception, with a turn-out in October 1991 of over 80 per cent at its
second general election in two years.) In Hungary, as early as October
1990, only 27 per cent bothered to vote in the second round of local
elections. In Poland's municipal elections in May 1990, turn-out had
fallen to 42 per cent, with a mere 34 per cent voting in Lodz, Poland's
second city. Although turn-out rose again (to 61 per cent) for the
critical November 1990 presidential elections, won by Lech Walesa, a
huge 60 per cent abstained in the October 1991 general elections. In
the then Soviet Union, denied democratic political choice for seven
decades, 'voter apathy' quickly succeeded enthusiasm's first blush. In
Moscow, in March 1989, 83 per cent voted in the multi-candidate
elections to the Congress of People's Deputies. A year later, an average
70 per cent voted in the elections to the Russian parliament; in some
constituencies the turn-out was already less than 50 per cent, and under
the electoral rules run-offs were needed. By December 1990, only 20
per cent of voters in Leningrad, as the city was still called, turned out
for a by-election. The view that 'voting makes no difference' was already
widespread. The democratic revolution had come in a mere matter of
months to levels of public inertia comparable with, and in some cases
much greater than, those recorded in Western presidential, parliamentary and municipal elections. 'They know how to cry "Down! Down!
Down!",' declared the already cynical far-right leader of the Soviet
Liberal party, Vladimir Zhirinovsky, 'but they don't know how to be
constructive. Our most thoughtful people are sitting at home. It is very
dangerous.' These were alarmingly early days for such developments.
But in this failed utopia doubt, misperceived as 'patience', had for
decades shadowed ringing political declaration; disbelief, misperceived

as 'resignation', had for years dogged socialist professions of faith in the future.

But while some 'sat at home', others – the nimble, the quick-minded, the light-fingered and worse – were out in the open, liming the twig and lining their pockets. Crime, aggressive hedonism's twin brother, soared in the aftermath of every socialist fall, including in what had been the Soviet Union. With old authority's gold braid in tatters, there was a forty-fold increase in bank robberies in the former East German state of Brandenburg in the first year of freedom. In Poland in 1990, the number of burglaries increased by 176 per cent and robberies became more violent. Rising volumes of extortion, embezzlement and counterfeiting, as well as of prostitution, drug-related offences and the use of guns in the commission of crime were also reported. There were marked increases in the murder-rate in (for example) Czechoslovakia, Poland and the former Soviet Union. As the 'reform process' deepened, crime statistics and court evidence suggested that those seeking money-for-nothing were becoming less inclined to let others stand in their way. Many of those making money were provokingly putting it on show, or conspicuously consuming their profits; those not making it were choosing increasingly violent compensations for their sense of injustice or failure. 'Money', said an East German sociologist in June 1990, 'is now a constant topic. It has entered into personal relations in a way it never did.' Defeated expectations, the cascade from the West of tantalising images of well-being, the new freedom of movement, inadequate policing and the uneasy combination of new wealth and falling living standards turned some hustlers from petty theft to armed robbery, and even to the organisation of vicious protection rackets. Gang crime – particularly violent in Moscow, including in its food markets – drug trafficking, alcohol smuggling and prostitution rings were reported from many ex-socialist capital cities.

In July 1991, a large quantity of cocaine was found even in Cluj, in Romanian Transylvania, and a Colombian, an Italian and several Romanians were arrested; in October 1991, Polish customs officials seized £19 million worth of cocaine in the Baltic port of Gdynia. Russian criminal gangs, engaged in shoplifting, prostitution and smuggling rackets, were active in Finland; Hungarian mafiosi returned to their freed homeland from American exile; young women from Eastern Europe were said by Interpol to be finding their way into organised West European prostitution. Porn-shops and brothels became commonplaces in East European cities; Moscow set up its first vice squad; in

Poland, by 1991, there were reported to be a quarter of a million drug addicts. 'A society that is disintegrating,' opined Hungary's deputy chief of police, 'is fertile soil for criminals.' Again, this was too simple. Certain kinds of crime, especially financial crime and systematic theft from the state, were an integral part of the communist system. With new opportunities, new (and not so new) crimes and sharp practices were being added to old. Thus, as soon as the reins upon private property were let go, high-ranking Soviet government, military and party officials, schooled in corruption, were found to be buying their official *dacha*s at knockdown prices. Such was the scale of it that the then Soviet parliament was forced to intervene in July 1991 to stop the acquisitions, most of them being cynically made by men of the *ancien régime* who had been ostensibly opposed to the reform process.

Almost everywhere in the declining socialist world, as popular insecurity deepened, there were similar tales of opportunism and economic crime. In Poland, in August 1981, half a dozen senior state bank officials were arrested for siphoning off unthinkably large sums of the impoverished state's funds into private business enterprises. In Hungary, 1,200 police officers had been arrested for corruption by the end of 1990; in Cambodia, as liberalisation developed in 1991, official corruption grew at such a rate that public acceptance of the reforms themselves was said to be being imperilled. In Nicaragua, in June 1991, it was revealed that even the Sandinistas had given themselves and their activists 'thousands' of houses and farms – some of over 10,000 acres – as property handouts on their fall from office in the previous year. In China, liberalisation brought increasingly abusive recourse to child labour and the exploitation of prisoners to produce export goods. Even in Germany, former East German officials working for the Bonn government's Treuhandanstalt, the agency empowered to dispose of and privatise the East German state's assets, were found within months of its commencing work to be involved in a '500 billion mark' scam involving the illicit sale, on the cheap, of former state-owned land and property to West German entrepreneurs, in return for bribes and pay-offs. It was precisely this kind of crime which had a pedigree in the socialist utopia. Its range had been wide, from petty factory-theft (on a vast scale) to the purloining of goods at every stage in the chain of distribution, including the looting of freight trains. It had encompassed systematic stealing from state shops during the so-called 'third shift', when, after closing hours, employees would sell off the shop's goods (at higher than the fixed prices) and pocket the proceeds. A 'culture of theft' had created every variety of racketeering in scarce public resources, sometimes involving a socialist republic's highest state officials.

But now such crime grew potentially more threatening to the social order. 'Socialist discipline', once honoured not only in the breach but also in the observance, was being dispersed by the new freedoms as inequalities widened. Moreover, with the old grip of central authority weakening in every sphere, the authority of the police, additionally tarnished by association with past abuse of power, weakened with it; the ostentatious weeding-out from their ranks of the more brutish did nothing to restore it. Demoralised by the odium in which they were held, and which could now be freely-expressed, many – as with the Tsarist police in the Bolshevik Revolution – cast off their uniforms and melted away into other employment, if they could find it. Those who remained at their posts, under-qualified and under-trained for the tide of crime that rose around them, had (those who were honest) a difficult choice: to 'crack down' and risk accusation of old-style 'repression', or behave in a 'new democratic fashion' and be accused of weakness or dereliction of duty. In Bulgaria, in September 1990, the police complained of having been 'turned into a laughing stock' and of being 'unprotected, abused, powerless, manipulated and abandoned'. The conversion of a police force from being mere agents of a regime to becoming custodians of civic order – and custodians on whom individuals could rely – was no easy matter. Moral authority had to be earned. Yet, there was no time (nor adequate enough resources and manpower) to earn it, while the increasingly emboldened criminal fraternity made hay in the confusion. 'How,' asked Yuri Osipov, deputy commander of the St Petersburg Special Branch, 'can we pit an underprivileged militiaman earning £18 a month against a call-girl making £60 a night?'

There was no direct answer. The indirect one, generally uttered sotto voce by random passers-by of the older generation, was that 'this would never have happened' under Brezhnev, or Honecker, or Husak, or Zhivkov; even that 'things were better under Ceausescu'. 'Under Zhivkov's regime,' Zhivkov himself asked rhetorically, 'were the stores empty? Was there such high unemployment? Did destruction [sic] and rocketing crime exist?' No one answered him as he wrestled with his accusers. Another commonplace could be heard in China in June 1991, a year after the Tienanmen massacre. 'Life was hard, very hard, in the time of Mao, but at least we knew where we stood.' A nostalgia, perverse in some, had begun to develop. It was not for the repressions but for the certainties of the old orders, when the trains ran on time and everyone knew their stations. Indeed, instinctive Stalinist reflexes lay close below the surface of the new democratic attitudes. They were not to be dispersed by a half-turn to freedom, and one which had occurred under duress. In 1990, Gorbachev was still describing the Party in time-honoured fashion as a 'holy matter'. Party radicals, he declared, were 'opportunists' and 'careerists', the old Stalinist slurs. Those who left the Party and 'sought refuge elsewhere', he 'view[ed]' with contempt'; his multi-partyism was plainly skin-deep. As late as December 1990, and still in fine communist fettle despite the liberalisation, Gorbachev announced that he would 'never accept the Party becoming a parliamentary party'.

Four months later, the strands of liberalism and Stalinism continued to be intertwined. Gorbachev, architect of his country's democratic revolution, could be heard even in April 1991 declaring that his more reformist opponents were 'seeking to destabilise society'. In the old Stalinist days such a charge would have been a certain prelude to, and pretext for, a trial for treason or disappearance into the gulag. More extraordinary (and Stalinist), Gorbachev on the same occasion demanded a 'stringent regime of work' in 'key sectors' of Soviet industry, together with the 'immediate restoration of a vertical structure of subordination from bottom to top' in centre-republican relations. Gorbachev's ambivalence, simultaneously liberal and illiberal, simultaneously for and against the old order – while 'the people' floundered for a sense of direction – was not merely that of a Russian wrestling with self, but Janus-faced: anti-Stalinist and Stalinist, democratic and undemocratic, together. (It did not prevent him being one-dimensionally denounced by arch-conservatives as a 'bourgeois'.) Against such confusion, with a new and more authoritarian tsar, Tsar Boris, marching upon Moscow as pretender, a coup was attempted in all but Stalin's name. In Hungary, such conspiracy got no further than, for example, the setting up by hardliners of a Ferenc Munnich Society, in the name of an interior minister of the bad old days. In Albania, they founded a 'Committee for the Defence of Enver Hoxha' which demanded that the dictator's statues be re-erected. Similar groups of malcontents, officers without units, cadres without a party, bureaucrats without an office, had formed behind closed doors in every collapsing East European country. In Russia, as elsewhere, the old order was inextricable from, and laid hands on, the new. The very language of

Stalinist political discourse was heard on the lips even of the most dynamic and seemingly emancipated of reformers.

Thus, just as the coup plotters of August 1991 promised (using a Stalinist term of art) to 'liquidate' what they described as 'criminal military formations' – the self-defence Home Guards in the Baltic states for instance – so the reforming Polish Solidarity government promised in the same month to 'liquidate' one thousand state-owned firms. The term was avoidable: the thousand firms were in fact being privatised. In July 1991, Gorbachev, using another such Stalinist formulation, described Yeltsin's proposal that Russia should have its own army not as an error of judgment – if such it was – but as a 'deliberate provocation'. Yeltsin himself, in his autobiography *Against the Grain*, even called an attempt on his life, in which he ended up in a river, a 'premeditated act of provocation'; an allegation in the Russian parliament in May 1992 that he drank to excess was likewise dismissed as a 'provocation'. In Western liberal democracies, what Stalinists termed 'provocations' are opposing views and dissenting judgments. 'What defamation! What provocations!' Ceausescu shouted at his accusers a few hours before his execution. Stalinism, among other things far worse, was a lexicon of specialised feeling with its own language by which to express its dementias. Thus, in June 1991, Soviet hardliners suggested in incorrigible fashion that the 'occupation of the Soviet Union' was being planned by 'Western intelligence sources'; in the past, scapegoats' trials would have followed. Similarly, as late as March 1991, *Pravda*, using the once-classic Stalinist (and communist) method of smearing opponents with suggestions of physical debility or mental disorder, published a 'socio-psychological portrait' of Boris Yeltsin. It accused him – without particulars – of 'being ill', of a 'sluggish way of articulating', and so forth; the August 1991 coup plotters spoke similarly of Gorbachev, by reflex. Once, this would have been terrifying, a preamble to annihilation. Now, even if shorn of its terrors, it represented the moving of the old muscle beneath the skin. But it went deeper still, such darkness, being bred in the bone, or in the 'Russian soul'. Stalinism was merely one of its possible embodiments.

As the communist system sank into its terminal corruption, the corrupt were heard accusing (as they had always accused) others of corruption. Yeltsin, for example, was accused by the KGB of being involved in fraudulent currency deals, of recruiting members of a criminal Moscow gang as his personal bodyguards, and so on. 'Call him to account!', shouted delegates to the twenth-eighth and last official Soviet Communist

Party congress in July 1990, as Yeltsin walked down the long aisle to the podium. The lawless called for law and order; the cowardly demanded 'respect for our glorious armed forced'; baseness, calling for the defence of the 'healthy [conservative] forces in society', chased baseness into a common oblivion. Indeed, as liberalisation continued in the former Soviet Union and Eastern Europe, and more covertly in China also, the old habits died hard, or did not die at all. Yeltsin, in April 1991, called for a 'purge' of remaining Party officials by forcing them to face democratic election – defeat at the ballot box remained a 'purge'. Lech Walesa had similarly told a congress of citizens' committees in April 1990 that if he were to become president he would use special courts to 'purge' communists from office. 'Elimination' of opponents kept its place in the vocabulary even of the reformers.

The past shadowed the present, however transformed. The Chinese, notwithstanding their 'open door' economic policy towards the West, described the Tienanmen Square Statue of Liberty, erected by students in May 1989, as a 'treacherous icon to alien American ways'; democratic dissenters were 'despicable buffoons'. Ramiz Alia, pretending to reform-mindedness as communism's last president of Albania, showed his true colours in calling attacks on his Stalinist predecessor, Enver Hoxha, 'barbaric'. And Lech Walesa, archetype of the anti-communist proletarian of Eastern Europe, set up, as president, a small parallel presidential cabinet of his own, doubling the government's functions. With appointees given ministerial rank, it would, he declared, 'oversee key policy areas' nominally in government hands. Its model, which it perfectly reproduced, was the communist politburo; Walesa's former chauffeur, Mieczyslaw Wachowski, became the new regime's éminence grise.

Below the threshold, or under the floorboards, of democratic revolution, pre- and anti-democratic reaction flourished in many and complex forms. Walesa, searching for a metaphor for the new order of his dreams, declared in October 1990 that 'we want family businesses, with dad the managing director, mum the trade unionist, and the son the proletariat;' yes, 'the proletariat'. At his presidential inauguration, he specifically invoked 'the workers and the peasants' of communist incantation, describing them as the 'joint managers' of 'our homeland'. Moreover, the language of the market plainly took some learning; for many post-communists it remained the theatre of 'speculators', dangerous and exotic, part welcomed, in equal part resisted. Thus in April 1991, Walesa – as ever speaking for millions – was declaring himself 'frightened' of capitalism. 'I don't like capitalism,' he said, 'but I like its capital, its dollars, its effects.'

Ambivalences such as these were rarely so candidly expressed. It is also probable that few of post-communism's leaders thought differently from Walesa. Moreover, as the economic plight of their nations worsened, and mindful of the fickleness of popular temper, many of them appeared to find democratic attitudes hard to sustain. It was plain that Walesa and Yeltsin, like Gorbachev, preferred to rule by decree. 'Today,' announced Walesa in November 1991, 'Poland needs a president who on the one hand will not disturb the nascent pluralism ... but who on the other hand will be a dictator in the executive process.' In societies with, at best, the shallowest democratic traditions, the habit of authoritarianism in the leader was matched by expectations of, and even desire for, authoritarianism amongst the led. The new fashion of the democrat in the former Eastern Europe and the Soviet Union was to share power with others; the impulse of the old authoritarian (frequently the same person) was to acquire, keep, and even enlarge power for himself. And should chaos begin to encroach, including chaos willed or provoked by political opponents, it was the older reflex which came into the ascendant.

In Poland and Russia, and in Bulgaria and Romania, for example, the subversion of reform by varieties of denigration and obstruction – overt and covert – also continued deep into the period of transition from command economy to market. Ex-communists, above all, hoped to make capital, in many senses, even from crime and bloodshed. Systematic diversion or withholding of commodities in short supply aided every political attempt to prolong the distresses and confusions of the transition. Gang crime assisted the purposes of those who decried the immoralities of the market; the discovery of officials with their hands in the tills of the new order nurtured the know-nothings, for whom all change was obnoxious. Bureaucrats anxious for their jobs hid behind the complexities and failures of privatisation; republics, bent on consolidating their independence, starved the centre for their own political advantage. Mafias, old and new, battened on every deprivation, and cheats spread their wings in the sun.

As in the case of the police, the dilemma for political leaders lay in the conflict between a general desire, which they shared, for whip-cracking, and a public recoil, of which they had reason to be wary, from whatever smacked of the old communist abuses of power. The 'authoritarian alternative' constantly beckoned. Lech Walesa, Zviad Gamsakhurdia in

Georgia and Vitautas Landsbergis in Lithuania succumbed to it, the first intermittently, the second with determined but vain purpose, the third while pretending otherwise to himself and to the Lithuanians. 'The people believed in you,' deputy Sazhi Umalatova complained to Gorbachev in the Soviet Congress of People's Deputies in December 1990, disappointed with his vacillation. 'The people have been cruelly deceived. You should leave your post. There is no master in the country. Without a master we cannot go anywhere.' A year later her wish was granted. This too, was the voice of the people, and as representative as any in Mother Russia.

Lech Walesa, although continuously resisted by the Polish parliament, often gave way to his authoritarian promptings. In August 1990, after having promised to 'create an order that is a sort of storm' – Mussolini's language to the word – he was urging that voters' names be marked on their voting slips in the approaching presidential election, 'so that, afterwards, I would know how everybody voted.' He did not appear to be joking. Elected, he was soon variously threatening to dissolve parliament if it refused to pass laws in the form he desired, seeking decree powers for the government so that it might bypass parliamentary obstruction, contradicting government decisions, issuing competing bills from the presidential office, and warning, as constitutional head of the army, that he would use 'all force and means' to defend Solidarity's ideals of 1980. In June 1991, the former union leader was threatening to put air traffic controllers 'under military discipline' if they went on strike; in November 1991, he was seeking powers not only to nominate the prime minister but his cabinet as well. By then, one in four of all Poles thought that communism had been replaced by a 'dictatorship'; a mere one in nine believed that a democracy was emerging in Poland. In February 1992, he was again threatening the dissolution of parliament 'for a year'; in April 1992, it was revealed that his officials had drawn up contingency plans for the imposition of martial law.

Walesa's language was sometimes violent, and frequently plebeian. In November 1990, he wanted a 'good professional army' in Poland which could 'pick anyone's eye out, or break their leg, so they do not meddle in Polish matters.' Leg-breaking was a recurring metaphor; in April 1991, he complained that he could not 'drive the government too fast' or they would 'break their legs'. 'I want to get all of you involved,' he told steelworkers in October 1990, after a diatribe against intellectuals, 'in order to smash everything that hinders us.' These were the sentiments of the Romanian miners when they bludgeoned Bucharest, and an echo of Yeltsin's rough call to the Moscow crowds to 'roll up your sleeves and show your fists'. In his office, Walesa kept a statue of Marshal Pilsudski, his political hero. Polish head of state from 1918 to 1922, Pilsudski returned after a coup to lead an authoritarian regime – with a thin democratic veneer – from 1926 to 1935. 'I will obey the law, but the law must not obstruct us,' the former shipyard worker was fond of declaring. The head of his personal secretariat in Gdansk, Krzysztof Pusz, was less circumspect: 'we just need someone with a whip.' (Whips in Polish hands are, for Jews, a terrifying image.) For some, there was a blunt proletarian charm in Walesa's desire, *à propos* the rising volume of economic crime in Poland, to 'leave thieves standing in nothing but their socks'. For others, it recalled instincts less comic.

At the same time, as whole nations floundered, the urge to order was to be expected. (Even Havel, objecting to an outbreak of protests in April 1991 over the then ousting of Slovakia's nationalist prime minister Vladimir Meciar, allowed himself to declare that 'in 1989 we went into the streets so that we would never have to go into the streets again'.) 'We have no one to believe in,' complained an old man at Bucharest's Ghencea cemetery – where the Ceausescus were secretly buried – in June 1991. 'Yes, he was a tyrant, but we built a metro, apartment blocks, schools. Now, no one works and nothing is done. Nothing.' This was untrue. But with so many millions trained out of their energies and capacities for self-reliance by socialism, the hankering for a saviour to solve the nation's problems was evident, especially in the older generation. And on the shoulders of every actual post-communist leader an inordinate burden of expectation rested.

To do what? Above all, to satisfy desire: from the desire for plenty, to the recovery of lost lands. Past, present and future (both lost histories and lost prospects) had to be rescued. Principle needed to be restored, but dogma, the dogma of 'isms', rejected. Such expectations could not be met; they would have been beyond a Solomon. The deposed monarchies, too, began to yearn for their lost crowns and palaces. Simeon of Bulgaria, Leka – son of Zog ('big bird') – of Albania, Michael of Romania, the Karadjordjevics of Serbia, Zahir Shah of Afghanistan, Bagration of Georgia, the Habsburgs, and even the Romanovs in the shape of the elderly heir to Russia's tsars, Grand Duke Vladimir Kirillovich, stirred. Moreover, after the long suppression of national feeling by 'proletarian internationalism', the urge everywhere to national renaissance under a national leader broke swiftly upon the changing scene. The sense of ethnic particularity, as in the Balkans and Transcaucasia, in the Baltic states and Central Asia, had long been crudely overridden by 'socialist solidarity', or repressed by fear and force, including mass deportation and killing. But old belonging and old hatred, especially in the peasantries of the socialist world, had merely been reduced, not cancelled, by the 'fraternity' of the socialist order. Now, democratic freedoms gave licence to their expression.

A new constellation of nationalist elements came into being in almost every post-communist country. It was disparately composed of conservative communism's 'patriotic forces', long-standing anti-communists with traditional pride in nation, religious revivalists and monarchists, those longing for strong government and economic independence, anti-capitalists of left and right recoiling together from the corruptions of the market, and ethnic dogs-in-the-manger of varying stripe, baring their teeth or yelping at every alien footfall. There were sufficient fears and hopes to unite, as well as to divide, them; utopian dreams of salvation under God, King, or People's Hero to inspire them; new and old angers to drive them to action. Those who did not lend themselves easily to such nationalist emotions were nevertheless touched by them; those who were firmly opposed to them quickly learned, as in the bad old days, to keep their own counsel.

'Never again a Bulgaria under a Turkish yoke!' shouted (communist) Bulgarians protesting in July 1990 at the post-communist restoration of the rights of Bulgaria's Muslims. 'Germany for the Germans!' roared the crowds in Leipzig in March 1990; 'For the Tsar, Rus [the old name for Russia] and Our Faith!' cried the slogans in Moscow in July 1990. 'Great Russia,' declared Boris Yeltsin as he was sworn in as Russian president a year later, 'is rising from its knees . . . Russia will be born again.' It was grandly spoken. It was also a step towards the reconstitution of that Great Russian nationalism which in the past made smaller nations tremble. Indeed, between the virtues of nationhood justly redeemed from subjection and the vices of nationalism stirring to renewed rampage, it was quickly hard to distinguish. Croatia, reborn and clad in its old chequer-board colours – recalling, to the frightened, the fascist Ustashe regime – was soon in brutal combat with the spirit of ancient Serbia. Vladimir Meciar, Slovakia's first post-communist prime minister, swiftly spoke out against property restitution to 'Germans, Hungarians and enemy collaborators'; Solzhenitsyn preached an exclusive 'salvation' of 'our own people'. Demonstrators in the German Democratic Republic, who had set out on the path to a democratic revolution by shouting 'Wir Sind Das Volk' (We are the People), within weeks were chanting 'Wir Sind Ein Volk' (We are One People), as once the Nazis had declared the Germans to be 'One People, One Nation' and had prepared for war. Independent Estonia's 'Heritage Society', proud of a recovered national purpose, contained numbers of former Estonian SS members.

Like any man, but more so, the enthusiast for nation can be scoundrelly or noble; or, more confusingly, change chameleon-like from one to the other under the eye of the observer. In addition, communists and ex-communists adopted the nationalist cause with seemingly little qualm and often with relish. Intolerance was their second nature. Slobodan Milosevic, the Serbian communist leader and son of a Serbian Orthodox priest, supervised the seizure of Croat and Bosnian territory – while Serb irregulars set in motion a policy of 'ethnic cleansing' against Bosnia's Muslims – but claimed the unity of a pan-tribal Yugoslavia as his objective. His foe, Franjo Tudjman, Croatia's arch-nationalist leader, had also been a life-long communist, fighting with Tito's partisans during the war. The nationalist Slav leaders, Yeltsin in Russia, Kravchuk in the Ukraine, Shushkevich in Byelorussia, had all been Party bosses. In Romania, leading figures from Ceausescu's inner circle of sycophants re-emerged after his fall as authors of racist anti-Hungarian tracts. In Poland, some of the most extreme nationalists were former members of the communist apparatus. Support for Slovak separation from the Czechoslovak republic was strong in the opposition communist party. In Cambodia, the Khmer Rouge became the most fanatically nationalist of the warring factions. Now they claimed it to be their new mission to protect the 'Khmer race' – whose numbers had been sharply reduced under their own aegis – from being 'swamped' by Vietnamese, Thais and other non-Cambodians. But then in France, too, communist mayors could lead street protests against 'aliens'; the mayor of Clichy-sous-Bois, a fully paid-up Party member, even described 'blacks and Arabs' in Clichy as 'a pack of hyenas'.

Historically, the move from communist allegiance to the cause of an extreme nationalism, and even to fascism, had already proved not to be a long leap for some. It had been a side-step, rather. However doughty the record of many communists in the struggle with fascism, the Nazis had recruited half their numbers among Germany's working class, including from its communist 'vanguard', whole sections of which in some German industrial cities 'went over' to the Nazis. The proletarian, and not merely the plebeian, found a comfortable enough home in both movements. Today, the French National Front, the German neo-Nazis, the Belgian Flemish Bloc, the Croatian Black Legion, British skinhead gangs and all the rest of them – including the rougher end of Milosevic's Serbian national movement – have at least one booted foot planted deep in plebeian life and proletarian labour; the far-right German Republican Party leader, Franz Schönhuber, an ex-communist as well as an ex-Waffen SS NCO, found his strongest support among German working people, East German and other East European migrants to West Germany included. Those who have felt their interests to be unrepresented in, or threatened by, the existing political and economic system have at some point always become susceptible (even when not succumbing) to the attraction of extreme measures, in order to 'do something' about it. The more actively impatient or desperate, the more susceptible they are. However, in the absence of a charismatic leader to galvanise the defeatist, the majority (in this post-Nazi era) has in general preferred the option of welfarist inertia, often in the belief that no solution at all – and certainly not a solution of blood-and-thunder – is available for its problems.

But in the wake of the communist collapse, many a slumbering beast, dulled for decades by containment in its fetid compound, stirred once more. At the level of geo-political manoeuvre, new governments from Transylvania to the Transcaucasus immediately began to rehearse old arguments and to sharpen their weapons. In the streets, and in individual hearts, old fears and fancies showed themselves to be eternal. New compacts and ententes – such as the post-Soviet 'Commonwealth' – might be forged between newly independent nations. But old urges to annexation of territory, or to the resumption of long-suppressed national and ethnic struggles, perilously began to tempt many to action, including young people who had no previous direct experience of them. As entire states, such as the Soviet Union and Yugoslavia, ceased to be sovereign entities, the danger grew greater. Where neighbouring nations intruded themselves, had legitimate historic interests, or feared instability as populations began to move in search of haven, the danger was heightened. Thus, Germany 'took initiatives' in Slovenia and Croatia, and, without 'Europe's approval, recognised their independence in December 1991. Hungary, which was buying weapons from the disbanded East German army, sympathised in the Yugoslav civil war with Croatia; Romania, at historic loggerheads with Hungary and Ukraine, took the side of Serbia. Neighbouring Austria, suddenly in the market for anti-aircraft missile systems, drew closer to Slovenia, Albania to Kosovo,

Italy to Albania, and every nation which might be affected braced itself for the arriving refugee influx. Similar nervous effects, waxing and waning, were felt in other areas of national and ethnic conflict, potential or actual: in the Baltics, in the Trans-Dniester region, in Transcaucasia, in Muslim Central Asia.

In some, revival of nation and ethnicity, as in the Transcaucasus, seemed to provoke a perverse desire for trouble. 'We defeated our monolithic enemy,' complained Havel, 'and now we are looking for enemies in each other.' Equally strong, however, was the urge to order, which resisted early pressures to settle old scores, for example against Russian minorities in many of the former Soviet republics. Nevertheless, in many places, the new lumpen, driven to the margins of the civic order by unemployment, joined hands with the atavistic survivor of the communist decades; the returning émigré made common cause with the universal Rambo *de nos jours*, toting his weapon in yet another 'armed militia'; a Black Legion of German neo-Nazis joined the fighting on the Croatian side in the Yugoslav civil war. Relatively few seemed troubled, in the savage conflict between Serbs, Bosnian Muslims and Croats, or Armenians and Azeris, that such ethnic fears and hatreds had been a proximate cause of two world wars. It was as if, for some, the recovery of national identity required the accompanying sound of gunfire. Minorities might quake at the memory of other times when their host communities had been in such travail; heroes-in-headbands, undaunted, exchanged fire in sight of the West's film-crews, vicariously eager for the fray. Moreover, as in Ulster, much of the reviving hatred was sectarian, tribal and intra-proletarian. That is, it was inaccessible to and ineradicable by pacific or rational endeavour.

In Lithuania, the Polish minority was soon being roughly handled; in Moldova, the Gagauz (Christian Turks) and the Russians; in Romania, the Hungarians; in Serbia, the Albanians, among others. But in Bulgaria, the Turks, after decades of cultural repression at the hands of the communist regime, resumed their Turkish names, returned to their mosques, were permitted to wear traditional costume and to practice circumcision, and recovered the right to have Turkish taught in their schools. In the former Soviet Union, a multi-national empire where the very concept of a 'Soviet people' had been an artifice, no less than 65 millions, or between a quarter and a fifth of the entire population, lived in areas dominated by nationalities other than their own. Russians, for example, constituted more than 20 per cent of the inhabitants of the independent Ukraine – where there were no less than 120 different minority groups in all – more than a quarter in Estonia, a third in Latvia, and nearly 60 per cent of Kazakhstan's urban population. There were more than 4 million ethnic Hungarians, to take another example, in 'Yugoslavia', 'Czechoslovakia', Romania and the Ukraine. In the 4.5 million strong ex-Soviet republic of Moldavia, annexed from Romania in 1940, there were 3 million Romanian Moldovans, one million Russians and Ukrainians, with lesser numbers of Gagauz, Jews and Bulgarians. Two million ethnic Germans, too, were seeking an autonomous republic for themselves in the former Soviet Union.

In Belgrade, extreme nationalists were complaining in July 1991 of 'hordes of Romanians, gypsies and prostitutes from the Ukraine flooding into Serbia without control'. Franjo Tudjman, in Croatia, fanned Serb fears by refusing to condemn wartime Ustashe atrocities, when hundreds of thousands of Serbs, among others, were killed. In March 1990, in Tirgu Mures in Romania, there were violent attacks on ethnic Hungarians by armed Romanian peasants, wielding knives, axes and pitchforks. As ever, history was invoked to justify such violence and blame laid, as it generally is, at the door of the victim. Not only had Romanians been subjected to past Hungarian dominion, but Romania had been invaded by then-fascist Hungary in August 1940, with ghastly massacre and deportation on Hitler's behalf. *Ergo*, today's Hungarians in Romania must continue to be punished, as Ceausescu also punished them, even if the Romanians – when they joined the Axis – conducted themselves in like manner; their Seventh Army helped to murder thousands of the Jewish population of neighbouring Odessa. The heavens themselves might weep over it, but a species of ethnic paranoia everywhere began to rear its head. Albania accused the Serbs of 'planning the genocide' of the former Yugo-slavia's Albanian minority; the Serbian chief of staff accused Germany of having designs, through its support for Croatia, on the warm-water ports of the Adriatic; Ukrainians, Poles and Lithuanians, all now asserting themselves as independent players on the world stage, harboured near-pathological feelings about each other. Catholic and Orthodox, Christian and Muslim – and Muslim and Muslim in former Soviet Central Asia – Slav and Teuton, Russian and non-Russian, Czech and Slovak, Serb and Croat, Tatars, Yakuts, Cossacks and even Ingushi tribesmen in the Caucasus began to move again to the rhythms of ancient grievance. The ethnic merry-go-round, slower in some places, faster in others, was once more in motion.

War-cries that a particular people, sometimes the numerical majority, sometimes an embattled sub-group, were 'second-class citizens in their own country', joined the whirlpool of economic dislocation and defeated expectation. Instead of soaring living standards, there had been a perceived bonanza for the few, whom paranoia would always identify as the outsiders, and the old hardships for the many, whom the same paranoia would identify as the natives. In the former East Germany, after forty years of Soviet occupation, the denizens of the grim housing estates cropped their heads and began to react with a violence which was soon 'normal'; there were school pupils, apprentices, and army conscripts among them. The police, ill-equipped, demoralised, scared and sometimes sympathetic to the gangs, made what response they could, and sometimes barely any response at all. Unemployed (and employed) youth in Berlin, Leipzig and Dresden had been prone, even before the communist fall, to neo-Nazi protest and brawling, and attacks on immigrant 'aliens'. Now, so analysis ran, they and their equally disillusioned elders in the former East Germany were being told, in effect, that the last four decades of their country's history, as well as the previous two decades, had been a disastrous error, and their lives and efforts wasted. Some experts shrugged off the *Fremdenhass*, or xenophobia, as the standard aggression of the bored and disaffected, or a mere outcrop of the 'skinhead scene'; most of the violence was committed by teenagers, and even by children as young as twelve. Others, observing the swift (and organised) spread to prosperous West German cities, especially in North Rhine-Westphalia and Bavaria, of the East German pattern of attacks on immigrants, refugees, asylum seekers, gypsies and others, were prematurely alarmed at the prospect of another collective psychological breakdown in Germany, the second in little over half a century. Yet others feared, as a potentially lethal future combination, a working-class led nationalism, in which thwarted post-communist ideals of 'solidarity' and community were turned to the defence of race, class and nation.

The problems of the former East Germany were particularly serious. Thus, in Leipzig in 1990, and in part due to the exodus of young people to the West, the rate of marriages had fallen by 60 per cent in one year, and the birth-rate by 40 per cent; the fall in the birth-rate was 50 per cent for the country as a whole. A third of the city's workforce was unemployed, and 15 per cent of all calls to the switchboard of the

Nikolaikirche were said to be from people contemplating suicide. The notable absence, or self-repression, of nationalistic euphoria in West Germany at the time of reunification added to the sense of void in the Eastern *Länder*. Their people, the message of this lack of enthusiasm appeared to be, might be Germans too, but they were nevertheless a costly incubus, measurable in tens of billions of marks per annum. Indeed, few spirits, whether German or non-German, soared in contemplation of the new giant, with its combined population of 79 millions. Saddled with its heinous history and complex burden of unease as butcher of millions, it lay sprawled across the face of Central Europe, funnelling large sums in grants, loans and other assistance to the former Soviet Union, Poland and Hungary, as well as to its own new hinterland. As economic inequality, unemployment and disillusion increased in its Eastern provinces, in cruelly bleak settings of environmental damage and urban dereliction, it would have been more surprising, given all the circumstances, if neo-Nazi thuggery, inarticulately representing those excluded from the promised largesses of the market, had not increased *pari passu*.

In July 1991 an official survey, conducted for the office of the German ombudsman, had found that between 15 and 20 per cent of East German youth were 'ready to condone violence against foreigners', of whom there were then 120,000 in the East German population of 16 million. Before the fall of the Honecker regime there had been attacks on Vietnamese, Mozambican, Cuban and Angolan 'guest workers'. Indeed, as early as 1981 the existence of 'extreme right-wing tendencies' among young East Germans had been officially recognised in a little-publicised report by the East German interior ministry's Central Criminal Institute; assorted skinheads, 'Nazi punks' and 'Faschos' – with children of high communist officials among them – were already involved in attacks on 'guest workers' and in violence associated with football matches. In October 1987, more than two years before the fall, thirty skinheads wielding 'iron chains and baseball bats' had irrupted into a rock concert at East Berlin's Zionskirche, shouting '*Sieg Heil!*' From the end of 1987 to the end of 1989, when the Honecker regime was overthrown, nearly 500 separate neo-Nazi incidents had been investigated by the East German police.

Now, young people were 'expressing themselves more openly still'. Sociologists were at hand with explanation. The issues were most commonly held to be those of 'transition', of 'identity', and of 'second-class' citizenship *vis à vis* the West Germans. Or, East German youth, having 'lost its ideals', had 'not learned how to come to terms with temptations to wild behaviour under democratic conditions'. They had 'no foothold' or 'felt unwanted'; the commission of acts of violence attracted the attention which they lacked and needed. More elaborately, they were 'intolerant of nonconformity as the result of the legacy of the previous system', or were 'attracted to extreme politics' because they were 'just emerging from dictatorship', and so on.

The run-down housing estates of Dresden – which boasted, *inter alia*, an organisation of 'Saxon Werewolves' – were a main source of local youth violence. But by mid-1991 many other East German towns and cities contained bands of youths prowling the streets in search of 'foreigners' and trouble. A year earlier, in May 1990, '200 skinheads' in Nazi regalia, calling themselves 'national-socialist political soldiers', had formed themselves into a human swastika in (of all places) Berlin's Marx-Engels Platz. In November 1990, facing a gang of '500 skinheads' yelling *'Heil Hitler!'* and 'Bring Back Mielke!' – the former head of the Stasi – the Leipzig police had panicked and opened fire, shooting one of the demonstrators dead. In April 1991, on the 102nd anniversary of Hitler's birth, there were marches in several East German cities, including Leipzig. In the same month, the first Poles crossing the border into Germany after the lifting of visa restrictions were greeted with skinhead cries of *'Sieg Heil!'*, stones and spitting, together with shouts of 'Foreigners out!', 'Out with Polish pigs!', and 'Germany for the Germans!' In their turn, gangs of Polish skinheads were in the streets of Warsaw during the 1990 presidential election chanting 'Down with Mazowiecki!'; in March 1991 similar gangs rampaged through Warsaw Old Town, fighting the riot police and breaking windows. Attacks on non-white foreigners occurred in Hungary and Czechoslovakia also, with swastikas appearing on the plinth of St Wenceslas' statue.

'Kill the scum!' they shouted in Germany outside the hostels of immigrants and asylum-seekers, who in 1992 were entering the country at the rate of one thousand each day. In Berlin, in May 1991, apartments occupied by African workers were stormed by skinheads; two Namibians fell from balconies, critically injured. Two months earlier, a Mozambican immigrant worker had been pushed by a gang of youths from a moving train and killed; 300 youths, some armed with clubs, knives and tear-gas, even tried to attack his funeral procession. In September 1991, at Hoyerswerda, a lignite mining town near the Polish border, '200 jackbooted skinheads' laid siege for almost a week (to the cheers of bystanders) to two hostels, from which some 250 Mozambican,

Vietnamese, Nigerian, Ghanaian, Yugoslav and Romanian asylum applicants and immigrant workers had to be evacuated. A home for the mentally ill, some of whose occupants were beaten up, and even a children's convalescent home containing victims of the Chernobyl accident were assailed. There were attacks on a hostel for Cubans in the Eastern town of Brandenburg, a hostel for gypsies in Recklinghausen in West Germany, and a hostel for Romanian and Vietnamese refugees in Rostock in the East. Buildings were stormed, petrol bombs thrown, heads broken. There were many such cases; in 1992 it was reported that the number of attacks on foreigners in Germany was running at four times the level of the previous year. In addition, the far right parties were making significant gains in regional elections. In December 1991, the Federal Agency for the Protection of the Constitution estimated that there were 40,000 members of more than 60 extreme right-wing groups and organisations in Germany – such as the German People's Union, the Free German Workers' Party, and German Alternative, of whom 4,500 could be counted militant neo-Nazis; two-thirds of them were said to be in the former East Germany. But a Dresden member of parliament estimated that these groups had 15,000 supporters in Saxony alone. In Cottbus, south-east of Berlin and one of the centres of the neo-Nazi revival, there were perhaps 2,000 sympathizers.

In the former East Germany there had been little of the (uneasy) self-confidence of post-Nazi West Germany, where guilt was replaced with wealth and self-hatred camouflaged by efficiency, geniality and comfort. In the East, the burden of responsibility for the Nazi past had been simply, if psychotically, transferred to the West Germans alone. At the same time, Nazism's personality and 'style', its buildings and many of its personnel had been silently incorporated into the Stalinist regime. For decades, old excrescences of German behaviour were deemed not to exist in the socialist utopia, or were glossed over. It was only after the collapse of the Honecker regime, and prior to reunification, that first Hans Modrow (in February 1990), and then, more formally, the democratically-elected East German government (in April 1990), accepted 'joint responsibility, on behalf of the people, for the humiliation, expulsion and murder of Jewish men, women and children' in the Nazi period. A parliamentary resolution, passed on the day of the new democratic government's formation, asked the 'Jews of the world' for 'forgiveness'. The stern reply from Israel, not-Christian, was that 'the shame of Germany will never be erased'.

In 1990, East German moods had darkened, despite the hopes of economic and political renewal. Here and there Grosz-like scenes had begun to be re-enacted. Bedraggled Soviet soldiers on low pay and short commons could be seen selling uniforms and weapons – 25 marks for a hand-grenade, a pistol for 100, a Kalashnikov from 200 to 1,000 – at flea-market stalls. Others went about begging. Soviet war memorials in East Germany, granite in granite settings, were vandalised and graffiti-covered; down-at-heel shoppers were 'sure' that the Stasi were 'behind the Faschos'. The shorn-headed, gloomily abusing their emerging freedoms, attacked the luckless passer-by and the scared alien. Gypsies, the age-old scapegoats – perhaps half a million had been exterminated by the Nazis – began once again to be a target for the spleen of others. There were now said to be some six million in Central Europe, with 2 or 2.5 millions in Romania (around ten per cent of the population), perhaps half a million in Hungary and in Slovakia, and substantial but smaller communities in an arc from Poland to Bulgaria. Among many other trades and occupations, they were dealers, casual field-hands, musicians and hoarders of ill-considered trifles, both honestly and dishonestly acquired.

As borders opened, gypsies were freer to cross frontiers which their traditions and culture did not recognise; and their trading in goods and currencies began to suffer insult and violence from local people. In July 1991, at Mlawa in Poland, after a car driven by a gypsy had knocked down three Poles, killing one of them, crowds shouting 'Death to the gypsies!' and 'Poland for the Poles!', attacked and looted a settled colony of gypsies – some of them prosperous gold merchants and car-dealers. Their wealth was said by one of the crowd, again using the old Stalinist lexicon, to be 'provocative'; some 1,200 Polish gypsies fled the violence to Sweden, but were refused asylum. The following month, in Northern Bohemia, skinheads fought running battles with gypsies, leaving one gypsy dead and several injured. In Hungary, where expression of anti-gypsy prejudice is a commonplace of idle conversation, some 60 per cent of Hungary's prison population were said to be gypsies. In Romania, as fancies grew wilder under stress, you might hear that President Iliescu was a 'gypsy paid by Moscow'. The old suggestion that gypsies were all 'thieves and pickpockets', or child-snatchers, or possessed of the evil eye, dogged them in their settled communities and in their increased itinerations. In turn, and more 'provocative' still, the new freedoms led gypsies in some Central European countries, such as Hungary and Romania, to form their own

self-defence and political organisations, incurring the hostility which
was once directed at the 'uppity nigger'.

But it was the neurosis of anti-semitism which made the most
widespread as well as the most open of returns. The Leipzig rallies of
late 1989 had had their ugly aspect from the outset; cries of 'Jews out!'
could be heard amid the din of triumphant anti-communist protest.
Once more, 'release from repression' was the favoured sociological
explanation: that which had been taboo could now be spoken. Yet the
habit, for example, of ascribing Jewish forebears to political opponents
or faction rivals in the belief that it is an insult, or as a prelude to and
legitimation of a mean or violent act, had always been part of communist
history in Eastern Europe and the Soviet Union. (It is also part of anti-
semitic reflex the world over.) In the late 1930s, the Soviet Union had
given entry permits to Jewish exiles and refugees from Nazi persecution
only if they were Party members. Individual Jews, such as Stalin's
henchman Lazar Kaganovich, might be Stalinists themselves, but it
earned them no remission from Stalinism's terrifying rigours. The
Warsaw ghetto, an area of 700 acres, was obliterated by the post-war
Polish communist regime as if it had not been; the Holocaust itself was
reduced to little more than a footnote in the histories of Eastern Europe.
In concentration camps preserved as memorials in Czechoslovakia, in
Hungary, in Poland – as in Majdanek or Oswiecim (Auschwitz) – the
fact that Jews had died there by the millions was barely mentioned, or
avoided altogether. The truth lay in the unspoken. It was the silence
which was telling.

There was much, from some points of view, that required to be
hidden. The newly-independent Lithuanian government was quick to
exonerate thousands of Lithuanians whom it described as having been
'wrongly accused' by the previous Soviet authorities of being Nazi war
criminals. But new post-fall access to the hitherto sealed archives of
Eastern Europe and the Soviet Union began to disclose the full extent
of willing, and even enthusiastic, local participation in the deportation
and annihilation of their Jewish populations. Not only did the existence
of hitherto unknown ghettos and camps come to light, but also new
evidence of the scale of collaboration in atrocity on the part of the Poles
and Hungarians, Croats and Slovaks, Russians and Ukrainians (including of their police forces). Against it, the long-standing exclusion of
Jews from the Czech politburo, or the anti-semitic campaign conducted
by the Polish communist regime in 1968, were trifles.

Jews, like any other people, have been capitalist and anti-capitalist, communist and anti-communist, liberal and illiberal, members of every party and movement, and of none. Whatever their differences, they have also been aware – with fear or pride, anxiety or unconcern – of a common ethnicity, despite generations of admixture. This awareness has been matched, or more than matched, by a sometimes morbid interest in them on the part of those who are not Jews. This interest is potentially most morbid when it is based upon, and constantly returns to, what Adam Michnik, the Polish-Jewish intellectual, has described as a 'strange fascination with blood and heredity' and with the 'racial background of grandfathers and great-grandfathers'. Beyond it, lies the fanaticism of dreams of a nation's 'purity' – a Christian state without Jews, a Muslim state without Jews or Christians, a Jewish state without non-Jews. And beyond that, requiring a step taken only by a few (unless specially dire circumstances attract the many), is the lunacy of genocidal ambition. But it is in its more banal, or vulgar, forms of expression that most Jews encounter anti-semitism, whether directly or indirectly, explicitly or by innuendo, if they encounter anti-semitism at all.

In the fall of Eastern Europe, it began immediately, as with the cries of Leipzig. It lay, by innuendo, in the common assertion – perhaps commonest in Poland, but common too in Romania and Slovakia – that this country or that was 'being sold to the bankers'. In the discourse of anti-semitism, conscious or unconscious, every banker may become a Jew, even if not every Jew is a banker; the archetypal Jew, at such times, is never a Christ and rarely an Einstein. (Indeed, any individual who is disliked may become a Jew, even if he is not one.) Especially in periods of economic insecurity or crisis, banks and capital, buying and selling, and (even more) wheeling and dealing, are habitually associated – in the popular landscape of the mind – with Jews, either undisguisedly rapacious or refurbished with a sanitised name and a sophisticated manner. 'First we were occupied by the Soviets for forty years,' declared a spokesman for an East German neo-Nazi group, presenting the 'politicised' version of the old racist story. 'Now we face colonisation by the international Jewish captialist conspiracy.' The involvement of any Jew in the swiftly spreading corruption suggested that corruption itself was Jewish. When one of the alleged malefactors in a case of Polish fraud turned up in Israel, it served to confirm, with a nod and a wink, that Jews could be found in every swindle, even if tens of thousands of crooks, large and small and of varied provenance, were at work throughout the collapsing socialist system. 'Jewish managers of government companies impoverish the country with their swindles, while

Polish children starve,' was how Boleslaw Tejkowski, leader of Poland's National Community Party, put it.

In Romania, in July 1991, it was being claimed in widely-disseminated broadsheets that Jews 'controlled' the government, that 'Israel' planned to 'make Romania into a Jewish colony', and that 'the Jews' were 'plotting with the IMF to turn Romanians into street-sweepers'. Even the Association of Polish Victims of the Third Reich – one-fifth of Poland's entire population, including the Polish Jews, died, half its housing stock was destroyed, and some one million Poles were employed as slave labour – circulated leaflets claiming that the government of Tadeusz Mazowiecki planned to 'turn Poland into a valley of Jews'. 'I don't want to be in a Poland transformed into a Jewish colony,' declared Stanislaw Tyminski, the presidential candidate in the 1990 election. The notion that the Jews were 'coming', as purchasers of the nation's patrimony, as manipulators of power, as new oppressors, became pervasive in Eastern Europe. So, too, did popular fancies that various leading political figures, including Vaclav Havel and Tadeusz Mazowiecki – and even the Pope and President Bush, according to Boleslaw Tejkowski – were concealing their real identities as Jews. The crushing defeat, in the Polish presidential election, of Mazowiecki, a devout Catholic, was attributed in part to the rumour, spreading rapidly among those predisposed to believe it, that he was a Jew in sheep's clothing. Similarly, when Vaclav Havel boldly visited Bratislava in March 1991 to protest at the consecration there of a memorial to Slovakia's wartime puppet-leader, Father Josef Tiso – hanged after the war for his complicity in the deportations of 60,000 Slovak Jews to Auschwitz – the crowd greeted him with cries of 'Go home to Prague, you Jew!' as well as of 'Judas, Judas'.

In July 1990, it was disclosed that the Polish secret police, in a country where only some 6,000 Jews remained of the original population of 3 million, had throughout the communist period kept lists not only of Jewish associations and of known Jewish individuals, but also of people with 'Jewish-sounding names'; the wearing of a yellow star would have been in closer accord with tradition. Lech Walesa had a habit of calling himself, on public platforms, a 'true Pole' and 'clean'; to a Polish audience the significance of the Nobel laureate's assertion of purity was as plain as a pikestaff. In August 1990, he made his position and his reflexes clearer during a public dispute with Solidarity's liberal Citizens' Committee for Democratic Action, a few of whose members – perhaps two or three – were of Jewish origin. They should, he exclaimed at the meeting, 'declare their origins. I am from the bottom level of society. People there don't like a lack of clarity. They don't like things being hidden.' Franjo Tudjman, the Croatian leader, was plainer still with his audience in the summer of 1991, declaring in public that his wife was 'pure Croat, neither Serb nor Jew'; 'thank God,' he added. In Budapest, where Stars of David were scrawled on certain candidates' election posters from the very beginning of the 'new democratic era', a group of prominent members of the Hungarian Democratic Forum, speaking for what they called the 'national majority', bluntly declared during the 1990 elections that 'people of Jewish extraction' could not be 'true Hungarians'. The old 'Magyar doctrine', which had sought before the war to classify Hungarians by racial origin, was making its reappearance.

These were minority currents for all the majoritarian rhetoric. Nevertheless, they were the same currents which had flowed in the Thirties, and which had been partially dammed during the communist blockade of national emotions. Flowing again in April 1990 in Lodz (with its dire history for the Jews, and no remaining Jewish population), citizens' committee election posters throughout the city were daubed with graffiti insisting that Mazowiecki was a Jew; anti-semitism was described by an observer as 'public and unchecked'. In the same month, in Kielce – notorious for the murder in 1946 of forty-three Jewish survivors of the Holocaust at the hands of a Polish mob – a concert by a visiting Soviet-Jewish folk group was attacked and broken up by a local skinhead gang throwing smoke-bombs and shouting anti-semitic slogans. There are no Jews in Kielce. At a demonstration outside the presidential palace in Warsaw in August 1991 of elderly people seeking higher pensions, the crowd set up a chant of 'Jews to Israel!'; at meetings of the Polish political right, anti-semitic literature was on open sale. Anti-semitic obsession became common in Romania also, and was clearly reflected in the periodical press. 'In parliament and in the government,' wrote *Romania Mare*, 'it rains Jews by the bucket.' In September 1991, anti-semitic hostility to Prime Minister Petre Roman was alleged to have been a major factor in forcing his resignation. '*Juden Raus!*' said the graffiti in Berlin and Warsaw; the word 'Jew' was written across the election posters of Free Democratic Alliance candidates in Hungary and Solidarity candidates in Poland. Jewish cemeteries were desecrated in Croatia, in the former East Germany, in Hungary, in Poland, in Romania, in Slovakia.

'Jews,' shouted a nationalist gang from Pamyat (Memory), breaking into a meeting of the Soviet Writers' Union in January 1990, 'your time is over!' 'The Jews,' declared Anatoly Buylov at an earlier Writers' Union meeting in November 1989, 'appear to be the only nationality that is interested in our ruin. They are everywhere.' 'Many,' he added, were 'hiding' – as, nine months later, Lech Walesa also thought and said – 'under different names and another nationality'. Pamyat, with its programme to 'preserve Russian culture' and its passionate argument (from the 'Russian soul') that Russians had 'suffered more than other people', blamed the Jews even for the empty shelves. Shortages, they announced, were 'caused by Jews'. With the serialisation of *Mein Kampf* available from early 1991 in Moscow's *Military History Journal* ('in response to readers' demands'), old phobias resurfaced in military circles too, and in ways that recalled Tsarist times. At a Soviet Army Day rally in Moscow in February 1991, not only did banner slogans declare 'Yeltsin and Co' to be 'servants of Zionism', but accusations were heard – and repeated at a Leningrad rally on May Day, 1991 – that 'Jews' were now being 'favoured at the expense of Russians'. General Albert Makashov, a defeated candidate in the Russian presidential election of June 1991, went further, picking out for special abuse Alexander Yakovlev, for a time one of Gorbachev's closest advisers and a Jew, and placing him at the head of a list of 'enemies of the people'. In June 1992, the city of Lvov even decided to name one of its streets after the Ukrainian nationalist leader, Semyon Petlura, notorious (among Jews) for his instigation in 1918 of pogroms in the Ukraine in the wake of the Bolshevik Revolution.

While some laid Stalinism itself at the door of the Jews, for others Stalin's approach to the 'Jewish question' became, in fond retrospect, one of his signal virtues. 'He only wiped out Zionists, speculators, and enemies of the people' – all three thinly-coded terms for Jews – said a woman bystander at a United Workers' Front demonstration in Moscow in May 1991, which had been called to protest against the diplomatic rapprochement with Israel. And while Pamyat made clear its desire to see the Jews depart *en masse* from Russia, as they were already doing, the United Workers' Front criticised them as 'traitors' for leaving. Jews, sometimes attributed with almost sole responsibility for Bolshevism itself – 'this was an Empire of Satan, built by Jews,' said a passer-by in Cluj in Romanian Transylvania in May 1990, referring to the Romanian communist system – could also be singled out for not having done enough to oppose it. Thus, the chief rabbi of Romania, Moses Rosen, was typically focused upon as a target of reproach for having 'collaborated' with Ceausescu, while a veil was discreetly drawn over the acquiescent role of Romanian Orthodoxy, the national faith, throughout the communist period. 'I gave my hand to the devil,' answered Rosen, in an impressive but insufficient apologia, 'but I was not Faust. I did not sell my soul.'

In the former Soviet Union, as throughout Central Europe, silence generally greeted the signs of anti-semitic revival. Gorbachev, voluble on many subjects, permitted Jews to leave the Soviet Union but for several years kept a measured distance from the wider issues. Only in October 1991, at a ceremony marking the fiftieth anniversary of the Nazi massacre of Jews at Babi Yar, near the Ukrainian capital of Kiev, did he deplore the Soviet Jewish emigration, belatedly declaring it to have resulted from government and public failure to condemn anti-semitic hatreds. Boris Yeltsin, who, while Moscow Party chief, had studiedly welcomed Pamyat representatives to his office and had been photographed smiling genially with them, eventually made a brief public reference to 'unacceptable fascist and anti-semitic organisations'. Lech Walesa, whose own presidential sails had filled during the campaign of innuendo against Mazowiecki, set up a Council for Polish-Jewish Relations which met for the first time in March 1991. Its purpose was to 'stamp out anti-semitism', and to 'stop the word "Jew" being used as an insult'. Most liberals in the new democratic orders, however, including those who had played distinguished roles as dissenters in the communist era, said nothing on the entire subject. In Central Europe and the former Soviet Union, the risk of being branded a 'Zionist' or a 'Jew' was evidently a risk not worth taking, particularly for a politician. The prosecution of a noisy Russian anti-semite, Konstantin Smirnov (a factory worker), ended in Moscow in October 1990 with court uproar, as he was sentenced to two years' hard labour for 'inciting inter-ethnic hatred'. 'I suffer for Russia,' he characteristically shouted in the bedlam, while denouncing the 'Yiddish verdict'. 'Beware of Yids!' read the T-shirts worn by some of the demonstrators in the court-room.

The search for deliverance from communism, and for a return to the 'normal', was taking its toll. The transgressor Smirnov, too, was one of its victims. Like the long misery of the Jews at hands such as his, his 'suffering for Russia' spoke to an ancient story. With the fall of the socialist utopia – its columns tumbling like those of King Solomon's temple – an old life was resuming, including the old life of the Russians and the Jews. For hundreds of thousands of Jews it was ending in disregarded flight, and for tens of millions of Russians (and Central

Europeans) in that darkness of 'soul', illuminated by outbreaks of passionate expectation, which the Jews had once shared with them. To its pre-communist atavisms, the legacy of the communist era had now been added. It was a world whose future exaltation, material and spiritual, would be a labour of generations, if it could be achieved at all.

FIVE

Thinking Again

The recent times of upheaval have not only been times of release and of trouble, as the Psalmist puts it, but of transformation both of intellectual fortunes and intellectual perspectives. Of all the intellectual convulsions those of the left were the greatest, even if there was (relatively) little sign or sound of it.

Some Western socialists sought to rally their spirits in any way they could. Many more were put to confusion, and, their confusion being continuously before them, fell silent, waiting Micawber-like for something to turn up. Others, especially Marxists in the West, still hoping that their time might come and that capitalism's difficulties were greater than theirs, often preferred to believe that what had occurred accorded with arcane left prediction and called for no pronounced reaction; Gorbachev believed that the 'discrediting of socialism' was 'only a passing phase'. Of fundamental re-evaluation of left positions – as distinct from a hurried casting overboard of principle for electoral reasons – there was little; of confession of error, of recantation, of making intellectual amends, even less; of open acknowledgment of utter socialist failure, almost nothing.

Instead, here and there, a former intellectual guru of the left might murmur his regrets at the outcome of decades of socialist endeavour. He would claim to have been always opposed to its excesses; half-heartedly propose an amended, or more democratic, version of socialist theory; mutedly declare the continuing relevance of the socialist ideal, and lapse once more into silence. Some, it seemed, were keeping their heads down in hope, until the 'turn to the market' itself turned into failure, social crisis, war, fascist restoration and the revival of socialist prospects. Two hundred years ago, the surviving aristocrats of the French *ancien régime* nurtured similar hopes, huddled together for mutual comfort amid the relics of their former lives.

Like the French nobility, the left had lost most of its estate, in its case an intellectual estate, but an estate for all that. It had lost, one might say, an intellectual fortune in its ideological pills and potions, its old apophthegms and nostrums. Its philosophy of class, its history of class, its economics of class, its politics of class, its (latter-day) sociology of class, had lost most of their former dominion. The guilty intellectual fetishisation of the proletariat was exposed as false coin; the left's decades of self-confident propagation of obscurantist theory were part of the history of alchemy, not science. Yuri Andropov, Gorbachev's predecessor, had typically proclaimed in 1983 that the Soviet Union had 'entered a period of perfecting developed socialism'. Instead, it had been the beginning of the end.

Where individual members of the Western intellectual left were communists, or nostalgic ex-communists, they found the organisations to which they had belonged for their adult lifetimes, or whose 'lines' they had followed at a greater or lesser distance, disbanding around them, or suffering social democratic mutation. Not long before, they could still have fancied themselves – in France, in the former West Germany, in Italy, in Britain – as members of the ruling class of a future socialist utopia, and as advisers to, or scribes for, its prospective Grand Viziers. Except in isolated pockets of continuing influence (India's West Bengal, for instance), such hopes vanished. Where they had had more modest aspirations as all-knowing critics of their own and every other social order, they had found their study floors cave in beneath them. There were elements of farce in it. But in the waste, and sense of waste, of entire intellectual lives, and in the loss of faith and face, there was also much that was tragic.

Few on the left could credit, or allow themselves to credit, that it was not only 'Stalinist communism' but socialism itself which had been discarded in the Soviet Union and Eastern Europe. Even fewer could believe that tens of millions of 'real proletarians' had come to perceive socialism, as well as communism, as a failure. The form of society which socialists, middle-class socialists in particular, had chosen for the working-class had been rejected by the majority of the working-class itself. Unspoken, and unspeakable, was the sense of one 'loss' in particular: the loss of that world which was 'not capitalist', and whose mere existence, however flawed, betokened the possibility of living by other than the laws of the market.

Lost with it was much of the socialist sense of election and special virtue. As the scale of 'real' socialism's delinquency became clearer, and as former socialist leaders – emerging from the shadow of ideological untruth – themselves began to disclose its iniquities, the claim that socialism occupied higher moral ground than capitalism fell by the wayside. The false syllogism which stood at the heart of the left's *amour propre* was exposed. Its first term was that socialists alone cared for moral ends, chief of them equality and social justice; its second, that the pursuit of equality and social justice was an abiding virtue; its third, that socialism and socialists were therefore virtuous also. To a dogmatic socialist, socialism not merely expressed but exhausted the politics of conscience. Its indignations, its protests, its struggles, its victories possessed – to a socialist – an inherent moral quality which was not found in the actions of others.

A Hazlitt might argue that it is in the 'spirit of dogmatism' that 'all idle theories have their root.' But to a socialist, dogma was more truly a body of ethical principle, self-evidently sound, by which the socialist lived, moved, and had his being. No believer committed to a faith ever believed differently or less.

From what did the moral confidence of socialists, so rudely shaken – but not shattered – derive? First, it rested in a belief, or fixed principle, that the human condition could be ameliorated and should be ameliorated, and that socialist theory and practice indicated the means and provided the models by which such amelioration could be effected. 'The Golden Age of the human species,' wrote Saint-Simon in 1814, at the dawn of modern socialism's illusions, achievements and disasters, 'is not behind us, it is before us. It lies in the perfection of the social order. Our children will one day arrive there. It is for us to clear the path.' In such assertion lay the well-head of socialist assumptions as to the meaning of progress and the progressive, and of socialist claims to an exclusive lien upon both of them. Marx added the spirit of Judaic prophecy (and intellectual rigour) to the French aristocrat's wishful thinking, appointed the proletariat Mankind's redeemer – in every sense its *deus ex machina* – and confidently awaited the socialist millennium. It was a confidence passed on not only to his followers but to socialists of every sect and persuasion.

Such confidence rested, secondly, upon a belief, corroborated by moral first principle and confirmed by intellectual inquiry, that socialism contained an historically transcendent moral critique of capitalism, and would prove in practice superior to it. When the world of 'real socialism' collapsed, morally compromised and in practical discredit, the claims of the left to special insight – whatever its reservations about the particular

form of socialism created in the Soviet Union and Eastern Europe –
were struck full on the chin, staggered against the ropes, and fell.

At first glance, the categories of right and left themselves seemed to
have been transcended. The advocates of the market in the socialist
countries were the 'left-wingers' and the 'progressives'. The defenders
of socialism and the proletarian interest were the 'conservatives' and
the 'rightists'. The disorientation of the Western left, indispensable foil
to the right, also deprived the right of part of its defining purpose.
Without the propulsion provided by its anti-socialism, the latter too lost
some of its intellectual momentum and sense of direction.

In the 1970s, the advancing fortunes of the intellectual right in the
West had owed much to the intellectual left's increasing obscurantism
and dullness of mind. Indeed, the 'rise of the right' was less a cause
than a symptom of the left's failure. Yet, so comprehensive was the
communist fall that the right too was taken aback. Many of its
intellectuals, especially the Burkean conservatives, were incredulous to
find communism being swept away for a capitalist restoration; they were
even, in their own way, disdainful of the seemingly headlong enthusiasm
of former socialists for the market.

But no confusions could have been greater than the left's. The
market philosophy, which yesterday had represented 'Thatcherite
greed,' social Darwinism, vulgarity and even 'evil', was today being
taken up by erstwhile communists in the name of progress and popular
well-being. Socialist aspiration was being rejected as misguided or even
wicked. Collectivism, the left's high road to human emancipation, was
not merely being abandoned to the right's 'bourgeois' conceptions of
freedom, but the entitlement to be free of socialism was, horrifyingly,
high on the new post-socialist agenda. The freedoms of an unequal
society were being preferred to the servitudes of an egalitarian, or
quasi-egalitarian, order. In such a preference socialist aims seemed to
be of little purpose. It even looked as if 'the working classes' of the
socialist countries had decided that they, too, stood to do better in the
world of private enterprise – which everybody believed they had been
taught to fear and hate – than in the socialist utopia.

The left also had to face the discomfiture that socialist collectivism
was being freely equated with fascism. Hitherto, the argument had been
dismissed by most socialists as a right-wing extravagance which was
beneath its attention. Not only were Stalin and Hitler now held to be
equivalently tyrannical as persons, but the systems over which they
presided were being asserted, without demur, to have been equally evil.

'State socialism' and 'national socialism', it was being said, were not significantly distinct. Both systems had been autocracies directed to the creation of 'slave empires'; both had sought to impose a uniformity of thought and behaviour on entire societies with the aid of security organisations as large as armies; both had killed their foes, or driven them to death, on a scale to beggar imagination, the one in concentration camps, the other in gulags. Both had been driven by ideological obsession, and each had ended in (equivalent) disaster. They had even had the same kind of art and architecture.

Capitalism, the left was being told, was not only more democratic than socialism could ever be, but also more moral. Social justice and egalitarianism were either meaningless or unattainable, or both; and, if attainable in any degree, more likely to be attained in a plural and free market society than in any other. It was not the competition of the market which conduced to anarchy and a Hobbesian state of nature, but the doctrines of class and class struggle. Indeed, market competition was positively benign, as well as productive of wealth, when set against the ruinous outcomes of class conflict. Socialist meddling with the market, not the market itself, was the *fons et origo* of economic turmoil; socialism was a destructive intrusion into the natural order.

Furthermore, it was not the pursuit of the interests of the working class but the 'spirit of entrepreneurship' which was the true arm and instrument of progress towards a prosperous, just and (if one wished) egalitarian society. Socialism could not even produce enough to keep its citizens in potatoes. It was effort in the market, not the building of utopias, which led to the general comfort of the people. True morality lay not in 'dependency' on the state, but in 'dignities' which were self-earned. It was not passivity but the assumption of responsibility which should be rewarded; the capitalist not the socialist ethic which, properly weighed, would be found to be the more humanistic. For if the exercise of 'market freedoms' produced greater prosperity and promoted greater invention – and did so more efficiently and more swiftly than under any other dispensation – this was in itself a moral and humane value.

Also coming to the aid of the left's rout was the assertion that the right's political and economic presumptions worked 'with the grain' of society, while the left's worked against it. Socialism, it was argued, was impossibly predicated upon changing human nature. But the non-proprietary, non-competitive, selfless, egalitarian-minded individual of the ideal socialist republic was pure artifice, a figment of the utopian imagination. Even the attempt to create such an ideal order necessarily required cruel imposition, force, and falsehood; and socialism-in-practice had inevitably depended upon them. Desire for private property, acquisitiveness, competitiveness and self-seeking were attributes of human nature; to take measures to repress them had proved a foolish and costly business. Moreoever, these propensities were closely associated with identity and self-esteem, creativity and human effort. To assault one set of deep instincts was to cause damage to them all.

The socialist might think it in some way base to 'truck, barter and exchange', but it was an error to think anything human alien, and to act to extirpate it. The right had therefore turned back (in triumph) to Adam Smith for its 'commonsense' corroborations. 'It is not from the benevolence of the butcher, the brewer, or the baker that we expect our dinner,' said the Scots economist, 'but from their regard to their own interest.' *Homo sapiens* had his own ways, and senseless at the last any mere ideology which was founded upon their denial. Nor was the wisdom which the right claimed to find in Adam Smith his alone. Had not Aristotle in his *Politics* asserted, for instance, that 'with every man busy with his own, there will be increased effort all round'?

The oldest arguments of the anti-socialist case came flooding back as socialism stumbled and fell. Differences in individual talents, endowments and aspirations, to say nothing of differences of perception as to what constitutes achievement in the first place, made nonsense of the case of the socialist egalitarian. Indeed, society had a duty to nurture, reward and promote such differences. Citizens of the socialist countries had themselves grown tired of egalitarian social experiments carried out in their names; the pressure for a 'return to the normal' had derived in large part from the insistence of individuals upon their individuality. The resilience of human nature had, in other words, triumphed over all that had been done to confine it.

Other awarenesses were thrust upon the left, and had to be swallowed in silence. Among the most galling was that socialist states had not been able to organise their societies and economies better – that is, more productively, more efficiently, more happily – than could have been achieved under democratic conditions in a market order. Every socialist knew, *in pectore*, that had the future socialist states of Eastern Europe been left in 1945 to their own capitalist choices and devices, their citizenries, from the Baltic to Bulgaria, could not possibly have ended up so beggared. It was similarly plain that the Soviet Union, without the burden of the Bolshevik Revolution, would have been able, seven decades later, to feed its own people.

The conclusion which the right drew from this record, and which it put under the left's recoiling noses, was that the 'laws' of market freedom were as fundamental to economic progress as the laws of gravity or relativity were to physics. Related to this proposition was the assertion that Western liberal democracy, as a form of human government, was the 'end of history' and acme of perfection. Beside it, socialist government and the command economy were the work of the devil. The individual's needs and desires, so the right declared, could never be adequately enough known, nor understood, to make the socialist regulation of them a rational, let alone a moral, project. Adam Smith, said the right, had been wiser than all the vain armies of socialist planners in holding the view that 'no human wisdom or knowledge could ever be sufficient [for] the duty of superintending the industry of private people, and of directing it towards the employments most suitable to the interest of the society.' Socialism, the left was being told, was organised ignorance and harm. Capitalism alone could conserve that precious spirit of spontaneity and freedom which made for human happiness and progress.

In the moral history of the left there had been no intellectual challenge to its ideas and purposes comparable with this one, nor a juncture so awkward. It was a challenge which it failed. The left protested, where it protested at all, that the ethic of market capitalism not merely ratified private greed and selfish desire, but made public virtues of them. It was callous in its unconcern for the outpaced victim of headlong competition; it was pharisaic and insufficiently Christian; it was less libertarian than it seemed, and more authoritarian than it professed, in practice; it was a philosophy which rewarded strength and penalised weakness. Even Marx made a fleeting reappearance. The form of 'personal freedom' which was currently being celebrated by the right amounted to nothing more than what he had once sardonically called 'the right to an undisturbed enjoyment of mere chance'. In the name of liberty, blind Fate, the goddess of the market, had been permitted to defeat and displace the rule of Reason. (Had the left known enough of its own scriptures, it could also have invoked Lenin: 'Down with the kind of freedom offered by capitalists with banks, and private factories, and enterprises, and speculation! Down with such freedom!' he had exclaimed in 1919.)

The common good, declared those among the left who were still standing, could be served only by a common purpose. The market could not in fact do what the socialist state was accused of having failed to do. It could not meet a community's public and social needs, nor could it furnish to those with little purchasing power the wherewithal of a secure and contented existence. Even with the best of intentions, and in the most flourishing of free markets, there was much that no individual could do for himself. What force, if not that of the benign socialist state, would consider it to be its moral duty, as a matter of policy or conviction, to make good all such defects? ('God will provide, but who will provide *until* God provides?', asks the Jewish joke, or dark riddle.) Individual goodwill, the left insisted, was an unsteady prop for the needy. Even the Good Samaritan could, on a bad day, be deaf to entreaty.

There were other ethical objections, most of them not made by the left, to the 'marketisation' of human relations. They were objections shared on the right by paternalists who despised, *de haut en bas*, the morality of the vulgar rich, the rentier and the market stall-holder. The needs of 'customers' and 'consumers' were an impoverished theme, paternalists thought, for a political and civic life. Not everything under the sun could be managed by the price mechanism and minimal social provision; self-interest and anti-socialist bigotry could not make good the absence of other principles. The materialism of the free market and of the 'self-made man' was ethically insufficient and without a redeeming social purpose. Indeed, a life spent in the market was as much a life wasted as one spent in failing to construct the socialist utopia.

And, asked the patrician, what of the old familiar order of hierarchy, established privilege, rule of law, religious observance and tradition? Did not Edmund Burke prescribe to politicians the task of acting as 'trustees for the nation' and as 'good stewards of its traditions, its values and its riches', rather than being merely the custodians and managers of its markets?

The market might well be the locus of a large part of human energy – the part discounted by socialist folly – but what eternal values were to be found there? Had not every ethical system, whether secular or religious, sought to compensate for and transcend the values of the market-place? Could the acquisition of wealth for its own sake be considered a virtue? How could 'competition' govern, or be permitted to govern, all human relations? How could schools and hospitals, galleries and museums, libraries and opera houses, institutions of charity and academies of higher learning, be made subject to the criteria of virtue esteemed by their bookkeepers? In any case, no state known to man had been able simply to abandon its economy and society to 'market forces'. The very idea was as utopian as any socialist panacea. There was no such thing as a 'free market'; here, mannerly right and left were at one.

But the ruder and more confident of the right regarded social justice and equality as 'bluffs', and made powerful objection to the left's 'egalitarian crusades'. They perceived egalitarianism to be simply the vice of leveller-envy made over into a virtue. Its pursuit led directly to the bureaucratic misallocation of resources, passive reliance upon welfare, the grey depression of incentive and (its corollary) the abuse of power. Aristotle, the Hellene, knew better than Marx, the Semite. 'Equality,' said the former, 'means giving the same to those who are alike,' not giving the same to those who are unlike.

Yet, surely, whispered the near-mute left, socialism's aspiration to a fraternity of souls – in this life – was preferable to the severance of man from man under regimes which celebrated the individual ego? In principle, perhaps, answered the unsentimental right. But in practice socialism had proved to be bleakly destructive of civic society, while in capitalism even the relations of the market (or those relations above all) were fully human. Society and culture advance by invention, but collectivism had suppressed such invention. The right welcomed and made way for individual excellence, but the instinct of the socialist was to compensate the mediocre for the merit of others. Nor could the left shrug off such reflexes; the socialist impulse derived from them. Hence, said the right, socialism had failed. And so it had. A few socialist intellectuals sought spiritedly to confront the ideological challenge in mid-defeat. Most shrank into silence, and for good reason.

The political parties of the Western right were increasingly emboldened by the growing socialist debacle. In particular, the British Tory Party, under Mrs Thatcher, proclaimed the nation to have been 'demoralised' by the past application of left nostrums. The electorate was told of the need to 'restore initiative', reduce dependency on welfare, 'roll back the frontiers of the state', promote an 'enterprise culture' and so forth. 'Socialist' public utilities were privatised, 'superfluous' regulatory institutions were abolished, voluntary association was privileged, obstructive trade union powers were curbed, and 'markets' were created in public and social institutions where none had previously existed. Taxes were cut, or were attempted to be cut, and welfare provision was either (modestly) reduced or access to it made harder. Some public bodies lost subsidy, others were dismantled. 'Wealth creation' was given precedence over the needs of the halt and the lame, 'family values' were lauded, and the principle of responsibility for self proclaimed from the rooftops. Socialist potions, even in dilute form, were held to be poison. Non-socialism was both an antidote and a bracing tonic.

Astonishingly – from some points of view – many socialist politicians broadly agreed, in the East as well as in the West. Though few would yet say so, they appeared (from their actions, not their words) to concede that the old socialist game was up. Even though significant proportions of Western electorates still appeared to espouse 'socialist values', particularly as to public provision, a new consensus was being established. Indeed, some politicians of the Western left, in their new-found enthusiasms for the market, for individual freedom, for choice and so on, moved well to the right of many moderate rightists. (In consequence, the right had to remain further right than it might have wished, merely in order to be distinguishable from pro-market leftists.) Left politicians even shied away from the word 'socialism'. Embarrassed by their ideological inheritance, they were fearful of being tarred electorally with the socialist brush. The right's old enemy was camouflaging itself with the right's colours.

In France, the resulting political confection was dubbed 'Chanel socialism', and its exponents the 'caviar left', the '*foie gras* left' and so forth. As socialist politicians began to try to vacate the worlds of public ownership and public provision, some left-wing intellectuals sought to restore their sense of purpose and their morale by taking up the cause of constitutional reform, citizen 'empowerment' and the 'deepening of democracy'. Others continued to condemn varieties of social injustice and inequality, but now usually without specific reference to socialist means or socialist ends. Even the term 'social democracy' was treated with inhibition.

In other words, much of the ideology and most of the institutions of capitalism now seemed to be being acquiesced in politically, both East and West, by former socialists and communists. Yet, left intellectuals in general remained silent. Moreover, the legitimacy of capitalism as a socio-economic system continued not to be accepted by socialists whole-heartedly, or at all, despite a seeming abandonment of socialist ideas and institutions. Unable to acknowledge the scale of their defeat, socialists, East and West, nevertheless began talking the language of markets and of profit, but with neither aptitude nor conviction. Ex-leftists assumed the uneasy guise of deft managers of the capitalist interest, while simultaneously nurturing the remains of their socialist commitment; converts to the doubtful virtues of competition and consumption hankered in secret for their old allegiances to the working class and the producer.

These were the confusions of ideological failure. 'Thinking again' had brought the surrendering left to many of the right's positions, as captives in war, disarmed and unmanned, find themselves on unfamiliar hostile terrain. In the West, to be caught in the uniform of the left was now to be judged (at best) an innocent dupe of idealistic folly, at worst an historic enemy of truth and reason. Conversely, the right, even in left estimations, had lost some of its negative anti-democratic and anti-progressive associations. It had acquired a new aura, often grudgingly and suspiciously bestowed, of being right on many matters, above all those to do with the centrality of the market in human affairs and the virtues of individual freedom. Here, right was right, and left was wrong.

This was a serious moral defeat. It was disorientating that what had always been seen as the right's inherent amorality could triumph over the left's highly ethical value system, as the left esteemed it to be. Socialism's moral recoil from private property in the means of production, for instance, had itself been rejected, including on moral grounds. But socialists, East and West, also knew (to take the example of private property) that once the rights of private property had been 'conceded', it would require all the efforts of state and law to give such rights substance. Private property would have to be physically protected by the post-socialist state's servants, rights of inheritance would have to be guaranteed across the generations, property values would have to be sustained by, and would do much to determine, the state's policy choices, and laws in many fields would have to be tailored to the task of establishing and maintaining the legitimacy and certainty of property and other market transactions. To a socialist, once the pass of private property had been sold, or 'sold out', all else followed.

The sense of identity of the left, sustained by the self-validating world of 'left culture', also lay in its perception of itself as the party of the most interesting and intelligent people. Now, the left found that its ideas were widely thought to be neither intelligent nor interesting. But more grievous was the harm done by socialist failure to the left's sense of self-regard, which had been nurtured upon the assumption that other moral people shared its values. In socialism's heyday, to be a socialist was felt (by socialists) to be synonymous with being a good as well as a progressive person. And to consider oneself a good and progressive person was, plainly, an essential element of an individual's moral self-esteem. (I know this, having felt it myself.) This party – using the term in its broadest sense – was unprepared for its awakening to a world in which 'socialism' was being thought by many to signify something misguided or evil, or both, and in which the word itself could barely be spoken without discomfort.

A fraternity of the elect had been founded upon unquestioned assumptions about class, the iniquities of 'the bourgeoisie', Western imperialism, the continuing 'struggle' onwards and upwards, and so on. Now, almost overnight, the assumptions evaporated and the fraternity dwindled. Sense both of direction and of identity came under severe pressure. Once, some on the intellectual left had found a sustaining life in the worst of socialist pretensions. A certain kind of 'Marxism' had its own snobberies even. Thus, Richard Gott, a journalist of the British left, visiting Nyerere's socialism in Tanzania in 1971, felt able to declare in the *Guardian*, in the high period of such folly, that 'rootless Socialists from all over the world seem to home in on Dar-es-Salaam, and I have long since given up being surprised at greeting friends here last seen in Hanoi or Havana.'

Mutual validation of purpose, inflated by its dissemination in left books, periodicals and newspapers, and through public meetings and demonstrations, sustained a whole structure of self-referring truth and self-confident assertion. Outside its moral consensus, those who were not *parti-pris*, not members of the 'party of the good people', were perceived as inhabiting a penumbra of unenlightenment and of simple-minded error. Their language and interests, perceptions and preoccupations, were all felt to be equally alien. Not subject to external test, its evidences unverified and counter-evidence unadmitted, every socialist assumption appeared true, every conclusion proven within the unbroken left cocoon.

Some few cocoons remain intact. The rest are fractured, and most of the moths and butterflies which were in them have flown. Out of one cocoon, voices (such as that of Wang Zhen, the vice-president of China) could be heard arguing, in August 1991, that 'the future of socialism, without any doubt is glorious and bright'. Two years earlier, out of the same cocoon, Jiang Zemin, the Chinese Communist Party's general secretary, had foreseen the 'final world victory of communism' and a 'communist future for the human race'. Out of another cocoon, in May 1990, the North Korean dictator Kim Il Sung proclaimed communism to be the 'only road for mankind'; out of the Vietnamese cocoon, socialism was said, in June 1991, to be the 'only way to happiness and freedom'. Even in the West, a few stray voices from the cocoon continued to speak, in the old way, of 'bringing new layers of working people into struggle', and so forth.

The sharing of a particular construct of reality, and the sense of identity it provides, may plainly be directed to public ends, as well as being hallucinatory in a more private and personal fashion. As a political construct of this kind, socialism was sufficiently well organised at its zenith to possess its own well-thumbed texts and crowded congregations, together with its own forms of intercession. It provided reassurance and a sense of purpose to the converted, and served as a powerful attraction to the politically homeless. Socialism had both gods and fallen angels. The working class was its kindly light, and imperialism, capitalism and the universal machinations of the right its unholy trinity of demons. They were the fixed poles of a 'common left culture', a common way of seeing, thinking and behaving, a common way of life: the 'life of the left'. This left culture invested its beliefs, many of them drawn from (and much elaborated in) books, with the force of a natural reality. It took the wafer of hope-for-social-justice to be the body of a sufficient political programme; it took truths, half-truths, verisimilitudes and figments of the imagination to be all one substance.

Intellectual error and worthy moral aspiration, real analytical discovery and the arrogance of political power, combined forces to wreck the societies upon which they turned their redemptive attentions. Yet, the attractive force of left illusion was so great that even lies and violence could not deter, and did not deter, thinking men and women from embracing falsehood wherever they found it. Among communist die-hards there was credulous nostalgia for the memory of 'Uncle Joe' even after disclosure had been made of the horrors of the Stalinist period. As late as November 1986, with only three years of the dissolving Soviet imperium remaining and with Mikhail Gorbachev already in office, a Marxist intellectual and doyen of historians such as Eric Hobsbawm could still express relief that the 'Soviet zone of influence' in Eastern Europe had, for three decades, survived the 1956 Hungarian uprising. 'Thank God,' he commented. ('I think the British Communist Party has deserved well of the British people,' he added for good measure.)

Jewish intellectuals are prone to ardour for a cerebral cause, but are rarely disposed to the active sustaining of the crueller forms of unreason. Intense moral unease, plain signs of despair, dissident objection and fatalistic surrender are more common Jewish responses to the Pharaonic tyrant. But the dangerous fidelities of socialist belief made possible every clerkly treason, whether on the part of Jew or gentile. In East Germany, for instance, the mere expression of 'anti-socialist sentiments' was a crime for which many went to gaol. Yet 'left culture', in its cocoon, was always able to invest such improper anathemata with their own logic and moral purpose. No true loyalist would have thought to protest against them. On the contrary, they were a badge of faith. The impulse to establish and impose a commonality of socialist purpose, whether by 'democratic centralism', 'collective discipline', the 'closed shop' or whatever, was universal in socialist instincts and thought-processes, and almost always took predence over liberal scruple.

The 'socialist way of life' was a matter of faith and fraternity, higher purpose and varieties of coercion, from moral suasion to violence. It shaped not only individual perceptions but individual aspirations also. It was therefore surprising, at least on the surface, that so many 'committed socialists' appeared to set aside so quickly their beliefs and reflexes, forego long established habits of public polemic for silence, and – in some cases – so quickly assume ways of thinking and acting which, in the cocoon, had been tabooed and even punished.

The essence of the matter was more complex. Many left political reflexes, including Stalinist reflexes, survived the transition, as I have pointed out in a previous chapter, and this was not surprising. Economic duress, not free choice, had dictated the turn to the market. Often the choice was made, in Eastern Europe and the Soviet Union, with little knowledge of what it would entail; and once made, 'market behaviour', with its new sets of premises and expectations, was having to be arduously learned. In addition, the substratum of political and economic truth which underlay socialist error made the complete abandonment of socialist theories and practices difficult, even for the most enthusiastic of post-socialist converts. They had been brought up, and had had their understandings formed, in societies which saw the spectre of exploitation in private property, class in the conflict of interests, and the root of all evil in the capitalist system.

Socialists, and ex-socialists, East and West, knew too that socialism had not invented the working class. It was present in the economy and the division of labour, as both Marx and Adam Smith had demonstrated. What socialists *had* imagined, however, were the supposed virtues of the working class as a body on the one hand, and its 'world-historic' role on the other. It was an instance, one of the most disastrous, of left truth as the ground of left error. It had been but a short step from such error to counterpose to the (imaginary) 'unselfish interests of the proletariat' the 'selfish interests of the owners of capital', and the script for the 'class war' had been written. By the time the communist parties of the world had decided, as did the Communist Party of the Soviet Union in January 1990, to 'demystify the concept of the working class' – having mystified it for decades, to the point of near-pathological abstraction – it was far too late. The proletarian socialist boat had foundered.

There was somewhat more to this type of left fancy (or delusion) about the working class than met the eye, a fancy which could turn a Caliban into an Ariel by sheer force of wishful thinking. There was the unctuous self-coddling of those who believed themselves to be more 'fraternal' in their sympathies than the next man; there were those for whom the facing of unsentimental fact did not serve their emotional purposes as well as a diet of sentimental fictions; there were those, even, for whom the mere existence of the 'underdog' subconsciously gratified their own sense of security and well-being. 'When a man is tired of what he is, by a natural perversity he sets up for what he is not,' wrote Hazlitt, not knowing of today's, or yesterday's, vicarious proletarians of the middle class, but speaking to their case as if they stood before him. 'If he is a patrician in rank and feeling, he would fain be one of the people. His ruling motive is not the love of the people, but of distinction; not of truth, but of singularity.' Once, there were many such in socialist ranks, driven by the peculiarity of their circumstances and motives to outdo others in their socialist ardour. Where the Jew, frequently enough the archetype of the intellectually privileged outsider, took to left-wing extremes – from Marx onwards – such estrangements played their part.

But 'stooping to the level' of the proletarian could be a costly business for the middle-class socialist intellectual. In some egregious cases, it involved changes of dress and accent, vocabulary and manner. Indeed, there were few left-wing intellectuals who did not at some time feel constrained to show, or to pretend, that they were not really intellectuals at all. To be thought to be the member of an 'elite' was at odds with the desire to be seen as an egalitarian. Thus, the presentation of an intellectual analysis on behalf of the socialist cause might be deliberately vulgarised lest it be thought to bear too many of the stigmata of a middle-class manner. Tom Nairn, writing on popular sovereignty in the *New Left Review* yet needing to cite both Bagehot and Burke, felt bound to keep a safe distance from such oracles of conservative thought. Bagehot, therefore, became 'a Victorian gentleman called Walter Bagehot' – both a distancing and a nursery-tale description – and Edmund Burke, vulgarly, 'the organ-grinder to Bagehot's monkey'. This uneasy patois was the price to be paid for class condescension.

A leaven of the vernacular, or the plebeian, permitted those left intellectuals who employed it to think themselves, as well as to be thought (by some), men of the people. Eric Hobsbawm was capable of it even when speaking of Nietzsche in an interview with the *Guardian*. 'At a time when, superficially, everything seemed to be . . . rolling along nicely, moving forward . . . here was this guy [sc. Nietzsche] saying "it isn't really like this at all."' 'This guy' was the vernacular badge of belonging. Such play-acting involved – I know it, since I did it myself – the crossing of a Rubicon: from an instinct for fastidiousness of intellectual manner, to a more carefree, or careless, ease of address which, on the one hand, rendered a subject more accessible to the uninstructed but which, on the other, tended to crass oversimplification of the truth. Socialist fabrication, and hence error, was in part constructed upon a foundation of intellectually vulgar short-cuts.

The defence of these short-cuts, to which a great deal of socialist thought and doctrine was reduced for popular consumption, was itself a vulgar business. It involved the defence of much which was intellectually indefensible in socialist thought and socialist values, ranging from the bogus 'dialectic' to the unexamined moral assumption that socialism was virtue. It was a defence which observed no Queensberry rules in the coteries of the Western left, let alone in the Soviet Union or Eastern Europe. The notion that a 'social democratic' or liberal-minded deviant from socialist articles of faith was not a dissenter but had committed *treason* was second nature to many 'committed socialists'. A confidential Chinese Communist Party document, first published in October 1991, described Gorbachev as a 'careerist, opportunist and traitor', who had been 'violating the principles of Marxism for more than six years'; the 'nihilistic' Gorbachev had 'betrayed socialism', declared the Greek Communist Party in December 1991. When the fit was upon even democratic socialists, let alone Marxist-Leninists, heresy could be smelled in any new idea, and apostasy in a mere difference of opinion. Where Marxists found a backslider's position to be 'bourgeois', democratic socialists could as readily find it 'elitist'. It was a distinction without real difference, and a judgment just as final.

Matters were obviously more serious where socialism became tyranny-in-power. The pantomime rigours of socialist earnestness in the

West, although related, were of lesser significance. In 'real socialism' those of whom orthodoxy disapproved could be diagnosed as mentally ill, or be otherwise consigned to oblivion. Ladislav Adamec, the communist prime minister of Czechoslovakia at the moment when communism fell, described Vaclav Havel as 'a nobody, simply nil' only days before the latter's apotheosis. This was the authentic voice of the 'dictatorship of the proletariat', pronouncing judgment upon a dissenting 'bourgeois' intellectual. In exactly the same totalitarian style – that of reducing a foe, an opponent, or merely someone who was disapproved of, to an impalpable nothing – Boris Pugo, future plotter against Gorbachev, was described by a leading Soviet journalist as an 'absolute zero' at the time of the former's appointment as Soviet interior minister in December 1990. Likewise, the mayor of St Petersburg, Anatoly Sobchak, reported in September 1991 how Anatoly Lukyanov, one of the leaders of the attempted coup against Gorbachev, had advised him 'not to worry' about Gorbachev since the latter had 'a nil rating anyway'.

'Neutralising' a rival took many forms. In February 1991, hardliners in the Greek Communist Party, one of the most rigid, had declared themselves ready to reveal 'matters of concern' in the 'private lives' of members of a more liberal Party faction. Todor Zhivkov described members of the dissident Club for Glasnost – one of them shortly to become president of Bulgaria in succession to the fallen dictator himself – as 'scum'. The new democratically elected president of Georgia, Zviad Gamsakhurdia, was similarly quick to diagnose his opponents in classic Stalinist fashion as 'not normal'; that is, mentally unbalanced. They described him in the same way. The treatment of dissenters by psychiatry was a part of such reflexes.

Inflexibility of thought and brutishness of manner, left and right, have always responded in similar fashion to the objections of the dissenter. In the socialist case, the increasingly alarmed defence of orthodoxy during the 1980s expressed a fear of the fate which had previously been reserved to socialism's heretics and apostates: the same oblivion. The 'landmarks of the socialist tradition', the *New Left Review* was nervously complaining in the spring of 1986, were being 'washed away in a flood of revision and amnesia'. That is, identity itself was being endangered. A Kim Il Sung might erect large graven images of himself equipped (so it was said) with elevators and underground shelters, in order that the landmarks themselves might be rescued in the event of a political earthquake. The left intellectual in the West had no such bolt-hole.

At the heart of the socialist fear of 'revision' always stood the anxiety, as in every threatened creed, that tampering with any one of its articles of faith could imperil and subvert all the others. Some socialists, knowing better than their critics the hidden flaws in their belief-system, always knew of their vulnerability to accusations that they were pursuing a political chimera. 'There is no good reason to believe that the "socialist enterprise is illusory,"' wrote one of socialism's minor gurus defensively in the *New Left Review* in 1985, when there had long been many good reasons to believe it. Against the fear that the rock of faith might prove on closer examination to be made of compacted sand, left intellectuals worked hard to construct an outer bulwark against the always encroaching tide. Its cement would be that of intellectual certitude, or at least the appearance of it, at the level of theory. The Marxist version of socialism was therefore made internally consistent intellectually, and its political embodiments clad in iron; its premises might be built on utopian stilts, but its battlements were imposing. From within, the fact that delusion was part of the fabric was barely visible. From without, it was as clear as daylight. The drawbridge was raised to exclude every doubting Thomas; within, a fraternity of intellectual onanists gradually went blind to truths known to every non-Marxist Tom, Dick or Harry.

The fact that capitalism, for instance, was not simply 'exploitative' but possessed 'other features', was something which had been 'neglected' by left sociologists because of their 'personal values', earnestly explained an English professor of sociology, Richard Scase, in June 1991. What 'other features' of capitalism had they missed? They had missed the fact, Scase declared, blinking in the light, that it was 'not emotionally, psychologically and materially totalitarian'. To have made such a 'discovery' would once have been impossible in most left circles; to have admitted it the rough equivalent of a foolish burst of conversation in a conventicle of Trappists. Even a modest 'revision' such as this – and the 'amnesia' which went with it – remained difficult for most socialists, and not a few ex-socialists also. Their view of the world, and that of many social democrats too, remained fixated on a life beyond the capitalist order. The suggestion that, after the 'phase' of what used to be called 'late capitalism', there was only more of the same to come, or that 'post-capitalism' would itself turn out to be another stage in a capitalist continuum, was beyond the intellectual grasp of most leftists.

Why? Because the idea of the transcendence of capitalism as a precondition for human advancement was so deep-rooted in the soul of the socialist, in all that soul's varieties and mutations. The contrary assertion by the right, that the abandonment of socialist theories and practices was the true prerequisite for human progress – and that the turn to the market was 'progressive' in precisely the sense given to the word by leftists – remained outrageous. In consequence, a large part of the post-socialist political dispensation was inaccessible to left processes of ratiocination. To its adherents, socialism was the very principle of reason. To be told instead that socialism was irrational, because *contra naturam humanam*, was barely assimilable. Thinking again, beyond certain narrow limits – those governed by the parameters of socialist assumptions – was thus out of the question.

The fact that the Soviet Union and Eastern Europe were slouching towards capitalism, as well as towards the old Enlightenment utopia of the 'bourgeois' (with its 'bourgeois freedoms'), did not therefore have the effects on the left that its enemies might have imagined. The left's fixed notions of 'progress' might have been unhinged, but in most socialist heads and hearts – silent though most of their tongues might be – the moral claims of the collective over the individual interest remained prior. Some form of common ownership was still felt to be morally more desirable, in the case of public goods, than their private dispersal. The market allocation of rewards and resources continued to be regarded as a form of unreason. Entire populations might have had their well-being set back by decades under the socialist aegis, and now required rescue by drastic capitalist intervention. But it had disturbed far less than the right might think the left's sense of the moral superiority of socialist theory. Part of the reason was that without the goal of socialism for which to strive – or a goal akin to it – and without something like a socialist amelioration of the human condition in prospect, the Judaic in every individual is prone to feel that there is little to live by, and in extreme cases nothing to live for. (Everyman is, to some degree at least, a Jew.) Without the sustenance of a belief that there is a global tide in the affairs of men, whether supervised by God or by a secular doctrine, thought itself, as well as hope, can for some lose all focus. Left thought, with its obscure conflicts and sectarian excoriations, might have become increasingly infantile and regressive, and the emancipation of mankind no more than an incantation or *mantra*. But its mental props and toys were also fixtures in the firmament of a thought-system, a thought-system which made at least partial sense of the world we live in.

At the last, however, the defence of illusion had taken such priority

over the encroachment of reality that the left had lost much of its grip
on the world around it. The German Democratic Republic, declared
Barbara Einhorn and Mary Kaldor in the *New Statesman* in November
1989 – a month before the GDR collapsed in political and economic
ruin – was 'easily the most successful economy in Eastern Europe . . .
It does not have a debt problem.' Nicolae Ceausescu's speech of
rejection of democratic reforms to the Romanian Communist Party's
last congress, also in November 1989 and only a month before he was
executed, was an 'exemplary model of creative tackling of present-day
problems' and a 'genuine thesaurus of social and political thinking',
according to a fellow politburo member. The British *Morning Star*, its
circulation reduced to the minuscule, described itself – also in November 1989 – as 'read by wide sections of the working-class movement
and democratic forces'.

Such false judgments (and falsehoods) were, at best, characteristics
of a condition in which the ideologue's fancy took charge of observation.
Yet, it was done in the name of a doctrine whose presumption of
superiority lay in its claim to get behind the 'mere world of appearance'
to a truer world within. In the thick of its own untruths, it preached the
truth to others; on the basis of its professed deep reading of history and
motive, it made its superficial but overweening judgments and
predictions.

As late as February 1988, and on the verge of the socialist collapse,
Eric Hobsbawm, described at the time by his journalistic presenter as
'one of the most cogent voices in the land', announced that the capitalist
system was 'obviously extremely unstable. I think there's going to be
enormous numbers of revolutions and shifts [a tic-word in left jargon]
within the capitalist system . . . The major danger at the moment is for
the whole thing [capitalism, not socialism] to collapse under its own
contradictions.' In conditions of intellectual asphyxia, but sustained on
the one hand by a matrix of systematic thought, and on the other by
the mutual validations to which I referred earlier, error of judgment on
this scale was easily arrived at. Hobsbawm – among the worst of
offenders – then gave frank as well as unwitting testimony to the
perils of the Marxist schema while casually elaborating upon the
'advantages of being a Marxist'. 'Things which might otherwise be
"trivial pursuit" actually get fitted into a pattern – or you think you can
fit them into a pattern. In some ways the real problem is to write in
such a way as to make it all hang together in your own mind, or at any
rate if it doesn't hang together in your own mind, *to try and pretend to*

*readers that it looks as though it hangs together so that they feel maybe that
something has been explained'* (*Guardian*, 26 February 1988; my
emphasis).

Pretending to others that something had been explained, when it had
not, was the besetting sin of Marxism. It was also one of the principal
causes of its intellectual failure. In the heady days for the left of the
continuing Cold War, of left hysteria about the dangers of 'capitulation'
to 'revisionism' and 'reformism', of admiration for the Italian Marxist
Antonio Gramsci, of belief in capitalism's 'decomposition', and of
various forms of 'extra-parliamentary agitation' – usefully responded to
in turn by the 'repressive bourgeois state' – left prognoses of the kind
delivered by Hobsbawm and by many others were still unembarrassed.
It was possible to refer to the 'class struggle' without evoking laughter.
The nuclear apocalypse could also be forecast with an unseemly ardour.
Today, rises in the numbers of the unemployed in capitalist societies
must provide the left with the perverse pleasure it once obtained from
the contemplation of a nuclear armageddon. 'It is probable,' declared
Edward Thompson in September 1982 in Budapest – a period which
turned out to be that of 'late socialism' not 'late capitalism' – 'that we
will have a nuclear war in the next twenty years. This war will bring to
an end European civilisation'.

The enthusiastic imagining of catastrophe is not the special property
of left thought, even if it has always played a large part in it. But wishing
the Seven Plagues of Egypt upon one's own house has been specific to
it. In unemployment under capitalism, socialists looked – and some still
look – for a means to 'teach people a lesson' about capitalism's claims
to superior virtue. In social deprivation, left intellectuals looked, and
some still look, to see redistributive socialism's fortunes restored and
their own fortunes with it. The locust years, the years of the lean kine
in an uncertain market, are the years in which the socialist looked, and
still looks, for the sun to shine upon him. However, it also became clear
to many Western socialists during the 1980s, as socialism in the East
sank into deeper trouble, that to live in such amoral hope was
insufficient. Something politically more attractive was needed, if socialism East and West were not to reach their climacterics together. It was
in this period that most Western reform socialists began arguing not for
a new model of 'socialism' – the very use of the word diminished
sharply – but for an 'extension of democracy', 'democratic accountability', 'decentralisation' and so forth. (The fatal equivalents in the East of
this new emphasis were 'democratisation', 'pluralism' and a multi-party

system.) The pursuit of socialism as such began to recede, both in the East and the West. In its place came ideas of democracy as a 'buttress of social advance', of power being 'brought to the people', of 'empowerment', 'enablement', 'citizen rights' and so on.

In the West, the argument for 'greater democracy' was a surrogate for the lost old-left case against the capitalist state. In the East, exhausted by decades of socialist aspiration, a similar argument quickly became a ground of action against socialism itself, and justification (in the eyes of some) for a capitalist restoration. In the East, apparatus authoritarians became overnight pluralists and implausible freethinkers; in the West, often equally narrow politicians of the left suddenly espoused, or tried to espouse, a rainbow coalition of new causes. In the East, even hardline communists had been trying during the 1980s to come to terms with universal youth's tastes and with the 'youth culture'. In the West, left parties attempted a pop redesign of their 'images', trying to put aside the more obvious stigmata of work and struggle, and the last traces of the collective persona of the proletarian.

Much of this was new falsehood for old. Party truth is, of course, party truth, right or left. But for Western socialist parties to pretend to reconcile in one programme – as some did – the interests of capital and labour, of production and consumption, of industrial expansion and environmental protection, of sexual puritanism and sexual freedom, was ideological imposition. In the history of the Stalinist left, the Orwellian misappropriation and abuse of terms such as 'democracy', or 'liberation', or 'progress' had come near to poisoning their truths at source. But it had also set a poor precedent to more benign left innovators, who were now set upon investing many of the same tormented words with new, or 'updated', meanings.

Socialism, having always been morality's holy fable, had *ab initio* required the services of wordsmiths in the elaboration of its ideas. In its Marxist form it had attracted, or seduced, intellectuals the world over to compose entire libraries of scholarly recension, or embroidery, of its sacred texts and inscriptions. This had been Talmudic work, work upon the shibboleths of faith, work which had both developed and imprisoned the faculties. It had also rendered the adept unfit for flexibility or variety of thought. When the hour for re-thinking struck, most socialists and ex-socialists – in particular Marxists – had been too long habituated to the security provided by a few favourite dogmas and by the elaborate constructions built upon them. To embark freely upon new inquiry, or depart far from the beaten tracks which linked one moral and intellectual landmark to another, was a task beyond the reach of many. For all the boldness of socialist assertion, socialist failure revealed the doubts and timidities which underlay it. They were doubts and timidities which habits of left concealment, and of self-deception as to the true nature of the socialist record, had done nothing to diminish. 'For many years, being a Marxist and a communist, I wasn't anxious to write about Russia because you'd get into trouble. You couldn't write without actually deciding that the official line on most things was horse-shit.' The gratuitous vernacular is the signature of Hobsbawm. 'So it was easier,' added the historian of Europe and Empire, 'to keep off it.'

In compensation for, and in further concealment of, disablements of this kind, socialist intellectuals had always struck heroic moral poses with words and slogans. The rigmarole of left-wing role-playing required it. But the effort required for a 'bourgeois' intellectual to betray his instincts – 'class instincts', a Marxist would have called them – and pretend to be a socialist egalitarian (with 'horse-shit' at his finger-tips) was, for some, a very great one. To be thought radical, revolution-ary even, and worthy of the term 'comrade', demanded intellectual sacrifices, the sacrifice of truth among them. To an extent, the effort of it could be minimised by recourse to left rhetoric and empty gesture. But the use of such devices also had the effect of compromising those who employed them, above all in their own eyes. Moreover, habitual resort to rhetoric corrupted much of left thought. Like any other intellectual short-cut, it was a form of intellectual betrayal. At its heart, the problem was that of 'left culture' itself, composed as it was of a great deal of theatrical fancy. Close to the surface, including in the most inappropriate and improbable of circumstances, lay the archetypal image of the revolutionary socialist as a warrior 'in struggle'. Trevor Griffiths, the English Marxist playwright, described himself, in April 1986, in a fashion typical of such postures, as 'trying to be a communist in the belly of the beast'; or, a Jonah set bravely to his purposes within the leviathan of British capital. When in April 1991 the Red Army Fraction assassinated Detlev Rohwedder, head of the German Treuhandanstalt, it called in a leaflet for an 'intensification of struggle' against the 'leaps of the imperialist beast'. 'Beast' comes easily, as a word, to the fevered imagination.

Most of this remained at the level of a striking of poses. 'I prefer those who chop off people's heads to those who celebrate those who chop off people's heads,' absurdly declared the French composer, Pierre Boulez, in July 1989, as he left Paris to avoid the bicentennial of the French Revolution. In all such attitudinising, the Great Lie lurked. Furthermore, individuals of the left, in order to keep up radical appearances, could be driven from falsehood to falsehood and excess to excess. The intellectual failure of socialism owed much to this process. 'Lech Walesa's revolution,' announced John Pilger in February 1990, 'could not happen in Britain, where the right to strike and the right to assemble and associate have been virtually destroyed.' But the right to strike, the right to assemble, and the right to associate had not been 'virtually destroyed' in Britain in February 1990. The assertion was either a form of hysteria, or the struck pose of the tragic actor who, in his own estimation, thereby becomes a friend of the people, or even a hero. This left instinct for lilliputian self-dramatisation came in many forms, and on many subjects. Even redundancy notices could be described by trade union leaders as a 'purge'. A Tory prime minister could be denounced by Labour MPs for 'ruthlessly crushing dissent' and 'trying to destroy the human spirit in Britain'. Even a moderate socialist politician, in the grip of such passion, could call on his political *confrères* to 'smash' the 'decrepit, effete [British] constitution'. The verbs to purge, to crush, to destroy, and to smash came directly from the left's lexicon of rhetoric and gesture. Moreover, if the left hero's cause could be made out to have been trampled underfoot, preferably by 'beasts', the subsequent flexing of verbal muscle over it became the more emotionally satisfying.

In such heroisms, an enemy of the left was required by the left to be 'ruthless', just as capitalist 'oppression' was always the necessary foil to socialist 'emancipation'. In order to fit into this manichean structure, certain events, facts and persons required to be demonised, and others allocated to an opposing pantheon of virtues. But to square complex truth with schematic fancy was rarely possible without half-truth, exaggeration, or falsehood. A British government proposal that the long-term unemployed should do 'work trials' with potential employers while receiving unemployment benefit was a 'step towards forced labour'. British workers, declared Michael Meacher, a Labour shadow cabinet minister, in April 1989, were 'the most oppressed in Europe'; 'legions' of 'teenage dossers', said a Labour journalist, inhabited the streets of London; the national health service, said another, was 'shutting down', and so on. 'Forced labour', 'most oppressed', 'legions', 'shutting down' and the rest of it were all variants of a similar style of falsehood. Perverse and even masochistic, with the excitement of the false image savoured, they were truth-corrupting. It was a style which could take leave of all morality in its striving for effect. 'Like Germany in 1945, Britain after Thatcher will be a scene of destruction. Those who will need to rebuild what has to be restructured,' declared Eric Hobsbawm in July 1988, 'need a preliminary survey of the bomb-damage.' For a Jew to have asserted such a parallel was particularly inappropriate.

Socialism's fatal flaw, the flaw of all authoritarian utopias, was to seek, especially when opposed or resisted, to wrestle men and women towards its ends in a half-nelson of fantasy and falsehood. 'Our party and government showed great restraint,' Li Peng, the Chinese prime minister, said blandly of the Tienanmen Square massacre in June 1989. 'We do not believe there was any tragedy in Tienanmen Square,' said Jiang Zemin, the secretary of the Chinese Communist Party. (The spirit itself cries out again the lie of it.) Always quick to detect and denounce moral blindness in others – even to the extent of finding madness in it – the left has paid a justly high price for such moral transgressions. The tendency of all sects may be to protect adherents from knowledge of their own falsehoods, and from awareness of the truths of others. But the left, the party of the good and the true (in its own valuation), suffered very greatly for it. For the immoral socialist to oppose the immoral capitalist has now deservedly become harder then ever.

The full extent to which intellect could be corrupted by socialist habits of mind and training became plainer after the fall in Eastern Europe. The suffocation of intellectual and academic freedom, and the staffing of institutions of higher learning with individuals steeped in a culture of resistance to imagination, had come, in many fields of the arts and sciences, close to bankrupting the spirit of inquiry itself. Outside the small circles of the dissident community, autonomy of thought was found to be at a premium. Freedom of expression itself required to be freed from the inhibitions which had confined it. Old textbooks by the million, which had dimly reproduced the orthodoxies of state, had to be discarded. Entire university faculties and departments of faculties – in law, in history, in philosophy, in economics – had to be shut down, or re-staffed and re-ordered, and their old disciplines, being rooted in socialist theory at its most immobile, cancelled. In Albanian art schools, with 'socialist realism' rejected, there were no teachers at all to teach an alternative curriculum. Everywhere, new syllabuses, new systems of teacher training, and new books had to be introduced. This was the beginning of a cultural revolution on the grand scale. In many educational institutions teachers overnight changed their opinions. In others, as in East Germany, thousands were fired.

Yet, once more, not everything was as it seemed. Intellectual placemen in the socialist system had frequently gained their positions less by true faith than by the profession of faith; left rhetoric and gesture reigned in the world of 'real socialism' as it did in the latter's Western simulacra. To surrender the convictions which an individual had never held therefore required no great effort – only the quick removal of the Marxist mask, and the disclosure of the persona it had long hidden. In other cases, Marxist intellectuals believed, or had come to believe, what they professed, and suffered a corresponding intellectual disillusion and disorientation. In yet other cases, senior academic time-servers of modest intelligence proved difficult to dislodge from powerful positions, for a time frustrating every effort at intellectual renovation. Such resistances sometimes involved a clinging to the lost spars of true faith, as well as to mere office. Indeed, the left world-view, although possessing a bookish sense of history and historical purpose and an abstract shaping vision, had too many roots in common-sense assumptions to lose its purchase entirely. Beneath the turbulent surface of the new democratic and capitalist tide, there was a socialist (as well as a neo-fascist) anchor, however rusted. Even where the notion of a root-and-branch reform of socialism was accepted, to the point of trying to cast out most of the latter's traces, caveats and reservations came early. 'It took Britain centuries to get where it is today,' observed Gennadi Gerasimov, then Soviet foreign ministry spokesman, in April 1989. That is, there would be political and economic reform in the Soviet Union, but no miraculous transubstantiation should be looked for. It was a discreet form of nay-saying, or refusal to surrender at once to the 'triumph of the market'. Only in September 1991 did Gorbachev bring himself openly to pronounce communism a 'failure'.

Others, ostensibly responsible for abandoning an old order to which they were still committed, made the turn to democracy into a complex masquerade. 'We do not want to follow any model, including the model of bourgeois democracy,' declared President Iliescu of Romania in January 1990. The multi-party system, over which he was shortly to begin presiding, was an 'historical irrelevance'; a 'genuine people's democracy' – the old, bogus socialist concept – was much to be preferred. Other socialist diehards, such as Fidel Castro, warned in June 1991 that 'the people' would soon 'wake up to the pains of true capitalism'; the 1991 congress of the Cuban Communist Party dismissed multi-party politics as 'garbage'. For these last defenders of the faith, 'genuine liberty' still lay at the end of the socialist, not the capitalist, path. In the North Korean time capsule, every citizen remained bound by Orwellian decree to wear in his lapel a portrait of the Great Leader, a living god whose powers had been effectively absolute since 1948. He continued to present himself as the embodiment of popular democracy; organised unreason continued to govern the nation's bankrupt economy and culture. Indeed, as the socialist fall became general, two new hybrid species of begonia were declared in North Korea to be 'immortal flowers' and were named, respectively, *kimilsungia* and *kimjongilia*.

Some socialists in the West tactically chose the hour of socialist debacle to redirect attention to the 'authoritarianism' of liberal democracies, pointing to the imperfect state of their civil liberties, or of their markets, or of their social conditions. One of the most feverish, the British Labour MP Tony Benn, would declare Britain in May 1989 to be 'fast becoming a one-party state', with 'democracy itself under attack'. A year previously, as the socialist world had begun to enter its revolutionary crisis, he had been denouncing the 'systematic destruction of democratic institutions' in Britain, the 'wholesale control of information', and so on. 'We have to re-establish,' he had announced in March 1988, 'the rights of freedom of thought, freedom of speech, the right to be heard, and the right to be different'; in his own public declarations, frequently repeated and often published, lay the proof that these rights existed. But the implication of such arguments was that the model towards which a post-communist reformer might be aspiring, even if it took 'centuries' to get there, was a chimera. British democracy, it was being said, was not merely flawed but *unreal*.

In the reflex left falsehood of it, there was further evidence of a phenomenon I have already discussed. In the counter-attack on the 'corrupt and undemocratic institutions of the British state' – which could even be described unblushingly by the left as a 'police state' – there was another Orwellian abuse of words. (The word 'corrupt', in particular, cannot be so lightly used.) In May 1989, it was further asserted from the same despairing quarters that it was 'sanctimonious' to claim that 'British society somehow embodies the values of pluralism and the right to dissent'. This judgment as to the humbug of the British political system was co-authored by, among others, Tony Benn and Meghnad Desai, an Indian academic at the London School of Economics. The latter was shortly to accept a life peerage, and allow himself to be transmuted, without evident embarrassment, into 'Lord Desai of St Clement Dane's'.

Violence on the left, like violence on the right, has come in many forms, intellectual violence among them. Intellectual violence itself has many forms, but one common feature: it assaults the accepted truth, and in its precipitate course is capable of violating the very language it uses and its ordinary meanings. In its grip, the British journalist Neal Ascherson, joining in the 'new' left's refocusing of its purposes upon the 'destruction' of democracy, could describe (in July 1991) the tradition of parliamentary sovereignty not merely as 'archaic' – which it is – but as the 'central cancer' of the British political system. Its other disorders, which included the 'despotism of Downing Street', were, he said, the symptoms of this 'cancer'. Cancer? Despotism? Our hold on the truth is at the best of times hard to secure; 'despotism' and 'cancer' were, not to put too fine a gloss on it, lies. In this case, they were the characteristic lies of the left. Similarly, when Benn described George Bush in January 1991 as a 'fanatical leader', sense itself was unhinged. Yet, it had often been precisely by such excess – the badge of much left intellection, including in the past my own – that the credentials of ardour could be demonstrated to the like-minded. But it was also by such excess that the left brought the political agnostic to despair, and by such excess, among other things, that socialism was itself defeated.

The 'true' leftist has rarely been deterred by, or made to feel apologetic about, intellectual error and political failure, however gross or obvious. If he had been so deterred, the history of left falsehood would not have been so continuous, nor so plainly repeated by each generation. In December 1978, Malcolm Caldwell, a London University lecturer who had been invited to Cambodia by Pol Pot, was brutally murdered by unknown assassins in his Phnom Penh hotel. Of the land which despatched almost its entire urban population to the countryside in pursuit of the phantom of 'total revolution', 'abolished money' and slaughtered droves of its citizens, including most of its intelligentsia, the victim had spoken approvingly. The 'tertiary, urban sector of the economy', said Caldwell, had been 'totally unproductive' – 'totally' a familiar adverb of left excess – and had 'served only foreign interests'. It had therefore been 'dismantled'. As to the forced rural labour (a true forced labour, in which hundreds of thousands died, not the hysterically perceived 'forced labour' of Western welfare projects), 'every effort was made', Caldwell had declared, 'to match tasks to the labour available, so that no category of person was left functionless and no task was left unattended to for lack of labour'. The result had been a 'triumph for the revolutionary forces'. Indeed, 'the forethought, ingenuity, dedication and eventual triumph of the liberation forces in the face of extreme adversity ought to have been cause for worldwide relief and congratulation, rather than the disbelief and execration with which it was greeted. But we have to understand,' Caldwell insisted, 'that what the Cambodian people accomplished struck fear in the hearts of all those who at present control the "free" world's food production "business" to their own immense profit. And it is they to whom our "free" media must respond rather than to the *call of truth*' (my emphasis). Here, many of the main varieties of left falsehood, and of particular pleading, are concentrated in a brief space. Characteristic are the implicit claim to a monopoly of truth, utopian extravagance, sardonic dismissiveness about the 'free', and the intellectual left's old vicarious enthusiasm for the labour of others. They were the very stuff of left judgment; and despite every defeat and failure, they continue *sub rosa* to be so.

Indeed, resistance to thinking again about the socialist collapse has been more than a rearguard action. It has instead been marked by a refusal, authentic in its own fashion, to accept that the left utopia is finally shattered. 'The Soviet Union did exist, does exist and always will exist,' declared Sazhi Umalatova, the former Soviet people's deputy, in March 1992, three months after the 'Soviet Union' had disappeared. There have also been various attempts to reinstate, at least in words, the old left premise that its beliefs are historically progressive, and that the introduction of a market economy to formerly socialist societies represented both a retreat and a regression. Some on the left have put the entire 'revolution' of 1989 in quotation marks in order to signify scepticism as to its staying power, or to suggest that nothing of substance occurred. Alternatively, if there was a revolution, it could not properly be termed an 'anti-socialist' revolution since the regimes which were overthrown were not 'genuinely' socialist in the first place. In February 1990, Eric Hobsbawm went further: the revolutions in Eastern Europe were not even anti-communist, since 'communism was never established in Eastern Europe'.

Many have tried to take refuge in the belief that it was Stalinism, rather than their own faith, which had been tried and found wanting. Others, fearful that even the mildest form of left programme could be sucked down in the general wrack of socialist fortunes, have denied not only the relationship between 'communism' and 'socialism' but also that between 'socialism' and 'social democracy'. Others, like Hobsbawm himself, have preferred to stress the social and economic progress that the countries of Eastern Europe allegedly made under socialist dominion. 'Any number of them', he announced, 'are a good deal further advanced as economies and in every other way than was conceivable in 1940.' Particularly extraordinary was the assertion made in September 1990 by Frederic Jameson, a leading American Marxist academic, that it was 'wrong' to say that socialism had been a 'failure'. 'A new stage wouldn't be taking place [today],' he maintained, 'unless socialism had been successful.'

This position was akin to the contorted suggestion that socialism's crash had been 'objectively' – another left adverbial term of art – in its own real interests, and pointed the way to socialist renewal. One extreme version of this claim came, characteristically, from Tony Benn, who could be heard declaring in July 1988 that 'the most important effects of the Gorbachev reforms on the world as a whole' were likely to include a 'strengthening of the influence of socialist ideas everywhere'. A year later, he was persisting: the 'changes' in the Soviet Union had 'put socialism back on the agenda'. Such delusion was not confined to the British far left. In October 1989, Gerald Kaufman, Labour's then shadow foreign secretary, speaking in Gdansk, thought that 'democratic socialism' had actually been the 'objective' of the upheavals in Eastern Europe. A middling view, or rationalisation, adopted by the Archbishop of Canterbury in November 1989, was that the 'defeat of communism' was 'not a victory for capitalism'. That is, the revolutions, even if not (*pace* the wishful-thinking left) in the interests of socialism, were not a triumph for capitalism either. A sub-variant of this position, taken up by Professor David Marquand, a former Labour MP turned social or liberal democrat, was that capitalism *had* triumphed, but 'only because it is no longer capitalism'. What this convolution meant was that a 'reformed welfare capitalism' had succeeded in the battle with socialism only because it had become 'socialistic' itself. Similar in content was the position of the socialist Jacques Delors, President of the European Commission: it was not capitalism *pur sang* which had been victorious but the 'mixed economy', in which 'liberalism' is 'blended with some state intervention'. That this *is* capitalism in one of its several politico-economic forms was not admitted, or left unsaid. Another tack or feint of the left intellectual was to seek to distinguish, as did Marquand, between the 'economic theory of socialism', which had been 'discredited', and 'its ethic', which had not. Instead, the 'values of community and fellowship' were more necessary than ever. That a fascist, too, might espouse these values, in his own version, was passed over.

Among the far left, East and West – from Hanoi to Hampstead – a very different and near-paranoid position could be found. Yes, there had been an anti-socialist revolution, or counter-revolution. And, yes, it was indeed a revolution which represented a victory for Western capitalist interests. But it had all been a plot. This was a mirror image of the near-paranoid far-right version of what had occurred: a series of fake revolutions had been carried out by, or on behalf of, crypto-communists, whose long-term purpose was to restore communist rule with the aid of Western credits. The far right's counterparts on the left believed, instead, that 'foreign imperialists', the CIA, and other 'anti-socialist forces of reaction' in the West, acting hand-in-glove with their agents in the socialist countries – described in the Chinese version as 'right opportunists' – had sought to 'topple socialism from within'. A variant of this type of left case, proposed by the *New Statesman* at the end of 1989, suggested that some Western interests, above all those of the 'West's bloated national security apparatus', were 'threatened' by the changes in Eastern Europe. 'Arms manufacturers', the magazine fantasised, were 'weeping and wailing and gnashing their teeth' at the fact that 'the enemy doesn't want to fight any more'. In other words, these interests, simultaneously bellicose and lachrymose, could have recovered their composure had the revolutions in Eastern Europe and the Soviet Union failed. At the same time we were being invited, from the right, to imagine the quiet satisfaction of 'red' sleepers as the revolutions made their conquests.

No less fanciful was the near-instantaneous claim, on the part of many on the left, that they had always supported, and were now celebrating, the collapse of the Soviet and Eastern European socialist systems. 'Today', wrote W. L. Webb in the *Guardian* in December 1989, 'there's no point in trying to do anything other than let joy be unconfined.' There were those who were now ready to say, in the twinkling of a socialist eyelid, that the fallen regimes had always been 'brain-dead'. Some were even prepared to maintain, eating their ideological hats, that Marx had been 'selectively read', and that, reborn, he would surely have ratified the fall of the communist order. Among the individuals who leapt through this hoop were some who managed simultaneously to hold most of the available positions on what had occurred. Thus, it was possible for the same person to assert hotly that no anti-socialist revolution had taken place, but that if it had, he was in favour of it. In some cases this feat of left acrobatics, or tail-chasing, was achieved by means of believing, or pretending to believe, that the upheavals in the socialist system were essentially 'democratic revolutions' and signified nothing, or nothing of grave import, as to a wider socialist failure.

The least honest of all sought to claim, under this rubric of self-deception, that the left's democratic prayers had been answered by the events in Eastern Europe and the Soviet Union. In order to sustain such a position, much of socialist history had to be swiftly rewritten. The East European 'communist revolutions' of the mid to late 1940s now became *coups d'état*. The last four decades were turned from a flawed record of struggle for socialism against the odds, to a period of the 'darkest times'. Men such as Vaclav Havel, yesterday an anaemic liberal intellectual, today became – to Tom Nairn, the Marxist political historian, for example – a hero of 'sceptical, anti-dogmatic humanism', the 'spiritual president of the new Europe' and so on. Others, doing their best to resist the triumphalism of the right, tried to find that socialism had not lost and that capitalism had not won; rather, that liberal democracy was the true *victor ludorum*. But when all such arguments, many of them conducted out of earshot, failed to convince even their authors, a last left solace lay in the hope that, whatever had happened to the socialist system, it would not and could not last.

Here, the left's Hebraic instinct for catastrophe made its reappearance. It whispered in the ear of the left, cupped to every promise of disaster, that there was no hope of long-term stability in the nations of the former Soviet Union and Eastern Europe, and that the late convulsions offered no prospect of real or lasting progress. If socialist fortunes – though not the *anciens régimes* themselves, which few wanted – were to be at least partially restored there, such an outcome would need to await civil war, the resurgence of nationalism, and even the full-scale revival of fascism. Here, a simple and universal left proposition lay embedded: the red flag would always be the swastika's only true opponent, as the red ensign was of the skull-and-crossbones. In any event, so these new left promptings suggested, a market capitalism could not at a stroke be installed on the ruins of socialism, or perhaps not installed at all, in a time of capitalism's own 'global crisis'. Nor, the discomfited left told each other *sotto voce*, could thriving new political systems rest upon a basis of mere anti-communism and shallow democratic practice. Much more secure political foundations would be needed. And even if the right's arguments were to be partially conceded, the failure of socialist illusion had been succeeded only by the vain pursuit of the illusion of the 'free market' and its tacky, short-term seductions. The masses, like the stave-wielding Romanian miners, would wake up soon enough to the follies being newly imposed upon them. Marx, the left optimist mutedly declared, would still have the last word.

Old prophecy was here clinging to the course of events, whatever new turns it might take. The vision of left ages, supported by its testaments, was not to be put off by a passing dialectical negation. The reason (or unreason) of the schematic thinker, with the key to the universe still in his pocket, continued to oppose and threaten the reason of the liberal sceptic. In the intellectual realm, Marx's revolutionary Hebraism – the Hebraism of the recurring jubilee of 'liberation' – still posed its challenge. It was a doctrine, the doctrine of faith, which knew nothing at all of true rethinking.

But Marx had mistaken and misjudged many things in his necessity-driven cosmos. The increase of capital did not *necessarily* increase the numbers of the proletariat, as he predicted it would in 1849; modern technologies have reduced them. The worker does not *necessarily* 'perish if capitalism does not employ him'; modern welfare has prevented it. It is not *necessarily* the case that the 'more developed are market relations, the greater is the degree of labour exploitation'; the opposite is nearer the truth. Again, the growth of wealth under capitalism has not made the 'enjoyments of the capitalist increasingly inaccessible to the worker'; on the contrary, in many cases. And as the material conditions of working people under capitalism improved, the 'golden chains' which this improvement forged came to be preferred by the working class itself to the iron shackles of socialist production. With the abolition of private property under socialism, the proletariat had been intended (by Marx) to disappear. But the proletariat remained in dull subjection throughout the socialist system. Most critical of all to socialist theory, private property, so Marx had declared, was a 'fetter upon the forces of production'. But private property had had to be restored throughout the collapsing world of 'real socialism', in an effort to revive its moribund 'forces of production'.

These were not mere corrections of prophecy, but inversions of it, including inversions of socialism's central values. The 'knell of capitalist property', which Marx had heard ringing constantly in his ears – the tinnitus of the professional revolutionary – had not sounded. A tocsin for socialism had replaced it, with proletarians themselves among the bell-ringers. Marx had looked forward to the 'muck of ages' being swept away. In the view of some, it had swept back in triumph. Even at the price of the loss, or severe curtailment, of individual freedom and the mass confiscation of possessions, the socialist economies had not prospered. It had also been intended by socialism that the 'expropriators' who ruled the world's capitalist system should finally be themselves 'expropriated'. Instead, it was socialist property rights which were abolished by socialists, while the legatees of the old owners, and in some cases the old owners themselves, were restored to their fortunes.

Marx had thought that his *Das Kapital* was a final refutation of Adam Smith's *Wealth of Nations*, but both had turned out to be mere chapters in the history of economic theory. Communism, wrote Marx in the *Communist Manifesto*, 'aimed at the abolition of bourgeois individuality, bourgeois independence, and bourgeois freedom'; they were all being restored. The high road to socialism, policed in the former Soviet Union, some said, by no fewer than 30 million bureaucrats of one kind and another, had been a blind turning and a dead end. Communism, Marx had predicted, would 'abolish the present state of things'. Instead, the present state of things had abolished communism.

In the teeth of this degree of prophetic failure – as terrible, almost, as if the Messiah should turn out, at the end of days, to be Satan – an intellectual world had disintegrated. The graven images of socialism, many of them profitable for nothing, had fallen from their pedestals. Some eyes that had been shut were opened; the folly (and intellectual vanity) of left idol-makers had been revealed. Smiths and carpenters were now bent to the construction of a new and more resplendent image of Capital, or Aaron's Golden Calf; an altar laden with precious objects stood before it. In the past, a Moses would have descended from on high – with the Ten Commandments or a *Communist Manifesto* – to grind such a god to powder, or at least attempt to do so. Now, drowning the diffident murmurs of intellectuals and the shouts of a few fearful bystanders, the sounds of hammering filled the air.

SIX

Playing at God

To the atheist or agnostic who contemplates the world of the faithful, the case for religion seems to rest on anxiety about mortality, puzzlement about the origins of life, and vain dreams of salvation. Conversely, the religious, looking over their shoulders at the irreligious or 'faithless', find in them a suppressed fear – which the former believe cannot be met without 'faith' – of the finiteness of their own existences. The religious also think that they discern in the irreligious a hankering, which the religious consider unsatisfiable, to ground their actions in a sense of moral obligation which is not beholden to belief in God. At their most dismissive, the religious perceive unbelievers to live (like beasts) for the day, gratifying only themselves. Under this construct, the latter proceed like oxen to the shambles and without a sacred thought for the morrow. They may be 'saved' – for who can know the mind of God? – but it will take some doing.

Of all atheist judgments of religion, the most fatally ignoble and gratuitous were those of Marx and Marxism. Scoffing at the 'opiates' of others was eventually amended on the left to a sociology of religion, which made of the different faiths a benign bestiary of 'comparative' follies. But the damage to Marxism, not to religion, had been done. When so much of socialist faith itself narcotised the understanding, the casting of stones at God and his various servants became more than a simple Marxist 'contradiction'. No more persuasive was Marx's perception of religion as 'mere idealism', as if Marxism were not idealism also.

In the Marxist schema, the left's progressive 'materialism' – a rootedness in, and engagement with, this world – was set off against the reactionary (and hence right-wing) 'mystifications' of reality peddled by anti-socialist enemies of the people. Where socialists pursued the interests of Man for the proletariat's sake, so the socialist argument ran, anti-socialists promoted only their own interests and dunned the poor in the name of God, Family and Nation. Socialist materialists were concerned with this rough earth, anti-socialist idealists with that blue yonder; the former with this life, the latter with the next one. It was by such idle diversions that the deserving were cheated of their worldly due, and fobbed off with the promise of a *post-mortem* reward at the Last Judgment, or in Heaven.

Such criticisms of the spirit of religion will always possess their own validity and attract their own audience. Moreover, in the Marxist critique there was once more a substratum of left truth, upon which an edifice of left falsehood and violence was typically constructed. For violence and falsehood – ultimately vain – were required if profession of faith was to be discredited and the faithful isolated. Physical violence against the religious, against their places of worship, against their priests, deterred observance, profaned the sacred and disabled religious intercession. Marx's unease with the faith of his fathers, an unease which at some time almost every Jew has shared, had exacted a high price. Hebraism disowned became the politics of a general irreligion; the rejection of old faith a new faith to save the world.

But the world was not saved. Marx's socialism had run its unrelenting, and unrepenting, course; and most of the world, especially that part of it ravaged by 'real socialism', sighed with relief at its passing. More important in the longer run, the world's religions, coiled in hibernation in communist societies after decades of anathemata pronounced upon them, had begun to stir even before the fall. Indeed, their stirring hastened the fall. Uneasy Marxist intellectuals, brought up to unconcern, or at worst contempt, for all faiths but their own, found themselves before the opening doors of churches and other tabernacles. Within, they glimpsed the ritual genuflections of the religious – or superstitious – and listened, estranged, to the sounds of sermon and prayer. Words such as 'sin', or 'holy', or (particularly) 'god', had not merely an unfamiliar but an alien resonance to their ears. Socialism had trained the past decades to its own sense of taboo; the taboos were being shaken off as if they had never existed. The socialist, who had made the 'politically unenlightened' into strangers in their own land, now felt a stranger himself amid the quickly re-forming congregations of the religious. He could not lend himself intellectually to their obeisances; but he found himself politically on his knees before the forces of the religious revival.

Habituated to sectarianism and faction, leftists were truly at home only with the internecine. Where Christian sects – the Roman and the Orthodox, the Orthodox and the Uniate, the Catholic and the Protestant

– were at odds in the post-communist world, the Marxist, observing from a distance, could recognise as familiar only their 'struggle' for influence or for favour with the new regimes. The rest, if it had to do with, say, contests (as in the Ukraine) over disputed church properties, or the redrawing of diocesan boundaries, or the appointment of bishops, or the recovery of the dusty appurtenances of worship, was as strange to a Marxist, or ex-Marxist, as the riddles of Tertullian. It appeared, and some of it was, mediaeval. It also appeared to be, even where it was not, the world not of the living but of the dead; more the removal of the cerements, or grave cloths, of the long-buried than the re-vesting of faiths reborn and in the ascendant.

The left agnostic, and more obviously the atheist of the left, felt a particular recoil from the energies which enthusiastic, or 'fundamentalist', religion inspired. All religions might have their virtues, and lament the same vices with worthy motive. A socialist could also agree with a man of God to condemn certain worldly sins – Covetousness and Sloth, for instance – and Christian Socialists, among others, had easily married one faith with another. But a 'fundamentalist' *rejection* of the modern world and its degradations was too severe a doctrine for the socialist 'materialist' who had sought both to embrace the world and to change it. Resort to the supposed authority of the Word of God, a return to pre-lapsarian sources of wisdom and a rejection of secular authority pointed into deeper darkness. Not even socialist failure could convince socialists, and many ex-socialists, that the defeat of contingency and human frailty must await the Last Day; and even the most messianic (or Judaic) of socialist utopians would hesitate to make entire common cause with a dancing *hasid* or fulminating imam.

Nonetheless, the left now had to face and accommodate many unwelcome truths. One was that the failure of socialism had given a new lease, or licence, to anti-secular recipes for human redemption. The 'Islamic way of life' exerted an ever stronger appeal – and there were many to argue its justice – at a time when all perceivedly 'Western' doctrine, socialism included, was thought to have revealed itself both as irreligion and impractical humbug. Buddhism raised itself from decades of repression as Asian communism began to founder; socialist-influenced secularism came under increasing pressure at the hands of 'fundamentalist' Hinduism in India; Jewish zealots were more than ever convinced that they inhabited a latter-day Sodom and Gomorrah. In Israel, patrols of the hyper-faithful sought out breakers of the Sabbath, denounced the pork-eater and defaced 'provocative' posters. Believing

that the Messiah might appear at any moment, the ultra-orthodox
required that their world be made fit to receive Him.

The secularist and the materialist (in every sense) had had this kind
of thing coming to them for a long time. Socialist and capitalist
materialisms, East and West, had done much to shrink man's sense of
the living world to the narrowest compass of aspiration-and-gratifica-
tion. But if the passage from production to consumption and back again
was sufficient unto the day, it was not sufficient for the night, or for
those who dream of another way of living. Where even calamity,
whether private or public, comes to signify little more than an interrup-
tion of pleasures, man's life and death themselves come to mean next
to nothing; or a merely temporary grazing on the earth's already over-
grazed surface. If spiritual mountebanks, mocking reason, then stepped
into this vacuum, it was those who had betrayed reason, often in the
name of reason, to whom the greatest historic blame attached. Those
on the left who had tried to build a world where nothing was sacred
could not persuasively complain if they were challenged, or even
threatened, by the pious, proclaiming from the pulpit that the entire
world was holy, holy, holy. It was too bad for the inveterate scoffer if a
novel or a foreskin, a ham sandwich or a condom, should then become,
themselves, the stuff of anathema and loathing.

Nor, once the gates of clerical irrationality had been opened, could
'conscience' alone, the lode-star of the liberal-minded, serve to withstand the onrush of those claiming to live by God's law, and insisting
that others do so also. Secularism might invest the 'right to choose' – in
questions as to what to eat, how to dress, or under what conditions to
copulate – with a privileged moral status. But when the choice, once
made, offended the prohibitions of newly-emboldened religion, the dust
raised by the collision between ethic and ethic might not easily settle.
The West's capitalism and the East's socialism had come close to
creating, between them, the world's first near-universal secular culture.
The moral crusade against such a culture gained strength and spirit
from the fall of its socialist pillar; the prospect that the 'values of profit'
might now rule the entire globe promised (to some) a 'new world order'
wholly governed by a market ethic, but to many others this was no ethic
at all.

However, those who would redeem the world from such an outcome
were themselves a motley crew. Elderly Christian patriarchs called for
capitalism and the market to serve the cause of human freedom; the
pampered princes of the church enjoined 'being', rather than 'having',

upon resourceless millions newly freed to a post-communist world of aspiring consumption. At the same time, Islam, the church militant which Christianity had failed to be, came out of its corner fighting. It fought for the Faith, it fought the apostate, it fought to preserve the sanctity of its holy places, it challenged the infidel. 'Militant wrath' some Muslims called it. In the view of Islam, proselytising with aroused fervour, Christianity had long been impoverished by tolerance of doctrinal backsliding and was now near-vanquished by the secular spirit of the age. Islam, with its religious powder drier by far, could – declared the Ayatollah Khomeini in March 1989 – yet 'save all nations'. Britain, too, where a third of the population declared themselves in 1989 to have 'no religious beliefs' and two-thirds of young people 'never' went to church, 'like all else belongs to God', said Khomeini.

In the view of most Jews, a Khomeini, like most Muslims, was no more than a 'fanatic'. But in the view of most Christians and many Muslims, the orthodox Jew, bent to his devotions, was a fanatic also; and few Jews or Muslims believed that there were many devout Christians at all. The greater truth was that each religious confession had, each in its own way, suffered from the encroachment of the secular tide. Each, particularly in the last decade, had sought to revive the ardours of its faithful. In the faltering of socialist faith and the *fin de siècle* pessimism of the intellectual, each had found opportunity for renewal; Islam and Eastern European Catholicism had in part succeeded. Even Islamic Jihad's kidnappers were bold, or shameless, enough in August 1991 to call on 'the world as a whole' to 'adopt Islam as an ideology, a code of law, and a system'. By 1991, in contrast, almost a half of all Americans, according to poll evidence, did not think religion 'very important', while a majority admitted that they were no longer able to 'tell right from wrong'. Indeed, such was the scale of Western Christian unbelief that it had begun to appear as spiritual blindness even to unbelievers.

This same (nominally) Christian West had always reacted to Islam with a degree of anxiety, and sometimes with outright hostility, especially in the latter's intermittent periods of militant recrudescence. Now, Islam in its turn was proving aggressively quick to detect the old animus of the West in every protest against its perceived unreason. Objection to superstitious excess was judged historic 'ignorance' or racism; Western fear of the 'fanatic' was shrewdly exploited by manipulative acts of terror; the acts of terror were themselves denied, disowned or blamed on others. With sentiments of aggrieved innocence, and as if helpless in the face of Western malice, the more sophisticated intellectual apologists for Islam sought, or even insisted upon, the West's respect for the achievements of Islamic history, culture and tradition. The West, despite its superior physical strength, was no match for an adversary so complex. It might, with its own counter-violence, bury Iraqi soldiers in their desert trenches, but could gain no lasting victory by such methods, nor by any others.

Some in the West, puzzling feebly over the revival of its old 'predicament' with Islam, pointed to the latter's refusal of the Western liberal's distinction between Church and State, God and Caesar, as if this were the historic root of the 'mutual incompatibility' between Christianity and Islam. But in 1991 Polish Catholic bishops, for example, were similarly calling for an end to the separation of Church and State in Poland. The troubling rejection of the boundary between the secular and spiritual realms was a familiar issue in Christendom, and not at all a specific problem posed to the West by Islam. That there might be, and that there might always have been, a finally unbridgeable chasm between Islam and the West, for all the cultural splendours of their meeting in Moorish Spain, few in the liberal West were impolite enough to mention.

This chasm merely grew wider after the 1979 Iranian revolution. Its radicals openly proclaimed that relations with the West would 'pollute' the 'purity' of the Islamic republic. Had a Western Christian or Jew offered a like judgment of the world of Islam, Muslims would have poured on to the streets in holy outrage, fists raised to the heavens. Catholic theologians might justly declare that there could be no peace among people without peace among religions. But Khomeinite Islam, inflaming itself with execrations of its satanic foes, knew nothing of this, taking up arms equally against variant Muslim sect and neighbouring Muslim nation. Indeed, war was faith, and faith was war, according to this most unmerciful Islamic doctrine. In February 1989, reviewing the long (and futile) years of Iran's war with Iraq conducted under his aegis, the Ayatollah Khomeini, sage of sages, declared that the 'spirit of revolutionary Islam' had 'only materialised because of the blessing of the war', with its millions of dead and injured, its aims unachieved and the nation's coffers emptied. 'Our war,' Khomeini added, 'was the war of the right against the wrong, and that war can never come to a conclusion.' It was also a war against fellow Muslims.

In the same month, the Ayatollah, with expressionless composure, had announced that 'world arrogance' was 'afraid of our revolution'.

This also was too simple. Rather, tapping its head from what it hoped was a safe distance, world arrogance had observed the revolution with the incomprehension of ages, with disbelief and with its own righteous anger. That the 'Islam of today' was 'dynamic and epic-making', as its radicals claimed, the West was (foolishly) not prepared to credit; that it was seething with an alien and unholy frenzy was more to its taste as a final judgment. Those with a longer view of history might suggest that Islam was once more 'advancing' on the West, scimitars flashing, and required a 'new crusade' to stop it. Disheartened non-Muslims, bewailing the decline of their own faiths, might even find some virtue in Muslim religious fervour. But most wished a plague on all such passions, and the swift use of as much Western muscle as might be required to teach the 'barbarians' a lesson.

Meanwhile, Khomeini, who had already issued his *fatwa* against the author Salman Rushdie for *The Satanic Verses*, was leaving what turned out to be his last instructions to his Shi'ite clergy. These instructions, to a Christian or Jewish eye, were less other-worldly than they might have been for Western comfort. But Western comfort was not the Ayatollah's business. Islamic clerics, their spiritual mentor enjoined, 'should be fully aware of the issues of the time', including political issues, and be 'familiar with the ways of dealing with the economic system which dominates the world'. Why? In order, the Ayatollah declared in February 1989, that the clergy of Islam might possess the 'intelligence and shrewdness necessary for managing and safeguarding a great Islamic or even a non-Islamic society'. But in what circumstances, it might (and should) have been asked, would an Islamic cleric find himself 'managing a non-Islamic society'? When Iran's ambassador to the Vatican, of all places, declared in the same month – as socialism's crisis, on another terrain, deepened – that he was personally willing to carry out Khomeini's order to kill Salman Rushdie, more than the niceties of diplomacy were being infringed. At all such junctures, and there were many during the decade, certain suppressed questions arose. Was the world here facing purposeful strategy, or disorder of mind? If the former, what strategy, and what purpose? Were the hijackings, the suicide bombings, and the hostage-takings the political froth of the savage moment, a foaming at the mouth in generally turbulent times? Or were they directed towards specific moral-political ends, however vengeful or hate-ridden the means? Were the ends deserving of others' respect, however unwilling? And if the last, what were those ends?

There was little doubt that even where internecine Muslim conflict, often carried to the death, obtruded, the principal *casus belli* and impulse for the hatred of others was the cruelly unresolved Palestinian issue. Here, there were no moral bounds, and certainly not the bounds of Western expectation, which went untransgressed. 'If, in retaliation for every Palestinian martyred in Palestine,' Ali Akbar Rafsanjani, regarded as leader of the 'pragmatists' of the Iranian revolution, declared in May 1989, 'they [sc. Islamic militants] kill and execute, not inside Palestine, five Americans or Britons or Frenchmen, the Zionists would not continue these wrongs.' This was a murderous suggestion. Its author, the genial-seeming Rafsanjani, later to become president of Iran, was the speaker of the Iranian parliament at the time he made it. Its transgression of the law of both God and man, even if dictated by a sense of sore (vicarious) grievance and injustice, was entire; to act upon it would be to violate the moral order itself. Beyond it, whether for Jew, Christian or Muslim, there is nothing.

The 'challenge of Islam' lay not so much in the declaration itself, violent as it was, as in the fact that too few Muslims, Iranian or non-Iranian, Shi'ite or non-Shi'ite, would have regarded it as vicious *per se*. Many would have regarded it as the normal coin of Muslim discourse on the Palestinian question, and fully justified by the failure to resolve the issue. Few could, or would, conceive it to be a Muslim's moral or religious duty to oppose a declaration of this kind. Worse still, when such suggestion became deed, and words became killing, the same kind of moral indifference was sustained. In such a blank predicament – of faith without guilt, and crime without sin – neither conscience nor reason can have purchase. Belief, the belief of hopeful interlocutors with Islam, itself fails. All men may be wicked, and act wickedly, but absence of moral duty to express dissent from evil-doing is rare. When a Belgian imam, himself a man of God, spoke out against the fiats of Khomeini, he was promptly assassinated. Against this, the fact that hijackers or hostage-takers were not men of notable moral scruple was a relatively insignificant matter. They might speak of 'holy war' and 'revolutionary justice', or term themselves of the 'Party of God', but they were merely a small part of a larger 'moral culture'. And this culture had become as base in faithless Western eyes as the West appeared decadent to Muslims. Certainly few Christians could easily see God's will being done in the beating of elderly hostages kept in darkness (nor in Israeli arm-breaking of Arab captives). It was equally hard to find virtue in the death-sentence pronounced by the former Iranian interior minister, the cleric Hojatoleslam Ali Akbar Mothashemi, against 'all the participants' in the 1991 Middle East peace conference, Muslim delegates included. 'They will be executed,' he declared before the Iranian parliament in October 1991.

That amputating a malefactor's hand from the wrist, or leg from the ankle, might be thought by the god-fearing to be in accord with divine injunction also stood on the inaccessible far side of a chasm, even for those without qualms at American recourse to the electric-chair and gas-chamber. Likewise, the clerical promise of 'paradise' offered to the suicide-bomber, or martyr in war against the 'infidel', was a promise to shake the Christian's Kingdom of Heaven to its very foundations. (That a mere mortal could make such a divine promise, playing at God, was as much outside Jewish comprehensions as were Christ's own similarly blasphemous intercessions.) And although a Catholic worshipper might venerate a sliver of the True Cross or a saintly forefinger dry as dust, neither Christian nor Jew could celebrate, as did Khomeini in his clerical instructions of February 1989, the 'torn off pieces of the bodies' of martyrs, freshly bleeding. If some Shi'a Muslims on the tenth day of the month of Moharram, commemorating the holy martyrdom of the grandson of the Prophet, flagellated themselves in grief with razor-sharp clusters of blades attached to chains, Christian moral distaste was somewhat less easy; self-flagellation is known to Christian zeal too. To Jews, forbidden to cut or otherwise disfigure themselves in the paroxy-sms of mourning, the practice is obnoxious, just as is the sacred iconography made of Christ's gaping wounds and agonised dying. If love is part of the divine scheme of things, as it is believed and preached to be by the Christian, during this decade it was little sermonised upon in Islam, let alone practised between Muslim and non-Muslim, or Muslim and Muslim.

The Western liberal, wringing his hands, had 'toleration' and 'respect for other cultures' constantly on his lips in an effort, mostly vain, to stem the perceived unreason. Christian and Jewish religious services, and even the display of Christian and Jewish religious symbols, might be utterly banned in Saudi Arabia, say, where study of Freud, Marx, Western philosophy and Western art were also forbidden. But the 'true Christian' turned his cheek at such offence (inviting another), and refused to follow the intolerant model. If the Holy Koran denied that Jesus died on the Cross, and the Jews denied that Christ was the Son of God, the Christian himself would ecumenically forgive such trespass, inviting all-comers to his lands to worship their gods as they saw fit in mosque and temple. Tolerance and forgiveness might not be requited, but at least they set a moral example.

It was not catching. Ali Khamenei, Khomeini's successor as Shi'ite vicar-on-earth, announced in December 1990 that Salman Rushdie, apostate author, 'must be killed even if he repents'; even, God help him, if he were to become 'the most pious man of his time', he would 'still burn in hell'. This was not merely cruel, but cruelty with a vengeance. Similarly without mercy, in July 1989 Abdullah al-Mashad, one of Egypt's leading Islamic scholars and head of the 'Fatwa Committee' at Cairo's el-Azhar university, theological seminary-of-seminaries in the Muslim world, called on 'all Aids victims' to be 'killed' in order to 'stop them from harming society'. Such a pronouncement stared Western humanism in the face, and outstared it. 'We must purge society,' he continued – not only under Stalinism was the word 'purge' thus domesticated – 'of the Aids patient *and those like him*, because his existence causes public harm' (my emphasis). There was no treating with such a morality. When a 'strict' Birmingham Muslim came before Birmingham Crown Court in July 1989 on a charge of murder, after cutting his own teenage daughter's throat (in front of her mother and sister) for attending meetings of Jehovah's Witnesses, he pleaded 'provocation'. 'She had to be taught a lesson,' the accused declared. There could be no 'multi-cultural' bridge to cross an abyss so wide.

During the decade, the Western liberal and Western illiberal alike were continuously made aware, unless they turned their backs on it entirely, of the undiminishing distance between sets of ethics which did not often speak the same moral language. Such distance might be narrowed physically by Muslim immigration to the West, or by politically widespread sympathy, especially left sympathy, for the Palestinian cause. But the Islamic death penalty for apostasy, or execution in public by the sword after Friday prayers (as in Saudi Arabia), or the enthusiastic welcome in several Islamic countries for the attempted August 1991 coup in the Soviet Union – a 'magnificent act', Libya's Gaddafi instantly called it – were of an alienness hard to encompass. Looking forward fatalistically in January 1991 to the coming Gulf War, or 'mother of battles', a PLO official declared, 'We know it could mean even the destruction of the Israelis and ourselves. But our people say "Let it be".' Fervour is one thing, and common, even necessary, to all faiths and causes; fatalism, whether as a pious quietism or individual resignation, is known to all cultures. But combined extremes of fervour and fatalism, to the point of countenancing the prospect of mass suicide with enthusiasm, real or feigned, merely bewilder.

The Muslim intellectual has always warned the Western observer of Islam against the stereotype of the Muslim 'fanatic', according to which every Muslim is represented as in some sort a Khomeini. He has justly resented the overlooking of what he himself sees: the 'ordinary, tolerant, gentle religionist' of Islam going quietly about his daily business, immune to clerical or political inflammation. But this anti-cliché, necessary to the whole truth as may be, is also too simple. Acting faithfully under the impulse of pulpit injunction, and most often living in societies with little tradition of civic liberty or intellectual freedom, the Muslim *homme moyen* has rarely shown great capacity for resistance to the tides of local religious feeling; the higher the tide, the less the resistance. 'Whoever will not rave like the rest, is suspected,' wrote Romain Rolland in 1916, of the fevers of the then war-party. A crowd in Teheran or Tripoli, when its dander has been roused against the 'imperialist', the 'Zionist' or some other satanic figure, leaves little elbow-room for the dissenter.

Nor is the Islamic intelligentsia itself short of swift apologists for unreason. That the Muslims have 'suffered too long at Western hands', and that they have been 'pushed towards extremism' are the commonest reflexes. Most Muslims will themselves deny the distinction between a 'liberal' and a 'fundamentalist' party in Islam. 'For me,' declared Sher Azam, president of Bradford's Council of Mosques, in July 1989, 'you are either Islamic and hold to your beliefs; or you do not hold to them and you are not Islamic.' The conviction, shared by Muslims who could not properly be described as 'fanatics', that all that needs to be known is to be found in the holy books of Islam, also makes for a restricted conception of the limits of free-thinking. Even modernising Islamic thought remains deeply anchored in anti-secular premises; the sixth century casts a deeper shadow over the Muslim intellect than does biblical antiquity over the Jewish thinker, the zealots of 'Judaea and Samaria' notwithstanding.

Nor is there much to compare, in modern Christian or Jewish impulses, with the strange whetting, to near-orgiastic levels, of some Muslim appetites by the prospect of final engagement with the foe; and nothing akin to the diatribes of incitement which accompany invitations to it. When the Muslim warrior mounts his charger, reason has cause to flee for shelter. The infidels, declared Baghdad in the Gulf War – cursing the United States as 'the Great Satan' – would 'wallow in their own gore'; the Iraqis would 'make the [allied] invaders eat fire'; 'no opportunity' would be given to them to 'remove their dead from the pools of blood in which they float'; the very desert sand would be incarnadined. 'Smite the evil invaders, and tear them to pieces,' Baghdad radio enjoined its warriors, 'strike at their necks, chop off their fingers, turn their bodies into fragments of flesh, let them have no foothold.' This was bellicosity with a difference. 'O Iraqis, O Arabs, O Muslims who believe in justice,' the radio intoned in January 1991 – a brother Muslim state having been sacked and pillaged – 'your faithful and courageous forces have launched their lightning land-attack, bearing high the banner saying God is Great, and crushed the armies of atheism as they were advancing.' There was no such 'crushing'. Iraqi forces were in tragic mid-debacle, the struggle hopeless. The 'unsheathed swords of Iraq' (the 'glittering scimitar' is no racist image) would 'not be sheathed again until Jerusalem returns to its kinfolk', a military communiqué declared, as the Iraqi forces fled in disorder. A dire and brutal carnage, as at Mutla Ridge, had been unleashed upon them, but victory, Baghdad insisted, was theirs; the infidel, not Iraq, had 'fallen in the mud of crime and disgrace'. It had been, this vast defeat under the 'new Saladin' and 'minaret of mankind', an 'epic, valiant battle' which would be recorded by history 'in letters of light'. But the real battlefield was a wasteland, and the Iraqi army had suffered a rout.

Preceded by blood-curdling and gloating imprecation, and followed by lyrical but false claims of triumph, the very mode of doing battle – in words and deeds – defied the understanding. Vainglorious gesture and suicidal impulse, protestations of innocence and murderous intention, crowded one upon the other. Men ran to their deaths with open arms, or surrendered at the first sound of gunfire. Minds darkened by the demonisation of the adversary, blood ran hot and cold from one instant to another; the flames of sabotaged and burning oil wells reached to the high heavens; looted air conditioners and lipstick, leather luggage, string beads and silver tea-sets, unmatching women's shoes and refuse trucks, Kuwait zoo animals, food mixers, toilet paper and TV sets, were this war's booty. It was impossible to comprehend, and the West withdrew without trying. It had approached closer to the eye of the Islamic storm than ever, at least in modern times, but was none the wiser for it. Nor could the West fully face up to its own awareness that there were few pulses in the Muslim diaspora (including among 'ordinary, tolerant, gentle religionists') which had not quickened at the thought of an Iraqi victory over the Great Satan.

Western incomprehension was composed, in large part, of recoil from passions too unpredictable and too strange to fathom. The Jews, especially those of the Middle East, know the Muslims better. The average Anglo-Saxon or American could make little of being termed a 'vampire' by a white-bearded Ayatollah. The orthodox Jew would have had less difficulty with the call to God, by an Algerian fundamentalist preacher in June 1991, to 'make the Earth open' and 'swallow Algeria's [insufficiently Islamic] security forces'. Once, in distant times, this was the language of Christian anathema too, as well as of traditional Jewish cursing. Now, polite (or anaemic) Christianity – though not the strident TV evangelist – disavowed such religiose fury entirely, while the Jewish curse had become domestic, or private. When Saddam Hussein described President Bush, in October 1991, as a 'poisonous snake created by Zionism' the resonances were mediaeval. But it could also be said that only Islam had maintained and re-charged its ancient fervours. In the collision of energies, as well as of cultures, the West was marshalling its new technologies of production and war against an old but aroused religious spirit fiercely resistant (thought not immune) to secularisation. When even the King of Jordan, seemingly not much given to excess of Islamic passion, in February 1991 declared the Gulf War to be a 'war on all Arabs and Muslims, not just on Iraq', this was but a short step – a step taken by many other Muslim spokesmen – from pronouncing the War to be part of a 'Christian crusade' against the entire Islamic world.

The hostilities between Muslim and Muslim, between Jew and Muslim, and (surfacing briefly but dangerously) between Muslim and Christian were plainly more than rhetorical, even if marked by a sanguinary prose and a poetical hatred. For, like world socialism itself, the legacy of secular nationalism in the post-colonial Arab world was disintegrating. The increasing satanisation of Zionism and of Western motives, together with the magnification of the Palestinians' cause, helped, or seemed to help, to fill the political void, providing a growing lumpen-intelligentsia, religious and lay, with an apparent unity of ideological and moral purpose. And as socialist belief and Soviet support for the PLO, for example, waned together, so a redoubled zeal both for Islam and the collective 'Arab nation' might make-good flagging hopes, lost resources and an uncertain sense of direction.

But this also was only part of a larger upheaval. With the retreat and dissolution of Soviet power, client dictatorships and military autocracies, hitherto held in place by Moscow, tumbled; China, which had once made its own heavy political and economic investment in the Third World, as in Tanzania, had already retreated. As 'pluralism' invested the Soviet Union, and an entire creed – transplanted to many African (and North African) countries as the socialism of one party – failed, so 'reform', 'democracy', 'the market' and, in most cases, elections became the new watchwords of progress from Angola to Zanzibar and Zimbabwe. In Ethiopia, the last 'Marxist-Leninist' government to be set up on the planet (in 1987) fell in May 1991, and its brutal ruler, Haile Mengistu, fled the country. Benin, also 'Marxist-Leninist' since a military coup in 1972, as well as corrupt and despotic, dropped Marxism-Leninism as its ideology of state in December 1989, and no longer required its civil servants to address each other as 'comrade'. In dictatorial Zaire, languishing under Mobutu's rule since 1965, '*citoyen*' was dropped in April 1990 as a form of address, and '*monsieur*' and '*madame*' were once more permitted. Guinea-Bissau, once regarded (under Amilcar Cabral) as a shining Leninist outpost in West Africa, fell to the reforming tide; Algeria lurched into free market reforms and, with chaotic outcome, multi-party elections; and even Nelson Mandela announced in July 1991 that the African National Congress 'would not follow socialism' in South Africa when it came to power.

Nor were such changes and convulsions confined to Africa. In Nicaragua, the electorally defeated Sandinista leaders ('we have to be pragmatic') turned to running supermarkets and private airlines. Fidel Castro, who had removed his last troops from Angola in May 1991, became the Prospero of a lost tropic island. Michael Manley, Jamaica's prime minister and once – with Castro – the fiercest-sounding socialist in the Caribbean, was also preaching 'pragmatism' by June 1989, before resigning in April 1992. In India, in 1991, bureaucratic 'socialist controls', which had done much to stifle the nation's economic progress, were being dismantled. Pakistan's Benazir Bhutto had jumped even sooner; by early 1988 she had openly discarded the socialist beliefs on which she had been elected to office. President Mohammed Najibullah, too, in neighbouring Afghanistan, had by January 1988 declared that his government was now 'non-Marxist'. But not even this volte-face could prevent his overthrow by the *mojahedin* in April 1992.

In many other countries, greater ideological confusion than ever succeeded these evaporations of socialist doctrine. In the old world of Islam, from Samarkand to Somalia, suppressed Islamic movements and

Muslim spirits had long been astir. Now, in some places, overthrow of
one-party despots made possible the reappearance of Islam's clerics
and their followers on the streets; in others, as in Algeria, they came at
a bound from worship to the forefront of the political process. In large
swathes of the Third World, 'Marxism-Leninism' and even a fierce
brand of imported Maoism had once provided the rhetoric of denunciation of the West, and shaped the intellectual perceptions of substantial numbers of the educated. Such doctrines had spoken the language
both of resistance to the West and of progress beyond it; of superiority
to the capitalist world and of (secular) faith in the people. In many
countries, as socialism collapsed, an old contest was rejoined. But now
it would increasingly take a new form. With socialism no longer a
significant player, the West's blandishments – in the guise of the
economic liberation of the market and the 'civilising' influence of liberal
democratic political practice – would now have to encounter an anti-
Westernism of recovered indigenous culture and belief, Islamic belief
included. It viewed, or affected to view, the markets of Western
capitalism with as much distaste as the exploded nostrums of the
socialist heathen.

Pressures quickly mounted in Muslim and Muslim-dominated states
– in the Maghreb, Egypt, Pakistan, Sudan and the Yemen among others
– for the observation of Shari'a, or Koranic domestic law. In non-
Muslim countries with large or restless Muslim populations, including
India and Nigeria, a new turbulence of pride and expectation was
everywhere apparent among Muslims. Muslim bodies, including in
Britain, demanded increased respect for Muslim interests and customs,
sometimes dividing the Muslim community by their agitations. Together
with their counterparts in Western Europe, the Muslim Brotherhood in
Egypt, Sudan, Syria, and Jordan, the Jamaat-i-Islami Party in Pakistan,
the Islamic Regeneration Party in Tajikistan and Uzbekistan, the
Al-Nahda Party in Tunisia, the Islamic Party in Malaysia and many
other movements, nationalist and separatist, large and small, pacific and
violent, became more energetic in the pursuit of the various dimensions
of the Islamic cause. In some countries, these fraternities and parties
formed governments; in others, as in Egypt, they were a parallel power,
dominating wide areas of public life, with Iran and Saudi Arabia vying
for influence as their paymasters. From Afghanistan to Burma, Palestine
to Malaysia, and the Philippines to Indian Kashmir and the Chechen-
Ingush Republic in the northern Caucasus, the same cause was
implicated in simultaneous insurgencies of varying scale and intensity,

some of them long-standing. To a Jew habituated to hearing 'Zionism' decried, frequently by Muslims, as an organised global movement of the earth's mere 14 to 15 million Jews, it might seem inconsistent that the spokesmen for more than one billion Muslims should routinely declare themselves to be 'the Muslim nation', a vast supranational diaspora of the like-minded in faith and tradition.

Indeed, the geo-political implications of a renascent Islam knew no boundaries. In Afghanistan, after the *mojahedin* were victorious, Shari'a law was swiftly imposed and the *chaddar*, or woman's veil, restored; from Sudan, a focus of Iranian influence, 'fundamentalist' doctrine began to make itself felt among Muslim minorities from the Horn of Africa to Kenya. Islamic radicalism, which is in part resurgence of religious faith, in part expression of rediscovered national identity, passed as easily from Iran into Pakistan and Afghanistan, or over the borders of the collapsed Soviet Union and even into China, as along the Gulf or the southern littoral of the Mediterranean. There were, in addition, some 50 or 60 million Muslims in former Soviet territories, including Azeris, Uzbeks – between one and two mosques a day were being opened in Uzbekistan in 1991 – Tajiks, Turkmens and over thirty other Muslim ethnic subgroups, many straddling the frontiers of Islamic nations to their south. 'There is now a struggle for the soul of Central Asia,' declared a CIA official in February 1992, 'and Turkey, Iran, Saudi Arabia, Pakistan and the US will all play a part'; 'secular' Turkey (its strategic significance growing) and Iran quickly established themselves as the main protagonists in this intra-Islamic battle. Even in China, an 'Islamic revolt' in Xinjiang border region, armed by Afghan *mojahedin* calling in the name of Allah the all-merciful for the 'Victory of Islam over Marxism-Leninism', was 'put down' by force in April 1990. But the struggle for Muslim self-rule in Xinjiang continued.

On the borders of Greek Thrace, European Turkey and Southern Bulgaria – where the former communist regime had sought to force assimilation upon the Muslim population – there were substantial Muslim minorities whose affinities could not be divided by frontiers. That most Albanians, 90 per cent of the Kosovars, 44 per cent of the Bosnians (converted to Islam under Ottoman rule from 1463 to 1878) and large numbers of Macedonians were Muslims added to the imbroglio of Yugoslavia's disintegration. In Bosnia, where Muslims voted overwhelmingly in March 1992 for independence, the ensuing civil war claimed thousands of Muslim victims, as massacre and forcible expulsion were cruelly resorted to, under Serbian inspiration, to prevent the emergence of a 'Muslim-dominated state in 'Europe'. Turkey, Iran and other Islamic nations, with arms shipments and volunteers, in turn sought to come to their co-religionists' aid, perceiving the Serbs and Croats – although at one another's throats – as united in a Christian assault on Islam.

The Libyan revolution had for its part fished even in Northern Ireland's troubled Christian waters, supplying the IRA with arms and money. That the latter should have mounted a mortar-attack on Downing Street during the Gulf War was no coincidence, as Yasser Arafat himself indicated a few weeks later. 'When Saddam Hussein called on "good Muslims" to attack Western interests, who was he referring to?' Arafat was asked by the journalist Isabel Pinto, in an interview published in the *Guardian* (4 March 1991). 'To the IRA perhaps, as has been seen in Britain,' Arafat answered. The IRA were hardly 'good Muslims' – indeed Arafat's entire reply was astounding – but the point he had made was sufficiently plain. There was even an attempted Islamic coup, allegedly backed by Libya, in Trinidad in July 1990; its leaders were arrested.

The Muslim diaspora also constituted a settled community of hundreds of millions of peaceable brothers-in-faith. But Muslims on the move – part of that wider movement of peoples discussed in an earlier chapter – had recently brought Islam from India, Pakistan and Bangladesh to Britain; from the Maghreb and West Africa to France, Italy and Spain (to go no further in Europe); from Turkey and many other Islamic countries to Germany; from Indonesia to Australia; and so on. There were even 100,000 Palestinians in Detroit. In 1991, there were estimated to be, at over 30 million, more Muslims in Europe than there were Scandinavians. There were some 15 million Muslims in European Russia, perhaps 4 million in the former Yugoslavia – close to the number of Jews in Israel – perhaps 3 million in France, of whom some one million were Algerians, 2.5 million in Albania, 2 million in Germany (the great majority Turks), and over 1.5 million in Britain.

In some countries, Islam was at home. In others, it was a settler of ages past and deep-rooted in its culture. In others again, it was a recent stranger, welcomed and unwelcomed. In Western Europe, Muslims formed part of minority communities which variously fought to coexist with, adapt to, or resist majority values, sometimes with the host's toleration and support. In different ways politicians of majority and minority benefited from, or exploited, the immigrant presence. Minority community leaders sought, or struggled, to represent the community's intrests in the political system, to guide loyalties divided by the pressures of estrangement and assimilation, or to prevent surrender to local 'decadence' and the abandonment of tradition by the younger generation. In West Africa, the Vatican reported in July 1990, revived Islamic energies for proselytisation on old colonial territory were challenging, and being challenged by, Christian evangelism. In Kano in Northern Nigeria, for example, blood flowed in October 1991 between Muslim and Christian gangs in running street-battles over such evangelism. In Kaduna, some three hundred people died in May 1992 in ethnic and religious riots involving Nigerian Muslims and Christians. Elsewhere, too, Muslim-Christian hostility erupted. In Cameroun, in January 1992, Muslim youths clashed with police over the choice of a site, said by local Christians to be sacred to them, for a new mosque in the capital, Yaounde; in Sanabou in Egypt, in May 1992, twelve Christians and one Muslim died in inter-religious violence, said by the Egyptian interior ministry to have been 'stirred up' by Muslim militants. In other parts of the Islamic world an ancient torpor reigned.

Those who were most uneasy at the new presence of Islam in the West – many of them hostile to all immigration – could be heard arguing that 'Europe', or 'European civilisation', or even 'European Christian civilisation' was 'under siege'. They shifted nervously over demographic statistics; or noted with alarm, as they had once done with the incoming Jew, the contrast between the insipidity, and sometimes the absence, of local allegiance to faith, or home, or work, or education, and the religious fidelity, domestication, and habits of application of the once-poor migrant.

An old contradictory response, well-known to the Jews, also raised its head. The continuities of minority culture and the maintenance of minority identity were simultaneously admired for their conservative virtues, and blamed for their ghetto-like persistence. But where the cause of Islam began to turn, usually at the prompting of minority community radicals, to demands against the host community (as in France and Britain) for the absolute right to eat, dress, be educated or slay animals in a particular fashion and no other, conflicts sharpened and violence might threaten. Where militant Islam went on the offensive in already nominally Muslim polities to pursue, often with guns and bombs, the setting-up of an Islamic state or the full imposition of Shari'a, states of emergency might be declared (as in Algeria in June 1991), and the jails fill to overflowing, as in Tunisia in May 1991, in Algeria in July 1991, and in Islamabad a month later. Even when militants in Algeria won an overwhelming victory in democratic elections

in January 1992, the army moved swiftly to stop the Islamic Salvation
Front gaining the political prize, a state of emergency was once more
declared, and thousands of Muslim radicals were detained. Islamic
'fundamentalists', believing that they were doing God's will, would
often be accused by fellow Muslims of 'subversion', terrorism, or armed
conspiracy to seize power; in turn they might even call, contrary to
Koranic prescription, for a *jihad* against their benighted, or insufficiently
Muslim, brethren. As in confrontations with the Great Satan, the
former would profess innocence of every ill intention. They merely
sought, as every good Muslim should – so they would protest in court,
sometimes before being sentenced (as in Jordan, Algeria and Tunisia)
to hang – true Islamic rule, 'democratic', 'participatory' and god-
fearing.

In May 1991, such pressures drove the Pakistani government, now in
command of the capacity to build nuclear weapons (as Iran, Iraq and
Libya also sought to be), to accept Shari'a, rather than the constitution
of Pakistan, as the nation's supreme law. Opposition demands to
entrench protection of the parliamentary system and basic rights,
including the rights of women and non-Muslim minorities, were
rejected. Two months later, death by hanging was made mandatory in
Pakistan for defamation of the Prophet. Sudan, locked in civil war with
Christians and animists in the south of the country, had also introduced
Shari'a law in March 1991. Included in its provisions was the death
penalty for apostasy, and public whipping for petty crime. 'Anyone who
betrays the nation,' the Sudanese leader, General Bashir announced,
'does not deserve the honour of living.'

But it was Ayatollah Khomeini's *fatwa*, pronounced in February 1989
against the English-educated writer Salman Rushdie, which aroused
the greatest frissons of enthusiasm for, and hostility towards, the
Muslim revival. 'I inform the proud Muslim people of the world that
the author of the *Satanic Verses* book ... and all those involved in its
publication who were aware of its content are sentenced to death,' the
Shi'a sage declared; 'I ask all Muslims to execute them wherever they
find them.' An assailant who died in the act, or in the effort to commit
it, would be an instant martyr to Islam and be admitted to honour in
heaven. A bounty of one million dollars – a sum which would be raised
to 3 million dollars if the killer was Iranian – was placed upon the
luckless author's head. Hojatoleslam Mohammad Ali Tashkiri, Iranian
delegate to a meeting of the Islamic Conference Organisation in Riyadh

in March 1989, described the *fatwa* without more ado as 'the sentence
of Allah'.

Rushdie, Indian-born, Muslim by family, Rugby and Cambridge
educated, and resident of North London, had suddenly found himself
within Teheran's jurisdiction, under Koranic interdict and at the mercy
of the long arm of a holy assassin. An English left-wing intellectual by
acclimatisation had been struck by an Islamic thunderbolt. The body
and soul of one of Britain's 1.5 million (or so) immigrant Muslims –
five times the numbers of British Jews – had been reclaimed by his
fathers. Bradford Muslims burned his book with appropriate impreca-
tions, and significant numbers of the indigenous intelligentsia declared
their secular outrage for the offence being done by faith, and an 'alien'
faith at that, to the principle of intellectual freedom. Some of the latter,
in their vicarious sense of embattlement, contrived (against the odds) to
cut absurd figures. 'To threaten the life of one British writer is to
threaten us all,' wrote the novelist Alan Sillitoe in a letter to a
newspaper, addressed from the Savage Club. Politicians with large
numbers of Muslims in their constituencies jumped this way and that.
Some betrayed life-long ideals in the 'interests of race relations'; some
muddied the issue as best they could; others stayed silent. Some
Muslims marched for the frightened Rushdie's blood, some (though
only a few) dared to speak out against the *fatwa* and counselled
'moderation', and others (the majority) kept their partially-English
heads down, waiting for the Islamic storm to blow over.

The Satanic Verses, whatever else it might be, was, closely read, the
autobiography of an anglicised Muslim fabulist, Salman Rushdie, who
takes the name – among his other aliases and alibis in the text – of
'Salman the Persian'. It is, among other things, the tale (not always a
very good tale) of a Muslim migrant's spiritual journey in both Albion
and Arabia; a storyteller's and fib-teller's journey, Rushdie's own,
between cultures. It is a journey restlessly conducted, back and forth, in
his own head, or imagination. 'Salman' and the other characters, all of
whom are chips off the author's block, move through an Arabian Nights'
sequence of dreamed lands, dreamed scenes, and dreamed circumstances. They even dream dreams within dreams, until the reader is
shaken off the trail of the author's wrestling with his own provenance
and experience, and is lost. The book's irony, given Rushdie's fate, is
that at its narrowly self-preoccupied heart is the inner life of a man
wandering (or at large) in worlds of fact and fancy, reason and
imagination, where Islam – like some distant Xanadu, wished-for but

also feared – is the object both of scorn and nostalgia. No Jew who has lived his life within the same dilemma could fail to recognise the burden, in every sense, of such a work of the imagination. It contains hidden truths and attractive falsehoods, nose-thumbings at inherited faith and secret longing, pleasure in the display of mastery of adoptive feeling and language, dissatisfactions with self which are temporarily made good by the act of writing, and much else which comes from the no man's land between belonging and estrangement.

More important, Rushdie – or his various *alter ego*s in *The Satanic Verses* – plainly feared the possible outcome of his authorship of the work, in particular for 'polluting the word of God with my own profane language' (p.367). Even the future arguments of the real victim-to-be are rehearsed: 'Where there is no belief, there is no blasphemy,' the author asserts (p.380). In his dangerous chapter, 'Return to Jahilia', whose sometimes scabrous character outraged Muslim opinion for its insults against the Prophet and his wives – even though the chapter is, or appears to be, the account of a dream – Rushdie transposes his prescient anxieties into the musings of the fictional Salman. 'And now Mahound [an offensive name for the Prophet] is coming in triumph, so I shall lose my life after all. Baal asked: "Why are you sure he will kill you?" Salman the Persian answered: "It's his Word against mine"' (p.368). The idle fantasy of the self-frightening Muslim child – Islam, like Judaism, creates a world both of fears and pleasures – has become an adult nightmare. 'The next day . . . Salman the Persian is dragged into the Prophet's presence. Khalid, holding him by the ear, holding a knife at his throat, brings the immigrant [*sic*] snivelling and whimpering to the *takht* . . . The Prophet begins to pronounce the sentence of death, but the prisoner begins to shriek the *qalmah*: "La ilaha ilallah! La ilaha!" Mahound shakes his head. "Your blasphemy, Salman, can't be forgiven. Did you think I wouldn't work it out? To set your words against the Word of God."'

In this fable, Salman the Persian, or the Rushdie of Rugby and Cambridge, 'swears renewed loyalty' – as the author attempted to do in his 'public conversion' to Islam in December 1990 – and is not sentenced to death by the Prophet. 'Let the wretched fellow live,' says the novel (p.375). Here, life did not imitate art. On the penultimate page (p.546) of the book, Rushdie returns to his anxiety about what he has written. Another *alter ego*, now called Salahuddin, speculates, in this fiction of obsessive thought and toying fancy, about how he is 'going to die for his verses'. And, at the very last, Salahuddin, resigned to his fate, 'could not find it in himself to call the death sentence unjust'. But Rushdie, as real life caught up with him, was less accommodating.

In the British passage of post-*fatwa* events (holy and unholy), inward rumination and outward declaration upon the 'Muslim threat', upon 'fanatical' religion, upon imagination, upon the 'foreign' fiat against a citizen of Britain, upon the law of blasphemy, upon the rights and limits of intellectual freedom, upon public order and incitement to violence, upon the virtues of Rushdie's book, and upon the costs of his protection by the state's servants contributed to a whirlpool of unease and excitement. Voices of vain lament declared that in 1970 there had been a mere 3,000 Muslims in Britain. By the year 2000, said the stricken, there could, or would, be 'over 2 million', the great majority mosque-going. There were already said to be more Muslims than Methodists in Britain; by 2000 there could well be more observing Muslims than confessants of the dwindling Church of England. This signified (to some) that Britain was no longer, or would soon cease to be, the green and pleasant, Anglo-Saxon and Christian, land of their fondest fancies.

The weakly hopeful, seeking to hold their own against the foes of 'multi-culturalism' and the enemies of goodwill and toleration, looked to Iran to amend its ferocious judgment. At the death, in November 1989, of the Ayatollah Khomeini – 'God's spirit in the body of time' and a 'manifestation of pure truth' as the Iranian government's official statement called him – such hopes rose. It was not to be; the death sentence was repeated. Indeed, by June 1990, Khomeini's successor, Ali Khamenei, was calling for the still-surviving Rushdie to be 'handed over to British Muslims in order that God's decree be implemented against him'. The head of the Iranian judiciary, Muhammad Yazdi, solemnly declared that those who possessed the means to kill the hidden author, but did not (or refused to) do so, would have committed a 'great punishable offence as well as a sin'. In March 1991, the bounty upon the writer's head was doubled. Bookshops in Britain stocking *The Satanic Verses* were fire-bombed; in July 1991, its Italian translator, Ettore Capriolo, survived an assassination attempt by an assailant said to be Iranian; its Japanese translator, Hitoshi Igarashi, was stabbed to death eight days later. 'Today,' said a spokesman for the Pakistan Association in Japan, alleging that the killing had been carried out by an Iranian, 'we have been congratulating each other. Everyone was really happy.' But what, he was asked, of others' hostile reaction to such a murder, and in such a cause? 'They have to learn a lesson,' he replied, in the manner of the Birmingham father who cut the throat of his daughter. 'We don't care about their reactions.'

Most non-Muslim intellectuals, unused to terrorism against a book – even if habituated by now to hijacks, hostage-taking and the destruction of aircraft – had long ago reeled away from the scene. Incomprehension, beyond a certain point of effort, settles into passive anxiety and silence. They had thought the matter, from the beginning, to be 'intolerable', an 'outrage', an assault upon 'reason'. They had insisted, or had tried to insist, that the book in question was a mere fiction. They held, especially if they were themselves without religion, that notions of blasphemy were outdated. They signed protests, presented petitions, held meetings, and went back, non-plussed, to their desks and pre-occupations.

Rushdie himself, in his act of 'return' to Islam (and in justifiable fear of death), had formally 'witnessed' in December 1990 that Allah was 'the only God'. But the Muslim sword of Damocles was not lifted from his head, and a year later Rushdie was retreating from his conversion, describing it, in December 1991, merely as an 'attempt to make my peace with Islam, even at the cost of my pride'. By February 1992 he was calling it a 'mistake'. His self-appointed judges, some of them fellow-British Muslims, and even fellow-British Muslim intellectuals, had from the outset not been satisfied with his (modest) degree of contrition, or had declared his 'conversion' bogus, or both. The victim, who had also succeeded in disillusioning his non-Muslim and non-religious supporters by his 'conversion', strenuously denied that he was acting in bad faith. But Shabbir Akhtar, a fellow-Cambridge Muslim intellectual, pronounced him still a 'sinner', and his act of conversion to have been 'paved with bad intentions'. Coils of truth and untruth, of stubbornness and courage, of simple misjudgment and complex evil-doing (or wickedness) lay entangled together. Rushdie refused to 'withdraw' his book; shop managers and assistants refused to sell, and also refused not to sell, the offending volume; Islam's clerics refused to withdraw, or claimed they had no power to withdraw, Khomeini's *fatwa*; the British government refused to accede to Teheran's demands for the delivery of Rushdie to Islamic justice; intellectual opinion engaged with the issues, and then in general refused to engage with them further.

Koranic experts, Muslim and non-Muslim, fought over rival interpretations of Holy Writ and of the applicability of the decree of a Shi'a cleric to other Muslims. (Followers of the Shi'a tradition of Islam make up some 10 per cent of all Muslims.) Some said that the Koran, allowing for mercy, did not sanction an irrevocable death penalty for blasphemy. Others insisted that it did. Some said that the offence Rushdie's book had given to Muslims fell short of 'waging war upon God and his messenger', for which the alternative Koranic punishments are to be 'killed or crucified', to have the hands and feet 'on alternate sides' struck off, or to be exiled. Others argued that the book's abuse of the Prophet by a Muslim was tantamount to such a waging of war. But what if Salman Rushdie was not a Muslim at the time of the offence? Could a non-Muslim be put to death for insulting the Prophet? And even if Rushdie was a Muslim – on the principle of once a Muslim always a Muslim (or once a Jew always a Jew) – were not repentance and commutation of punishment allowed for?

Some said that, since God not Man is the judge of all things, it was for God to accept or reject Rushdie's act of 'conversion'. Others declared themselves fully satisfied with Teheran's stony rejection of it. The argument that true Koranic Islam stood upon the twin principles of 'balance' (al-adl) and 'compassion' (al-ahsan) was offered up to the obduracy of the hard-hearted. Chapter was set against chapter and verse against verse. It was even argued by a few that there was no religious ground at all for the fatwa: 'Whoever wants to believe, let him believe, and whoever wants to disbelieve, let him disbelieve,' was one Koranic text urged in vain against the merciless party. 'There is no chance of the fatwa being removed,' declared Sayed Quddus, a Bradford Muslim leader, in January 1991. 'It is Islamic law. He must die.'

Die? In Britain? A British citizen by adoption? At the hand of a Muslim carrying out a deceased Iranian cleric's orders? For a bounty of dollars? The questions were asked across an intellectual chasm, while the victim moved from hide-out to hide-out. Dr Kalim Siddiqui, a British Muslim of Indian extraction, London University education and Iranian persuasion – who simultaneously professed obedience to the British rule of law and approval of the fatwa – led one faction of the unyielding; in May 1992, he even declared, ex cathedra, that the fatwa would be 'deemed to apply to anyone who ignores the line that has been drawn by us on the sands of history'. Quick to see a crusading enmity against Islam in most Western judgments and open about his urgings upon Teheran to maintain the fatwa, to Siddiqui the death sentence was an expression of Islamic justice. Rushdie's book, he believed, was 'part of a global war declared on Islam by the West', and merely a continuation of an old colonial enterprise by other means. 'Rushdie scum!' and 'Kill the bastard!' shouted the less erudite at demonstrations.

A British Muslim cleric, Inayatullah Zaigham, publicly referred (with 'un-British' odium) to Rushdie's 'rat-like existence'; Imam Bukhari of New Delhi's Jama Masjid mosque, one of Islamic India's great centres of worship, called him a 'blasphemous dog'; he was portrayed throughout the Muslim world as a horned, demonic figure.

The British state's protection of the author notwithstanding, a paralysis of the will in the face of a multiple challenge – moral, intellectual, cultural, legal – could be observed in official responses to the strange and complex plight of a British subject. British Muslims, while claiming to 'want to be good citizens', openly demanded a fellow-citizen's head; yet incitement to murder, an offence in English law, went unchallenged and unpunished by the law's guardians. 'I hope he will be killed,' declared Mohammed Ismail Janjua, president of Dudley mosque, in February 1989. He was one of many Muslims in Britain to utter the murderous sentiment. 'If he takes his book back we would forget him. [This was the 'moderate' Muslim position.] If not, I would be prepared to kill him.' The British law ignored it. 'The book has no place in a civilised society,' said Kalim Siddiqui in October 1989; 'this author and his book have got to go.' 'He is up for the high jump,' Siddiqui declared in February 1990; 'the *fatwa* and our presence in this country will keep Rushdie pinned down for the rest of his life,' he added in May 1992. Other statements in public of this kind, many of them promising the apostate a violent end, were allowed to pass.

A variety of reasons was adduced for turning a deaf ear to Muslim excess at the price of the rule of law. It was argued that a tradition of 'colourful rhetoric', however homicidal, must be allowed and, in a 'multi-cultural' society, lived with. Or, to proceed against an offended British Muslim temporarily beside himself with zeal would be to invite the prospect of further trouble from other British Muslims, likewise offended. Or, to light upon and punish one individual in the Muslim community for what all felt, and many said, would be to create the first British martyr of British Islam. English liberals might cite the refinements of John Stuart Mill on freedom of opinion, or the certitudes of George Orwell on freedom of speech, but neither was a match for the promptings of Koranic faith and the curses of the outraged. It was best, so the official view appeared to be, to let well alone.

But the incorrigibly alien, professing to be ready to kill the author of a novel, was arguably less serious a cultural adversary than the part-assimilated Muslim intellectual. An alienness which makes no bones about its distance from the values of the society it inhabits can be directly confronted and, if it comes to it, fought. The individual who combines knowledgeable admiration for, with suppressed resentment of, his adoptive home and culture is a potential challenge more redoubtable by far. Shabbir Akhtar, with a Cambridge philosophy degree and writing in *Muslim News* in January 1991, described the sequence of events in the Muslim pursuit of Rushdie as an 'episode in the insecure career of Western destiny and identity', both of which had been 'suddenly brought face to face with genuinely Islamic tempers of mind and devotion'. Salman Rushdie himself, Akhtar briskly declared, did not matter. Here, articulate reason, or seeming reason, eschewing the street-cries which demanded the burning or hanging of the author, appeared to move the argument to higher ground. 'Khomeini's edict,' the Cambridge man continued, 'was not against one self-indulgent novelist but rather against the civilisation that has historically supported many anti-Islamic excesses other than Rushdie's literary impudence. And how does one implement Khomeini's ruling?' Akhtar asked sardonically, but safely, in the pages of *Muslim News*. 'There are, sadly, technical difficulties in any attempt to execute the entire British literary establishment.'

The word 'sadly', however wicked, could be discounted as a mere flourish. Behind it, stood a partially-cultivated moral insouciance with which it is harder to treat than with the more obvious, and more innocent, diatribes of the zealot. Although sentenced to death, Rushdie, declared his fellow-Cambridge Muslim, did 'not matter'. Instead, a timely and merited blow had been struck by the Islamic 'temper of mind' against Western 'identity' and 'civilisation'. But 'technical difficulties' stood in the way of carrying out the Ayatollah's edict; Rushdie's execution was not that easy. At the same time, Akhtar went on in his article to insist, Islam was the 'intellectual religion *par excellence*'; it was, said Akhtar, a religion which knew the 'true value of the scholar's ink'. But earlier, to a different and largely non-Muslim readership, the same Akhtar (in the *Guardian* on 27 February 1989) had made no mention of the 'technical difficulties' which 'sadly' stood in the way of 'execut[ing] the entire British literary establishment'. For his *Guardian* audience, Akhtar had objected – in the measured tones of an adoptive English man-of-letters – that the 'prevalent image' of Islam as an 'anti-intellectualist creed' was 'one of the many ironies and paradoxes generated by the Rushdie episode'. With this degree of evasive sophistication, none could deal. Better a simple man's murderous oath than the philosophical countersigning of a death-warrant.

Akhtar was not alone. Non-Muslims, and in particular staunch believers of other faiths, found their own grounds for moral reproach of the author. Sometimes such reproach was severe, even where the critic might disapprove of sentencing a man to death for what he had written. No Voltaire, Michael Dummett, an Oxford professor of philosophy and devout Catholic, held it to be a 'disgusting thing to defile what other men regard as holy'. The Archbishop of Canterbury, Dr George Carey, finding that *The Satanic Verses* 'contained an outrageous slur on the Prophet', could 'well understand' the 'devout Muslim's reaction' to it; Billy Graham, the American evangelist, 'sympathised' with Muslim protests against Rushdie's work; Cardinal Decourtray of Lyons, distinguished for his ecumenism towards the Jews, thought the book an 'offence against religious faith'. The former American president, Jimmy Carter, agreed: *The Satanic Verses* was an 'arrow pointed at religion in general'. The book was declared to be 'certainly a blasphemy' by Kurt Waldheim, the president of Austria, passages in whose own life were a blasphemy beyond the reach of any Rushdie.

In Britain, from right and left, and even in the centre, sentiments were heard which in their own ways fanned the flames set burning beneath the author by an Ayatollah. Lord Dacre, the Tory historian, violently declared in writing that he 'would not shed a tear if some British Muslims, deploring [Rushdie's] manners, should waylay him in a dark street and seek to improve them'; the voice of the mob, with a genteel Scots accent. Norman Tebbit, the right-wing British politician, called the author an 'outstanding villain' and 'the world's richest multiple renegade'. (References were frequent, among Rushdie's critics in Britain, to the money he had earned from his best-seller). He was, said Tebbit with considerable spleen, 'an unwelcome, impertinent, whining guest', with a record of 'despicable acts of betrayal of his upbringing, religion, adopted home and nationality', the latter an allusion to Rushdie's past expressions of hostility to Thatcherite Britain. The lawyer and civil libertarian, Francis Bennion, described him as 'not worth defending' after his seeming 'conversion' to Islam. John Berger, a Marxist (or former Marxist) writer and a Jew, accused Rushdie of 'irresponsibility' and of 'playing at being God' in his 'arrogant fiction'.

But 'playing at being God', far from being aberration, is the common currency both of religion and irreligion. It provides the impulse for every construction of a political utopia and guides the pen of every writer of fiction. God, in one form or another – from the sublime to the ridiculous – is a familiar figure as an adoptive persona. An Ayatollah, a Pope, an Archbishop or a Chief Rabbi can not only think themselves to be God's messengers or apostles, but, if sufficiently encouraged by others, invest themselves with the very divinity they worship. The 'little man' too, even without the formal trappings of the godhead, may fancy himself to be blessed, and capable of bestowing blessings – moral and practical – upon others, even if it only be upon his immediate family members. It was in the name of God, in whatever shape or form, that most moral and political philosophies had their first founding. And it was in the name of God, in our own times, that Catholic Christendom pitched itself into the battle with communism as if the mediaeval wars of religion were unfinished. The revival of Islam's pride and the overweening claims made on behalf of the humble story-teller's art had God about them in similar fashion; but there was no 'playing at God' as effective as that of Pope Wojtyla in Eastern Europe.

The latter's achievements were substantial both in religious and worldly political terms. By October 1990 even the Soviet Union had divested the state of its right, or duty, to 'propagate atheism' and had restored its citizens' religious freedom. (Gorbachev himself was a baptised Christian.) The religious revival had been under way in Eastern Europe and the Soviet Union for a decade and longer; now it began to reap its particular fruits. In Poland, in western Ukraine, in Czechoslovakia, in the Baltic States – but not in Hungary or East Germany – the Catholic church had served as a focus of resistance to communism's ideological pretensions. By extension, it was seen to be the defender, bold or patient, not merely of faith but of civic liberty in general. And at communism's toppling fall, it was the Church which stood in many countries of Eastern Europe as a symbol, even *the* symbol, of national revival. In East Germany, however, where roughly half the population was Catholic, the Roman Church ('we did not believe in demonstrations') was little inspired by a Polish Pope's example, and played only a small part in the 1989 upheaval. Here East German Protestants led the religious way. In Leipzig and other East German cities, their church premises became the Jacobin clubs of the revolution.

Just as Coptic Christianity in Armenia had been felt by generations of the faithful to bar the way to Islam, so Polish Catholicism, in particular, had for decades squared its shoulders to state Marxism; and in Poland, communism's ravages had failed to pick the Church's bones clean or chase its congregations into the Party. Some churches, however

– in particular, the Orthodox Church in Russia, in Romania and in Bulgaria, although not in Georgia – played a largely compliant role in such trials of faith. There were many hierarchies (Catholic, Protestant, Jewish, Muslim) which rendered little to God and a great deal to their local Caesars. In April 1988, the Romanian Baptist Assembly, for instance, in a telegram to Nicolae Ceausescu, declared its 'love, esteem, and gratitude to the genial builder of modern Romania'. In November 1989, a month before Ceausescu's execution, Patriarch Teoctist of the Romanian Orthodox Church fulsomely congratulated the dictator on his 're-election' as Party leader. Cardinal Lekai of Budapest, the Chief Rabbi of Romania, the Grand Mufti of Sofia – there were many others – each in his own way did much to sustain regimes which harassed and stifled faith and the faithful. In Bucharest, Ceausescu had destroyed a dozen churches, two monasteries, a synagogue and almost the entire Jewish quarter of the city to build his gargantuan People's Palace. Everywhere, especially in the regimes' early years, priests (and nuns) had been set to hard labour, mortified and even executed. In Albania, as the regime collapsed, Tirana's Orthodox cathedral, turned into a sports hall by Enver Hoxha, reopened, and priests reappeared who had been in jail for twenty-five years. Where faith had proved incorrigible and ineradicable, communist parties had also placed their own hirelings in the pulpit; the KGB had Russian Orthodox priests on its payroll.

For decades, there had been much for the religious to endure and most of it was borne in silence. But it was in the name of endurance, too, that many clerics, bowing simultaneously to the Will of God and the Will of the Party, had long ago made their peace with the Devil. As the Devil had relented, backing away in most countries from state-imposed atheism at an early stage of the final revolutionary crisis, many priests who had pursued a policy of accommodation with local regimes were to be heard claiming vindication for their years of pious acquiescence. Long-standing secular dissenters, as in Hungary, knew better; there, disillusion with the Church matched disillusion with the Party. Elsewhere, church-going, where permitted at the worshipper's own risk, had for some been as much an act of political defiance as of true faith. After the revolutions, with the ends of defiance secured, the churches would lose part of their congregations. This was so even in devout Poland, where 96 per cent of the population counted themselves as Catholic by faith, if not by constant observance.

The Western left, as well as the ideologues of the communist regimes, had their own simple equations between religion and obscurantism, and (latterly) between religious revival and the return of 'reaction'. They could understand little of religious impulses, nor contemplate – without private disdain – the act of worship as an aspect itself of the 'return to normal'. Yet, the force of religious affiliation would not be gainsaid; it swept, or helped to sweep, all disparagement before it. The priest re-emerged from the shadows, swinging his censer, and choirs recovered their voices. The faithless might jeer, or look on in huddled bemuse-ment, but expression of religious feeling quickly regained its ancient composure. 'As soon as the sheet of ice which has been put over everything cracks, the mammoth comes alive,' Eric Hobsbawm sardoni-cally declared. But the suggestion that the revival of faith was a mere resurfacing, in a hail of ice-age gravel, of primordial instinct was the old left's customarily simplifying imposture. (The unspoken and false premise of it was that base instinct was one thing, and socialist reason another.) Instead, the cause of religion in Eastern Europe became, in a revolutionary decade, a determining political issue. It stood not only for the raising of a Lazarus from the dead, but for pluralism of affiliation; not only for the darkness of a clerisy reborn – as the left would see it, by intellectual reflex – but for the return of a nation's traditions to the light of day.

The most active single instrument of the crusade for Christian restoration in the lands which communism was vacating was the Polish Pope Wojtyla. As the secular priests of Marxism-Leninism gave up the ghost, new cardinals and bishops – in Czechoslovakia and Romania, as well as in Vietnam and China – took their places on the moral and ideological thrones of flagging communist nations. In Poland, as the red flag was lowered, the red hat reoccupied, or sought to reoccupy, the state's inner sancta. East European countries one by one re-established diplomatic relations with the Vatican, as they did also with Israel. The Ukrainian Catholic church, forcibly merged with Russian Orthodoxy by Stalin, was restored. Ancient Catholic archdioceses, such as that of Lvov, now found themselves bisected by, and pushing against, modern state frontiers; old conflicts between the Latin and Greek rites, Catholic and Uniate, revived, as if they had never been stifled. Religious liberty and political convulsion reunited the German Protestant church and (briefly) led Lutheran pastors into government office. It permitted Jews to leave Albania, and even brought the Moonies' leader, Reverend Sun Myung Moon, to a meeting with Gorbachev in the Kremlin. In ways which had become unfamiliar to Eastern Europe, Christian moralities also quickly made a public reappearance. Thus, the East German Protestant church, to general indignation, gave refuge in January 1990 to the fallen East German leader, Erich Honecker, upon his conditional release from detention on charges of treason and corruption. 'The Protestant church,' said a spokesman, 'has always tried to be a voice for the dumb and the weak. Now he, too, is among the weak.'

But it was Papal Catholicism, Polish both in spirit and in fact, which did most to arouse and direct the ardour of a popular Christian revival; the Vatican had had the great foresight, in 1978, to elect as its *pontifex maximus* a cardinal from Krakow. By 1979 Wojtyla had made his first pilgrimage to Poland as Pope and addressed millions of the faithful. Within a year Polish Solidarity had thrown down its historic gauntlet to Warsaw. A year later, an assassin, allegedly set to the task by the Bulgarian security services on the KGB's behalf, attempted to kill the Pope in St Peter's Square. His progress, and the progress of the Church's ideological confrontation with the battered regimes of Eastern Europe, was not checked. The Pope urged Solidarity on after its first failure; expressed his support for the self-determination of the formerly Catholic nations of the communist empire; and repeatedly proclaimed, with unshakeable faith or prophetic superstition, that at the time of the Bolshevik Revolution the Portuguese Virgin of Fatima had predicted the ultimate 'conversion of Russia'. In June 1991, the Pope announced Russia's coming spiritual rebirth to a vast crowd at Bialystok on the Polish-Lithuanian border, scene of past pogroms. In August 1991, he offered immediate moral sympathy to Gorbachev, as the leaders of the coup against him placed him under house arrest in the Crimea. In the same month, he spoke of his 'closeness' to embattled Catholic Croatia, but not to Orthodox Serbia.

This was much more than the spiritual shepherding of his flock. The Pope, during the historic decade in which communism had come to grief, had been a main actor in its drama and dénouement: a protagonist, not a witness. Lech Walesa, above all, had been the Pope's political right arm in Poland. Once the ground of communism had begun to quake in earnest, the shipyard worker became something more than a mere *amicus curiae* for the Bishop of Rome. From his proletarian days of agitation in Gdansk to his (no less proletarian) entry into the presidential palace, Walesa had openly declared his fealty to his Polish brother. 'I'll do anything not to disappoint the Pope,' Walesa exclaimed in November 1990, during his presidential campaign. In February 1991, the new president of Poland made a state visit to the Vatican – the first foreign journey of his presidency – in order to 'bring thanks for everything which the Polish people owes your holiness'. 'Jesus Christ be praised!' he declared, as the Pontiff, raised to the near-divine by the Gdansk worker's obeisances, took his hand. It was a redolent moment not only in Polish history but in the revived history of Christendom in Europe; the symbolic moment of communism's defeat by an alliance of prelate and proletarian.

Its outcome in Poland was, for some, discomfiting. In compensation for 'atheistic communism's' moral depredations, the church girded its loins to the old anti-secularist fray. It sought, above all, to drive the anti-Christ from the classroom and the maternity clinic. Thus, Polish Catholic bishops fought hard, or too hard, to make abortion a crime in a nation where prior to communism's fall 600,000 Polish women a year had had resort to it, and where, after the fall, abortion remained legal and freely available. Bills to criminalise abortion, to permit abortion and to call a referendum on abortion came before the Polish parliament. In February 1991, a Church-sponsored bill to ban abortion even in cases of pregnancy following rape or incest was rejected; in July 1992, a bill making doctors who performed abortions liable to up to two years' imprisonment was passed by a large majority at first reading. Pastoral letters warned of the 'mortal sins' which attended the taking of unborn life; but only 11 per cent of Poles, it was said in March 1992, were persuaded. (A deputy minister of health, Kazimierz Kapera, was even opposed to contraception and, like the Imam of Cairo, pronounced homosexuals to be 'deviants', although he stopped short – being a Christian – of urging that they be killed.) Nor did Poland's bishops hesitate, as in the elections of October 1991, to declare from the pulpit that the newly-democratised 'mandate of believers' should go only to those candidates who stood for the 'defence of human life from the moment of conception'. Uneasy memories stirred over these priestly pleas for the 're-moralisation' of Poland's 'social and political life' and at clerical intrusion into the interstices of daily existence. The period during which the Church had stood, sometimes alone, in opposition to communist rule began to appear, even to some priests, as a simple and obstinate golden age; Poland's pre-communist anti-clerical tradition was also aroused. Opinion polls in 1991 found that as many as two-thirds of all Poles wanted the Church's influence in public life 'limited'; some post-communist neo-democrats, often communists in all but name, began stridently calling for the church to 'keep out' of politics altogether. On his return to Poland in June 1991, the Pope himself was driven to disclaim any 'tendency' on the part of the Church to 'take over any sector of public life which does not belong to it'. Yet, on this same visit, the Pope, celebrating high mass at Koszalin for 30,000 officers and men of Poland's armed forces – there had been an earlier 'military pilgrimage' in October 1990 to the shrine of the Black Madonna in Czestochowa – described the Poles as having been 'always a nation of knights'.

The Jew, among others, might look upon this kind of Wagnerian flourish, more Gothic than Catholic, with early foreboding. The sombre Central European tones in which the Pope, during a visit to Prague in April 1990, had described communism as a 'tragic utopia' were evidently capable of darkening further; a history of suffering, foreign imposition, hatred, faith, mass murder and thwarted national aspiration were the black ground of Polish thought and endeavour. When Catholic conservatives, of whom the Pope was the exemplar, expressed the belief that Poland had a 'mission' to 're-Christianise the spiritually impover-ished West', the Jew might tremble. A call for a 'return to Poland's Christian roots' and its 'Christian-oriented traditions' meant not the resurrection of the rabbinic Galilean, but the reappearance of the Slavic knight-errant in a horned helmet. In Moscow, too, a drawing of a mediaeval knight, together with a banner in the black, gold and white of the Tsarist imperial state, provided the back-cloth to a meeting in February 1992 of right-wing 'patriotic forces', at which 'Zionism' was accused of being the source of Russia's problems.

At Wloclawek, in June 1991, the Pope declared not only that the 'true sources of European culture' lay in 'Christendom' but that these sources were 'created by the ancient and modern martyrs'; an Iranian cleric might see Islam in such terms also. The Greek philosopher and poet, the Roman soldier and jurist, the Judaic moralist and prophet, and a host of martyrs other than the saints of the Catholic *ecclesia* had simply vanished in the land of Auschwitz. 'Poland, of course, is a Christian society,' said the faithful Walesa, echoing his master's voice, 'and must be fashioned according to the fundamental moral values of Christianity.' Poland's 3 million Jews, lost in the charnel-house, might never have existed.

An intendedly elevating morality was being planted, or re-planted, in a dark soil. Old spiritual values were being newly proclaimed in the name not of a true catholicism of spirit, but of a 'united Christian Europe' and a 'unified Christian continent'; both phrases recurred frequently in the Pope's homilies and speeches. 'Must not the salvation

Christ has given us be again spread to the furthest bounds of Europe?'
asked the Pope at Trausdorf on the Austrian-Hungarian border. It was
essentially the same question as was put, even more imperatively, to the
Shi'a clergy by Khomeini, of the Teachings of the Prophet. These were
in each case warrior accents, but fitting enough in a crusade for moral
virtue. Pressed into the service of the 'Muslim nation' and 'European
Christian culture', their resonance was different. In the name of *fides
rediviva*, the Pope accused contemporary Western Europeans of 'wal-
lowing in sensuality' and, again, of betraying 'true European culture'.
So might, and did, the imams speak of the 'decadence' of the West. 'All
these comforts in the sensual realm,' the Pope declared, 'in sexual life,
in the pursuit of various pleasures and all sorts of lust, do not raise men
to Europeanism.' But this was the Europeanism not of the Hellene and
the Jew, nor of the European rationalist and the sceptic, but the
Europeanism of the conservative Christian-in-Europe; a different, even
if related, matter. 'I preach no message but the Gospel,' the Pope
explained in Finland, in June 1989. But the Gospel is silent upon the
'true values' of Europe.

In the moral confusion of communism's fall, the Pope restlessly beat
the bounds of the post-communist order, an order which he had done
as much as any individual to bring into being. In the rubble of the
'tragic utopia', he was quick to refuse endorsement to the new utopia of
the market. Instead, he warned against the 'vast atheist movement'
which, he said, was now attempting to build in Eastern Europe and the
former Soviet Union a 'new materialist society' on the ruins of the old;
he gave priority to the 'dignity of the person' over the claims of mere
'economic theory'. 'Christian Europe' responded to and echoed his
message, in whole or in part. The victorious Hungarian Democratic
Forum openly appealed to 'European Christian values' in the 1990
Hungarian general election. Liviu Petrina, one of the leaders of
Romania's National Peasants' Party, called for the 're-establishment in
Romania of Christian morality', adding that the 'morality of society'
came from 'Christian peasant stock'. Tadeusz Mazowiecki, a devout
Catholic who tended to resist such invocations – and lost his presidential
contest with Walesa, who did not – declared his 'great respect for
Christian ideas' but refused to 'convert [them] into a political programme'. Indeed, the Papal view of the 'true' nature of Central Europe
was both a divisive and shaping vision. 'There is a chasm', announced
an editorial in the *Independent*, in effect endorsing the Vatican's geo-
political outline of the future, 'between those countries whose experi-

ence lay within the boundaries of Christendom, and those whose cultural and political development was stunted by centuries of Ottoman rule.' In the first category the newspaper placed Czechoslovakia, East Germany, Hungary and Poland; Romania, Bulgaria and 'most of Yugoslavia' in the second.

Both the Christian and 'the Turk', symbol of Islam, had made a belated reappearance on the European stage. Indeed, with communism swept from the world scene, the Cross appeared to be staking its claim to the soul of the new Europe, presumably before the Jewish capitalist or the Muslim migrant could get his clutches on it. Russia's 'European past', declared the right-wing (ex-left) English Catholic journalist Paul Johnson, could be recovered by 'allowing the Christian religion once more to occupy the forefront of life'. Russia, said Johnson, over-simplifying, was 'at heart a profoundly Christian country', and 'Christian consciousness' her 'chief title-deed to her European status'. In June 1991, the Pope (playing at God) chose Warsaw, a city haunted by the ghosts of Christ's own people – the Jews – to proclaim the Christian alone as the true spokesman of the 'values and traditions that once shaped Europe'. The same values betrayed, and the same traditions maintained, had not only dealt out murder to millions, but murder under the supervision of unknown numbers of the baptised, the Catholic faithful included.

The Pope, lost in a particular moral darkness which could never be dispelled, now attempted to address the issue in whose shadow the dilemmas of post-communism could seem the puniest of matters, and which had put 'European civilisation' itself into question. The attempt failed. A Polish pastoral letter of January 1991 had expressed a somewhat vague 'regret' for 'all cases of anti-semitism which were committed at any time or by anybody on Polish soil'. Six months later, at Radom – some one hundred miles from Oswiecim, or Auschwitz – the Pope himself struggled with the Holocaust, and lost, banally likening it to that 'vast cemetery of the unborn', as he put it, whose lives had been claimed by abortion; and repeated the morally maladroit analogy, despite Jewish protests. (In November 1991, Filipino officials, no wiser, described deaths in a typhoon as 'like the Holocaust'.) In Wadowice, the Pope's birthplace, he made a passing reference to its former Jewish community, describing it merely as 'not with us any more'; the fact of mass murder was avoided. Such obliqueness was a familiar symptom (to Jews) of moral failure. Indeed, the benign vacuity of 'not with us any more' might be thought to point into a spiritual abyss, as profound as that left behind by the Polish communism whose wake he was attending.

Awkwardly caught up in a tacky – or ungodly – web made in part of his own spinning, and further assailed for it, he now called for a 'special effort' from the Polish Church to 'overcome the damaging stereotypes and established pattern of prejudices [as to the Jews] still lingering here and there'. But although the 'stereotypes' and 'prejudices' to which the Pope referred might have their own moral importance, only a handful of Poland's Jews had survived, and remained in the country, to be 'damaged' by them. For a Pope spiritually to disengage, or appear to disengage, from the oblivion of millions no longer 'with us' was of another order; it might make even the angels in heaven, they too with Jewish names, weep out loud. But Pope Wojtyla was not alone. Auschwitz had been described since July 1947, under communist decree, as a monument to the 'martyrdom of the Polish and of other nations'. (But then 'Jew' and 'Jewish' are difficult words to utter, including for some Jews themselves.) It was a similar spiritual blindness which had for so long dictated the Vatican's 'non-recognition' of Israel, the same 'Israel' which is at the heart of Christian prayer. Proposals to 'normalise relations' were announced in July 1992, but the country of Christ was one of the few which, by self-denying ordinance, the Pope had been unable to visit.

The Jews' historic refusal to acknowledge a fellow Jew as the Son of God has had a long coda, with murder one of its principal themes. Yet, the accusation that the Jews 'killed Christ', a false accusation which underlay much of this murder, was always at odds with the heart of the Christian message itself; that Christ 'laid down his life for others'. But it was on this dire battlefield that the 'Jewish problem' was created and the hosts of its victims, physical and moral, fell. They were not all Jews, even if it was most often the Jews who would lose their lives and possessions, and the non-Jews (and anti-Jews) their souls. Indeed, even Popes can appear to lose their ethical way when the subject at issue is the Jews. For Pope Pius XII to have kept silent while Jews were being herded into a building off St Peter's Square on their journey to the death-camps was, after all, sin, for which (according to Christian moral design itself) he would ultimately have to answer. For the Vatican to have helped leading Nazi war-criminals reach sanctuary in South America – admitted by Cardinal Franz König in January 1988 – was likewise sin. It was sin, too, and in Christian terms, for the French Catholic church to have given protection and shelter for more than forty

years (in a succession of Benedictine abbeys, including the Grande
Chartreuse) to Paul Touvier, sentenced to death in absentia for war-
crimes as Lyons Milice chief. At the same time it was possible to see, if
the matter was considered with care, that much of this sin was almost
helpless. Wickedness committed against Jewish 'others' – whether
perceived as less than human, more than human, or merely different –
may seem, to the morally astigmatic, less heinous than it is; to the
morally blind, no crime at all. Popes are not exempt from this moral
law, or any other.

Historically, or in the first instance, the 'Jewish problem' was a
problem identified by non-Jews to be so. That is, the Jews were felt by
non-Jews to be a 'problem' when the latter contemplated the objects of
their interest, hostility, or obsession. This 'problem', in which the Jews
stood at the centre of varying concerns about them on the part of non-
Jews, was thence transmitted to Jews in the form of consequences which
the latter have had perennially to suffer. Of the antiquity of the
'problem' there can be no doubt: the First Epistle of St Peter describes
the Jews as 'an holy nation, a peculiar people'. Sometimes sufficient
in its intensity (as I have already suggested) to throw the most
compassionate of Christians and the most all-merciful of Muslims into
moral confusion, the idea of Jewish particularity has dogged every Jew's
footsteps. The Jews themselves have the most vivid sense of such
particularity, and Mosaic authority (they believe) to sustain it. But no
Jewish feeling of divine appointment or elect virtue can match the pains
of being singled out as an object of special preoccupation, let alone of
odium or obsession. Moreover, the peculiar judgment of the Jew as a
'problem' does moral harm to those whose perceptions come to be
governed by it. 'Christian love' can be brought to dust when an
exception is made of the Jew (as a Jew); the Muslim zealot can be
driven to break the Koranic injunction to respect the religion of others
when he basely stoops to make all Jews the target of his angers; the
Vatican can flout the law of nations in order to single out the 'Jewish
state' for denial of recognition.

Such dislocations of response can also aggrandise the labour and
thoughts of some 15 million Jews into aspirations for 'world conquest'.
A Middle Eastern nation the size of Wales or Denmark, and with a
smaller population than Switzerland's, can be turned into a Goliath; the
ordinary Jew going about the business of life into a species of centaur.
If there were 1,000 million Jews in forty-five different nations, many of
those nations almost wholly Jewish, as there are Muslims and Muslim

nations, and if Judaism's leaders were with fiery declamation urging a Talmudic order upon an exhausted planet, a 'Jewish problem' might then be said to exist. But it is not so. Nevertheless, such a problem is thought to exist, and the thought of it has continued to be father to many deeds, large and small, whose pretexts (as ever) continually vary. In the post-Nazi era, it is less the Jews as such than Israel, and Israel's existence in the Middle East, which have become the main focus of an old preoccupation. At its heart, there stands not so much the fate of the Palestinians – over which, despite their plight, the world is relatively little concerned – as the 'problem', once more, of the Jews. 'In the Palestinian issue,' Ali Khamenei, Khomeini's successor, declared in June 1990, disclosing where preoccupation lay, 'the goal is the obliteration of Israel.'

Direct expression of hostility to the Jew as Jew has been rendered morally awkward or unseemly (for most) by the memory of such hostility's Holocaust excesses. It can, however, be transposed, in reasonable moral comfort, from Judaism and the Jew to 'Zionism' and the Israeli. But some lack even these scruples. The fundamentalist Hamas movement, based in Gaza, called upon Arabs during the Gulf War to 'take up arms to kill the Jews'; in October 1991, its offshoot, Hizbollah-Palestine, declared 'killing the Jews' – and not merely the Israelis – to be 'the promise of God'. Or, as Islamic Jihad put it after the bombing of the Israeli embassy in Buenos Aires in March 1992, the 'war' against Israel would continue 'until Israel ceases to exist and until the last Jew in the world is eliminated'. Such animus has few bounds. 'Hit Israel with chemical weapons now!' shouted worshippers spilling out of Amman's mosques in January 1991 during the Gulf war; 'the [Scud] missiles soothed my heart,' said a Tunis schoolmaster of Saddam Hussein's bombardment of Israel. 'Allahu Akbar!' shouted the Palestinian, invoking the Almighty as he stabbed to death a randomly chosen Israeli bus passenger in December 1990.

This was to play at God in a most particular fashion, in which spleen and fervour, fixation and mission could between them distort judgment, promote hatred and justify every violence, post-Holocaust Jewish counter-violence included. Here, reason itself could be unhinged. Israel laid claim to an identity founded upon the Rock of Ages and a literal interpretation of the Bible, chapter and verse; but the Iraqi ambassador to London, Azmi Shafeeq, placed inverted commas around the very word 'Israel' when he wrote of it. While Jews asserted themselves in Judaea and Samaria as if under God's own command, President Hafiz

Assad of Syria, at a Ba'ath Party rally in Damascus in March 1990, declared that Israel should be subjected to a 'holy war as long as time'. Sheik Abdul-Karim Obeid, the fierce Shi'a cleric subsequently taken hostage by the Israelis, called from the pulpit for the 'expansion of the Islamic revolution and the destruction of Israel'. The Jews crowded to the Wailing Wall in January 1991 as the Gulf War became more intense, while *Al Qadissiya*, the authoritative Baghdad newspaper, looked forward to a 'new era, after we have completely annihilated the bastard entity of the Zionists.' 'Iraq and Palestine,' Yasser Arafat declared a few days later, 'will be together side by side, and after the great battle we will pray together in Jerusalem, God willing.'

God, however, was not willing, leaving all His gun-toting spokesmen, whether Arab or Jew, on their own racks. The former feels in his heart that the entire state of Israel is built upon 'holy Muslim soil'; to the latter, the same state is God-given and God-endowed. Moreover, the Jew, Zionist or non-Zionist, hostile or sympathetic to the Palestinian cause, harm-doing or peace-loving, believes he knows what all such declarations as those of an Assad, or an Arafat, or an Obeid have in mind. By conditioned reflex, and sometimes with hysteria, he links them historically to an unending chain of circumstance and tribulation. Knowing the past consequences to himself of old habits of palliation of the foe, he is now less prone to bend to the demands of others. From the massacre of the defenders of Masada nineteen hundred years ago to the missile attacks on Tel Aviv in the Gulf War, he sees only one great sequence and connection of assaults. When German neo-Nazi groups are trained at PLO camps in Lebanon, as they were reported to have been in the 1980s, he sees, or thinks he sees, an old nexus of evils; when the president of Austria is shunned for his Nazi past in the rest of Western Europe but received in the Vatican by the Pope and by Chancellor Kohl in Munich, and welcomed in Arab countries – in Kuwait as in Iraq, in Jordan as in Syria – the Jew draws his own conclusions.

In many non-Jews, the Jews' preoccupation with their own 'fate' evinces little sympathy and not much interest. It is the lot of all men to suffer; 'Jewish suffering' merits no greater privilege than the suffering of others. To insist upon the special status of Jewish griefs, as the Jews are widely perceived to do, is (for some) yet another ground for unease at Jewish pretension. It is even (for some) an 'explanation' of the suffering in the first place. Indeed, it is a common enough experience for a Jew to hear it said, or implied, that the Jews, by their own sense of

particularity, have 'invited' others to single them out for particular
attention, including the attention of the violent.

Moreover, few non-Jews can be expected to follow the path which
many Jews habitually take in their examination of the runes of daily life
for evidences of anti-Jewish odium. Should it be disclosed, as it has
been, that Libya has given funds not only to the IRA but to the British
National Front, the Jew will on the instant make the 'anti-semitic'
connection. If Russian Pamyat is shown, as it was in March 1990, to
have links with the KGB and the police, the Jew, at least, 'always knew
it'. Or if Vienna's Institute for Conflict Research should reveal, as it did
in July 1989, that '40 per cent' of Austrians are 'anti-semitic' – in
October 1991 '20 per cent' of Austrians even thought that the rights of
Jews in Austria should be restricted – the findings take their place for
the Jew in an established topography, which he carries about in his
head, of ill-feeling. 'Let them go to Alsace-Lorraine, let them go to
Alaska, let them go to the Baltic states, let them go to any of those
places, but we cannot accept Jews on our land' – meaning the land of
the 'Arab nation', comprising 14 million square kilometres from the
Gulf to the Atlantic – announced Colonel Gaddafi to the 1989 Belgrade
summit of the Non-Aligned Nations. The Jews, by ancestral habit,
make a mental note of it and (increasingly) stiffen their guards. They
generally expect non-Jews to take note of it, too; but, equally generally,
non-Jews do not. When even John Strugnell, the Harvard divinity
professor and at the time chief editor of the Dead Sea Scrolls, told an
Israeli newspaper in November 1990 that 'what bothers me about
Judaism is the very existence of the Jews', to non-Jews it might seem an
academic's *jeu d'esprit* or (at worst) 'in bad taste'. To Jews themselves, it
could sound like the distant echo of the trump of doom.

Such dichotomies of perception make mutual understanding between
Jew and non-Jew about the nature and significance of 'anti-semitism'
almost impossible to establish. Few Jews, including anti-Zionists, can
be convinced that anti-Zionism is not anti-semitism in thin disguise;
few non-Jews, including pro-Zionists, can conceal their impatience with
the Jewish habit of translating oppostion into 'prejudice' and criticism
into the hostility of the 'anti-semite'. Yet, no force on earth can now
stop a Jew hearing 'Jews to the ovens' even in a casual slight, let alone
in the grimmer forms of aspersion. To many non-Jews, however, the
Jew is not only flawed by his own 'racism', but is a 'touchy' or 'thin-
skinned' creature. 'If he were a man' he would take such blows as came
his way in more Job-like, or Christ-like, fashion. He would also allow

hostility to be either the effect of his co-religionists' own misconduct or, more vaguely, further evidence of the old Adam in all men. But such will as there is among Jews to make this leap of imagination – from seeing themselves as singled out, to seeing themselves as at one with others – is constantly held in check, or even set in reverse. The desecration of Jewish cemeteries from Carpentras in France to Oradea in Romania, from Edmonton in North London to Nitra in Slovakia, and from Naples to Buenos Aires, reminds all Jews of what they are. '*Sau Jud!*' was even written on Bertholt Brecht's grave in East Berlin's Chausseestrasse cemetery in May 1990, in the mistaken belief that he was a Jew. 'Bizarre,' said Alexander Koulakov, one of Pamyat's leaders, of the Carpentras outrage in May 1990, when the interred body of an old man was exhumed: 'You should take it out not on the dead but the living.'

The more extreme forms of response to the Jews – those which deal in the Jewish 'peril', the Jewish 'conspiracy' and so forth – also prevent many Jews from seeing the world with the modest equilibrium and rational goodwill which are expected of them, by friend and foe alike. The suggestion, taken from a sample extremist pamphlet, that 'the Jew dreams of world domination', or 'controls the financial and economic life of the world' – controls the press, too – or 'has the power to instigate crisis in order to ruin whole nations', presents the Jew to himself as a Titan. But many, and perhaps most, Jews, in their own distorting mirrors, see themselves (at their very grandest) as King Davids in a world of plebeian Goliaths. Often, they are in their own eyes mere pigmy figures among giants, and lamed in their possibilities by their Jewishness, rather than endowed by it with special opportunities of influence and power. Nevertheless, 'Jewish conspiracy' theories, in one version and another, are widespread. Nor are they confined to the leaflets of street paranoiacs, in which the Jews might be variously accused (in Poland in November 1990) of 'running the government', (in Moscow in May 1990) of 'causing shortages in the shops', (in New York in June 1990) of 'plotting the financial destruction of black people', and (in South Africa in March 1990) of 'creating the Aids virus'. Such aspersion has its polite forms and its impolite; expresses a variety of emotions from the fastidious to the thuggish and from outright dementia to discreet recoil; and works its influence both upon the members of clubs and upon the citizens of whole nations.

Even in Japan, where there are perhaps to be found 200 Jewish families in all, a spate of best-sellers – the most notorious of them by

Masami Uno, published in 1987 – assured the Japanese that there was a 'Jewish plot' to 'destroy Japan'. In New York, in June 1989, the spokesman of the 'rap group', Public Enemy, declared not only that the Jews were 'wicked' but that they had 'their hands right round Bush's throat'. In August 1990, an article in the British *Spectator* asserted that the communist takeover in Romania had been carried out by '1,100 Moscow-trained Romanians, 900 of whom were lapsed Jews'. At Czestochowa, in August 1989, Cardinal Josef Glemp declared (in a sermon) that the media 'in numerous countries' were 'totally at the Jews' disposal'. Six months later, President Assad of Syria was making a similar assertion. 'Zionism', often a synonym for Jews as such, was, he said, 'now active everywhere', 'infiltrating' the 'countries of the former Soviet bloc', its influence 'clear in the media' of the post-communist world. A Japanese writer, a black New York musician, a *Spectator* contributor, the primate of Poland and the president of Syria might agree on nothing else, but on 'Jewish power' they were at one.

Since the late nineteenth century, and especially in the Nazi 1930s, something called 'international Jewry' has been continuously held to be both the expression and instrument of Jewish aspiration for influence in the world, and even (in the wilder versions) 'world conquest'. To Hans Klein, Chancellor Kohl's chief spokesman, it was 'international Jewry' which in November 1989 had objected to Kohl's proposed visit to Auschwitz on the Jewish sabbath. According to the *Independent* in June 1990, Jacques Attali, a former adviser to the French President and a (Jewish) banker, was himself 'specially interested in the workings of international Jewry'. In the same month, Jean le Pen, the leader of the far-right French National Front, was charged with 'racial defamation' for accusing the same 'international Jewry' of sinister machinations against the 'interests of the nation'.

Such preoccupation with the imagined collective actions of Jews as Jews is a burden both for Jews and non-Jews. For both, it stands in the way of true judgment. It inextricably mixes fact with fancy, and (for both) places profanation of man and God – as when three-quarters of the Jews of Europe were annihilated – in the same scale with common-place human phobias and estrangements. That is, it makes too few of the discriminations which reason requires. It also makes it hard for Jews to distinguish between the freedom of opinion of others about them (as Jews) and evil intent. But this blindness of the Jews is, at its heart, due to larger causes. It is ultimately derived, whatever their own faults, from the unspeakable crimes committed against them, not as men or women but as Jews. Such crime is itself a burden; few can gain insight or elevation from the scrutiny of it. When Hitler declared, on 23 January 1942, that 'the Jews must clear out of Europe' and that 'if they refuse to go, I see no other solution but extermination', even the spirit of moral censure cannot easily follow. When he said, on 27 January 1942, 'where the Jews are concerned, I am devoid of all pity,' fear itself is halted in its tracks, frozen.

The Jew thinks he knows – and it may be so – that such pathological obsession with the Jews is not finally distinct from lesser-order preoccupations with the same subject. It is not necessary to agree that 'any and every nation which fails to exterminate the Jews in its midst will sooner or later finish by being itself devoured by them,' as Hitler put it on 31 August 1942, to hold the lesser-order view that Jews are 'active everywhere' in pursuit of their supposed interests as Jews. But the two views do not appear to a Jew to be as distinct, one from the other, as the non-Jew might wish. Nor are assertions, choosing at random from the British press, that the 'Jewish lobby' in the United States is 'omnipotent' (*Independent*, 13 September 1991), or that it has 'tentacles' (*Guardian*, 14 September 1991), or that the Jewish community of Nice is 'big, powerful, influential and vengeful' (*Guardian*, 27 September 1991), distinct enough from those of an age-old mania.

In the contest between rival notions of collusion and conspiracy, paranoia clearly plays the largest of parts. The extravagant fear, in some Jews, about the degree of collusion which exists between their foes, real and imagined, is matched by the equally extravagant fears of them which some non-Jews manifest. (For what else but fear is expressed in allegations of 'omnipotence', of 'mighty' lobbies with tentacular reach, and of 'vengefulness' combined with inordinate power?) History itself sometimes appears to conspire against the restoration of reason and balance. From year to year, trials of evil-doers, such as an Eichmann or a Barbie, have stirred buried memories and passions. Cases of gross financial malpractice involving Jews – a Robert Maxwell, for instance – fit a stereotype, or confirm an odium. A lingering process of Jewish reparation-seeking, or the discovery of the true biography of a public figure (a Waldheim, a Karajan), recall infamies partially forgotten, or renew perverse hostilities towards their victims. A voyeuristic, and even for a few nostalgic, interest in the old trappings of state sadism – its jackboots, its corpses, its other 'picturesque' relics – releases into today's air the grave-odours of the dead millions, for box-office and other types of commercial gain.

During the Gulf War, when Iraq appeared to threaten Israel with chemical and biological weapons, Germany, already accused of having contributed (with Brazil, among other nations) to Iraq's capacity to produce such weapons, attempted to come to Israel's aid. But it merely brought old Jewish antipathies and fears to the surface. 'Zyklon B – Mustard Gas – Nerve Gas – All Made by Germans for Jews' read a Tel Aviv street-banner, as the German foreign minister toured the sites of war damage.

Recurring accusations of Jewish collaboration in their own destruction, revisions of the facts of the Holocaust, and demands to 'draw a sponge across the crimes of the past' are paths to truth for some and profanations of truth for others. ('World Jewry,' complained the Croatian leader, Franjo Tudjman, in 1989, 'still has the need to recall its "holocaust".') Similarly, the placing of a Carmelite convent in an outbuilding of Auschwitz was desecration to the Jews, a sacramental act to its proponents. Again, the continuing of war-crime trials was for some the prosecution of the cause of justice, the pursuit of Jewish 'revenge' for others; for some, the upholding of the rule of law ('murder is murder'), for others its betrayal in a welter of unreliable testimony and unholy emotion. 'Unless you are a Jew,' declared the then British Home Secretary, David Waddington, in October 1990, when a bill to permit the prosecution of alleged Nazi war-criminals resident in Britain was being debated, 'it's very, very difficult to get inside the thing.' 'It was a long time ago,' said Viscount Whitelaw.

To most Jews, this insensate taking of a moral distance from murder – and genocidal murder at that – is incomprehensible and wicked, or a 'playing at God' which denies God and flouts the rule of law. But, at the very last, it is also taken for granted by many Jews. Moreover, it serves to justify in the eyes of the toughest-minded whatever moral or even violent intransigence they believe to be required in their own behalfs. If an official publication even of the Palestinian Red Crescent should deny, as was the case in December 1990, that Nazis murdered Jews in the gas chambers, then – the unspoken Jewish argument now often runs – so be it: obduracy of one kind will be met by obduracy of another. If Georges Montaudon's notorious *How to Recognise a Jew* is once more on sale on French bookstands; if a card-file census of all Paris Jews originally compiled under Gestapo instructions is revealed (as it was in November 1991) to be still in use; if a Paris appeal court rules, as it did in April 1992, that Paul Touvier, the Lyons Milice chief, should not stand trial on charges of crimes against humanity; or if

David Irving, the far-right British historian, declares, as he did in June 1989 in the *Leuchter Report*, that the 'infamous gas chambers of Auschwitz, Treblinka and Majdanek did not exist ever, except, perhaps, as the brainchild of Britain's brilliant Psychological Warfare Executive', then the Jews, so many Jews think, must give no quarter in the defence of their own interests as Jews.

The grounds for such obstinacy do not grow any less plain. At the Stuttgart trial in June 1991 of Josef Schwammberger, a Nazi camp commandant, young neo-Nazis outside the court shouted insults at the arrival of Simon Wiesenthal, the Jewish Nazi-hunter. In December 1991, a Bratislava poll indicated that 20 per cent of Slovaks did not want a Jew as a neighbour, and that 60 per cent thought the Jews 'had too much power'; one in five Austrians thought Austria would be 'better off without any Jews at all'. Video hate-games of German and Austrian manufacture, and in which the players may, for example, enact the roles of camp managers supervising the gassing of prisoners, were said during 1991 to be clandestinely in circulation in Europe. In April 1992, a Moscow synagogue was fire-bombed, causing serious damage. A super-market complex, including a shopping centre, restaurant, car showroom and tax-office, was built, despite vehement protests, on the site of the Ravensbrück concentration camp, where some 90,000 women died; even Belsen was daubed with neo-Nazi graffiti on New Year's Eve of 1991–92. If the Jew grits his teeth at all this, and vows to let few threats to him pass, he also ties a Gordian knot tighter, in which anti-Jewish (and anti-human) offence is met with Jewish aggression, as in the Middle East, and the aggression offends further. This is no longer the offence given by the 'greasy, mean Jew with bad manners', as a letter thought fit for publication in the *Independent* in August 1989 put it, but it is Jewish offence for all that. When Lord Denning (in August 1990) described Sir Leon Brittan, the former Tory cabinet minister, as a 'German Jew telling us what to do with our English law', it was a vulgarity of classical, but small, proportion; when 5 million Israeli Jews seek to tell 170 million Arabs what to do with their hostility to the state of Israel, it is a *casus belli*, or *bellorum*.

Most of this cannot be undone. Now, the Arab 'infiltrator' into Israel, with a gun in his hand, murder in his mind, and sometimes the Koran in his knapsack, encounters (among others) the armed Jewish zealot, with the book of Genesis on his lips and anti-Arab phobias to his nerve-ends. The Church of Rome's anti-communist crusade, which helped bring down an empire, drew gunfire even to the basilica of St Peter.

Jewish fundamentalists speak of the 'Kingdom of Israel' as 'the land which God gave Abraham', re-proclaiming their prescriptive right to the occupied territories of 'Judaea and Samaria' in the accents of the Prophets; Islamic militants invest their struggle to oust the Jew from the 'Holy Land' with, in turn, a holy and killing ardour. Since 1978 Pope Wojtyla has in his turn winged his way about the planet, in the name of the Cross, taking the salute of the faithful (from his bullet-proof Popemobile) in a battle for souls which has owed as much to Von Clausewitz as to the gospels. 'Playing at God' has become both a worldly and a worldwide business.

The Hebraic ingathering, or Aliyah, of the diaspora 'exile', including tens of thousands of Soviet Jews, is interpreted by the Jews both as the fulfilment of a bibilical vision and as the prelude to a miraculous 'final redemption' of Israel. By most Muslims it is seen as a further wicked encroachment upon Muslim land and the 'Arab nation'. The rest of the world, if it notices it at all, observes only another column of refugees proceeding from one place in order to arrive at another. Some, contemplating the migrations and associations of Jews, perceive race not faith to be their organising principle – only in December 1991 was 'Zionism' held by the United Nations to be no longer definable as a 'form of racism' – while many Jews are prone to see race not truth in all 'Gentile' objection to their conduct. But just as the word 'Jew' is, for some, a hard word to pronounce, so too, for others, is 'Gentile'. Indeed, both words signify, for Jews and non-Jews alike, mutual exclusion as well as difference. Although the latter is in origin Latin, not Hebrew, and was first applied to 'non-Jews' by the Romans – the nearest Hebrew word to it means 'stranger' – the term 'Gentile', for a Jew, still marks a boundary of race and of race-feeling, as well as of religion. 'Ye shall not eat anything that dieth of itself [sc. of natural causes],' pronounces the *Book of Deuteronomy*, of the categories of food fit and unfit to be eaten by Jews. But it need not be wasted. 'Thou shalt give it unto a stranger that is in thy gates that he may eat it,' the Jew is instructed, 'or thou mayest sell it unto an alien: for thou art an holy people unto the Lord thy God.'

To some, such discrimination is the ground of a justified anti-semitism, to others merely the sociologist's mark of 'belonging' and 'culture'; one man's prejudice may be another man's tradition. Yet, not even in biblical times was the strongest of all race taboos among the Jews, that against 'inter-marriage', strictly observed. King David, king of the Jews, was himself said to be of Moabite, not Hebrew, origin and married Bathsheba, a Hittite. Even Abraham, Jewish patriarch of patriarchs, 'went in unto' Hagar, his wife's Egyptian maidservant, who bore him a 'non-Jewish' son, Ishmael. The physical variety of Jewish appearance in the modern period, and (often) the indistinguishability of Jews from the rest of the population in the countries where they happen to be, testify, among other things, to a much greater degree of past 'inter-marriage' than has been generally acknowledged. As early as 1910, in Prussia, Austria and Hungary – heartlands of Jewish settlement in Central Europe – a quarter of all marriages involving Jews, and even more in such cities as Berlin and Hamburg, were 'mixed marriages'. (By 1900 the figure had reached 80 per cent in Denmark.) Despite it, from the destruction of the Second Temple in 70 A.D. to the annihilations of the Second World War, and beyond, the Jews have continued to be considered and to consider themselves the 'peculiar people' of St Paul's Epistle.

Today, the centre of gravity of the 'Jewish problem' has shifted from the diaspora to Israel. The focus of much old hostility and preoccupation has become concentrated upon a small territorial target – no more than an enclave in relation to the land-masses around it – and a small, but nuclear-armed, Jewish population. Here, the sense of the differences between, as well as the proximity of, three of the world's great faiths has sharpened. In one place, Jerusalem, so billions of the faithful variously believe, stood the Ark of the Covenant, the Cross of the Crucifixion, and the sacred point of the Prophet's Ascension into Heaven. It is a place which has the makings of a Golgotha for all, or one holy city. Here, priests, imams and rabbis, many of whom now play God's role in violent wildernesses of their own part-making, might, in their separately pacific ways, worship their gods, or God, together. Instead, Zion stands exclusively for Jewish restoration; Jerusalem is Islam's very own city, and no other's: Christianity, with a Jew as its saviour, pretends to be *primus inter pares*. Most Arabs (and even some Jewish messianists) will not accept the idea of a 'Jewish state' at all; most Jews cannot accept that the Arabs are equally semite; most Christians, *de haut en bas*, regard Jewish-Arab hostilities as a desecrating intrusion upon a private holy of holies.

Israeli leaders and their Jewish supporters consider the 'protection of the Jews' from their local foes to be their first duty. Palestinian leaders regard the recovery of their homeland, which some Jews dispute to be so, as a sacred obligation. To the Jews of Israel, it is the multiple mutual hostilities of the Arab nations which have helped to preserve them from destruction; to the Arab, it is opposition to Israel which is the cause-of-causes for the 'Arab nation'. Arab 'rejectionists' refuse all idea of negotiation with Israel; Israel's 'hardliners' reject all notion of compromise with the Arabs. The harshest critics of Israel see it as a 'brutal and expansionist society', an 'alien client state sustained by the world Zionist movement', or even, in the words of Crispin Tickell, former British ambassador to the United Nations, a 'poisoned splinter in the body corporate of the Middle East'. The harshest critics of the Arabs maintain the European colonial tradition of seeing as ignoble most that the Arabs do.

Between those who perceive Israel to be 'the Jews' last refuge', and those for whom Zionism is the right arm of Jewish world-conquest, there can plainly never be accord. Nor can there be identity of purpose between Jews who consider themselves to be 'citizens of the world', and Jews who consider themselves to be a race apart, with a private sense of obligation. As to the latter, from the time of Josephus, the Jewish historian of the first century A.D., there is record – as in his *Contra Apion* – of the objection of others to the religious non-assimilation of the Jews. To Marx, the Jew 'fancies himself justified in separating himself from humanity ... and waits on a destiny that has nothing in common with the destiny of mankind as a whole'. If so – and it is part-true and part-false, like every other socialist and Marxist theorem – the Jews have paid a high price for it. But then faith and loyalty to tradition are exacting; indeed, most Jews find true observance too demanding. Nevertheless, there are few Jews, 'assimilated' as may be, who can detach themselves from identification with Jewish fate and circumstance.

There are also few Jews who do not manifest an uneasy combination of a sense of superiority and a sense of disadvantage; few who do not feel at home everywhere, and many who feel at home nowhere. Despite the self-pity of Job and the lamentations of Jeremiah, however, the Jew can rarely be brought to accept that the divine scheme of things includes an already-written prospectus for the world's and his own utter desolation. On the contrary, despite the intense appeal, to the Jew, of a pessimism of spirit, there is also a paradoxical predisposition in most Jews to think it a 'blessing to be born'. Such a contradiction is expressed in the *Book of Ecclesiastes*. 'Whatsoever thy hand findeth to do,' the preacher enjoins, 'do it with thy might; for there is no work ... in the grave, whither thou goest.' This is the archetypal Jewish voice of obligation and despair. Only in the making of intellectual order – by interpretation, intercession and prophecy – can such despair be over-come, and obligation be discharged. But in each case Jewish intellectual presumption threatens. Indeed, from Moses to Christ, and Christ to Marx, it is in the ambitions of Jewish prophecy that there has been the most persistent of all 'playing at God'.

After 2,000 years of it we are no nearer redemption than ever.

SEVEN

Primum Mobile

The energy of human aspiration is the *primum mobile* of the social order. Lack of such energy is its *vis inertiae*. De Tocqueville, visiting the fledgeling United States, described the 'feverish impatience' with which 'all democratic communities are agitated.' But it was an impatience which in turn engendered a 'multitude of innovations', with 'a thousand simultaneous voices demand[ing] the immediate satisfaction of their wants'. Presciently, De Tocqueville had understood the febrile restlessness which, in our days, is both a spring of action and a source of violence, a fount of progress and an instrument (or angel) of destruction. The ground of our appetites for good and evil, it is the exercise of this energy which threatens the world and, with its inventions, lightens the burdens of existence; the same energy rewards and wearies the active, while lack of it disables and makes envious the passive. Given the hydra-headedness of all human effort and its range of outcomes, it was always too simple to have regarded Western materialism as merely a matter of 'consumption'; and equally simple-minded for socialists to have believed that societies could prosper while individual energy and the obligation to use it were in shackles.

The world is being despoiled, but for men's convenience and comfort; and Nature raped, but not merely for the rapist's own prosperity and advantage. The water, the air, the forests, the animals – 'every winged fowl', the 'creatures of the deep' and 'every creeping thing' – suffer increasingly direly from the depredations wrought by human energy, the self-same energy, or prime mover, which galvanises *homo sapiens* to both destruction and creation. In his thirteenth-century travels, Marco Polo, arriving in the vicinity of modern Baku (called by him 'Zorzania'), observed a 'fountain of oil' which discharged 'so great a quantity as to furnish loading for many camels'. The 'use of it', Marco Polo explains, 'is not for the purpose of food, but as an unguent for the cutaneous distempers in men and cattle, as well as other complaints.

And it is also good for burning,' the Venetian traveller adds; 'in the neighbourhood, no other is used in their lamps, and people come from distant parts to procure it.' Seven centuries later, the world consumes some 15 million barrels of oil a day, ransacking the earth and the seas for it.

With every year, or month, that passes, man loses more of that technological innocence which made a Marco Polo marvel in the province of 'Cathay' – modern China's Shensi, or perhaps Shansi, province – at 'a sort of black stone, which they dig out of the mountains, where it runs in veins. When lighted, it burns like charcoal, and retains the fire much better than wood, in so much that it may be preserved during the night, and in the morning be found still burning ... These stones may be had in the greatest abundance and at a cheap rate.' He could not know that the coal-of-Cathay would come to darken the heavens; that the climate of the planet would be altered by the consequences of human effort; that some '20,000' separate items of 'space junk' (including dead satellites and old rockets) would litter the earth's atmosphere; that whole animal species would be extinguished; that the 'eco-system' of human life would be itself endangered. Now, in green despairs, men see the very appearance of the world, which the Jewish God of Genesis saw at the Creation to be 'good', take on, even in broad daylight, new dark colours. The solace of Nature, reflection's most precious resource, has (for many) been diminished by anxiety for its future. For some, it is beyond human capacity to repair, or even beyond prayer.

Unheard-of nitrogen dioxide levels in the smog of Athens, the disappearance of a third of Sumatra's forests in only eight years from 1982 to 1990, the accumulated 'fifty tons' of garbage left on and around Mount Everest by climbers, the Gulf War's gross damage to the northeast coast of Saudi Arabia, harm both soul and body. Doubt, more depressed than apocalyptic, even questions whether, at such a rate of abuse by one human generation after another, the earth can or will 'abide forever'. The polychlorinated biphenyls now found in sea-mammals, and sometimes in human breast-milk, poison the mind also. The reduction of ozone cover, the leaching of pesticides into ground-water, the risks of nuclear power generation, the sounds of the tree-felling in Sarawak or the Philippines or the Amazonian rain-forest, the spillage of oil tankers, the indestructibility of toxic industrial wastes and many other similar phenomena assail the human spirit. Man's dominion over Nature and the 'multitude of innovations' it has promoted bid to wreck the world. But without such ravages, and despite the miseries and hardships of hundreds of millions, billions of lives could not be kept in reasonable contentment. An 'ecologically sensitive' system of global production and consumption which is 'fully respectful of nature' is unattainable except in the utopian mind, and to utopian prescription. H. G. Wells, in 1914, predicted that the 'steam-engine, the coal-yard and tall chimneys, indeed all chimneys' would in due course 'vanish quietly from our urban landscape'. But where they have vanished, they have not gone quietly; and where they remain, from old Cathay to the squalor of Polish Katowice, their effects are more toxic than ever.

Nevertheless, hysteria also stalks this field of anxiety and polemical special pleading. The 'primary product of the economy' is not 'waste', as Ivan Illich has excitably asserted. Modern society has not, or not yet, 'transformed the earth from an open breathing-space into a stinking junkyard'. If the West's vast productive output is directed more to satisfying the expanding wants of De Tocqueville's 'thousand simul-taneous voices' than to meeting their 'real needs', it is directed to their 'real needs' also. The West has not only sacked but also helped to maintain – and continues to maintain – economies and societies with lower levels of technical attainment than its own. Its industrial output saves lives, as well as threatening human health and well-being. Without the West's rapidly advancing technological revolution in the means of communication, the successful political revolutions against the state-socialist regimes might have been delayed; no 'iron curtain' could exclude, or resist the reach of, the information provided by television, photocopiers, fax-machines and private computer networks. The social-ist utopia fell, *inter alia*, to an electronic siege. Semi-conductors helped turn the 'thousand simultaneous voices' into a chorus of tens of millions.

However, at the same time as Western technical and economic prowess claimed their ideological prize, the idea that material prosperity and technological achievement were the sole criteria of individual and social progress had never been less persuasive, nor to so many. Even Japanese government surveys disclosed a decreasing interest in science and technology among young Japanese males, and 'signs of alienation from manufacturing'. Appreciation of the Japanese countryside, 'beau-tiful nature', history, tradition, and the arts were now said to hold pride of place in the Japanese scale of values over admiration for the products of advanced technology. As communism fell, the old assumption, a commonplace of Western thought since the seventeenth century, that prosperity is a pre-condition of 'progress', and the latter a necessary outcome of the former, had never been so disrupted. Far from the two terms being close to synonyms, the notion that increasing material prosperity did *not* necessarily bring in its wake a net improvement in the material conditions of existence, not even for the rich, had become a commonplace. Licensed inhumanity practiced in the name of science, disaster provoked by invention, and runaway injuries to nature inflicted by the continuous growth of knowledge could not be undone merely by more invention and more knowledge. Instead, many had become aware that material benefit and expert havoc rode the world in tandem. Nevertheless, the plenteous utopia, in which our wants – or the 'wandering of our desires' – are endlessly satiated, was not perceived by most to be an entire chimera. To suggest it, was, paradoxically, still to be a kill-joy. To point the crabbed finger of reproach, as some did, at the 'I want it now generation' remained (for many) an insult; to speak in direr vein, as some did, of 'leisure-fixated drones consuming for the sake of consumption', still seemed an outrage, even a class-outrage. Yet, increasing numbers of children, some as young as ten years old, might now (in the prosperous West) possess their own television sets, for example. Moralists, of left and right alike, bemoaned the existence of a 'dark underbelly of individual freedom', and belaboured its 'narcissism, compulsive striving and schizoid alienation', but such complaint was still mere froth upon the wave.

Worse still, anxiety was re-packaged and sold back to the anxious. Doubt itself became a cash-crop in the market. 'Green products' became the 'marketing opportunity of the Nineties' and whole industries 'talked green, but acted dirty'. Hundreds of billions of dollars were being spent in the United States each year on healthy antidotes and cures, designed to neutralise the effects of their purchasers' continuing greeds. Tens of millions in the West knew of the overwhelming need to reduce their levels of consumption and 'change their lifestyles', but few acted upon the knowledge. 'Sustainable economic development', energy conservation, 'organic' agriculture, pollution taxes, 'redressing the balance between rich North and poor South' and the rest of the 'green agenda' remained mainly for the birds. Instead, recycled paper and phosphate-free washing powders were added to the shopping lists of the more prosperous consumer. ('All the labour of man is for his mouth,' declared the preacher, 'and yet the appetite is not filled' – not even by brown rice and low-fat yoghurt.) The most awkward truths of all were that environmental degradation and spoliation were, on the one hand, an outcome of the rich world's excesses and, on the other, of the poor world's privations; and that the latter aspired to the condition of the former, with its higher levels of 'development' and its richer forms of pollution.

Organic compounds and heavy metals – including lead, mercury and cadmium – underwater and other nuclear tests, and an estimated 9 million tons of non-degradable rubbish thrown each year into the planet's oceans have given to nature, and to man, Pacific plankton contaminated with radioactive caesium, seals in Russia's northern coastal waters dying of radiation cancers, and fish found off the coasts of Britain with liver damage, bacterial ulcers, and strange raspberry-shaped tumours; 'God blessed them, saying "Be fruitful, and multiply, and fill the waters in the seas."' Indeed, in a specific act of grace, God, according to Genesis, particularly 'created whales', an act by which the awe-stricken might measure His benignity and power. The 'harvesting' of them, to use the modern term for the factory-ship's art, knows nothing of the divine. But then, to the Japanese – their reasserted love of Nature notwithstanding – cubes of whale tongue in a soup of noodles are a plain delight. In lakes of oil from Alaska to the Gulf, the sea-birds die; there is mercury in the seals in Liverpool bay; endangered turtles are soft on the palate in Bali. Whether the planet's atmosphere is warming (and, if so, to what degree) is still debated. But if it is not, another explanation must be found for changing weather patterns, the disappearance of 1,300 square kilometres of ice-shelf on the west coast of the Antarctic peninsula, and the shrinking of the Arctic ice-cap. At the present rate of temperature increase, with its consequence in a rising tide of waters, much of Bangladesh, part of Egypt and the English Fens, and many Pacific islands could be entirely under water (some say) by the year 2030; on some other Ararat, another Noah may come to rest. There will be grapes growing in Birmingham, but both the United States and the Ukraine – so the alarmists declare – will have ceased to be the granaries they are.

If fossil-fuel emissions (23 per cent of them emanating from the United States, with its mere 5 per cent of the world's population) and aircraft exhaust fumes increasingly swirl the globe, it is not only the sun's ultra-violet radiation from which mankind gradually ceases to be protected. Speculative thought is itself slowly penetrated, and the moral balance affected. Once, the stern philosopher considered man's petty fears for his body to be base, and thought derisory the contemplation of his frail physical self or his navel. Now, the problems of 'ozone depletion', or of the destruction of the rain-forests, or of the continuous elimination of plant, insect and animal species, are the stuff of a universal anxiety of spirit, an anxiety which far transcends concern with the small change of daily existence. A sense, which many might have thought had passed into moral oblivion in the 'age of reason', has returned to plague men's thoughts and given nightmares to many: the sense of there being unmanageable perils in doing violence to the natural order. Now, however, there is a difference from previous ages, since this sense is not superstitious but itself grounded in reason. Many of the dangers are either knowable, or already known. The times for biblical warning are past: 'Whoso breaketh an hedge, a serpent shall bite him' is a redundant injunction. Today, turning rare tropical hardwoods into chopsticks – in Japan, used once and broken after a meal – is a well-understood offence against nature.

One violation of nature breeds another. Animals have always been hunted and eaten, and parts of their bodies used for implements, clothes, adornments, fuel or utensils. But gratuitous violence against them, without even the excuse of 'sport' or scientific inquiry, seems to be another modern epiphenomenon of a general disrespect for the natural world. The statistics of cruelty to animals even in Britain, the 'land of animal lovers', have shown a great increase in recent years. Record levels of cruelty, both to wild and domestic animals, were registered by the Royal Society for Prevention of Cruelty to Animals in 1991. There is even a new category of harm-doing known to experts as 'animal abuse', and a new breed of malefactors called 'animal sadists'. Their recent misdeeds in Britain have included shooting cows in the eyes with air-guns, chopping off the legs of cats 'for fun' – for which two young Worcestershire men, aged twenty-two and eighteen ('I loathe cats,' said one) were jailed in July 1991 – decapitating gulls, starving domestic pets, tearing off the heads of ornamental wild fowl in parks and so on. These are, in the scale of things and *sub specie aeternitatis*, trivia; against other forms of violence, almost nothing. But they are also insults to life itself, their little indecencies made larger for being without purpose.

It is their purposelessness which perhaps gives the best clue to their meaning: the banally cruel, too, demand the 'immediate satisfaction of their wants'. Unreason is at least as 'feverishly impatient' as any other mainspring of action, and more than most. Even idleness is a propellent of sorts. Moral judgment accords a higher virtue to the 'constructive', but all human energy (to whatever end) is human, violent energy neither more nor less so. Indeed, to produce vari-coloured mink for the Western 'fashion market' by genetic engineering is also a violation of nature. Similarly, to modify micro-organisms genetically in order to create improved pesticides, and then to release them into the environment to multiply – as if this were the 'Eighth Day' of Creation – is not greatly distinct from the making of a diabolical mannikin, or *golem*. (This is especially so at a time when the evidence is increasing that genes can 'jump' between species more easily than was once thought.) If the human colour gene could be isolated, as has been the gene of gender, blacks might be turned into whites, and vice-versa. 'Gene practitioners' are already a registered profession, and genetic knowledge is now sufficient to create human clones and hybrids, whose own genes would be heritable 'from generation unto generation'. The alteration of cell-structures by genetical manipulation for purposes of medical treatment is one thing; the power of random creation vested in man is another. From erudite experiment upon the body of nature without adequate ethical constraint, to the lumpen tearing-off of the legs of cats 'for fun', is not a long step. The one merely requires more learning than the other, and a more articulate capacity to defend it.

The claim of science, or more properly of scientific method, is that it is directed to the 'eliciting of knowledge from ignorance and truth from error', as Julian Huxley once put it. At the same time, the scientific temper welcomes all new knowledge, not only irrespective of whether such new knowledge conflicts with old ways of thinking, as it often will, but also whether or not it poses dangers to man and insults nature, as it has increasingly done in the modern period. The acquisition by man of new authority over nature, including annihilatory authority, has not been matched by a similar expansion in his ability to control the noxious side-effects of the exercise of such authority. Nor has there been any increase in man's willingness to give a full moral accounting, to others, for the harm done to them in the name of scientific and technical progress. In the awesome danger of 'melt-down' in a nuclear reactor, or the risk of careless insemination with the frozen sperm of a wrong donor – as has happened in New York – it is easy to see how the speed and scale of the increase in human powers have outpaced experience of their consequences, outflanked moral reservations over their use, and defeated efforts to bring them under civic control. Even when scientific and technical development has become clearly self-defeating, as when there are no remedies for the effects of technical disaster, or when scientific 'progress' itself puts at risk all past human achievement, the high ground of debate – when there is debate – remains in the hands of the scientist or technologist, not his critics.

Instead, public attention is routinely given to matters of lesser moral significance, however important they may be in their own right, from the problem of 'technological unemployment' to that of, say, computer 'hacking' and fraud. That two million cars are scrapped every year in Germany, or that 'viruses' can be wilfully introduced into computer programmes, is not of the same moral order of magnitude as the fate of frozen embryos. Similarly, the ethical accountability of the inventors of new artificial computer-worlds for their creation of a 'virtual reality', into which an observer may (appear to) enter, cannot match that of the scientists of biological weapons' manufacture for their satanic labours. Yet, of the latter, almost nothing is known and less heard. Moreover, such is the complexity of the world inhabited by much modern scientific research that neither lay understanding nor moral judgment can gain access to it. Space research may cost 'trillions' of dollars; the 'electronic smog' of electro-magnetic waves, 'escaping' from personal computers and electronic games, may become so intense as to trigger and jam other electronic machines; the prospect may be nearing of *molecular-sized* computers. But, for the layman, such phenomena are themselves smog-bound in a miasma of technological unknowing.

Likewise, the fact that information-commands can now be electronically passed, as a matter of routine, from working machine to working machine still remains, with its implications, outside the bounds of average, or even above-average, comprehension. That an electronic switch can now be made from a single atom has, for many, no meaning whatever. That an individual, armed with a computer head-set and sensors, can now be, or seem to be, immersed inside and to be 'interacting' with a constantly-changing, three-dimensional screen image – thus permitting medical students to conduct an anatomical 'exploration' without a human body – leaves the electronically-illiterate no wiser. Further scientific work, dream-like or nightmarish according to (largely-uninformed) perception, is now being done on the means to project such 'virtual scenes' directly on to the user's retina by laser. So, too, is work to develop a 'teletact' pneumatic glove, which would not only generate force when it touched the screen, as now, but also receive 'tactile feedback' from a distant electronically-linked spectator playing the same game. Techno-sex, like killing by remote control, is at hand. And so on, *ad infinitum*.

No philosophy has yet encompassed the range of modern technics. It is possible that no philosophy can. Nor has any system of moral speculation fully engaged with it, being still unable to grasp with sufficiently comprehensive knowledge the implications of what man is now doing, and is capable of doing. In the mid-1980s, the Rand Corporation was even toying with the 'project' of harnessing anti-matter as a weapon to annihilate matter itself; it was being suggested that, thus 'harnessed', a gram of material with the weight of an air-gun pellet might be invested with an explosive energy equivalent to 50,000 tonnes of TNT. These energies are the energies of man applied to the energies of nature. The energies of the moral philosopher have not been equal to them. The bomb which, in one fell blow, killed 140,000 people at Hiroshima, contained only twenty-five pounds of uranium. Such disproportions (as in the case, too, of a switch the size of an atom) disable not only the direct victim of their powers, but the oblique observer of them also. In January 1986, the space-ship Voyager, eight years after it had been launched from Earth and 1.8 billion miles into its potentially infinite journey – yet still in contact with its scientific masters – 'discovered' a fifteenth Uranian moon. But who, any longer, thought much of it?

Even the setting foot upon the Earth's moon in July 1969, arguably *homo sapiens'* most notable scientific achievement of all, was a seven days' wonder. Eyes were raised in astonishment to the heavens, but only briefly, and returned to earth, and earthly preoccupation. In late July and early August 1971, James Irwin, the eighth man to walk on the Moon, travelled more than seventeen miles across its surface in a battery-powered Lunar Rover, reaching – via the Valley of Hadley's Rille – the foothills of the Appenine Mountains of the Moon. Yet, such technological fantasies made real appeared to have the power neither to instruct nor to inspire, nor even to charm. A New World was being discovered, but now without much notice and less thanksgiving; an historic landfall had been made by Man on a neighbouring secondary planet, but without arousing more than passing attention.

It was as if scientific progress, in its very rapidity and daring, had lost the capacity to surprise or enthral. But the appetite of the 'feverishly impatient' is quickly jaded: the 'multitude of innovations' that restlessness seeks soon palls. Moreover, anxiety, which serves to repress as well as to stir emotion, has with good reason learned to fasten its doubts upon the grosser forms of modern technological endeavour. Among the cascade of novelties showered upon an already-sated world, 72 million litres of 'advanced' herbicides were sprayed on South Vietnam during the Vietnamese war, destroying five million acres of forest. Some fifty nuclear weapons, and at least eight nuclear reactors, lie on the ocean floor as the result of naval collisions, fires, other accidents and sinkings. Astronauts have been immolated in balls of fire before audiences of millions, who move on quickly to other channels.

In the ruined world that socialism made, a comparable scepticism as to the virtues of capitalist growth now coexists uneasily with the desire for long-suppressed wants to be urgently satisfied. Not unlike the United States as De Tocqueville observed it in the 1830s, the newly democratised countries of Eastern Europe and the former Soviet Union now resound with 'simultaneous voices' (in tens and hundreds of millions) demanding their various gratifications. But theirs is a setting of particularly disproportionate destruction, in which environments have been comprehensively wrecked in exchange for lower standards of living than could retrospectively justify the vandalising of nature on such a scale. Here, there could be no balancing moral equation between material benefit and environmental harm. Forced industrialisation, the destruction of the village economy, the uprooting of peoples, the sacking of the landscape, produced insufficient amounts of convenience and advantage. Even the great economic and moral investments in public provision and collective action left their nations poor. In Soviet Asia, in rural Poland, in Romania and a few steps from the centre of Moscow, deprivation, sometimes gross, casts a dark shadow. With kindergartens and creches went maternal hard labour and poor housing; with cultural provision, lack of artistic freedom; with sanatoria, poisoned air.

Expectation was tailored to circumstance, and circumstance to expectation, in a vicious circle of low standards. Human energies, society's main resource, faltered or failed in a bureaucratic wilderness where minimum and maximum effort were equally rewarded, or unrewarded. In the end, with nature itself on its knees, one quarter of the Soviet population – or some 70 million people – lived below the poverty line of 75 roubles a month. Abandoned Trabant cars littered the streets of Eastern Europe after their owners had fled across the borders to the West. Craftmanship had been sacrificed to Stakhanovism, and proletarian health to (inefficient) mass production in poor working conditions. It was as if technology, mismanaged, could become an obstacle to convenience, reversing a law of human progress; as if invention could not merely be thwarted, but cancelled, by the greater ingenuity of the uninventive. At the unification of Germany, one in eight West Germans of working age was self-employed. In East Germany, the figure was one in fifty. To the last, the utility of the activities of the other forty-nine remained unquestioned; yet the body-work of the Trabant was made of compressed paper and cardboard.

The application of organised human effort under communist conditions had failed to meet a variety of commonplace needs. At the same time, and in ways familiar to the Third World, the combination of misshapen technological progress with pre-modern forms of living distorted daily experience to an irrational degree. 'We do nothing else,' declared an Albanian peasant in Gjirokaster in January 1991, 'but walk to our fields, cultivate them with our hands, and then walk home to watch television'; a journey of a few miles and a hundred generations. Technology had been intended to be placed at the disposal of 'new socialist man', who would thus become, in association with his fellows, master of all he surveyed. Instead, impoverished by socialism, with spirit of community drained, energy misapplied and technical development stalled, he found himself with neither his wants nor his needs adequately met. In the socialist struggle with nature, both assailant and victim had been left frustrated. In the West, the assailant has at least done better.

Indeed, progress under socialism demanded a multiplicity of knowing assaults upon objects and persons, places and traditions. Cultures, individual as well as national, were debased or damaged. Beliefs, models of behaviour – especially the aristocratic and 'bourgeois' models – aesthetic tastes, and styles of life came under the hammer, or were scythed away by the sickle. Such destruction of socialist man's natural and social environments has been matched in the West by the consequences of its own much more rapid technical progress. The 'advanced' West, too, has its shrunken Aral Sea, polluted Baikal and poisoned Volga. It has its own stunting forms of labour and its own moral indifference to it, its own macho-industrialism and mountains of ferro-concrete. It has imposed its own mortifications upon the spirit in its own urban subtopias, and similarly generated (in many) what Montesquieu called 'dejection of mind'. The stygian coking-plants, choking chemical vapours, acrid multi-coloured effluents, grey buildings and pale children of the socialist industrial world all have their counterparts, if less visible and less concentrated, in Western Europe's own backyards of dereliction.

Similar work processes and identical contempts for nature always made many distinctions between East and West too refined. There may be no Western statistic to compare with the '16 per cent' of the vast territory of the former Soviet Union designated by the former Soviet parliament as an 'ecological disaster area'. There may also be little in

Western Europe like the fiendish Copsa Mica in Romania, for instance, with its lead and zinc processing plants and carbon-black manufacture, the surrounding countryside and even the grazing animals blackened with the residues of incinerated oil and gas. But there is not much to choose between leukaemic children East and West, or between one dead river and another. And though ugliness is in the eye of the beholder, no beauty has yet been found in radioactive wastes, sewage pollution or trees consumed by acid rain, wherever they are.

Nevertheless, socialist uglinesses were compounded by wilful harms done to human sensibilities and a scale of wanton neglect of consequences hard to replicate in the West. Thus, Soviet nuclear reactors not only had gross design faults – not uncommon in experimental technology – but, despite being known to have them, they were installed and left to do their worst to man and nature. In the explosion at Chernobyl in April 1986, which propelled a lethal radioactive plume 36,000 feet into the sky and contaminated wide swathes of the Ukraine and Byelorussia with caesium 137, iodine 131, strontium 90 and carbon 14, it was not science fiction which became reality, but the law of scientific probability which was vindicated. It might be said that all nuclear reactors could explode in a similar fashion; there was a potentially lethal fire at the Windscale reactor in Cumbria in 1957. But the torpid failure to evacuate in time tens of thousands of local people in peril of their healths and lives, and the cascades of falsehood about the scale of the accident – radioactivity ranging from 1,000 to 20,000 roentgens per hour was reduced, in official pronouncements, to '0.0015 of a roentgen' – were *sui generis*.

So was the bleakest fact of all: that an accident which turned a nuclear reactor into a nuclear volcano was provoked by experiments being conducted late at night by two engineers. In violation of operating rules, and allegedly unaware of the risks of what they were doing, they 'uncoupled' the reactor's inadequate safety systems and set off a technological catastrophe beyond reversal or cure. (Much of the eighteen-mile disaster zone around the Chernobyl plant will be uninhabitable for centuries to come.) The reactor had been carelessly and cheaply built. Its materials were of poor quality; it lacked fail-safe devices; the engineers on duty in April 1986 were amoral. Indeed, it was a metaphor for an entire social system, which within five years of the accident was itself being buried in a sarcophagus of political concrete.

But even the sarcophagus at Chernobyl was to be poorly constructed.

Far from having 'sealed' the reactor, as was announced, birds, flying in
and out, made their nests in it, while it continued to leak radiation.
Inside the core of the 'entombed' reactor, which contained hundreds of
tons of graphite, it was even possible that the nuclear chain-reaction
could re-start. The risk of the leaching of radio nucleides into the
water-table and local rivers – and thence to the Black Sea and even to
the Mediterranean – had not abated, and cannot abate. Moreover, there
are some fifty primitive reactors, sixteen of them of the Chernobyl type,
in the former territories of the Soviet Union and in Eastern Europe;
some (as at Sosnovy Bor, 60 miles west of St Petersburg, and at
Kozloduy in Bulgaria) leaking, most of them poorly maintained, and at
least one (at Ignalina in Lithuania) built on a geological fault in a
potentially seismic zone. The lava-like flow of molten nuclear fuel and
the blue glow of Cherenkov radiation in puddles of water, observed by
frightened scientists at Chernobyl, was a graver matter than the 320,000
tonnes of noxious gases emitted each year by the Lenin steelworks in
Krakow; the monstrous births – six-legged pigs, two-headed calves –
and mutant vegetation now found in the area of Chernobyl much more
fearsome than the pall of sulphur dioxide (from the burning of brown
coal) hanging over Teplice in northern Bohemia. But, together, they
represented varieties of energy equally misused, and the *primum mobile*
in violent collision with human well-being.

The retreat of socialism in Eastern Europe and the Soviet Union left
in its wake not only a polluted landscape but tens of millions of their
peoples with reduced health, lowered expectation of life and the
sallowest kinds of spiritual depression. There were estimated to be 30
million alcoholics in the Soviet Union alone. In some countries, there
were almost Third World rates of morbidity and mortality; widespread
chest ailments and respiratory diseases, including (as in Poland) a high
incidence of tuberculosis; endemic cardiovascular disorders; and peri-
natal and maternal mortality figures far beyond the norm for Europe. In
Czechoslovakia, life expectancy was seven years lower than the average
in the European Community, and a full ten years lower in areas of the
worst pollution. This was not surprising: in parts of once-sylvan
Bohemia emissions of sulphur dioxide exceeded sixty-three tonnes per
square kilometre per annum. Heavy smoking – 67 per cent of Polish
men smoked – vitamin deficiency, poor diet and pollution brought
whole populations low. In Silesia, Utopia's citizens struggled with
chronic chest infections; in Volgograd, with birth defects (from chemical
pollutants); in Ulan Bator, with loss of teeth from exposure to uranium.

In the former East Germany, only 10 per cent of children under the age of three in Bitterfeld – with mercury in its river and sulphur dioxide in its air – were reported to have 'normal health'. In Katowice in southern Poland, hundreds of thousands of gas-masks had to be issued during 1990 to help its citizens to breathe; in the penumbra of Chernobyl, radiation sickness, leukaemia, and hypochondriacal fear of the onset of illness burdened the people.

Against the one-fifth of the planet's vast population which goes hungry every day, or the 180 million children in the world suffering (according to the United Nations) from severe chronic malnutrition, the legacy of industrial disease in the post-communist world is a relatively small matter. Nor is it distinct from, say, the historic legacy of the British industrial revolution, whose complex medical and social side-effects continue to be apparent in the old industrial areas of Britain. Dangerous photochemical smogs afflict many of the world's conurbations. In Athens, streets empty and hospitals fill when ozone and nitrogen dioxide levels reach physically intolerable levels; oxygen cubicles have been set up in the streets of Mexico City. Third World infant mortality rates can now be found in the United States, including in Washington, where black poverty and maternal 'crack' addiction have raised the capital's rate (at 23 per 1,000 live births) to the same level as in Romania. Indeed, black life expectancy rates, under the pressures of drug addiction and violence, have been falling in the United States since 1984. In Harlem, black men are now less likely to reach the age of sixty-five than if they lived in Bangladesh. There are many ways to drive the *primum mobile* of human energies into a brick wall.

In general, squalor takes universal forms and has effects which are common to all. *Vibrio cholerae bacterium* prospers in contaminated water and in refuse left uncollected under whatever social system. The spread of cholera in Africa and South America – it has also reappeared in Romania – during 1991 and 1992 knew no distinction of persons or of types of social and economic failure. In Western Europe, too, the signs multiply of civic standards under pressure, or even approaching organisational breakdown. The large increases in reported cases of dysentery and food poisoning in some British cities cannot be discounted, out of a false sense of insult to national self-regard, as symptoms of it. In the poor world, lack of services, dirt, malnutrition, joblessness, and lack of shelter draw whole communities into the gutter; in the rich world, hectic demand – De Tocqueville's 'feverish impatience' once more –

high costs, mass flux and dense congestion drive the largest conurbations towards stasis.

Some of the consequences converge in common and equally debilitating forms of stress upon the means of public service, from street-cleaning to medical provision, from safe water-supply to crime prevention. In the poor world, inertia accompanies the physical weakness of the people; in the rich, the effort to maintain standards in the teeth of compulsive mass demand for speed, convenience and cheapness is increasingly beyond the strength, will and application of those expected to make such effort. Ever-growing pressures upon hygiene, public transport, housing and the environment sap the energies of those whose task is to protect or provide them, and weary the victims of their decline or failure. Ten million tons of raw sewage pour into the seas around Britain per annum; *E-Coli* bacteria (the bacteria associated with human faeces) are routinely found in hamburgers, salads and ice-creams and in fast-food bars, pubs and even hospital kitchens. The sale of unfit meat, the use of harmful additives in food processing, the feeding of cattle on recycled animal offal, and the promotion of their growth with hormones or other dangerous substances are unhealthy responses to equally unhealthy but urgent demands.

In Britain alone, over 20 million fast-food meals were being consumed each week by the late 1980s. New 'food technologies', like other advanced technologies which human energies demand and supply, simultaneously solve and create problems. They work for human convenience, and undermine domestic skills; provide accessible satisfactions, and subvert the capacity for efficient spending on unprocessed foodstuffs. Their wares are attractive but often costly, with many leaving the consumer undernourished. It has also been noted in the United States that convenience-food advertising is disproportionately targeted at the poor, who can least afford an expensive but non-nutritious diet. The seductions of the seemingly convenient can even take the child from its mother's breast. At the end of the 1980s, barely one third of mothers in the United States with less than 7,000 dollars per annum of family income breast-fed their children, compared with more than two-thirds of the already well-off with more than 28,000 dollars. Throughout Western Europe, and especially in Britain, the industrial working class was also being continuously found to be in poorer health than others, as well as least disposed to give up smoking and least inclined to take, or heed, advice about diet. In north-west and north-east England, and in parts of Scotland and Northern Ireland, were to be found the highest levels of mortality from coronary disease in the world, run close by the similar proletariats of Eastern Europe. Conversely, falls in the British statistics for heart-disease deaths during the 1980s occurred, so it was said, 'entirely among the higher socio-economic classes'. Among the 'lower and manual groups' there was 'no improvement at all'.

At the same time, in the United States in particular, fitness and the search for the lissom body have become, for many, the object of the greatest effort. For some, it is the ego's main focus. American spending on health care in 1990 alone – when more than half the population of the poor world was said by the United Nations to have no access even to the most basic medical provision – reached a staggering 600 billion dollars, and was predicted to double or even triple by the year 2000. National hypochondriasis, medical and pharmaceutical extortion, real illness (including Aids), increasingly costly new medical technologies, and the desire (of some) to live for ever have between them driven health expenditure to unthinkable levels.

Here, hyperactivity and hypertension – the *primum mobile* driven towards self-destruction – are represented at their apogee. Even exercise can become a matter less of health than of continuous motion, and the search, or demand, for good health itself an unhealthy obsession. On the one hand, often-obese men and women – 20 per cent of Americans were said to be obese and 50 per cent overweight – feed themselves to stupefaction in an agony of plenty and dissatisfaction. On the other, the svelte, their skin taut across their cheekbones, seek a heavenly state of physical grace by passing through a purgatory of 'body-work', 'personalised fitness programs' and so forth. This is exercising on a treadmill. 'Feeling good', by the hard way of self-mortification, is now a billion-dollar industry. This cult of health in a world of sickness is as much religion as science, though with a degree of *angst*-to-the-bone which not even the Great Chiropractor in the Sky could lay His finger on. It is also an antidote, technologically driven in increasingly mechanised health clubs and gymnasia, to every hint of inertia. Here, De Tocqueville's 'feverish impatience' is to be found mounted on an exercise machine, or jogging itself into exhaustion.

Democratic energy, De Tocqueville remarked, is among other things 'extravagant'; the 'multitude of innovations' which the energetic citizen seeks are 'almost all attended with expense'. Indeed, the 'immediate satisfaction' of innumerable wants, as De Tocqueville long ago saw, demands 'recourse to the coffers of the State. Public charges increase in proportion as civilisation spreads.' Today, this 'recourse' has led to the provision of those public goods which it is beyond the reach of the private purse to secure: that is, 'the welfare state', 'welfare', 'welfarism', or 'welfare dependency', according to judgment. Here, the purposes of socialism and capitalism have in some respects coincided. In the latter case, state spending is designed to make good, in part, the defects of the market and amend its rigours. In the former, it was to construct a secure world of 'egalitarian' public provision.

The outcomes have been complex and contradictory. One man's necessary relief becomes the source of another's threadbare passivity, the release from insecurity in some the solvent of energy in others. In capitalism, welfare entitlements are placed, by some, on a par as 'rights' with the rights of suffrage or freedom of opinion. In the socialist world, they were the badge of a citizenship which had lost much of its other substance. In capitalist societies, such entitlements are now seen, by many, merely as supplements – of inferior moral status – to the rewards of the market. In socialist societies, they were part of the state's compensation to the individual for the sacrifice of his liberty on the altar of 'collective labour'.

Despite such complexities, socialists, by political doctrine and moral reflex, have always seen public spending and public provision as good in themselves, and even as the only means of addressing civic problems. But the low regard in which public goods are frequently held, also (it would often seem) by reflex, suggests that not every form of public provision has enhanced a sense of citizenship, or promoted public virtue. Indeed, disrespect for 'socialist property', especially in the heart of its continually pillaged production system, was one of the distinguishing features of the socialist system, as vandalism is of council building and other public property in Britain and elsewhere. Extensive social provision no more made for the creation of 'socialist man' in one system, than it has made for the nurturing of 'social' man in another. Despite vast expenditures on public well-being by the welfare state in Britain, for example, such well-being has proved elusive. Substantial sections of the population remain culturally deprived, badly educated, unhealthy and unhappy, as if the expenditures had not been made in the first place.

Many individuals benefited from post-war provision, taking advantage of new possibilities and conditions to make their way in the world, and to see their children prosper. But just as many, perhaps more, did not. They remained in an older, near-Dickensian kind of social thraldom beyond the reach of effective public assistance. It is also plain that it is not welfare provision *per se* which 'creates welfare dependency', but the combination of such provision with particular national, class and individual cultures, states of mind and predispositions. Low individual self-esteem can be reduced by the state-client relation; defeated expectations of the state and its bureaucracies further depress the already-pessimistic. Above all, transfer (to an excessive degree) of responsibility for self to agencies of public provision can reduce the individual's capacity for autonomous action. For some – a relatively small minority – state benefits invite predation.

The worst effects, sedulously denied by left intellectuals, are to be observed in the plebeian sub-cultures of Britain and the United States, where (for some) living 'on the dole' or 'on relief' becomes a self-perpetuating and permanent condition of sustained inertia. In such a condition, where the 'energy of human aspiration' may come close to extinction, a comatose state of existence is punctuated by routine welfare payments too small to provide comfort, but not so small as to compel a preference for self-reliance, and particularly not in circumstances of joblessness and inner city depression. 'It doesn't seem bad to me to be on the dole all my life,' said the bright but unemployed daughter of a Hull seafaring family to the *Guardian* in October 1990, 'it's what I've always expected.' Bitter protests against policies of welfare cuts (as in New Zealand and Holland in 1991 and in Spain and Greece in 1992) made clear that welfare benefits now meet cultural expectation, as well as economic need. Moreover, increasing reports of violence committed against the staffs of job centres and social security offices in Britain have given further clues to the nature of some of the emotions generated by the welfare relation. In central London in June 1991, for instance, a civil servant was 'pulled across a desk, knocked to the ground and kicked in the face' by a man 'angry because he could not have an immediate giro', or welfare payment: the *primum mobile* in a modern mutation.

Some elements of social provision in prosperous industrial societies are minimal and basic. Others arguably go to the outer limits of state management of the affairs of the individual. (In June 1989, Swedish social welfare authorities sent a group of young offenders on a six-month 'rehabilitation cruise', at a cost of £52,000 to Swedish taxpayers.) Professionalised welfare activities in some welfare systems have become a parody of productive effort; in other regards, public care of the needy represents a triumph of moral progress. It is clear, however, that where the scale of 'welfare investment' is greatest – as in the inner cities of the United States and Britain – there generally seems the least sign of civic redemption. Moreover, in most countries the cost of comprehensive social provision is becoming so high that, especially in times of recession, it is increasingly difficult even for wealthier economies to afford it. In Sweden, until provision began to be cut, welfare was absorbing more than half of the nation's GNP; in the north of England, 20 per cent of total household income at the end of the 1980s consisted of social security payments. The national health service in Britain costs some £35 billion per annum, the French health service £50 billion. Indeed, the very notion of free health care on demand had come into serious question in many countries by the end of the decade. Almost everywhere, charges were being levied for hitherto free social services, national insurance contributions were being raised, and the principles of welfare themselves were being re-examined, not least from fear of the *vis inertiae*.

In this debate, the right's doubts about the efficiency and cost of public provision and the effects of the welfare relation have clashed with the left's belief in the morally prior duties of the state to the individual, particularly to the individual in need. Moderates on all sides seek a *via media* of reform, in which 'cost effective' public provision, greater 'individual responsibility' for self, and the continued meeting of need might somehow be melded together. But almost any cut in provision, however modest, is hailed by objectors as an 'attack on the poor', and any organisational reform suspected of being a covert step towards the dismantling of public service. Likewise, almost any raising of the issue of citizen responsibility, or (worse) citizen duty, as a moral quid pro quo for state provision is dismissed as darkest reaction. Conversely, routine complaints that public services have for years been 'underfunded' and 'starved of resources', or that citizens have been 'let down' by the allegedly long-standing inadequacy of public provision, are themselves rejected as the special pleading of left lobbies.

The right in Britain consistently denies that the poor are as poor as is claimed. In office they have attempted to move from universality of entitlement to the 'safety net' principle in welfare provision; preferred loans to grants; frozen the level of certain welfare payments, and severed others from their linkage to rises in the cost of living. They have also agrued that there were fewer 'genuinely unemployed' than the statistics suggested, and 'tightened up' the rules under which the jobless obtained benefit by trying to insist upon proof of genuine effort to seek work. In New Zealand, in July 1991, a right-wing government caused uproar when it designated nearly half the population as 'wealthy enough to look after its own health, education, housing and retirement needs'. It adopted the pre-welfarist principle that those who could afford it should take 'personal responsibility for themselves'. The economy, declared the minister of finance, had been 'drained by years of overspending in pursuit of a utopian society'; now, it would live within its means.

It was an irony that while the prosperous Western economies were seeking to make a partial, or perhaps token, retreat from the principle of comprehensive state welfare, the post-communist economies had been driven by fear of civil conflict towards the introduction, for the first time, of Western-style welfare legislation. There were newly 'vulnerable groups' to be protected from the severities of the free market, and new armies of the unemployed to be shielded from absolute hardship by (minimal) benefit payments. There were also new taxes to be levied in order to fund new forms of social provision, new social organisations to be set up, and a new cadre of professional social workers to be trained.

At the same time, familiar claims of 'entitlement' to welfare could immediately be heard. The most bizarre came from the highest places of the collasping socialist order. 'Now that perestroika has entered its critical phase,' the doomed Gorbachev declared in June 1991, in his Nobel Prize acceptance speech, 'the Soviet Union is *entitled* to expect large-scale support to assure its success' (my emphasis). Such swift and energetic resort to the language of welfare 'entitlement' – why 'entitled?' – was an instructive reflex. The impulse to transfer responsibility to others while simultaneously putting them under moral pressure, only to turn sullen or aggressive if denied – the welfarist complex – had made its first appearance in post-communist diplomatic relations. 'If they [the West] just give us advice as to how to make our reform more radical without helping us with compensation measures,' Vladimir Scherbakov, the then Soviet first deputy prime minister, warned one month later in July 1991, 'the Soviet people will not stand a high level [of reform] . . . We cannot put further social pressures on people. *It is too hard*' (my emphasis). 'I'll tell the Italians,' Gramoz Pashko, the Albanian deputy prime minister declared in similar fashion in June 1991, as Albanian refugees struggled to enter Italy, 'that they need to do something to give these people jobs, to give hope, to invest in Albania and help to stop the problem.' The transfer not merely of moral responsibility, but of obligation, to the Italian authorities was Pashko's first instinct. What Albania needed to do for itself, cruelly impoverished as it might be, was a secondary matter.

In differences of judgment about what is morally prior in social policy, there is a deep ethical divide. Today, the left's refusal to make concessions to what is seen as ruthless 'Social Darwinism' is countered by the right's mounting disapproval of 'dependency' upon public provision. The anxiety of the altruist at needs unmet, or inadequately met, is now fully matched in the West by the growing unease of those who believe in at least some mutuality of obligation between the state and the individual. Wavering between one anxiety and the other is perhaps the commonest, and best hidden, of the policy-maker's and welfare administrator's positions. Conscience hopes not to be found wanting; practicality shies away from the utopian. But it is the taboo of class which, especially in Britain, stops candour in its tracks on most of the fraught issues of welfare. In Britain, mutual class recoil has not diminished during the post-war decades. On the contrary. But the sense of it is (for most) an unspeakable matter, and remains unspoken.

This is the case despite the gradual demise of the sentimental leftist, who had lived upon, and imposed on others, his fictions as to the virtues of 'proletarian culture' and the vices of 'privileged' lifestyles. Hostility towards what is perceived to be the increasingly base form of 'ordinary' wants and interests continues to be checked by polite inhibition. But resentments at the conduct of the powerful and the wealthy also remain largely repressed, or are de-fused by the synthetic indignations of the tabloid press. If De Tocqueville's 'thousand simultaneous voices demanding the immediate satisfaction of their wants' are thought to contain a large proportion of demands that are better left unmet, few are disposed openly to say so; if popular passions are aroused by the spectacular delinquencies of the rich, or by the unattractive antics of the 'royals', they generally abate before blood is drawn. Nevertheless, there is a fierce enough ill-will in anti-plebeian contempts whenever they focus upon issues of welfare. The language of 'scrounging', for instance, is the language of something close to class hatred.

Much of the (suppressed) middle-class hostility towards what are seen as increasingly 'debased' forms of working-class life and manners is also morally justifiable, even if social taboo prevents open and rational discussion of it. Class unease is as uncomfortable with the young desperadoes of the football terraces as, say, with club-wielding Romanian miners laying about their opponents. But it prefers in general to look away, swallowing its distastes, or speaks behind its hands about the behaviour and even the appearance of the 'universal plebeian'. Indeed, the 'real working man' of Britain and America has become less and less visible in the shabbiness of the dole queue, in the decline of working class self-respect, and in the indices of lumpen violence. But little or nothing is said about it in these terms. That the image of the employed, skilled, organised and free-standing proletarian has become (in many eyes) disastrously blurred, especially in Britain and the United States, with that of the unemployed, unskilled, and welfare-addicted plebeian is not really in doubt. Even the objects of such conflation have begun to accept it. 'I am working-class,' a London security guard told the *Independent* in November 1990. 'Someone on the radio said there is no such thing as working-class any more. If that is so, why,' he asked, 'are there millions of people claiming social security benefits?' The conception of the 'working class' upon which he was insisting was that of the 'universal plebeian'. Under it, differences of skill and trade, and even of employment and unemployment, are dissolved into a mere commonality of wants, where none can hear his own voice amid the tumult of De Tocqueville's 'thousand simultaneous voices', nor distinguish ethically between the 'benefits' of welfare and the rewards of labour.

As for the socialist utopias, they were no more classless, despite professing to be so, than market societies are, or could be. Instead, the 'model proletarian' of the socialist order, with his guaranteed employment and secure (if poor quality) access to state-subsidised housing, food and transport, was one of the fixed pillars of socialism's variant of the capitalist class system. Together with the members of the apparatus that set him to his often energiless labours, he stood – with his irreducible proletarian role in the productive system – square in the path of an evolution to a 'classless society', if such a thing could be imagined to exist at all. He also came to embody the very essence of 'welfare man', part 'working class' helot or serf, part state-dependent. As the socialist system collapsed, his helplessness in the face of the market made the rootedness of his proletarianism even plainer.

In both the socialist and capitalist systems, the 'working class' was never what it seemed. The true 'struggle' of working people, East and West, consisted (as it does for most people) in the pursuit of individual interest, even if such interest was collectively organised by parties or trade unions. To 'escape' from the factory bench into self-employmemt, and thus out of the proletarian condition entirely, was, and is, the dream of many in the West. In the East, it remained a forlorn hope (of the minority) until the socialist system was overthrown. Failing such 'escape', two forms of compensation for remaining proletarian, one economic, the other cultural, have been sought in all social systems. The first, especially urgent where no avenues of promotion exist, is to seek more money for labour by collective pressures. The second, a less tangible and more 'ideological' compensation, is to lay claim to the imaginary class superiority of working-class people (and their 'culture') over others. Socialism in its various guises – from conventional trade unionism to revolutionary communism – placed the need for such compensations at the very heart of its moral philosophy and sense of purpose.

In both East and West, belief in the moral virtues of the 'old working-class way of life' has largely foundered. In the former, where the whole structure of society (ostensibly) rested upon such belief, the market now offers these virtues a low reward; in the latter, they are withering away by attrition. Nevertheless, the bedrock of modern working-class life and 'culture' was formed by factory industrialism, and as long as this kind of industrialism remains, so too will the way of life and labour which it fosters. In the socialist system, the proletarian condition was officially celebrated, the better to keep the proletariat in thrall and as the supposed source of moral value itself. In the capitalist system, it was middle-class leftists, above all, who guiltily sang the praises of 'the working-class' in much the same way that the inverted racist sees virtue in every ethnic group but his own. A regressive Marxist politics and economics of class further sought to provide proletarians themselves – although they were rarely interested – with a theory and practice which might justify feelings of pride and aggression, solidarity and resentment, engendered by industrial life itself. In the socialist system, the destruction of the 'bourgeoisie' additionally cleared the way for the free exercise of proletarian vices and virtues. But it was continuous exposure to the brutality of the industrial environment in both East and West, accompanied by the atrophying of creative artisanal skills, which helped to complete the process of modern proletarianisation.

The legacy of this process in both East and West has been cultural, social and physical. Overlaying it in the West, and especially in Britain and the United States, have been the futher complex effects of the welfare relation, as I have described. In combination with the wide-spread post-war failures of the educational and urban planning systems, the continuing confinement of large numbers of working people to what are often no more than ghettos, and the gradually stupefying impact of 'popular' television culture, the 'working-class way of life', shorn of much of its communal strength, has been radically transformed from the proletarian to the plebeian.

An ubiquitous lack of self-regard has steadily replaced, in the plebeian younger generation, the older proletarian pride in skill, energy and effort, the very elements of human ardour. It has gradually depressed, too, the valuation placed upon education and technical training, once high among working people. The same lack of self-regard has intensified (traditional working-class) feelings of resentment at the achievements of others. 'He's a mouthy bastard,' a young Newcastle man told the *Independent* in October 1991, speaking of a night-club attack on the footballer Paul Gascoigne, 'and he thinks he's a bit of a celebrity. *He's getting a few bob more than me and he should expect a bit of bother*' (my emphasis). Moreover, as reliance upon state provision has increased with chronic unemployment, so, paradoxically, has the hostility felt towards the state provider. At the same time, deepening the problems of plebeian youth, the sources of security and self-advancement remain largely what they always were. The style of the 'universal plebeian', powerful as it has become, has not yet overtaken demand for skill, literacy and qualification. But the main consequence of the (now particularly British) refusal, and misuse, of those opportunities which post-war public provision offered has been that the historic legacy of class disadvantage has not in essence been overcome, however many individuals may have overcome it. In many areas of public health, housing, education and urban regeneration there has, in addition, been not so much the substance of amelioration of conditions, as the appearance of it; superficial change, without fundamental alteration; and, beneath the surface of social progress, not much social progress at all.

It is not only in Britain that such social stasis bars the way. For, now, the British plebeian has been joined by his closest likeness, the post-communist worker of Eastern Europe and the former Soviet Union. 'I hear from intellectuals,' Lech Walesa sarcastically declared in April 1990, to a mass meeting of steelworkers, 'that they would like a president who knows foreign languages, throws parties five times a day, bows nicely and is very polite. And I ask: "Can we afford such a president today?"' ('Intellectuals', he also told his laughing audience, 'say "the President should look different and wear a suit and tie."') Walesa's unease, commonplace in precisely this form in Britain, was here typically focused on education, skills, social graces, manners and even appearance. Mockery is its style; a dismal animosity, that of the dog-in-the-manger, its substance.

This kind of scorn for the intellectual as effete layabout – 'all knowing', Walesa jeered in another public speech two months later – is the true mark of the plebeian. The self-educating proletarian of earlier times generally had too much regard for knowledge to be quite so dismissive. But the 'feverish impatience' of the post-communist world was now expressing itself freely for the first time, and for other than official socialist ends. And when it began to speak, as through the mouth of a Walesa, it spoke in a debased class language all-too-familiar. Among the worst of insults that could be offered in June 1991 by a Liverpool Militant (or working-class Trotskyite) spokeswoman who had been affronted by Frank Field, the anti-Militant Labour MP, was that he was 'just a middle-class intellectual'.

The left apologist for these deformed working-class attitudes, however primitive such attitudes might be, would in the past always find in them signs of healthy class energy, or 'class consciousness', however misdirected. But when a six-pack of Marlboro cigarettes, a good pair of trainers and a Japanese video – the beads and mirrors of the market – began so quickly, and for so many in Eastern Europe, to overwhelm the ideal goals of old socialist aspiration, it suddenly became less easy for the left to discern in the enthusiasm for such things those distinctive virtues which it had once invented for the working classes. In fact, the escaping proletariats of the socialist system were disclosing, with barely a single faltering of step, identical tastes and interests to those of the 'universal plebeian' in the West. Old and real proletarian disadvantage was now set to be coated in a thin film of consumption, just as in the West. The worst of both worlds beckoned.

In the former East Germany's forlorn cities and towns it was the life-style of West Germans to which hopes turned. At unification, East Germany's own products – its shoes, its clothes, its electrical goods, even its most ordinary foodstuffs – overnight became undesirable, and almost unsaleable, in the country that had produced them. Long-repressed consumer hungers sought (and generally failed to find) De Tocqueville's 'immediate satisfactions'. Furthermore, at the elbow of each thwarted ex-communist shopper stood post-communist Welfare Man, swiftly resentful that his new 'entitlements' to consume were not being adequately met, or not being met at all. In Chelyabinsk in the Urals, there were riots and demonstrations in August 1990 over a lack of cigarettes and vodka. Similarly, a Romanian politician returned from a rural campaign-tour during the May 1990 elections with the view that voters were 'not interested in politics, but only in food, drink, women and gasoline'. The 'workers and peasants' of the socialist hymnal were stretching their cramped limbs in the new market. And when Romanian miners, rampaging through Bucharest in June 1990, claimed to have found 'naked and drugged young women' in the 'basement' of the university's famous school of architecture, other darker hungers (and hatreds) were briefly glimpsed, demanding satisfaction.

Workers wearied by decades of communist imposition and hardship were also reported, often with condescension and easy judgment, to be 'not used to working efficiently and well'. The communist system was said by the *Daily Telegraph*, in May 1991, to have bequeathed a labour force in Russia that was 'slothful, inefficient, surly and unprepared for change'. In Poland, the 'culture of honest work' had been 'destroyed', with many 'unused to serious work, and unwilling to begin'. Silviu Brucan, one of the (Jewish) protagonists of the Romanian revolution and a former editor of the Party paper, was forced to resign (in uproar) from the National Salvation Front in February 1990 after predicting that there would be 'only two classes' in post-communist Romania: 'clever people and stupid people'. 'Ideally', Brucan continued, 'clever people will be the rulers and stupid people will have to vote for their masters in return for some basic comforts.' The working class, he added, was 'incapable of governing itself'. Even Ivan Pavlov, the then hardline Soviet prime minister who a few weeks later attempted to oust Gorbachev, declared in May 1991 that Russians 'have no confidence that they can make their way through life by honest work'.

Such 'bourgeois' observations as Brucan's and Pavlov's, common as they were during the communist period, were normally kept private. But with inhibitions freed by glasnost, and as the first post-communist workers emerged into daylight, all tongues were loosened on the subject of the debased proletarian. Hitherto, he had been the 'hero of socialist labour'. Now he would be said, by foreign observers and erstwhile local communists alike, to 'oscillate between slavishness and aggression'; to be hoping to 'get rich without much effort' under capitalist conditions; to suffer from 'deep-rooted envy', and so on. Gorbachev himself, in his resignation speech of December 1991, complained of 'the sponging attitudes' which had allegedly impeded reform. It would be routinely repeated that anyone in the former socialist countries who tried to make money, or who began to 'do well', would 'find himself shunned'. When 2,000 Polish miners demanding higher pay stormed into Lech Walesa's

presidential residence in February 1991, the latter was greeted by abuse
which hoist him on his own proletarian petard. 'You betrayed us,' the
miners shouted, 'you are the same bastard as they [the communists]
were.' Among the bones of (class) contention was that the former
shipyard electrician's presidential salary was 'six times higher than the
average Polish wage'. The charge of 'elitism', a common plebeian
charge in Britain, had been quick to surface in Poland.

Labour is a Prometheus as well as a prime mover, and unchained can
move mountains. (Chained, it can move them also, although more
slowly.) In much of the modern recoil from old proletarianism, or the
cult of the worker, a lurking fear of this Promethean power still plays a
role. In middle-class socialist deference towards the virtues of the
imagined, or imaginary, worker precisely this class fear used to be
found. Indeed, fear of the collective energies of the industrial proletariat, especially when such energy is aroused to anger in its own interest,
is both the historic explanation of much 'bourgeois' policy towards
working people and a taboo class subject in its own right.

Such policy above all sought, and still seeks, to harness the energies
of labour to its own purposes, but only to the extent that such energies
are needed. (It is a need which becomes especially fitful in times of
economic crisis.) In addition, social strife and civic unrest require to be
averted by paying sufficient attention, among other things, to Prometheus' wages and conditions. Any tendency to rebellion – that is to the
redirection of working-class energy away from its working-class roles –
has always had to be contained or, *in extremis*, suppressed. The latter
task has now been eased, at least to some extent, by the failure of
socialism as a political alternative to the market system. But the necessity
of controlling, or taming, Prometheus will remain as long as the
economic compulsion to perform industrial manual labour (and the
exemption from such compulsion) divides the social order. That is to
say, it will remain for ever; or as far as the prophetic eye can see.

In benign social and economic conditions in the market, when all
prosper – if to different degrees – proletarian frustrations and hostilities
may abate, or even seem to disappear, in mutual benevolence and
accord. In other cases, the same favourable conditions can stimulate
Prometheus to strike while the iron is hot. Conversely, under conditions
of crisis, insecurity may in some cases depress Promethean energy for
conflict, and, in others, intensify every latent anger. In each set of
conditions, both kinds of emotion may be at war within the same
individual. In other individuals, fatalistic acquiescence, placidity, or

genuine satisfaction with labour – or a combination of all three – survive the worst of economic times and the worst of social conditions. But much more general is the pall of class depression which is created by a life of increasingly insecure industrial labour often carried on, East and West, in environments which are degraded and asocial. If the proletarian Prometheus of the previous generation suffered from it, his sons, with their diminishing self-regard and skill, have suffered more. Moreover, it seems today as if even the immediate meeting of the wants of the plebeianised younger worker, and the provision of a 'multitude of innovations' under the best of Western market conditions, could not appease the scale and increasing violence of dissatisfied plebeian desire.

Some forms of its thuggishness have become world-wide. Indeed, thuggishness is a large aspect of the character of the 'universal plebeian'. Here, the increasingly inarticulate word is made flesh; the flesh, in a modern market society, may be clad in style; and style, carrying (say) a stanley-knife – like the bludgeon of the bedraggled Romanian miner – may, often at a seeming whim, set to its targets. Political violence and the affrays of youth, and even urban gang warfare, have no doubt accompanied human settlement from its beginnings. Patriotisms, national and local, have never been slow to pick a fight; even violence for 'fun' is as old at least as the Roman gladiatorial contest. Today's routines and habits of violence, as I shall show in a later chapter, have become a somewhat different matter. The various and changing styles of this violence are akin to those of products in a vicious market; its Promethean aggressions and hatreds, with their ever swifter reflexes (both in males and females), often seem close to the rabid, yet are increasingly taken for granted. Violence associated with plebeian gangs in Western (and Eastern) industrial countries, and variously directed at racial minorities, foreigners, homosexuals and rival gangs, is also an increasing commonplace. It, too, now goes largely unremarked, except by its victims, or in circumstances where a dramatic excrescence of it may catch the headlines.

Plebeian 'queer-bashing', for instance, shadowy in scale, has been reported from many countries in the last years, including from the former East Germany. It is said by 'gays' in Britain to be greatly underestimated. Most street assaults, including on homosexuals, go unreported; 'gays' themselves claim, against police denials, that in Britain alone fifty 'gay' men were murdered between 1987 and 1991. Gang assaults on foreign students in Bath and Brighton – 'chased', 'spat upon', 'punched', 'beaten with sticks', 'robbed' – were said in

1991 to have become 'regular'; the local police refused to disclose the statistics of it, and a discreet silence descended. On university campuses, and in university cities such as Oxford, physical attacks on students by plebeian gangs are equally discreetly veiled, or lost in the data of urban violence. Attacks on Bangladeshis in London, for example – said by the community itself to be 'continuous' and 'routine' – intermittently flare into public notice; a mere shower of sparks in the darkness. Attacks on public servants, such as railway guards (common in France also), social security benefit workers, teachers and hospital workers (including doctors, nurses and porters), hardly make the news; in February 1992, the National Union of Public Employees even began 'self-defence courses' for nurses and other female hospital staff to protect them from 'attack by the public'. In May 1990, Salvation Army volunteers, too, were attacked in central London and their early morning 'soup run' in the Strand was suspended.

In settings of seeming enjoyment, as well as in those of resentment and depression, aggression may brandish its fists, or, sometimes in cold blood, take a knife from its pocket. Sporting victors punch the air, faces set in a strange grimace; plebeian violence accompanies the holiday flight, the football team, the rock band. It is a universal style. In October 1987, and from a host of instances, Canadian fans of the British rock group GBH – the acronym for 'grievous bodily harm' – 'chopped up tables with an axe on a Canadian ferry' after a concert by the group during one of its 'global' tours. Told of the incident afterwards, the lead-singer of GBH described himself as 'quietly proud'; a large part of the world has also learned to laugh, however uneasily, at such amorality, since condemnation has no purchase. The ancient village brawls of drunken folk tradition, or the violent horse-play of gilded youth, could in the past also turn nasty. But aggression without a moral hangover is another matter.

Holiday violence, once confined to places of near resort, is now packaged and itinerant. In the British plebeian case, much of the world has become its potential stamping ground. In the 1950s, British 'Mods' clashed with British 'Rockers' in Brighton, Margate or Hastings; moved from battlefield to battlefield on motor-bikes and Vespas; fought each other on British beaches. Today, the British take a third of all their holidays abroad, a higher proportion than in most other countries, and one which is rising. They 'buy' more 'package' holidays than any other European nationals, and pay less for them. Promethean aggression has taken to the air. Spain and the Balearics, the Canaries, Greece and the

Greek islands are the most popular of the 'package destinations', and the places which have borne the brunt of the plebeian trouble.

Moving in groups, and often sporting the colours of national and football allegiance, drunken jollity and (more commonly) drunken sullenness and unease can swiftly turn to pack vandalism and violence. The plebeian dog-in-the-manager, to whom I have already referred, bares his teeth ('the Spanish are shit, I hate them') at the local citizen. He bawlingly expresses his feigned contempt for the youth of the place, and above all for its passing women; then picks his fights and smashes his surroundings, often with female British plebeians egging on, or even joining, the mayhem, until violent desire is sated. The next night the ritual will be repeated; the next week by newcomers, who will be indistinguishable in conduct and aggressive expectation from those who have returned home to working boredom, or (less frequently) to unemployment.

In many places, most of the malefactors will have been, as I have myself observed, young British males, and most frequently from the old industrial working-class areas of Britain. But the 'English disease' has been catching, and many other European nationalities – Dutch, Germans, French, Spanish, Portuguese, Greeks and Italians – have caught it, if in proportionately lesser numbers. Thus, German youths were deported from Czechoslovakia in August 1991 for 'running riot' in Prague; 'one hundred' Spanish youths behaved likewise in December 1988 in the French ski resort of Chambéry, 'looting shops and houses' and 'smashing cars'. When the 'holiday season' is over, the locals, many of whom will have benefited from (and exploited) the brutish invasion, will clean up and repair for the following season. There will have been wreckage galore, bloodshed from stabbings, 'bottlings' and so forth, and – in Ibiza, in Majorca, in Crete, in Corfu, on the Costa Brava – even rape and a few murders. 'Hooliganism' will have been a poor word for it, 'cheap drink' an insufficient explanation. Thereafter, in the resorts, silence descends. The whirlwind of deformed proletarian energy has passed on, to re-form on the football terraces or in the streets of the inner city.

The Newcastle United supporter chased like a fleeing fox (at a motorway service station) by a pack of Millwall fans and stabbed in the neck was left with an embossed visiting card: 'Congratulations', it read, 'You have just met Millwall'. The 'Chelsea Mob', members of which were brought unsuccessfully to trial in January 1987, ran a 'planned campaign of violence to ambush rival supporters', also leaving visiting cards with their fallen victims: 'You have been nominated and dealt with by the Chelsea Head Hunters,' they read. Boots, to kick a rival fan unconscious – kicking is the commonest form of unarmed attack – and knives, particularly stanley knives or modelling knives, have been the preferred instruments of violence used by football gangs. Slashing foes about the face evidently has its own appeal; 140 stitches for a Chelsea victim, and 80 stitches for a Coventry fan (attacked in his car, and also robbed) have been a Saturday's sporting outcome. Leeds Crown Court was told in April 1988 that a Leeds United gang travelled around in its own hired 'aggro bus'; Southwark Crown Court heard in June 1988 how fifty Millwall fans stormed through a railway station in pursuit of its quarry chanting 'Kill, kill, kill!'; smashed jaws, severed arteries and knife wounds in the back have all featured in trials of football supporters. Reports of violence, as if savouring their detail, themselves become fevered, making it difficult to tell fact from fancy. Thus, it was alleged that at the Hillsborough football ground disaster in April 1989, when ninety-five people were crushed to death, some fans 'urinated on the police'; at the Heysel stadium in Brussels, where thirty-nine Italians died in 1985, it was alleged by the Italian press that Liverpool fans had urinated on some of the suffocated victims. In June 1990, after England's World Cup defeat, a man of thirty-three, remonstrating with a group of disappointed supporters who were creating a disturbance in the street after watching the defeat on television – 'we are all upset about it,' he told them, 'but just go home' – was kicked to death by two youths and a girl of eighteen. It was barely noticed.

These are no longer the crimes and excesses of youthful high spirits. Football-associated violence takes place not only at the ground, or in the immediate aftermath of a match, but en route to, or far away from, it. As with holiday violence, it too has taken to the air. If it is the violence of a minority, it is also most frequently the violence of packs. It is often associated with rival styles of dressing, sometimes in costly fashion, by which opposing fans identify each other. It involves aggression not only against persons but against places and objects, and even against the fans' own means of transport to and from a match; the wrecking of trains and coaches is now too common to attract attention. Weapons used are very various: knives, clubs, axes, crossbows, cork-screws, ammonia and tear-gas have been seized by police from fans pre-pared for trouble. Anti-personnel gas canisters were taken from British football supporters in Germany in 1988, and in Sardinia in June 1990;

even a home-made fragmentation bomb has been found at a football-ground in Holland.

Some of the violence is clearly planned in advance. Indeed, British fans have been heard vaunting that they are both 'harder' and 'more professional', or better prepared, than the fans of other nations. But even if violent British fans set the original example, others are now as 'organised' as they. Most of the aggressors who come before the courts in Britain are males between the ages of eighteen and thirty, though knife-carriers at football matches have been found to be as young as thirteen. (A Swindon fan, charged in 1991 with the murder of a rival fan aged seventeen, was himself only fifteen.) More important, neither the holiday-violent nor the football-violent are quite the welfare dependents or 'idle riff-raff' of popular prejudice and glib assumption. According to a report to the British Sociological Association in April 1990, 30 per cent of British 'football hooligans' – an inadequate term – who have been brought before the courts in the last years had clerical jobs and more than 20 per cent were 'skilled workers'. Since the late 1980s, there have been some 6,000 of these arrests per annum. In the lists which I have kept, there feature, in addition to a substantial minority of the jobless, also clerks, labourers and drivers, a British Telecom engineer and a British Rail employee, self-employed decorators and a shop manager, a hospital chef and an ex-Falklands War paratrooper, a 'porter', a butcher and a 'packer', a sheet-metal worker and a panel-beater, a cable layer and a 'computer tester'. Many of them spend hundreds of pounds a year – and some a few thousands – on the costs of tickets and travel at home and abroad. There is some evidence, the extent of it disputed, of far-right political involvement in these troubles. Varieties of racist chanting are common at some grounds; the aggression of some footballers has played to the aggression of their supporters.

It is the violence carried out by some British fans abroad which has generally been more intense, and involved more random attacks on local people and more vandalism, than the violence carried out at home; arrests abroad are even regarded by some fans as 'battle honours'. Abroad, football-related violence, like holiday-related violence, often deals in a frightened vaunting-over others with drunken insult. It can pick, again at a whim, on anyone who attracts notice or incurs disfavour – a passing stranger, a fellow-passenger, a shopkeeper, a public servant. It places at particular risk of attack blacks and others who are visibly distinct. For some British fans abroad, that which is most different from the familiar is most exposed to desecration. Most revealing of all, the pattern of such conduct discloses in British offenders abroad a powerful absence of self-regard, the great stigma of the debased proletarian condition. Self-humiliation (in the name of insulting others), as by urinating in public or by baring the arse to passers-by, is rarely absent from the most violent of such exchanges. Their 'highest' point, or climax, is often the point of greatest self-abasement. These are the self-flagellations of Prometheus' sons.

At first involving the aping of British forms of violence-and-vandalism, including its chants and insignia, such deeds – usually in less gross versions than the British – have now been reported from many countries. They include Belgium, France, Germany, Holland, Italy, Poland, the former Soviet Union, Sweden and the former Yugoslavia; even Algeria and China. After German reunification, a sharp increase in football-related violence was noted in several former East German cities. In Leipzig, Dresden, and Cottbus it was associated with the chanting of neo-Nazi slogans, post-match street brawling, attacks on immigrants and damage to public transport. But although one rampage was much like another, British rampages in the Heysel stadium in Brussels in 1985, in Stuttgart and other German cities in 1988, in Stockholm and Athens in 1989, in various Italian cities in 1990, and in Malmo in June 1992 were notorious for the harm and anger they caused.

In the centre of Stuttgart in June 1988, in an orgy of fighting and damage, cries of 'box-head bastards', 'get yer tits out for the lads', and (whilst rival fans were being attacked) 'fuck off, this is England' greeted passing Germans. A *Guardian* reporter described seeing British fans in Stuttgart shooting home videos of what they called the 'best bits' of the violence. In Frankfurt, in 1988, they sang 'Eng-a-land, a country so great, there's nothing so pure and so true', and, less lyrically, 'England here, England there, England every fucking where'. Wrecked ferries and trains, looted shops, vandalised bars, and punched, knifed and robbed locals marked the British plebeian passage. Counter-violence, arrest, official complaint and inflamed local reportage were the impotent responses. The Heysel riot and its thirty-nine Italian deaths were described in the Italian press as a 'massacre' and a 'slaughter'; the Liverpool fans were *'barbari'*, *'assassini'*, and even *'killer-tifosi'*; their emotions were 'cannibal passions'. According to leading Italian newspapers, wading in gore, the suffocating Italian fans – 'yellow, violet, cyanosed, with their tongues swollen' – had had their 'throats cut' (*sgozzati*), and their stomachs 'ripped' (*squarciate*) by stabbings. Liverpool supporters, said *Corriere della Sera*, 'jumped on the dead'; 'jackals' robbed the corpses. 'These are not people but sick animals,' crudely declared a Stockholm newspaper in July 1989; the Swedish police were said to have been 'stunned by the ferocity of English fans'.

Explanation was glib, and varied. 'It is in everyone to let out aggression,' said the unashamed returning supporter. 'It is an assertion of masculine identity,' said the expert at his elbow. A 'war game', a 'disturbed minority', a 'cultural inferiority complex', declared others, flailing for reasons; even, 'it is fun, they like fighting,' as a paper to the British Sociological Association put it in 1990. The reflex of the left analyst was, and always is, to see the 'hooligan' as 'more deprived than depraved'. Another was to blame the government, as did a Labour MP in July 1990, for 'failing to create a climate in which civilised behaviour can flourish'. The reflex of the right, equally banal, was, and generally is, to suggest a 'good flogging', as did a Tory MP in June 1990. Others saw the plebeian marauder as 'incited' by the alien, or 'driven over the edge by drink'. Yet others, dabbling with justification and near-approval, typically mixed token reproach with apologia: 'our lads' were 'over-eager', merely wanted to 'enjoy the success of their teams', were 'patriots' even if 'a little headstrong'. 'Proud, English and just crazy about football', announced a commentator in the *Independent*, also in June 1990, as British fans fought (and were attacked by) police in Sardinia.

The intellectual is plainly out of his depth with the energies of the plebeian. Class is a forbidden frame of reference. The voices of the fans, and of their families, are insufficiently heard, or, if heard, not listened to. The combining of misplaced moral zeal – for team 'pride' and national 'honour' – with abject acts of self-debasement is too complex to grasp. So, too, is the mixture of class depression with aggressive exhilaration, or self-contempt with the frisson that destruction evidently gives. ('No one likes us, we don't care,' sang shambling British fans in Sardinia). 'I like going for trouble as well . . . On a match day, you just can't help it, you just get all geed up,' confessed a convicted Darlington supporter. 'Some people were saying, "If they won't let us in [ticketless, to a stadium], let's wreck the town,"' reported a British fan, of the September 1989 Stockholm riot. 'A night of glory', said a Liverpool football supporter, of the panic-to-death of Italian fans at Heysel. 'I feel sorry for the people who died,' he declared, 'but we are still proud of what we did.' 'Violence always gives me a buzz,' a Leeds fan was said (at Leeds Crown Court in April 1988) to have told an undercover police agent. 'You have got to keep up the name of Leeds, we are the best fucking hooligans in the country,' he added. 'We were stared at and provoked,' said a British fan returning from the pitched street-battles in Germany in June 1988; in a plebeian pub, when danders are up, merely to catch a drinker's eye at the wrong moment can start a shambles, and end in bloodshed.

For most, this increasingly aggressive plebeian world – at home, on holiday, and in its entertainments – is unknown, or known only by media report and hearsay. The moral sphere it inhabits, in which a broken bottle can be thrust into the face of an adversary 'in the heat of the moment', is as distant as another planet, to many. The raucous 'disgust' of relatives at the custodial sentences meted out by 'foreign' justice against British delinquency, as expressed in Liverpool after the Heysel stadium verdicts of the Belgian courts, speaks to an ethics of its own. 'We started it [the attack and stampede] to try to save our lads,' said the sentenced son. 'This isn't justice, this isn't fair. Why should we have to put up with this?' demanded his outraged mother, morally supported by fellow-plebeians, including local Labour MPs in a largely plebeian city. 'Junk justice', declared Swansea's MP, Donald Anderson, of prison sentences handed out to Swansea fans after a rampage in Athens in September 1989.

When authority offers solace thus to the 'misunderstood' and 'falsely judged', the punished plebeian, as his fever cools, complains the more righteously of having been made a 'scapegoat'. The violence itself – this violence and many others like it – continues, even if the forms and focus of it may alter. The militant energies it expresses cannot be called back, for the *primum mobile* of aspiration, however deformed, has its own momentum. Ugliness-upon-ugliness, in a world which is being despoiled, discharges its own Promethean passions over others. 'If someone smacks you, you smack them back' is its ancient, Hebraic slogan.

EIGHT

Sounds and Visions

When a society's policymakers and intellectuals seem out of their depth with, and even scared of, the plebeian behaviour of increasingly large numbers of that society's citizens, the latter are both disconcerted and encouraged to find how extensive are the space and licence which such confusion permits them. The fastidious middle-class liberal will generally seek to retreat from what he sees as the base world of the *hoi polloi*. But, at the same time, the progressive in him will find some virtue in what he is fleeing. A related ambiguity affects most left judgments of the plebeian. 'Mass culture', for instance, is seen by the left as largely a culture 'manipulated' by the market and its interests. But, simultaneously, the same left's disdain for 'elitism' leaves it with few positions to take. When, in addition, 'folk culture' is as atrophied as it is in modern industrial societies, the left has little remaining choice but to privilege the 'popular', as the plebeian is generally called, over the 'bourgeois', and *vox populi* over *vox dei*.

Conversely, the socially immature, the uneducated, and the violent, instead of failing (as they should fail) to find themselves reflected positively in the social order which they inhabit – and often harm – cannot be unaware that the social order has been partly reshaped to accommodate them. This is especially, but not exclusively, the case in its culture. Much of television culture, for instance, has been remade in the plebeian, or debased proletarian, image. In its mirror, plebeian life, including that life at its most degraded, may look upon itself in a generally positive light.

Sometimes, the plebeian life is presented as a source of benign or undemanding entertainment for others; sometimes, plebeian energies, including the most vicious, furnish the night's vicarious excitements. In neither case is it common for this life to be judged. Instead, it is in general faithfully reproduced, and, being faithfully reproduced (without judgment), is both confirmed to itself and legitimated in the eyes of others. Nor can any of this now be altered in its essence. On the contrary; the plebeian image is a market leader, its popularity the guarantor of ratings, franchises, profits and, therefore, of further confirmation and consolidation. To stand out against the victories of unlettered Demos is 'snobbery' or, again, 'elitism'. But this particular battle is over. It is Demos, not the dignified aspiration of Jude the Obscure, which has even conquered large areas of the education system. It cannot now be brought to withdraw.

Few intellectuals wish to be seen in open engagement on this terrain, rightly fearing scorn. They have, or think they have, their own high ground to which to withdraw. Moreover, those who have rolled up their sleeves to the issues of 'standards', especially in education, have had their fingers burned. They have seen their integrity, their statistics, and their motives instantly assailed. Lobbies of pedagogues, criminologists, welfarists and others, themselves *parti pris*, have entered the lists, morally armed to the teeth, against the anxious critic. Politicians have cudgelled each others' heads, or belaboured institutions with reforms, until tired of their own efforts. Neither more love nor more money, neither more centralisation nor more decentralisation, neither more voluntarism nor more state direction, neither left nor right nor centre, has been able to drive plebeian resistance from the field. Contrary to the left's old insistence, it is not 'bourgeois culture' which is 'hegemonic'. Taste itself – in education and in entertainment, in public behaviour and in fashion, in moral judgment and in popular music – has been transformed.

Moreover, such taste in the mass has more cultural and economic power than ever. Electronic innovation is its right arm; sheer numbers overwhelm. The thin piping sound of old discriminations is easily drowned by demotic acclamation of the goal scored, and the 'kill-joy' worsted. The new French Disneyland may have taken 5,000 acres of rural woodland – equivalent to one fifth of the entire area of Paris – for its 12,000 space parking lot, make-believe erupting volcano, and other pasteboard American fictions. But it also found some 4 billion dollars of investment finance, and hopes for 11 million visitors per annum; a 'second phase' is planned for the mid-1990s. Against it, cerebral muscle-flexing is both idle and puny. On this scale – the biggest civil engineering project in Europe after the Channel tunnel – mass taste, cynically managed, seeks to carry all before it. Nor is it merely that 'images of New Mexico', or a 'taste of Manhattan', or (at the Newport Bay Club recreated by Disney in Marne la Vallée) the 'atmosphere of a

New England seaside resort', have been brought to the ruined French countryside, at a cost of billions; in the face of such resources, the frightened foe of plebeianism surrenders. To argue that such a folly is a 'cultural Chernobyl' is a lost cause. It will stand or fall by the criterion of market demand, not aesthetic scruple.

For a bathtime Donald Duck to displace the French huntsman in water-meadows a mere twenty miles from Paris was no simple Hollywood triumph. The disastrous over-refinement of Western intellectualism must bear part of the blame. In self-defence, it has sought throughout this century to find protection from the depredations of mass-man but has served only to strengthen plebeian instincts against the 'culture of the elite'. Mickey Mouse speaks for this reproach. 'Within five minutes I will be bored out of my mind,' plangently declared a fluent letter-writer to the *Guardian* in June 1991, of the inaccessibility of the modern British music and drama to which he had tried to listen. '*Rambo*, on the other hand, is good for a laugh if nothing else . . . The role of the artist should not be one of self-gratification,' he added. Indeed, the artistic and literary unmeaning (at third as well as at first hearing, or seeing, or reading) of much contemporary aesthetic production has a great deal to answer for in the popular celebration of hostility to effete 'high culture'. What the self-loving aesthete perceives as the 'philistinism' of others, is often no more than a preference for the comprehensible over that which is without perceptible meaning. As the critic Harold Rosenberg famously pointed out, much modern art 'makes us uneasy' out of 'uncertainty as to whether we are in the presence of a genuine work of art or not'. Few stay to decide; 'philistinism' has its field-day, and 'culture' gets its deserts.

Moreover, in an age when instant and easy communication privileges the telegraphic, the vulgar 'sound-bite', and the 'one-liner', a species of cultivated unintelligibility stands at the heart of the lost authority of 'the intellectual'. Convolution, like artistic obscurantism, arouses popular mistrust where, once, complexity suggested 'depth' and invited respect. Today, the ever more confident plebeian – himself lacking the craft of the proletarian who preceded him – sees not greater wisdom but lack of skill and sense in the over-refinement of 'the intellectual'. (This in part explains the middle-class left's old resort, discussed in an earlier chapter, to an ingratiating vernacular, in the hope of 'reaching a working class audience'.) Now, it is the standard of expressiveness of television's *hommes moyens* (the two-sentence news reporter, the chat-show host, the fashionable 'presenter') which daily sets the intellectual mean before a vast audience. To step out of its range of vocabulary or reference is to step, more than was ever the case, into an intellectual outer-space: an outer-space inhabited almost entirely by other intellectuals. They speak the same language, but it is a language which is largely incomprehensible to others.

Worse, in the world of modernism's artistic follies incomprehensibility has always come close to being considered a virtue in itself. In 1979, to take an example at random, the film critic Richard Roud could declare the 'greatness' of Buñuel's *The Spectre of Freedom* to reside in the fact that it was 'not immediately understandable'. (It was, rather, an 'object for meditation'.) Significant-seeming unmeaning, and insignificance rendered significant by the appearance of profundity, have also played their parts. They were among the means by which the middle-class audience's own growing lack of faith in what was being presented to it could be waved away with a vacuous flourish of brush or pen. By such means, artistic whim created, and spoke to, audience fashion; passing fancy stood in for meaning, and credulity made meaning of it.

To act the true prophet in a vacuum of unbelief is not easy. But where there is neither an agreed language nor a civic function, 'high art' has increasingly become an empty pose. Moreover, except to its practitioners and the circles of the gulled, it both looks and sounds empty. To this vacuity, the intellectual left, in its period of strength, made its own populist contribution. It did so by making 'self-expression' and 'creativity' synonymous. They are not synonymous – the first is, at best, a most uncertain means to the second – but false left sentiment, fearful of the plebeian, sought to make them so.

In the name of arts which, for all their intermittent splendours of achievement, had already lost much of their self-belief as well as their technique and social purpose, the artist has addressed himself less to the public than to his own imagination and his fellow-artists. Painting for fellow-painters, sculpture for fellow-sculptors, musical composition for fellow-musicians, architecture for fellow-architects (even 'quality journalism' for other 'quality journalists') have been the outcome of an increasingly self-imposed isolation from public tastes, good, bad and indifferent. Disdained further for it, artists have offended and excluded the public further, in reprisal. Yet, in the turn of market judgments, they have also been rewarded for the offence, as the bitten hand of the audience for 'high art' was trained (by market managers) to feed the offender. In such circumstances, absence of meaning – inventing its purposes as it went – became no obstacle to the approval of the *aficionado*. But though artistic producer and consumer might collude successfully, if temporarily, in rigging the market in 'high art', it was at a high price for 'the intellectual' in the public and plebeian eye. For most of the bedecked priests of such culture came rightly to be seen, by 'philistines', to have no clothes – to the damage of intellectual pretension itself.

The know-nothing is, of course, made happy to think, in the clash of cultures, that there is no discipline at all in the works favoured by the 'snob' or 'elitist'. ('I could do better than that with my eyes shut,' is one of the mottoes of the 'universal plebeian'.) Marks on the desert ground and across hillsides, inglorious cacophanies and toneless lyrics, random verbiage, pictures of soup-cans and heaps of stones, earned notice – and even wealth – for a few, but the disrespect of many. Yet, there were sufficient collectors and galleries, sufficient publishers and concert promoters, to sustain for a while every hoax and to promote every fiction. Some, rejecting the art of the finished work or the 'precious object', made an art of the incomplete, the broken, the conventionally valueless and the rejected. Others, contemning the classical and the formal, made the emptiest (and most repetitive) breaking of convention their claim to fame, as if iconoclasm for its own sake, rather than for the attainment of illumination, was an artistic value.

Prophecy in this period has spoken in inaudible or untranslatable tongues; the light of art has been shed on darkness, but the darkness has remained as profound as ever. Even singularity, being so strained after by so many, has lost its *éclat*; where all are singular, no one is singular. Having reached the outermost bounds of the 'shocking' – an eight-decade journey from the twelve-tone scale to the 'snuff movie' – there is at the last nowhere for art to go. Every 'advanced' position has already been taken. Some artists, retracing their steps, have gone backwards into 'post-modernism'; some have travelled hopefully in eclectic circles; some have persisted on the edge of futility and beyond; others have fallen into bewilderment or silence. The landscape of art has been tunnelled through, but beneath every tunnel is another deeper. That much of the edifice of 'the modern' has now fallen in upon itself, with few to lament its collapsed sense of direction, is no more than poetic justice. Noses have been thumbed, by artists themselves, at 'art' and 'culture' for nearly a century. The triumph of the plebeian is its main outcome.

Moreover, for all the effort of it, the 'bourgeois' had been only briefly 'shocked'. At the last, he was paying tens of millions not only for a Van

Gogh, but for the least decipherable of daubs, while Everyman, excluded more than he had ever been from the world of 'bourgeois' fancy, had surrendered increasingly to the shallowest stimulus at hand. Those who refused the emotional impoverishments of modernism at its most *outré*, on the one hand, and of cultural plebeianism at its most vulgar, on the other, crowded (some) galleries, museums and concert-halls in search of relief and solace. Arts-related and craft activities, as some British statistics showed, continued to occupy the attentions of many. But left assault upon 'elitism' in the name of John Citizen, an assault invited by the self-indulgent egotism of the few, continued to advance the cause of the plebeian.

'Sir Roy Shaw', the then chairman of the Arts Council, 'still seems to be locked into the notion that there is something special about certain types of art,' declared a letter-writing left critic in the *Guardian* as late as January 1987 – giving his address as the Shaw Theatre in London – 'and that these should be foisted upon the masses of this country. I am sure he still firmly believes', the writer added, 'that if car workers are given indigestion in their canteen by the incessant [*sic*] playing of string quartets all is right with the world.' But plebeian self-confidence has no further need of this type of amanuensis to plead on its behalf. In the maw of 'popular' television, 'elitism' is suffocated; 'snobbery' and its supposed impositions can be extinguished at the flick of a button. Even such cultural failures as loss of capacity in language – as many as one in six people in Britain are now estimated to have 'literacy problems' – are routinely met with swift countercharges not merely as to 'underfunding', but as to the 'elitism' of the critic. Indeed, these are as much catch-all plebeian alibis as the 'it wasn't my fault' of the football delinquent.

The reflex belittling of a disliked judgment as that of 'privilege' against common taste, is the left's last unkind legacy to political and artistic discourse. 'Like Latin, classicism these days communicates nothing but snobbery,' was another *Guardian* letter-writer's telling opinion, published in August 1991; a judgment which would consign both classicism and Latin, on the instant, to moral oblivion. It was asserted, in the same source, that there was a 'middle-class conspiracy to fund "serious art", at the expense of other equally valid forms'; a judgment which sentenced 'serious art' to exile in a middle-class no-man's-land, where no plebeian worth his salt would enter.

Such reflexes, and the scared apologias for 'popular' taste and habits, however base, which accompany them, have as little time for old elitism's fuddy-duddy correctitudes of language, say, as with its notions of just, or seemly, behaviour. Against whatever bears the stigmata of 'snobbery' or 'privilege', the vulgarities of demotic rule are able not merely to resist challenge over words 'not fitly spoken', but to prevail. A half-educated member of parliament may now refer to a government proposal as a 'piece of demented madness', or a prime minister confuse the verbs to 'lay' and 'lie' – only 'elitism' would now check it. If malapropisms, mis-spellings, split infinitives and the weariest clichés spread through 'the media' and every kind of public declaration, it is only 'snobbery' which would now draw attention to them.

A sample trawl in 1990 and 1991 of issues of *The Times*, *Guardian* and *Independent* could turn up 'adaption' (for 'adaptation'), 'addage', 'annointed', 'ariel' (for 'aerial', in the *Guardian*, on 25 March 1991), 'corruscating', 'disasterous', 'equivalant', 'existance', 'install', 'interlocuters', 'irrascible', 'ommitted', 'parrafin', 'peninsular' (as a noun), 'repentent', 'villified' and so on. 'Batallions', 'collossus' and 'viscious' appeared even in headlines, while the *Evening Standard* ran a story on 11 February 1992 entitled 'The Elusion of Grandeur'. But only pedantry would now trouble its middle-class head over such matters. That a London headmaster, no less, could object in June 1991 to 'didactic teaching', or that a statement the following month by the National Union of Teachers – criticising government education policies – could contain several grammatical errors, signifies failure only to the 'elitist'. And perish the 'bourgeois' thought that the uneducated could now be well-placed among the educators, or that the half-literate could be forming a nation's opinions and guiding its judgments. 'Criteria' as a singular is not, after all, a hanging matter; and language is a living force changing and developing with the generations.

Nevertheless, when the leader of a British teachers' union can assert, in September 1991, that 'a pencil and paper test in a practical subject such as science is daft', plebeian self-confidence has clearly travelled some distance, and begun to instal its coarseness in seats of substantial cultural power. The idle journalistic cliché-monger who speaks of 'rings of steel', 'bargaining chips' or 'ruthless purges' is a familiar, but relatively insignificant, figure. The inability of American astronauts to communicate, either articulately or interestingly, what they felt and saw on setting foot on the Moon – a place far beyond Man's previous Ultima Thule – was a more decisive matter. It was one of many ironies of this historic failure that a Jewish desperado-of-letters, Norman Mailer, should have been driven (in his book *Of A Fire on the Moon*) to put himself imaginatively in the space-travellers' places. In an unlikely astronaut's persona, Mailer took up his pen to describe what he had not seen, in the stead of the blockish voyagers who could barely tell mankind of their astonishing experiences.

In September 1991, America's College Board reported that the reading and writing skills of American high school classes in that year were the poorest on record. Commentators spoke, in passing alarm, of a 'revolt against reading' among American youth during the last quarter-century; and, more extravagantly still, of the written word as an 'endangered species'. (In Britain, one in four sixteen- to twenty-year-olds now say they have difficulties with reading.) Newspaper-owners justly took fright at what it portended: the proportion of eighteen- to twenty-nine-year-olds in America who were daily readers of the press had already halved in the last twenty-five years. It suggested that not even the combination of tabloid excess and contraction of language had sufficed to withstand the greater attraction of the visual image, and the visual sensation. In some areas of the press, populist brashness – designed to appeal to plebeian choices – was made into a virtue. But it also served to undermine the authority of many newspapers, without compensating advantage either in revenue or the quality of truth-telling.

The new spread of the unexpressive was a wide one; it was not only the interests of the readers of tabloids which were met, or were thought to be met, by abbreviated insights and monosyllables. In 'high art', too, and especially in the theatre, there were many signs of such losses being pressed into 'creative' service. The seemingly significant brevities, pregnant pauses, and gnomic commonplaces of the 'Pinteresque' appeared sometimes to be mere incapacity of expression. By positing the 'inadequacy' of language to convey depth of feeling and nuance of meaning, the tongue-tied writer – no Shakespeare, he – seemed rather to be seeking an alibi for his own diminished verbal skills. It made culturally possible the declaration in 1991 by a National Theatre guest director, Philip Prowse, that the words of the dramatist were of no more importance in the theatre than the work of the usherette. (Even the usherettes objected.) In often glittering counter-displays of torrents of words, particularly in the novel, some 'bourgeois' writers pitted increasingly elaborate artifice against such rationalisations for incoherence. But upon the enforced and despairingly over-refined style of such works, the long reach of a plebeianised culture, fists clenched, had again left its destructive mark.

Once, the preacher had sought to 'find out acceptable words'. The search was, and is, an arduous matter, of experience and learning, of sensibility and training, of memory and observation; and 'that which was written was upright, even words of truth'. The spreading culture of plebeian resistance to technique and training has gradually sapped – and even carried away entirely – skills of this and other kinds; it has been able to dictate, if sometimes at many removes, the terms of intellectual anxiety, and even the forms of art. Such developments drew from the plebeian-influenced left its own egalitarian theories of culture. Many of these theories pretended, sometimes with impressive confidence, that there were no distinctions of value between one cultural artefact and another. Only 'elitism', it implied, would make out a case to the contrary. Cultural and artistic preferences were contingent matters of time, place, standpoint and frame of reference, not of intrinsic merit or demerit. Not only beauty but also skill and meaning lay in the eye and mind of the beholder. All the world of human signs, plebeian signs included, constituted a text to be decoded, a sonnet of Keats at one with a graffito on the walls of the inner city. It was as if that 'pall of class depression' and disadvantage to which I have referred had settled even upon the groves of academe. Now, an adoptive plebeianism had come to redress that historic imbalance which had always sought to privilege the expressions of the select (or elect) few at the expense of the expressions of the many.

This was an old relativism clad in new, and often highly elaborate, fustian. Its own sign language was, paradoxically, inaccessible to all but a few intellectuals. Marx, in the *German Ideology*, had offered his own, similar version of it in the 1840s. 'The exclusive concentration of artistic talent in particular individuals,' wrote Marx – who hired private music-teachers for his own daughters – 'and its suppression in the broad mass, is a consequence of the division of labour.' In communist society, he direly promised, there would be 'no painters, but, at most, people who engage in painting among other activities'. One hundred and fifty years ago, the word 'elitism' was not yet in left vogue as a term of plebeian reproach for certain kinds of intellectual effort and expectation. But the emotion of it is an old one, as is the history of left justifications for feeling it; or for having, out of class guilt, to pretend to feel it. 'Whether an individual like Raphael succeeds in developing his talents,' Marx wrote, 'depends wholly [*sic*] on demand, which in turn depends on the division of labour, and the conditions of human culture resulting from it.'

The modern period's vicarious cultural democrats have been as fearful as their predecessors of being thought by others not to be egalitarians. But their task has become easier in the era of the 'universal plebeian'. The effort required of a Marx to reduce Raphael's art to a question of the 'division of labour' has not been required of those contemporary left intellectuals who have chosen to elevate the furthest extremes of plebeian behaviour and expression into parity of esteem with other forms of 'cultural production'. The violent feelings, sometimes sadistic, of 'heavy rock' – the music of class at its most self-hating – have even been roughly inserted, by a complementary intellectual violence, into the folk tradition of 'working-class protest music'. Other types of plebeian incoherence have been 're-read', without controversy, as 'intensity of experience', and thus ratified as expressive forms of culture like any other. It is a path which previous generations of left intellectuals, deferring to the proletarian as they now defer to the plebeian, often took. In September 1971, Jean-Paul Sartre solemnly declared that the intellectual 'must now write *with* the masses, in liaison with them. He must put his technical knowledge at their disposal. He is an intellectual,' Sartre allowed himself to say, 'because of the masses and through them; therefore he owes his knowledge to them, and must be with them and in them; he must be dedicated to work for their problems, not his own.'

This is, in its fashion, the *locus classicus* of middle-class left affectation. It epitomises the desire of some intellectuals to surrender to a world of which it imagines a great deal, but knows next to nothing. Moreover, the left error which invented 'socialist realism', privileged 'proletarian literature', and raised depictions of blast-furnaces to the status of 'high art' was an old one. It was compounded of egalitarian intentions, moral equivocation and utopian illusion, in equal measure. But where once it lent its intellectual energies to depicting proletarian manual effort in bright or heroic colours, it now does much the same with electronic plebeian angers and despairs. And just as during the communist period many a depressed East European made a nightly electronic emigration to the West, in the privacy of his home, so the 'universal plebeian' seeks refuge from the industrial world in a global village of thundering sound. And, at a safe distance, a sheepish intellectual watches, and may even clap his hands. The same intellectual, trembling in his boots, once tried to make his peace with the stolid, organised and puritanically self-respecting proletarian. Now that the latter is dead, or dying, the former has turned his attentions to the proletarian's multitudinous, uprooted plebeian offspring, consoling themselves with a hedonism tailored by the market to their unmet wants. However violent may be the hunger to satisfy such wants, and however un-nutritious the cultural *pabulum* on offer, the credulous expert follows youth (at an interval) in order to observe it at its commons. There was never such a humiliating mopping-and-mowing for the scraps thrown from youth's table.

In his September 1990 essay entitled 'How We Must Rebuild Russia', Alexander Solzhenitsyn objected fiercely to Soviet youth's 'soaking up' of the West's 'waste products' – including what he called its 'degraded pop music' – where 'once the Iron Curtain had defended our country from the best the West could offer'. But this was to ignore the powerful appeal of the 'universal plebeian' in bringing down socialist rule in the first place. 'Socialist culture', already in its intellectual dotage, did not survive its electronic encounters with Western 'popular culture'. Marxism-Leninism foundered, among other things, upon the rock of rock music, and sank (*inter alia*) in a tide of pop. In Bulgaria, during the decisive general strike of November 1990, even state radio and television, after joining the strike, played Beatles music and screened Pink Floyd's *The Wall*. In Albania, students successfully demanded (in February 1991) that the Enver Hoxha museum in Tirana be turned into a disco; in Cluj in Transylvania, during the darkest winter of the Ceausescu period, I saw the words 'Deep Purple' chalked upon a wall. Even in Ulan Bator, where British rock music had been popular since the mid-1980s, a Western-style rock group, The Honkh, led the protest demonstrations of January 1990, demonstrations which accompanied the collapse of communism in Mongolia. In June 1990, Stalinists in Sofia were referred to as the 'heavy metals' by spokesmen of the Bulgarian reform communist movement, while young people, in the same month, sang 'Hey Jude' in mass protest outside the city's House of Culture. In the Soviet Union, in Poland, in Czechoslovakia, in Hungary, rock and anarchic punk styles were sported during the 1980s in defiance of wooden proletarian convention, and at the risk of harassment and arrest. The night-stick was a blunt instrument against rock, but it is not surprising that it was used: the thesis and antithesis of Marxist dialectics were being capped by the synthesiser's all-conquering sound.

East had met West in an embrace from which a Solzhenitsyn might recoil. The same kind of demotic pressures which had been brought to bear upon cultural 'elitism' in the West had helped to suffocate 'socialist culture' as well. Pop music, in all its forms, was a world-force, corresponding to the universality of the plebeian emotions it reflected. The like and scale of it, magnified by technology, had never been seen before. 'If there are icons for this generation,' wrote Brett Easton Ellis, the young author of the murderous *American Psycho*, in 1991, 'they're in pop music.' He singled out the Italo-American pop-singer Madonna, whose talent lay in her 'willingness to transform herself and change images wildly'. Ellis made no bones about the seductive attractions of what he called (without disapproval) 'junk culture', with its 'fleeting pleasures'. 'It is hardly surprising,' he continued, 'that this generation has a nihilistic fascination with a culture that is so flagrantly superficial, so antithetical to idealised childhood notions of value, yet so in tune with adolescent experience.' 'Superficial' such 'junk culture' might be, but in the battle of generations and styles, East and West, the wounds it succeeded in inflicting on its adversaries and their 'notions of value' were deep ones. 'Adolescent' it might be too, but it was not innocent. (Plebeianism matures quickly and is old by thirty, the damage done.) 'We', wrote Ellis on behalf of the youth audience of the world, of which he still counted himself a member, 'are unshockable . . . This generation has been wooed with visions of violence, both fictive and real, since childhood . . . violence so extreme that it verges on the baroque,' its effects 'blunted by repetition'. The benign world of the Beatles had passed. 'The twenty-something audience' had 'seen everything'. Its attitude, jaded by 'zapping' from channel to channel of sensation, was, said the author of *American Psycho*, 'a cynical "I dare you to show me"'. Even sexuality was now 'overlaid' with 'freakishness', Ellis declared, and violence was its 'norm'. And so on.

The account of all this was as amorally 'sophisticated' in tone as the matters which were being discussed. But in the sense it conveyed of the speed of transformation, aided by technology, of the styles of 'junk culture' and of its 'fleeting pleasures', there was a glimpse of the wave which had struck the floundering socialist world, and which has struck hard at our own. Moreover, at every new surge of the plebeian tide, a 'serious' analyst (literary, musical, sociological and others besides) has immediately been at hand with apologia and explanation. If a film 'breaks new ground', as *The Accused* was said to have done in 1989, with its 'graphic portrayal' of gang rape carried out while a group of jeering men looks on, an expert apologist – in this case, astonishingly, female – could be heard declaring that rape had been 'too often glossed over in films' and 'left to the imagination', precisely as Aristotle recommended. But with this film, the female critic approvingly declared, 'the camera does not flinch from the unpalatable details of the attack.' It was a 'fair and honest attempt to convey the grim reality of rape'. Indeed, for a vast audience, growing vaster, 'grim reality' and the 'unpalatable' had come to possess their own savour, the grimmer and the more unpalatable the better. Like the unruffled *tricoteuses* who sat beside the guillotines of the French Revolution as heads rolled, this audience preferred its pleasures in the raw. And, standing in the wings, the chic, but plebeianised, intellectual applauded.

In explosive Los Angeles, murderous crack-dealing gangs – such as 'The Crips' and 'The Blood', who (among their changing sartorial styles) sport the colours of local football teams – kill for street conquest. An equally 'unflinching' film about their underworld, *Boyz N The Hood*, much praised and shrewdly made, triggered looting and fatal gun battles in and around the cinemas which showed it. Other gang-related films, such as *New Jack City* in 1991 and *Juice* (street slang for power) in 1992, elicited similar violent responses and earned millions; plebeian art had imitated plebeian nature and been itself imitated, to the point of further killing. It does not deter the 'new criticism', wary of being thought 'elitist' or old-fashioned, from its approbations; or, if more cowardly still, from sitting on its hands in silence.

The plebeian reach is a long one, and growing longer. In the uproar over child-abuse in Britain, it was not finally clear whether young, and sometimes very young, child complainants alleging 'satanic sexual abuse' had, or had not, regularly seen violent and frightening pornographic videos at home. A 'diet of horror', the lip-smacking tabloid press called it, joining in. Puzzlement therefore remained, in many cases, as to whether or not the children had imagined what (they said) had been done to them by family members, friends and neighbours. But without the influence of such films, few could adequately explain how children as young as five were able to invent what they recounted, if they were inventing it. In fact, there was much medical evidence, fiercely contested as it was (in some cases), to indicate that they were often telling the truth.

It was evidence, much of it uncomfortably derived from plebeian, or degraded proletarian, life-styles, which suggested a wider scale of sexual abuse than many bystanders appeared ready or willing to believe. Here, complex taboos of different kinds were at work to cloud judgment and to conceal feeling. They ranged from old taboos against sexual candour in general, to newer taboos – equally powerful – against candour about the 'universal plebeian' and his, or her, domestic mores. Yet, if a 'diet of horror' was indeed being consumed by those at whom fingers were pointed, it would hardly have been an exceptional matter historically;

vicariously enjoyed terrors have always possessed their relish. It was even less exceptional in the context of contemporary 'popular' tastes in violence; a 'nihilistic' and 'unshockable' fascination with visions (and videos) of one kind of horror or another is a commonplace. Indeed, a morass of synthetic, imaginary violence is now available, almost on the instant, to the 'universal plebeian' of the Western industrial world, and far beyond it. Nor is this the old violence, which was merely read. Brutalities seen in an emotional twilight and savoured in cold blood, or replayed in slow motion before the eyes, possess an immediacy beyond the reach of any written word. But even for the unaffected, for those left cold, habituation to violence as a routine is no moral progress. According to a British Independent Television commission finding, the proportion of viewers 'offended by televised violence' during the course of 1990 fell to a minimal 10 per cent. The Broadcasting Standards Council, mocked for its Grundyism, found in July 1990 that no fewer than 90 per cent of poll respondents said that they actively 'enjoyed' at least one 'type' (among alternative 'types') of violent film on their televised menus of violence. Only 'elitism', struggling uphill, could deny so many their pleasures.

Violence in music, on film and on television is often held – perhaps especially by intellectuals in awe of the physicality, or brawn, of others – to be 'not the same as violence in life'. (But the imaginative life, whatever its form, is life also.) There is no doubt, as apologists insist, that the myriad violences in question vary in 'quality' and 'purpose', as well as in their effects. The suggestion, however, that some of those violences, particularly the most gratuitous and banal, might express at close remove aggressive loss of dignity and self-esteem, or absence of love, identity and sense of purpose – plebeian wounds – is again a taboo subject. There remains to 'popular culture', notably in its surviving non-electronic forms, much which is consolingly unaggressive in its emotions. Yet, it is the case, too, that the more 'innocent' tones of some earlier pop and rock music have lost favour. Many of the links with an older folk tradition, still audible three (less plebeian) decades ago, have also been broken; it is not a coincidence that in this same period the 'culture of the working class', East and West, has disintegrated. Metallic stridency has advanced upon earlier forms of plangent self-pity; the sound engineer works acoustic wonders beyond the limited skills of the singer and musician; physical energy gains ground upon which talent cannot enter; the lyric is barely heard. Against such constraints, many of them shaped by the new technologies of music production themselves, new forms of popular musical expression continue to emerge, and to struggle for survival. But most become, or are made by market pressures, gradually indistinct from their manufactured predecessors. The technological sound of the recording studio, and the ring of the cash till, remain the loudest sounds of all.

If youth's wider aspirations cannot often be heard, or heard clearly, in its volumes, class (and race) depression and anger have been most audibly set to music, and with their own rhythms. In their turbulence, sound and feeling, vitality and exuberance remain. But the preoccupation with violence – with doing, and not merely suffering, harm – is also a constant presence. In close attendance, the record salesman, the disc jockey, and the amoral critic between them help to market whatever comes their way. There are few scruples. 'Have the razor-boys who recorded "Kill 'Em All" gone soft?' a *Guardian* headline asked on its 'Music Review' page in August 1991. Beneath this headline, the 'pop sensibility' of the heavy-metal group 'Metallica' (and related matters) was discussed in the characteristic style of the falsely jovial intellectual who is (with reason) frightened of the plebeian. 'Metal is a many-splendoured thing. The extraordinary GWAR perform a hypertheatrical stage show featuring sodomy, disembowelling and the slaughter of their would-be censors. Down in Florida, there's a boom in Death Metal, where the groups have names like Deicide and Obituary,' the critic enthusiastically explains. As for Metallica's music, it 'has been "evolving" for ten years from the "Thrash Metal" of "Kill 'Em All"'. This record is described, without hint of a value judgment, as 'fifty minutes of razorback riffs and rampant rhythms', an experience which is 'like being bludgeoned to death with crowbars of decibels'.

Their previous songs, the reader is informed, 'traditionally dealt in fear and anxiety'; their new release is 'almost friendly sounding'. Hence the newspaper cross-head, vicious in its own jocular way, which questions whether the 'razor-boys' have 'gone soft'. The critic further reports that 'Metallica' had received photos from American forces in the Gulf, 'proudly showing off bombs with "Metallica" painted on them', and that 'fighter pilots' had written to tell the band that 'a blast of "Kill 'Em All" was perfect mood-music for zapping Iraq'. No whisper of irony protects the reader from the impact of this verbal violence.

Thrash Metal, Speed Metal (with groups such as 'Carcass' and 'Napalm Death'), Hard Core, Death Metal – an American band is called 'Massacre' – and Cock Rock, which offers little to the dignities of women, have been described as an integral part of the 'international

rock movement', the voice of Anglo-American plebeian culture. But for
Death Metal to be praised, as it was by the *Independent* in August 1991,
and likewise without moral judgment, not merely as 'easily the best of
the bunch' but as offering 'serial killer chic' was to take an adoptive
plebeianism to its furthest and most gratuitous limits. Against the (at
best) terrified jokiness of it, 'snobbery' and 'elitism' might protest until
they were blue in the face; violence thus gilded over – no matter what
shape it took – and sustained by an entire industry of effort, was too
hard an obstacle for the merely word-armed opponent. Huffing and
puffing with his long-outmoded moral objections, the latter could do
nothing whatever.

The intensity of black plebeian angers, both real and feigned, and
the white liberal's fears of such angers, make critical assault on them
even less likely. 'Gangsta' black rap-groups, for example, use openly
violent language against their racial and sexual targets. In November
1991, the American rap-group 'Ice Cube', in a release called *Death
Certificate*, objected to a 'white Jew telling you what to do' and explicitly
recommended a bullet in the head for it. In June 1991, another such
rap-group from Los Angeles, 'Niggaz With Attitude', was idly singing,
or speaking, of meeting abuse with a sawn-off shotgun: 'When I'm
called off,' said the rapper, 'I get a sawed-off,/Squeeze the trigger/And
bodies are hauled off.' To the frightened critic who has laid aside his
moral faculties, it is merely a 'genre' sentiment, or 'ethnic' flamboyance,
or even irony. Such language is 'often very bitterly sarcastic and rude,
and will appear to our ears rude and crude', a leading British Queen's
Counsel told Redbridge magistrates' court in December 1990, of the
'lyrics' in an album by 'Niggaz With Attitude' which had been seized by
the police. 'But there it is, all part of the experience,' he declared. 'It
tells it like it is,' the advocate added in the vernacular – a familiar reflex
– after himself conceding that the lyrics were 'hateful', and aroused
'distaste, concern and fear'. *Do the Right Thing* (1989), a black-made
film about a fantasy New York riot which ends in burning and killing,
suggested both in its title and in its content that the way for blacks to
make progress was through violence. It was quickly re-presented by the
scared film-critic as no more than an 'art movie'; in the Los Angeles
riots in April 1992, life imitated art.

The corpses which bestrew the stage at the end of *Hamlet* not only
invite, but demand, a moral judgment, towards which the preceding
hours in the theatre have been driving the audience. Even the deaths of
the most wicked in Greek and Elizabethan tragedy are the object of

awe, whether at the power of the gods or the scale of human folly. Violence is not a purpose of art, but is purged by it, and fears aroused are also allayed by a sense of restored order, human or divine. Violence and death in Shakespeare's London, as in the rocker's and rapper's New York, were in the very air. But it was not violence which yoked 'life' and 'art' together. After seeing *The Revenger's Tragedy* it is doubtful that a groundling would have been inspired to stab his neighbour, in the way a fifteen-year-old Long Island boy was shot in the head and killed during one of the volleys of firing which accompanied screenings of the *Godfather, Part III*. Between the Elizabethan theatre and the streets of the city the existence of an imaginative wall made dramatic speculation about, and lyric judgment upon, 'life' the distinct realm of 'art'; when the average American or Briton spent some four hours each day watching television, a social or cultural life away from the screen had become, for millions of households, an interlude between pro-grammes. And if poll findings and programme schedules are a guide, for many the more violent the better.

Seeing, not reading, had increasingly – in all television-dominated cultures – again become the basis of believing, including for school-children. It was almost as if the Gutenberg revolution had not been. A British official survey, published in July 1991 and based upon infor-mation collected in 1988 from a large sample of 217,000 pupils in primary and secondary schools, disclosed that more than half of eleven-year-olds had television sets in their bedrooms. The average time spent on reading by eleven-year-olds was a mere three hours *a week*, while on average school pupils of all ages watched television for three hours *a night*. Another survey suggested that one in five of eleven- to twelve-year-old boys watched television every evening for 'five hours or more'. Signs of a modest reduction in sated adult viewing have not been matched in school children.

Reading, too, may be idle. But even when idle, it demands a certain minimum of energy and application, while (dependent on choice) simultaneously permitting and encouraging fantasy and speculation. Watching television may arouse the fancy, and (dependent on choice) inform, even if little remains. But, unlike reading, it is also compatible with a condition of entire inertia. 'Elitism', fond of pointing to statistics of educational failure, in general recoils at hours 'wasted' watching television; the 'universal plebeian' in general sees little harm, if not much good, in it. The anxious or over-anxious intellectual, observing what he perceives as the growing glut of information and the growing dearth of knowledge, says, with Saul Bellow, 'We are informed about everything. We know nothing.' In his turn, the cultural optimist celebrates the 'explosion' of new technical means, whether to entertain, to process data, to control production or to communicate with the spheres. In the meantime, American seventeen-year-olds, according to the US Department of Education, knew even less science in 1990 than they did in 1970, and the downward trend continues.

It was not only plebeian television and pop music cultures – the cultures 'snobbery' mostly disapproved – which were the objects of passive, or morally comatose, consumption. In the culture of modern industrial societies, it could be argued, the technology of mass communication (and of marketing hype) has kept the citizen-spectator at an increasingly remote distance from many different stages. In the glare of television arc-lights he could see, but not be seen. In other arts, too, the egotistical energies of a few, magnified by electronics, have blocked the genuine participation of the many. Moreover, not only was the physical presence of an audience rarely necessary to television, but (as with radio) an audience's seeming presence could be suggested. So, too, could its approval, when applause and laughter were – with increasing frequency – canned. Indeed, 'live performance' became a term of art for specialised circumstances which permitted the engagement of senses and emotions dulled to depression by the electronic.

'High' art, the select province of the 'elitist', was itself increasingly dominated by the same, or analogous, forces. The gallery-owner more than ever commanded the artist; vaunting theatre directors put out the light as often as they shed illumination on the drama; orchestral conductors commanded fees for brandishing a baton which no composer could earn. 'Karajan's Ninth Symphony' or 'Brook's *Dream*' gave, or sought to give, the interpreter, who had the technical medium at his command, absolute precedence over the composer and the playwright. Synthetic energy, as always technologically armed, inspired and assaulted the cultivated spectator too, who could be as submissive to technology's aesthetic blows as any slumped plebeian caught in a hail of television gunfire. In the theatre, in the novel, in classical musical performance, in the cinema, in architecture, even in the dance, it seemed increasingly the case that style (or fashion) thought first of an effect to be created – rather than of an artistic purpose to be expressed – and then considered what technical means might be employed to achieve it. Here, again, it was as if the more drastic the means the better, precisely as in the world of 'popular' culture. Spectacle has always dealt in such coin, and art without spectacle would be an impoverished thing. But art-as-spectacle is, on the whole, not different from art-as-sensation; and art-as-sensation, without more, is a thing even poorer. It is no less poor when 'high' art sanctifies it, than when 'video nasties' offer it as brutality and gore.

Against it, refinement of taste and integrity of purpose are constantly pitted, winning ground against the odds, whether cultural or economic, but losing more. The costs of technology, as well as the seductions of the market, shape (and even determine) the very forms of art and their contents. Moneyless sensibility is no match for the profitably gross. Across an entire culture – from grand opera to soap opera – audience ratings and sales figures count for more than financially unsuccessful intentions, however inspired. Moreover, the cultural tastes of the 'universal plebeian' stand conservatively, if silently, opposed to novelty and invention in every sphere but its own. These same tastes are, in general, also hostile to the efforts of the 'elitist' who defends 'old fashioned' forms of cultural expression, unless those forms are 're-packaged' and plebeianised for 'popular' consumption. Indeed, the 'popular', which 'brings in money', and 'minority tastes' (including the taste for the 'grand tradition'), which generally lose money, face each other in the market in increasingly unequal combat, as the dominion of the former strengthens.

Many artists, as many as those who have found continued inspiration under duress, have been driven from their courses by the hard combination of a need to sell their wares, on the one hand, and the absence of an accepted social role or civic function on the other. Market success has often been at the expense of fulfilment of purpose, not in pursuit of it, even if the instinct for self-protection should convince the artist otherwise. The best of writers, *in extremis*, remain capable of fine work; the painter or sculptor forced to outdo his rivals in excess, including excess of unmeaning, can turn excess itself to triumph. The search for effects, in 'high' culture as well as in 'pop' culture, may have outcomes of great artistic *éclat*. Even the merely spectacular, which makes its own demands both on art and technique, can answer to an audience's dreams. 'I am like a deep-sea diver,' Fellini once said, 'who *has to go* to the bottom of the sea [my emphasis] so that he can come up to tell what he has seen, so he can say, "I have seen many strange things, rocks and corals, beautiful fishes, monsters and mermaids."' If such 'strange things' are also 'box office', then the artist (across the culture) will prosper, sometimes at the expense of the audience. If it is not 'box office', the artist's work faces oblivion.

It was always so. Yet, today, fashion appears more arbitrary than ever, and 'fame' or 'success', except for a few survivors, more fleeting. Even accepted public or civic function – in the work of the state theatres or great opera houses – is not only increasingly vulnerable to, and shaped by, commercial pressures, but public function itself is no longer what it seems. Most of the national artistic institutions, far from giving voice to a living civic culture, are more nearly tourist attractions, 'flag-ships' or 'show-cases'. The British Royal National Theatre, for instance, like many other such theatres in Europe, serves no deep-rooted public purpose. To have a light shed on contemporary moral or spiritual dilemmas it is unnecessary to attend its productions. Without governing idea or direction, its principal intent, like many such institutions, becomes to keep its doors open. Shut down, the nation's self-knowledge, or knowledge of the world around it, would not be greatly diminished. The triumph of the plebeian, at however many (or few) removes, is further promoted by all such failures.

Many national cultural institutions have sought to 'sell themselves more effectively' by 'adapting to the market'. They have themselves adopted some of the demotic styles and plebeian attitudes of 'popular' culture. Yet, to the passer-by, these institutions are not much more accessible than they were. What happens behind their imposing frontages remains, for most, an Eleusinian mystery of the 'elite'. Even to many adepts, the mystery has less and less a redeeming spiritual or civic meaning. This is in part because the frontage is all, or nearly all; the sounds within, comic or tragic, those of spirits increasingly speaking – or singing – to themselves. Many vessels of 'high' art now ring hollow; much that hangs in the temple-galleries of the modern 'looks like art, but smells of money'; blockbuster advances and manufactured best-sellers provide the rigged hits of 'serious' literature's own tin-pan alley. This is inescapable in a market which puts such a premium on the promotion of 'stars', in 'high' culture as well as 'low'. Moreover, in Britain, the keepers of the public purse, saddled with other priorities in social provision, cannot or will not meet the levels of investment which the performing arts in particular require. And even if they wished to, the groundlings' distaste for 'subsidising' the 'pleasures of the elite' provides the political deterrent. Thus it is that even in 'high' culture the predator prevails, worthy institutions and individuals struggle against often arbitrary disfavour, and tastes are engineered into being or driven out of existence. But all these are relatively small matters, in weight and substance, when measured against the cultural significance and scale of the 'universal plebeian' tide.

The intellectual Jew-in-the-world, by disposition anxious, is ambivalent about 'popular' energies, however they are expressed, and however 'radical' he might be. (As I have pointed out, he is usually doubtful, even if only subconsciously, as to which way such energies might turn.) To a Jew, 'popular' culture, the culture of 'the people', often appears the culture of 'others', and the more plebeian, the more alien. This is so, however much (or little) he may try to approach it; it is so, even if he himself contributes to it; it is so, even if a prosperous fellow-Jew may choose to have a shaping hand in it. Turning aside from the 'universal plebeian' and his 'culture', as if by deepest instinct, the anxious intellectual Jew's reflex is to scan the world for signs and portents, looking first to the *appearance* of things for the truths they hold. Meanings must be found in what the eye beholds, and be then set in order by intuition, imagination and reason. In such work of the mind (and spirit), a sense of intellectual belonging is established beyond the plebeian reach, and a world made where Jew and non-Jew can be one.

But if the world of materiality might have once been kept at arm's length by such means, it can be so no longer. Anxiety increases. Offence to the natural order, once observed by intellectual Jews from a distance, induces a sense not only of guilt but of loss and isolation; Nature's reassurances cease to be a steadier thing than Man's fickle embraces. Violence against Man or Nature represents the power of physicality – a matter of awkwardness to most intellectual Jews – in its most alien muscular form. To a Jew, intellectual or not, the violent individual can seem another species, less-than-human. Yet, many of these perspectives are ideal, not practical. Thus, a Jew may love Nature in theory, but rarely botanise. And even if some Jews have acquired, or in some historic respects re-learned, newly practical and aggressive habits (out of self-interest, or, more often, from *force majeure*), the old habits, especially anxious habits of mind, remain.

Among them is a discomfort with places where no face is known, when a distant or atavistic sense of doubt or danger stirs. The physical demeanour or comportment of 'others' can suddenly estrange or deter. Even buildings and their styles can suggest the incorrigibly alien. Within the most creative and innovative of intellectual Jews, however 'radical', there is generally a cautious and conservative being who is unsure about 'how far he should go'. Surviving doubt about the toleration of others is often still a check to Jewish energies and endeavours. There are many examples of Jews, a minority of them wicked, who have swept such scruples aside. But there are many more who, out of anxiety, have deferred to it, and continue to do so.

Raking over, or breaking up, the ground of appearance, once such appearance has become familiar and without threat, therefore represents – to many Jews – more than a mere 'environmental' disturbance. Every transformation of place sets the anxious spirit the task of re-finding the way; every signpost altered makes the doubtful sense of direction waver. Tearing down buildings, like changing the law (or axeing the cherry orchard), stirs that which has become settled into new and unpredictable motion. The more dust that is raised, the less the prophetic eye can see. Political and cultural revolutions, even when radical Jews have been among their prime movers, promote 'trouble'; avoiding 'trouble', for many other Jews, is itself a prime mover. The utopian and messianic Jew – who exists in every Jew – desires change in his own and the world's condition; the conservative Jew – who exists in every Jew – fears it. In the conflict between tradition and alteration the Jew is simultaneously on both sides. Hence, in philosophical and artistic contention between the classical and the romantic, or the modern and the 'postmodern', the Jewish intellectual has a spiritual foot in all camps. The intellectual Jew entering the Parthenon and the Beaubourg, or the palaces of Nicolae Ceausescu and the Dukes of Urbino, feels at home in all of them. He also feels at home in none.

Jewish painters, sculptors, composers, writers and architects played their parts in the Modernist movement. But there are also aspects of the machine-culture of the twentieth century, and of its various appearances, emblems and emotions, which have always remained strange, and estranging, to the romantic and antiquarian temperaments of many Jewish intellectuals. The Temple of Jerusalem or the Bauhaus notwithstanding, the Jew is less a builder, unless the building be of intellectual systems, than a decorator; and less a mechanic than a driver. In the 'post-modern' reaction, the desire (of some) to find a way back to 'lost traditions', classical architectural forms, and a type of artistic 'good behaviour' – ephemeral projects, all – finds the Jewish intellectual as ambivalent as ever. The attempt to cast out modernist excess appeals to Jewish recoil from all blemishes upon the face of Nature. But the attempt to renew a sense of order and tradition, whether classical or romantic, Corinthian or Gothic, reminds the Jew that he is both part, and not part, of that same order and tradition. The Jewish intellectual, conscious of the accusations of 'vulgarity' directed at all Jews, is wary of the excesses of the Romantic tradition. But he cannot easily find his place in a world of classical restraint either, where all feeling – so he is prone to think – is at risk of being considered tasteless. Neither the pastiche of post-modernism, nor the cultural artifice of, say, a rural revival, offers the Jew a real intellectual home: the former, because it parodies real emotion, the latter because few Jewish intellectuals, or few intellectuals at all, are comfortable on horseback.

However, of all the possible varieties of Jewish intellectual unease, that with modernist architecture's lack of human scale, its too frequent insensitivity to the sanctities of place, and its forbidding materials, is among the greatest. Unfeeling makes for wickedness – including in Jews – and for uninhabitable surroundings; the Jew is, generally, a sentimentalist even if many Jews have had to learn not to display it. Stalinist bunker-blocks and mean council estates are also repellent to the Jew, since the life of the senses or emotions (so the Jew is inclined to think) could not survive them. High in his penthouse and close to the heavens, the Jewish real estate mogul, or crooked newspaper tycoon, is also capable of thinking that he has lost his soul, once his feet have left the ground. But since asceticism and denial of body and spirit – forms of unfeeling turned on the self – are avoided by most Jews, recovery of purity of heart, once lost, is hard; a return to earth, for the comfortable, still harder. In this modern no-man's-land, or labyrinth of possible dwelling-places, the preferred, or even natural, habitat of the Jew has become suburban: a retreat, or refuge, from the city which stops well short of the rural. (The Jew is an archetype in such physical and spiritual movements, as in others.) Here, so he thinks, belonging and anonymity may be secured, and combined as in no other setting. Here, the conservative in every Jew finds familiarity and order; and even the radical may await the Messiah in a garden suburb.

Paradoxically, this suburban world was 'post-modern' in spirit and style before the post-moderns. The Doric column and the neo-Georgian portico – although only a part, and a mocked part, of the present anti-modernist architectural reaction – were the vernacular of American suburbia long before the growth of resistance to modernist excess in the 1970s. The false antique and the reproduction of tradition (popular with some Jews) were the symbols not merely of aspiration to grace, but of rejection of the empty and spiritless aesthetics of the new. Those who had fled from modernism's ravages of the city decorated their houses, inside and out, with the symbols of their rebellion; the suburban cultural revolution, as it became more prosperous, hoisted coach-lamps at its door to signal that it would not surrender to a world of concrete. The neo-classical porch and the tapestry armchair were not mere whimsy and more than a retreat into the past. They were also rejections of the plebeian. It was in suburbia that the intensest cultural struggle was joined; a battle between neighbours, across families and even within individuals against the encroachment of the 'universal plebeian' – the fallen working class with access to the market, time on its hands, and energies increasingly undirected – and on behalf of the aspirations of the 'respectable', anxious to defend themselves from such disorders. With this kind of self-defence the Jew, who has had his own historic fight with plebeianism, has an instinctive, if guarded, sympathy; his secret history is that of a search for refuge from the ungoverned crowd, and of distaste for association with it.

But this cultural revolution, in Britain and elsewhere, spread beyond suburbia. Porticos, growing smaller, and other symbols of distinction – many destined to become plebeian signs themselves – began to appear not only in the most modest of new estates but on and in purchased council houses also. Yet, their original meaning was the same: the household, or at least some part of it, had refused or was resisting the plebeian. The critics of post-modernism have derided its 'posturing Georgianism', its 'shenanigans with arches, cornices and covings', its arbitrary mouldings and decorations, its 'chocolate box classical details', and so on. But on both the large-scale and the small, from the city office block disguised as a latter-day Italian *palazzo* to the earlier council-estate Doric, the cultural message has been the same: violences committed against the sensibilities, whether by the urban planner's rapine or the rampages of the plebeian – connected phenomena – are being opposed and rejected, even if in vain.

Modernism's scoffing at the 'sham graces' of the self-consciously antique expresses disdain for the 'cheap veneer' which such cultural reaction has allegedly sought to daub over the face of the modern. A high-technological age, modernism's spokesmen declare and imply, requires high-technological buildings; soaring modern aspiration-for-the-new demands to be embodied in the newest materials and forms. In this argument, the anti-modernist who is wearied with the new thinks he hears another: the aggressive city requires aggressive architects and aggressive constructions to reflect its temper. That is, edifices must express, not conceal, the spirit of place, and the activities which are conducted in or about it.

But, the traditionalist bystander might ask, is not the wearing of a cultural mask by the anti-human – as Jews well know – part of the history of architecture and building? Within the Roman Colosseum's over-arching grandeurs, men were consumed by wild-beasts for popular amusement. The functional, he might also argue, is only one virtue among many; to the eye, as well as to the soul, perhaps the least of them. Moreover, to hold technology in awe, the traditionalist will always declare, is to bow the head to a mere Golden Calf, or idol. Yes, but awe of technology, like awe of God, the modernist might reply, may inspire the building of great temples – such as the Beaubourg – to celebrate it, where all may worship and be inspired. But, returns the traditionalist, aggression and awe go uneasily together. Is not the Beaubourg the greatest of all modern monuments to urban violence? After all, here part of a city of real (not 'sham') graces was smashed by architectural aggression. A megalith was then raised in its place, which honours in fitting style the wounds done to civic feeling, and to the eyes, in metropolises the world over. Here, the traditionalist could well say, architecture clenched its fists to its violent task, like any other plebeian brawler. Brawn-and-brain, or mind-and-muscle, punched their way in the heart of Paris to a contemporary plebeian triumph, that of will over restraint, and body over civic soul.

But if this is the case, the counter-argument might run, it cannot be 'modernism' at whose door blame for such neo-Gothic or mega-industrial follies should be laid. 'Modernism' is a portmanteau term for a multitude of sins and virtues. Moreover, the spirit of the times is in the Beaubourg, a spirit which haunts the world. Ceausescu's 'House of the Republic', the Beaubourg's Eastern twin – it would be a twin soul, if either building had a soul – is six times bigger than the Palace of Versailles, and after the Pentagon the second biggest building in the world. Five years in the construction, it employed tens of thousands of workers. 'We are in the *Guinness Book of Records*,' its chief architect, Anca Petrescu, told me in April 1991. A whited sepulchre (with 2,000 rooms) of marble, gold and bronze, reinforced concrete and cherry-wood, stainless steel and crystal, it is socialism's greatest mausoleum. No imperial Trajan could have built on more orgulous a scale. Its 2,000 carved marble columns, raised in (pre-modern) praise of Romania's dictatorship, represent contemporary architecture's other great tribute to aggression. Indeed, the pretences of the Beaubourg and the House of the Republic are between them large enough to dwarf argument about the modern and post-modern. To make way for Ceausescu's folly, some 80,000 homes in what was once called the 'Paris of the East' are said to have been razed, and 200,000 people forced to move, many at forty-eight hours' notice.

'Yes, it is a symbol of the dictatorship,' said Petrescu, 'but was not Versailles a symbol of Louis Quatorze?' We must be 'objective' about it, she declared. It was a 'great creative achievement' – as is the Beaubourg – and a 'great national effort' even if made 'under idiotic conditions'. Ceausescu, the dwarfish *conducator*, or Romanian *duce*, had 'imposed an infernal rhythm' on the builders. Everything had to be done '*vite, vite, vite!*' He was, continued Petrescu, 'very demanding, like a Krupp or any other megalomaniac'; megalomania is the Beaubourg's mark also. 'He was intelligent but uncultivated, a peasant. Nevertheless he had a certain finesse. He might have had difficulty expressing himself, but he was very attentive to detail. He could also be kind. Charming, even,' she added. But 'master of the terrain, funds, and slave-like labour', he was, said Petrescu, 'in spirit a capitalist, for whom communism was the perfect instrument by which to dominate the workers' – part of the wider history of communist purpose everywhere. 'If any workmanship displeased him, even a small detail of marble carving, he could suddenly become very hard. The work had to be done again, without payment. I was exploited like everybody else; used, like everybody else, as an instrument. [She was twenty-five when chosen by competition to lead the project.] I was paid little. He exploited my creativity and imagination, but I exploited the opportunities I was given as an architect.' And, between them, as in Paris, patron and architect laid waste a once-pleasing and historic part of the capital city. An egoist he might be, but 'an idiot, no, not to do this,' she said, gesturing in the vast silence of the 'Hall for Treaty-making with Foreign States', columned in ghostly white marble and hung with crystal.

A monument of Stalinist classicism, with a Corinthian portico to outdo all porticos, it was communist plebeianism's ultimate anti-plebeian gesture. Each authoritarian master-builder, even when his intentions have been democratic or 'egalitarian', has wished to be thought an uncommon figure; he is making his own mark on the sand. But the order which he seeks to create, by increasingly insensate means, is more fleeting and elusive than ever. Indeed, today's wild profusion of styles in architecture – and not only in architecture – points to confusions of motive and purpose, and varieties of aesthetic theory and practice, such as have served in many settings to plunge the very spirit of community into disorder. The 'post-modern movement', neither truly post-modern nor a movement, is merely one more random style, or multiplicity of styles, among many. It is no more orderly than the modernist disorders it disavows, even if it embarked upon the creation of order with as much of a will as did the modernists themselves; Walter Gropius and Mies van der Rohe believed that they too were creating order in a surrounding chaos.

Rather, today's *pot pourri* of architectural forms and building methods, responding on the one hand to the hunger (of some) for continuous innovation, and to the seeming arbitrariness of civic and market choices on the other, has made incoherence itself into an aesthetic. The Piazza della Signoria or Prague's Old Town Square also present the citizen and spectator with a plethora of styles. But their materials, shapes and proportions are in concord. The mutually discordant aesthetic spirits of this age permit no such harmony. Between the brashest eruptions of modern technology and the rediscovered classical orders, as between the figurative portrait's photographic likeness and the furthest non-figurative abstraction, an aesthetic reconciliation is hard, or impossible, to find. To insist otherwise is merely one more style among many.

This incoherence, expressive both of fruitful-but-amoral energy and plain moral confusion, is part of the spirit of the age. There are even artists who claim, with seeming pride, to have no philosophy at all. Lucio Passarelli and Manfredo Nicoletti, Roman architects entrusted with the design of the new Museum of the Acropolis, which is being placed one hundred yards from the Parthenon, declared that their project was not only 'not ascribable to any particular school' – an unexceptional disavowal – but was also 'without preconceptions', a more serious matter given the setting. It was, they said, 'not a project to illustrate any philosophical tendency'; it was described by a critic as looking like a 'slab of sand-coloured cheese'. In such states of ethical blankness, unwitting violence against place is easy, as also are blows which are knowingly struck against feeling. Indeed, there may be delinquent buildings as there are delinquent people; buildings which seem as self-hating in spirit as any aggressive plebeian, and which, in their own ways, leave blood on the face of the city.

Yet, the beauties of the world as often survive to challenge their despoilers, despite the worst the latter may think to do. Constantly, the 'universal plebeian's instincts are challenged by the creativities and moral commitments he observes about him. There is, nevertheless, much to fear from that species of human animus which 'hits back' with its fists at whatever offends it. Moreover, it is the world made in the image of the plebeian, and made over to the plebeian, which appears to be hated above all by the plebeian himself. But his hatred of place, of buildings, of the very fixtures and fittings of a plebeian existence, once aroused, can also extend its arm. From quickly formed habit, from boredom, and (increasingly to come) in pursuit of neo-fascist purpose, a wider 'trashing' of objects (and persons) beckons. In Britain, the offence of 'criminal damage' already constitutes around '15 per cent' of all recorded crime; a 'vast amount' more of such damage is said to be 'hidden', or goes unreported.

Favourite targets include schools, council housing – especially vacated council houses – trains, railway lines, buses, public telephones and public amenities in general. Empty council houses in parts of the north-east of England were reported, in 1991, to be being 'stripped and wrecked by gangs within two hours of a tenant leaving' unless windows and doors were immediately bricked up by the council. 'You can hear them wrecking at night, bang, bang, bang all the time,' said a local witness. The volume of vandalistic damage to trains and buses, some-times carried out by the very young and ranging from the routine slashing of seats to outright attempts to derail trains, is increasing annually in Britain. 'Malicious acts' now account for more than 300 rail accidents (of various kinds) each year, including collision with obstacles placed on the lines, personal injuries deliberately caused, and derail-ments. In August 1987, a greenhouse, removed from nearby allotments, was set on the Norwich-London line and was struck by a train. In April 1988, children as young as eight – who could not be charged, being below the age of criminal responsibility – were caught placing a concrete post on a railway line near Bristol. In June 1990, three boys of eleven were charged before Bristol Juvenile Court with causing grievous bodily harm to a passenger, who required twenty-two stitches in a head-wound after they had thrown bricks through an express train's window. In August 1989, a section of railway line weighing a quarter of a ton, laid across the Oxford-London line at Hanwell by a 'gang of five or six young men', derailed a train, causing injury to passengers. It was a second determined attempt; an earlier passing train had pushed the line aside. In October 1990, in a sample week, there were twenty separate reported cases from widely different parts of Britain of concrete being placed on railway lines. In December 1991, vandals even cut through fibre-optic signal cables at Cowton in North Yorkshire; in the same month, a signalling control system for London's four main stations was set on fire.

The total costs of 'criminal damage' were estimated in 1991 to be running at about £1.8 billion per annum. In Britain, £50 million-worth of arson damage is done to schools in a single year; 'everyday' school vandalism adds another £50 million. This type of school trashing is three times as serious in London, the West Midlands, Tyne and Wear, Greater Manchester, South and West Yorkshire and Merseyside, as in the shire counties; between April 1989 and March 1990 alone, there were 182,800 'crimes against schools', according to the department of education and science, with the north and north-west the most seriously affected. Indeed, these and related indecencies are now 'universal plebeian' commonplaces, which have come to stand beneath the level of public notice. They are also increasingly accepted as a form of the 'normal'; there have been reports of public telephone boxes being 'deliberately wrecked' even in Peking.

Response has been dulled by familiarity, expert sociological explanation and apologia for youth's excesses, as well as by justifiably greater anxiety about violence to the person. But the mean passions of plebeian spite, roaming at large, merit close notice in their own right for the targets they choose. Oak saplings planted in Sevenoaks to replace the town's famous trees, felled by the 1987 hurricane in southern England, were snapped and broken by vandals a few hours before a civic ceremony in October 1988, held to commemorate the hurricane's first anniversary. A 2,000-year-old Roman mosaic pavement at Market Harborough was destroyed by vandals in August 1990; vandals cut through barbed wire and climbed forty feet of scaffolding at the west front of Wells' Cathedral in order to smash a mediaeval masonry canopy in July 1991. Historically, such desecrations of place and objects have generally had religious or political motives, or plain robbery as their purpose, while looting has always accompanied war and civil insurrection. Thus, some of the world's most exquisite mediaeval enamel-work was stolen in August 1991 from the thirteenth-century cathedral at Auxerre; in the 1980s, many of Lebanon's museums and grave-sites were ransacked and pillaged during its internecine war. The markets of the 'elite' set their own pace and price for the vandal, the world over; but it is the 'universal plebeian' who is, above all others, veritably on the move.

Between the kicking over and breaking of twenty-three British war graves at Ypres in June 1991 – which might, just, have been an incoherent political gesture – and the smashing of 112 headstones at Doncaster cemetery by an unemployed eighteen-year-old who explained that he was 'bored', there was the finest of lines. Such aggression, however, is less idle than it seems, and the complexities of ill-feeling from which it springs have deep roots, not least in the uglinesses which everywhere assail the mind's eye. 'Is this the city,' Jeremiah asked in despair of Jerusalem long ago, 'that men call the perfection of beauty?' If it was not so then, it is even less so now. Nor, now, is it prophetic lament which expresses best such feelings of recoil, but plebeian anger itself, growing as the unredeemed time passes.

NINE

Struggling with the Body

For every artist who sees as much of the divine in the human form as did William Blake, there is now another who neither wants, nor is able, to draw it well or at all. Such disengagements from the fellow-human, in the name of art, is more than a physical turning away. It is an aversion of the imagination, and in its silences speaks volumes. Nor is it only an artistic choice. It is a moral decision. In the space it leaves, the pornographer (among others) stands, today's leading portraitist of the human frame. In its essence and whatever its fleeting pleasures for some, pornography's arts and wiles do a particular harm, the harm of sexual violence, upon the vulnerabilities of human beauty. Worms shall destroy the integrity of this body in due time; to destroy it now, before its time has come, is a form of aggressive crime.

The connection between one desecration of the body (on paper, on film, on video) and another (in the flesh iself) is hotly, even sexually, disputed. But it hardly matters, except in law, whether one incites to the other. One ransacked body is morally much the same as another, and by whatever means the reduction is achieved. A woman may be attacked by a man in many ways. In the United States, according to official figures, there were 130,000 rapes in 1990, or 'one every four minutes'; according to research by the National Victim Centre, pub-lished in April 1992, the true figure was said to be some five times higher, at nearly 1,900 rapes each day, with over 60 per cent of the raped under the age of eighteen. The varieties of what appears to be hatred of the body, and self-hatred, have passed almost beyond fathoming. In some countries, Britain included, even violent attacks on pregnant women, and upon women accompanied by small children, are increasing. Violence against the person may remain a relatively small proportion of recorded crime in most countries – in Britain it stands at around '4 per cent' – and sexual crime may constitute a relatively small proportion of the violence committed against the person. But much of the latter, rape included, is believed to go unreported, and its nature or 'quality', often that of a seeming sadistic rage, begins to beggar description.

It is also clear that there are different types of men who are dangerous to women and capable of acting violently towards them, given occasion, circumstance and prompting emotion. In Britain, where it remains the case that fewer women than men are murdered, women have in recent years felt and reported an increasing fear of walking alone, and even of being alone in their own homes. Moreover, they have seen the worst forms of crime against women, which would once have turned every hair, taken increasingly on the nod with little stir; and they have had continuing cause to back away from aggressive maleness, with its plebeian cult of 'being hard' and its jaw set against feeling. Of all crime against women, it is opportunistic assault by strangers – even if more women than men in Britain are actually killed by relatives, lovers, and spouses than by strangers – which presents itself, in many countries, as women's most frightening prospect. This is so particularly in the heartlands of the modern city.

Women in need, with their cars broken down, seeking the way, lost in the city, even asking the time, may become the victims of heinous crime. In March 1986, Manchester Crown Court jailed for life for murder a young man of twenty-one, who, by chance, had come upon the twenty-nine-year-old victim of a 'mugging' which had just taken place in a street in Burnley; he 'stamped on her with such ferocity', the court was told, 'that the imprint of his boot was found on her stomach'. In June 1988, a similarly distressed girl of fourteen, lost in London after a day-trip alone to see a pantomime, was picked up, plied with alcohol and raped; dumped on the street in the early hours, but offered 'help' by two men in a passing car, they took her to a quiet street and also raped her. In May 1987, at Newbury, a woman of thirty-three, walking with a small child by the canal, asked the time of two men who happened to cycle by on the towpath; she was pushed into the canal by the men, who rode off laughing, and was rescued from drowning by a boy of fifteen. In November 1987, an unemployed labourer of thirty received a life sentence for battering to death and sexually mutilating a florist and part-time barmaid, aged twenty-one, whom he had come upon near the centre of Tranmere while she was looking for a garage after having run out of petrol; the marks on her body matched his teeth-marks. In June 1988, a seven and a half-months' pregnant woman of twenty-two, whose car had broken down on a motorway, was abducted while making an emergency telephone call, and found beside the road three miles on, killed by stab wounds to her jugular vein and with a fractured jaw.

This was a woman come upon, seized not by design but in passing, and by latent violence on the wing. In January 1988, Winchester Crown Court similarly heard how a sailor of nineteen had raped and (once more) 'stamped to death' a young woman of twenty-four whom he had come upon as she was walking home; a footprint on her stomach with the word 'Flash' helped to identify him. In March 1988, a woman walking her two-year-old child along Regent's Canal in London was sexually assaulted by a stranger and her child thrown into the canal; a student dived into the water fully clothed in rescue, and another chance passer-by gave the 'kiss of life' to the child. (Good Samaritans are at large also.) In June 1990, a Spanish *au pair*, walking home in south-west London, was stabbed and 'had her tongue slashed', the injury requiring fifteen stitches. In July 1992, a woman walking with her two-year-old son on Wimbledon Common was stabbed to death; the child, who had head injuries, was found clinging to her body. In June 1988, a *Guardian* reporter, Edward Vulliamy, who accompanied British football supporters to Frankfurt, described how a fan had 'picked up a bottle and casually smashed it across the face of a young woman sitting with two girl friends on the steps of a [closed] restaurant. She bled badly,' Vulliamy reported, 'from her eye and nose, her blood splattering the shutters of the café.'

Not even pregnancy, as has already been seen, can protect a woman from such hatreds and self-hatreds. On the contrary, some of the evidence even suggests that maternity can be a goad to violence, when the moral world itself seems to turn to darkness. In May 1987, in Liverpool, an eight-months' pregnant women of twenty-four was threatened with a screwdriver and raped while walking her dog in the park. In August 1988, in Lewisham High Street, a six-months' pregnant woman was 'punched in the stomach by two muggers' who stole £16 from her; her child was born prematurely by Caesarean section two weeks later. In June 1989, the Old Bailey heard how a night-club bouncer, aged twenty-six, subsequently sentenced to five years' imprisonment, had 'kneed' and punched his pregnant girlfriend in the abdomen, causing her to miscarry. In April 1990, Nottingham Crown Court was told how a man of twenty, sentenced to nine years' imprisonment, had 'stamped' (once more) on his seven-months' pregnant partner, killing the unborn child, whose foetus was found to have a fractured spine and other serious injuries. In October 1990, the Earl of Cardigan told Winchester High Court that, during a police operation to clear 'hippies' who were attempting to celebrate the summer solstice at Stonehenge, he had seen police hold an 'enormously pregnant' woman and 'club her'.

Clubbing or kicking a pregnant woman is a difficult thing to consider. Yet, in the scale of violence against women, it is a relatively small matter. When teenage youths from Harlem, out 'wilding' – or predatorily hunting their fellow human-beings – gang-raped and sodomised a twenty-eight-year-old jogger in New York's Central Park in April 1989, beat her on the head with a lead pipe and bricks, and left her for dead (in a haemorrhage of three-quarters of her blood) with a fractured skull and her left eye forced through the rear of its socket, they had merely proceeded further along an abyssal path. 'She wasn't nothing,' 'everybody was stomping on her,' 'they were punching her face "pow, pow, pow", it was fun,' the assailants said. This was neither 'black crime', nor distinctively American, nor of a brutishness without precedent or beyond belief. In October 1989, Edinburgh High Court heard how a woman of twenty-six found a man in her house who, with a knife to her throat, forced her to commit sexual acts and thereafter to get into the bath. Here, the assailant – found by the court not be be mentally ill, and 'from a stable background' – attempted to drown her, cut her throat, stabbed her in the stomach and 'attempted to poke out her eyes'. In February 1992, in Brixton in south London, a woman of twenty-seven, also the victim of sexual attack by a stranger, had her throat cut, the wound requiring 150 stitches; the bed upon which she was left lying was set on fire by her assailant.

At Nottingham Crown Court in November 1990, a man who, 'after watching a horror-video early on New Year's day', stabbed a woman to death in her home and then raped her thirteen-year-old daughter, was jailed for life. In April 1991, a man of thirty-one from south-west London who had beaten his girlfriend to death 'over a period of two hours' and 'stamped on her head', after smashing down her door with a pickaxe handle, was also given a life sentence. In July 1991, the High Court in London was told how a man of forty-three would stab pictures of women in 'books, catalogues and "nudie" magazines', had talked of 'getting' women whom he 'saw on walks', and carried a knife thrust down his trousers. In the same month, a man of twenty-eight, described as an 'extreme danger to women', was said at the Old Bailey to have told police, 'I just remember going crazy,' as he repeatedly stabbed and mutilated a sixteen-year-old girl before dumping her in a river with her neck broken. The aggressors, too, were often young; the 'wilding' youths in Central Park were aged from fifteen to seventeen. Not even this was distinctive. In September 1989, in Leeds, two boys of thirteen and fourteen were charged with the rape of a twenty-nine-year-old mother of three children; in December 1991, a fourteen-year-old boy was ordered by the High Court in Glasgow to be detained for nine years for raping a pregnant thirty-one-year-old woman, and setting her home on fire.

There are false rape and sexual assault claims, too, but they count for relatively little in the measure of these harms. And if even extreme youth can now lay violent, and sometimes killing, hands on women, so now not even the most elderly female can count on being immune from sexual predation. In Britain, there are many cases of rape and sexual assault of the old. In March 1987 in Oldham, for instance, two spinster sisters of ninety-two and eighty-one respectively were sexually assaulted before they were murdered; in October 1990, in West Yorkshire, a seventy-seven-year-old widow was left with serious internal injuries after a sexual assault by a twenty-five-year-old; in March 1992, a man of forty-five was charged at Pontlottyn Magistrates' Court in mid-Glamorgan with raping an eighty-nine-year-old deaf and partially sighted widow, after breaking into her home. At such a point, not only anger but satiety and disgust (always close at hand in account of crime) are, or should be, overwhelming. Yet, such instinct as there is, or was, to back away emotionally and intellectually from accounts of violence against women may itself be waning. In a world of violence in general – violence against children, violence against place and objects, violence against animals and so on – a new, and mostly covert, moral (or amoral) argument may now run. The female body is not the only biblical temple, or no temple at all; its integrity calls for no special privilege, when the whole world is under ravage. Moreover, where men do violence to women, so the debased soul may say, it is because the malefactors 'are violent', not because the special objects of their violence are women.

'Misogyny', it could also be argued – for there are apologists for everything under the sun – is 'merely' a sub-species of a 'misanthropy' larger in scope. But it is clear from the evidence that a specific desire, on the part of some men, to do injury to women as women, is a most particular thing, whatever name be given to it, and however complex its deepest motives. In some of the cases of assault by plebeian youth, studied closely, a violent assertion of 'manhood' – one complexity among many, and itself a short-hand term – seems to have been made. There are other cases more complex still which not even psychiatry can decipher. The discovery of the 'masculine identity' in a 'rite of passage' is one thing, and for many women (and men) unappealing, however necessary it may be thought (by some) to be; its assertion, if this is what it is, by means of doing severe physical harm to women is another. To kick a woman to death in the cause of male prowess is, or once was, only an act of Auschwitz, not of Central Park or south London.

It is not only male 'frustrations' and angers carried to excess in this gross fashion which arouse anxiety and fear. Rather, it is the ordinary (and increasingly characteristic) plebeian ideal of maleness itself which creates alarm. Under its rule, aggression is privileged and tenderness depressed, or even, at worst, extinguished entirely. In extremes of self-disgust, ugliness of manner may be celebrated as a degraded virtue. Such styles offer thin emotional prospects for women, even if there are plebeianised females who have themselves adapted to its norms, and even adopted some of its aggressive forms of gesture and conduct. The plebeian-football and plebeian-holiday war-cries chanted, en masse, in contempt of women are both a violation of feeling and, simultaneously, a crude expression of it. That is, they are typical plebeian emotions, typically expressed.

From such emotions, it is not only women who are in danger, but it is the female body which stands most commonly, and usually most easily also, in the path of its attentions. Many of the consequences, including in the extent of women's sexual unfulfilment and distress, are beyond the range of inquiry. But there cannot be much doubt that forms of physical *machismo* which are without grace and predisposed to aggression make a difficult appeal to the senses. (The British football fans in Germany in 1988 who permitted themselves to wear T-shirts with the words 'England boys, we are here, shag your women and drink your beer', promised little.) A combination of male self-hatred, a propensity to violence, and sexual predation is unlikely (from first human principles) to promote women's physical or emotional well-being. Unease with the body is also catching. In July 1989, the *British Medical Journal* reported that only 30 per cent of mothers in Liverpool, the most plebeian of English cities, breast-fed their babies, less than half the national average. The many different and complex reasons for this level of mass abstention from normal physical function can only be surmised; it is not unlikely that the association of the breast with male smirking is among them.

That some women, in such times as these, should have fought against the odds (and without signal success) to establish an alternative 'identity' for themselves from that imposed upon them by (some) males, was both inevitable and just. It was a means both of self-assertion and self-defence, not merely against men as individuals but against that large world which has been made in a male image, and sometimes in the most base aspects of it. The cause of feminism, albeit now on the wane, took much of its moral force and intellectual creativity from the argument that women-as-women are 'oppressed', and therefore require to be 'freed'. Seeing themselves above all as victims of male domination of various kinds, feminists sought to give priority to gender over other forms of human differentiation. For some, gender was the organising principle of analysis and theory, affiliation and action. It even became, for a minority of *ultras*, the criterion of truth – including artistic truth – and moral virtue.

The outcome was a modest change in some male perceptions of women's condition, some rearrangement of law, and some (relatively) minor enhancements of opportunity and reward. There were also two large failures. The first failure lay in the fact that gender, whether male of female, is not a criterion of truth and value; and for the *ultras* to insist upon it did not make it so. But although most men, and most women too, were unable to accept the extreme position, that same extreme position came wrongly, or maliciously, to be understood as the general position of the feminist movement. The second failure served only to reinforce women's disadvantage. An unintended consequence of feminist actions, it derived from the public rehearsal itself of the argument as to women's subordination to, and humiliation by, men. Even if some men learned from the argument, it stimulated many of the very men most in need of correction by it to redouble their determination to stifle women's (modest) efforts at self-assertion. In the most brutish minority, unpersuaded by such feminist complaints as that there are 'no memorials to the wife of the Unknown Soldier', ardour for insensibility was merely whetted. Nor did some women's protests and objections prevent for a moment the gratuitous use of the female body as a seductive market icon. After the women's movement had had its say, such use was more ubiquitous than ever. And in Britain most of the laws which were introduced in the 1970s, when the passion for greater equality was at its height, were being flouted a decade later. There might be equal pay laws, but in 1992 women's wage rates in Britain remained substantially less than those of men.

Moreover, the excesses committed against women in the Third World were unremitting. Lack of political rights, near-chattel status, hard labour and domestic violence were the lot of hosts of the world's women. 'Sex tourism' in Thailand, the Philippines and other South-East Asian countries, including southern Vietnam, drew increasing numbers of Europeans and other men. Between 1988 and 1991, nearly 16,000 Indian women were murdered or committed suicide in disputes over dowry; of the 140,000 Chinese who (on average) committed suicide each year in the 1980s, 70 per cent were women. If increasing numbers of women were economically active in Western Europe, they were also more vulnerable than men to economic downturns; if working, were still doing most of the domestic chores; and even where they had no children, had less leisure time than men. The 'equality' for which women fought may have been gained in small matters, but not in large. In 1991, one hundred governments in the world contained no women. Of British High Court and circuit judges in 1991, as few proportionately were women as ten years before. Moreover, as the *New Law Journal* showed in July 1991, a greater proportion of British women who killed their husbands was convicted of murder than of men who killed their wives: some measure, despite all the variables, of the status of the female and her body. It was a perverse consolation for the emancipationist that women, especially younger women, were shown in Britain to be drinking more and that more women were dying from lung cancer.

Women might be more prepared, according to feminists, to challenge the 'old patriarchal order', although there was precious little substantial evidence of it. A more telling index of women's position was the stereotypical woman of Western advertising, still preoccupied with the whiteness of 'her' washing, or inserting a phallus-shaped chocolate into a mouth forever pouting. Some feminists chose combat with the idea of God-as-male; others fought, with equally modest success, against 'men trying to control women's bodies' in matters of obstetrics, birth-control or the new technologies of reproduction. Many other, less secure women 'felt threatened' by feminist indignations. The disclosure that some fertility clinics in Britain had been providing artificial insemination, wittingly or unwittingly, not only to unmarried women but even (as the press put it) to 'virgins' who had 'no intention of ever having sexual intercourse or marrying', set a new anti-feminist hare running.

In the moral scuffling over 'virgin birth' that followed – it broke out in France also – the feminist combatants argued that 'sexual status' was 'irrelevant to becoming a good parent'. Anti-feminists believed 'virgin birth' to be like 'taking a dog into the family, except that there is no family'. The very term 'virgin birth' offended many churchmen. Feminists and their supporters argued that couples, married or unmarried, were 'not screened for parenthood', so on what ethical grounds, they asked, could a single woman be? Traditionalists, during the few weeks in which moral argument ran its course in Britain and was then lost from view, objected vigorously to the 'welfare' claim that an unmarried woman had a 'right to have a child'. Libertarians, on the contrary, described it as 'frightening' that the state might take on itself the 'job of deciding who could conceive'. Feminists provoked some men by declaring not only that virginity was a free choice, or a virtue – unexceptionable claims – but that women did not 'need sex to have a child'. The further suggestion that 'normal sexual relations' were the 'price women had to pay for conception' was swiftly attributed by anti-feminist men and women to 'lesbians'. The notion that human beings could express their sexuality in different ways was widely, if not generally, accepted; claims that the female should, if she chose, be entirely free of the male even in the act of reproduction was another matter.

For all that such arguments engaged moral attention, however briefly, it was physiology not philosophy which stood at their secret heart. That is, it was not so much women's rights as women's bodies which were the real centre of attention. Tabloid prurience, in particular, continued as ever to circle about 'women's issues' on behalf of the 'universal plebeian'. The self-appointed and ostensible role of such newspapers was as the defiant guardian of the 'sexually normal'. But there was evidence to suggest that, despite the fears of a new Sodom and Gomorrah, this 'norm' was secure enough not to require such (bogus) defenders. For example, an American survey reported in 1990 that the 'average American' had sexual intercourse 'fifty-seven' times a year with '1.16 sexual partnres', while no fewer than 98.5 per cent of the married declared that their spouses had been their only sexual partners in the year. Nevertheless, such seeming regularities, like the fondnesses of romantic fiction, were dwarfed by the forms and incidences of sexual abuse and crime, the scale of marital breakdown in industrial societies, and the multitudinous private turmoils of the continuing 'sexual revolution'. The more optimistic feminists believed that the 'oppressive' balance of relations between the sexes had been shaken, at least for some, during the 1970s. The movement for female 'independence', akin to the notion of political 'liberation' referred to in an earlier chapter, had been launched. The female as sex object, for instance, had been dramatically decried. Yet, at the same time, and with contradictory effects, the 'pleasure principle' – including, justly, that of pleasure for women – had acquired an elevated moral status; had even acquired the status of a right. The 'sex object' might thus become, at least in intention or theory, a full sexual subject in her own right, only to encounter a male whose insecurities were aroused by such female sexual assertion.

In these complex matters, there is no argument, particularly as to causes and effects, which could expect to go unchallenged. It is beyond contention, however, that the divorce rate has risen sharply in Western industrial countries in the last decade, even if the reasons for it have been greatly disputed. Anti-feminists, on the one hand, have been quick to argue that women's 'independence' exacted a high price in human relations. Feminists, on the other hand, have detected 'male chauvinism' in all such assertion, and 'liberated' men – another term of art – have generally stood by them, or made the effort to do so. Much of this debate, as the feminist wave itself passed, has now ebbed. Nevertheless, feminist polemics no more addressed men's own anxieties than men's insensibilities could address the reasons for women's profoundest displeasures. Nor did it assist male confusions that two contradictory propositions about men stood at the heart of the feminist cause.

One was, and is, that men and women are essentially the same, and therefore should be treated the same. The other is that men and women are essentially different, and therefore should be treated differently. Some feminists veered between one argument and the other, compounding every confusion, emotional and moral. Moreover, in the extreme feminist position of dislike of, or recoil from, men-as-men was the mirror of some men's (much more physically dangerous) hostility to women-as-women. 'Man-as-rapist', judged to be no better than an aggressor, latent or actual, was the blood-brother of the equally demeaning 'woman-as-whore'. Confusing, too, was the fact that public discourse about sexuality, and its various pleasures or torments, could often seem to be itself a form of sexual display, 'macho' or 'coquettish'. 'Why should any style of dress be assumed "provocative"?' asked a young woman of her media audience, trailing her own coat for appreciation. 'Should not women be free to dress as they choose without having to worry about exciting the appetites of men?' she inquired. In such a question, false ingenuousness, posing for approval, fluttered its eyes – but now it was in the cause of the asexual perception of women. To many bewildered males, this was itself playing with the seducer's fire; or moral hypocrisy pretending to seriousness of moral intention. Rising (consumer-style) expectations of sexual pleasure, however daunted by the fear of Aids, might also seem, to some, to be at odds with the just principle of a right to resist the desires, or consumer 'appetites', of others. Indeed, with the ratification of the claims both of sexual egalitarianism and sexual freedom, it became harder to object to the ever wider 'sexualising' of human relations.

Changes in sexual mores in the 'advanced' West have brought most young people, many young teenagers and even those once regarded as 'children' to sexual experience almost as a matter of expectation. This is true both of males and females, and at an increasingly young age. In New York, it was estimated in 1991 that no fewer than 80 per cent of high school students – or children – over the age of fourteen were 'sexually active'; in a Bronx high school, there was a brief eruption of 'scandal' when it was disclosed that more than half the girls in the senior class were pregnant. Nationally, two-thirds of American high school pupils and 80 per cent of college students, according to a survey published in July 1991, claimed to be having 'regular sexual relations'.

Nor was this a specifically American precocity. In a survey of 4,000 fifteen- to twenty-four-year-olds, published in August 1991, the University of Exeter's Institute of Population Studies found that 41 per cent of the male and female sample – in the south-west of England, not in the Bronx or Brooklyn – had 'lost their virginities' before their sixteenth birthdays. Of the 'sexually active' between the ages of sixteen and twenty-four, one in ten had had sexual intercourse with their partners on their first dates, one in eight within a week, and one in two within a month. An earlier survey, carried out by the Family Policies Study Centre and published in December 1990, similarly found that one in two girls and one in three boys claimed to have had sexual intercourse before the age of sixteen. Three decades before, in 1960, only 6 per cent of British boys and a mere 2 per cent of girls had made such a claim. The jump in thirty years from 2 per cent to 50 per cent in the case of girls, overtaking boys in their sexual experience, represented a moral revolution.

'Naturally' related, in some eyes, to earlier physical maturity, it was a 'catastrophe' to others. What its limits would be also puzzled specu-

lation. According to a report by the Economic and Social Research
Council, published in 1990, the 'average age of first intercourse' was
fifteen among British middle-class girls, but only thirteen-and-a-half
among working-class girls. A small-scale survey of 2,000 Americans of
both sexes, published in May 1991, found that one in five had 'lost their
virginities' *before* the age of thirteen; one in seven Jamaican boys,
according to an official health ministry survey published in February
1992, had sex before the age of ten. Even girls as young as nine have
been discovered by psychologists both in America and Britain to be
anxiously dieting for an ideal, or 'slim', body.

Here, the 'emancipation of women' and 'sexual equality' took on both
a new dimension and a new meaning. Sexual freedoms freely expressed
– sometimes with the active compliance of parents – were making
premature adults of many children, and leaving increasingly little time
for childhood. Moreover, given the 'regular sexual relations' of 'two-
thirds' of American high school children, the increasing precocities of
children even younger, and the growing alarms in many Western
countries (especially Britain and the United States) about 'child sex
abuse', it was becoming plain that the 'sexualising of human relations'
had begun to know fewer limits. In addition, accelerating rates of
divorce were leaving rising numbers of children everywhere in an
emotional limbo. In Britain, it was estimated that there would be 3
million children in step-families by the year 2000. Correlations between
abuse of children and circumstances of family distress or breakdown
are well established, even though such abuse can take place in the most
ordered of conditions. But the combination of family dissolution,
plebeian aggression, poor social conditions, male – and occasionally
female – sexual aberration, and the precocious sexual experience of
(some) children is not a promising ground for child welfare. The
rising incidence of sexual abuse of children, including increasingly
by other children and young teenagers, and of violence committed
against children, including by parents, are arguably to be placed
among the outcomes. And iniquity visited upon children, as research
findings have made plain, is commonly visited upon the children's
children also.

In October 1987, at the Old Bailey, the case was heard of a father
aged thirty-three who boasted to another man of how he had 'trained
his daughter', aged four, to have oral sex with him and said, 'Here, have
a go.' In the same month, in the same court, a man appeared who had
made his two daughters pregnant a total of eight times before they were

seventeen; one of his daughters had had an abortion at the age of twelve. In Cleveland in 1987, to growing confusion and uproar, 'widespread sexual abuse' in children referred to hospital (as well as in their siblings) – including a 'three-year-old with gonorrhoea' – was claimed to have been found by two pediatricians. Over 120 children, whose average age was 7.4, were thereupon taken into official care; but, as public and political pressures mounted against the two doctors, most were returned to their parents by the courts. In the turmoil, it ceased to be clear how many of the children might have been abused. A judicial report in July 1988 criticised the pediatricians for their 'over-confidence' in looking for abuse symptoms. The doctors themselves, even though they and the local health authority were successfully sued by some of the offended parents – for the distresses of having been temporarily separated from their children – refused to admit clinical error. Other doctors argued not only that many of the children had in fact been abused, but that the scale of abuse which had been disclosed was the 'tip of the iceberg'.

In Nottingham, in 1988, nine adults – eight from the same extended family – were sentenced to a total of forty-three years in jail on fifty-three charges of incest, cruelty and indecent assault against very young children, twenty-three of whom were taken into care. Here, the children's accounts of what had been done to them were corroborated by three adult women, evidence of a kind often unavailable or not forthcoming in other cases. An inquiry into 'large-scale sex abuse' in Humberside, including Scunthrope and Goole, between 1987 and 1990 and involving some 300 children, found evidence of paedophilia, 'sexualised behaviour' in the very young, and 'self-mutilation'. In Rochdale, in September 1990, allegations of 'satanic abuse' against parents, as a result of which some twenty children were taken into care, collapsed in a welter of recrimination; a legal inquiry, in which community embarrassment was at the fore, appeared to some to cloud both facts and issues, and to others to vindicate hurt parental feelings. But, contemporaneously, seventeen men and women, one of whom received a ten-year sentence and many of whom were members of the same family, were convicted at Maidstone on charges of buggery, rape and incest, involving thirty-two children over a period of eleven years. The judge spoke of a 'total breakdown of any kind of sexual or moral discipline'; social work findings in the case reported the 'almost routine sharing of children for sex among family and friends'.

Allegations of similar kinds of conduct, both proven and unproven, and sometimes involving large numbers of children, were reported from many parts of the world, including the United States and Australia. In the welter of British outrage at what the allegations disclosed – an outrage to which the tabloid press and some politicians were quick to contribute – there was much offence taken that the allegations had been made at all. In some cases, both social workers (as in the Orkneys in 1991) and doctors were condemned for their 'obsessions' with sexual abuse. In other cases, a wilderness of harm-doing to young children was revealed. By the mid-1980s, child care workers, a few of whom were also the subject of successful criminal prosecution for the sexual abuse of their charges, were reporting that sexual assault, predominantly carried out by males on family members, including their own children, had taken over from child neglect as a 'major cause for concern'. In the past, if family sexual abuse was 'common', as some sought to argue, it remained largely a guilty secret. Now, perhaps in part as a consequence of heightened public awareness, reports of child sex abuse to the National Society for the Prevention of Cruelty to Children (NSPCC) increased many-fold through the 1980s. The numbers of children officially registered by local authorities as 'at risk', including those classified as 'under sexual abuse', rose. At the same time, the widely reported delinquencies of those convicted not only of 'ordinary' sexual offences against children but of 'ritual' or 'satanic' abuse and sadistic sexual tortures, sometimes committed by parents, were beyond all normal understanding.

Not surprisingly, the integrity both of the children who claimed to have been the victims of such assault and of the adults who claimed to have detected it, was impugned. In the case of the 'commoner' forms of sexual abuse of children, it was the scale of what was being alleged which often ran into frank societal disbelief. It was not possible to decide whether there was a 'disproportionate' degree of child sex abuse in Britain – especially, some argued, among those of 'low intelligence and with time on their hands' – or merely a 'pathological interest' in the subject. It was also difficult to judge whether family ideals and community taboos were stronger in other countries, the first serving to inhibit abuse and the second to prevent disclosure of it. Whatever the case, the NSPCC continued to report a rising incidence of such abuse in Britain. In April 1991, the Royal College of Physicians recommended that all health authorities should have a specialist group of doctors available to examine children for its physical signs.

It seemed that there was not much of Blakean innocence destined to survive, if the world of adult experience was encroaching so far upon childhood, or upon the childhoods of some children. Even the vocabulary of 'traditional values' or of 'old-fashioned' reproach against 'decadence' was stilled in the face of offences, alleged and proven, which were outside the comprehension of most people. Moreover, when the arbiters of the sins of others – a priest, a judge, a director of public prosecutions – were themselves found morally lacking, every argument from rectitude faltered. The tabloid press, for its part, frequently trumpeted the facts of authority's crimes or peccadilloes with a gloating zeal that was itself near-pornographic. If such publicity brought perverse cheer to the sullen plebeian, it also drove moral scruple closer to exhaustion. A pope might rail at 'Western sensuality', but the plebeian who harboured violent fantasies about the female body, or was laying hands on his own children, was likely to have had his adult perceptions trained on the least sensual of diets. Under its promptings, any pulpit moralist could be a 'pervert', any policeman 'bent', and any doctor a danger to women. (The same impulse could make any Jew a crook, and any Muslim a fanatic or wife-beater.) Such moralities were the moralities of voyeurs, educated by videos and tabloids to simultaneous prurience and outrage. Indeed, the rapist or child-abuser doubtless outraged himself, as well as his victim, and gained an extra frisson from it. 'Conventional' morality, religious or lay, was no match for intricacies such as these.

Thus, the Vatican might defend the purity of its orthodoxies on contraception, or anathematise (say) the American movement for the induction into the Church of 'deaconesses' and 'altar girls'. But the moral purposes of such stances now barely seemed moral at all, in a world where amorality had assumed new proportions and lay moral preoccupation had shifted its ground. The great religions could not keep up – who or what could? – with the scale of the drug trade, or the flux of peoples, or the forms of crime. In circumstances where domestic or familial morality was also beginning to lose much of its meaning, and even children could become sexual objects, religious ethics, normally at home on such terrain, faced the risk of entire defeat. The Pope's apostolic letter, *Mulieris Dignitatem*, sought, by means of an old form of special pleading which had lost its moral purchase, to keep women in contented subordination in the name of their dignity as women. Islam fought harder and with even rustier weapons. In Algeria, in October 1991, as the tide of Islamic fundamentalism rose, the parliament wrestled over (and passed) a bill, later rejected as unconstitutional, to permit men to vote on behalf of their wives. Behind such measures lay wider (male) struggles, each conducted by its own lights and sometimes gaining as well as losing ground, to maintain a moral order – or the memory of it – by spiritual *force majeure*. In such struggles, however reactionary, there again lurked the sense that any moral order was better than none.

Women, whether in their roles, their rights, or their bodies, have always and for obvious reasons occupied male speculation, and often been at the heart of it. Their latent capacity to overthrow 'male reason', as men have traditionally seen it, has been quelled by domestic authoritarianism, political denial or moral sanction; they have been 'kept in their places', in the most repressive circumstances, by all of them together. Traditional moral and religious codes on relations between the sexes, male-written, were designed, at least in part, to meet male obsession by reducing women's scope to arouse it except in conditions controlled by men. 'Women's liberation', however else it has been perceived, threatened such control. In threatening such control, it threatened the 'order' which not only served to reduce women's rights, but also to confine (some) men's preoccupations about women to manageable dimensions.

The Jewish marriage service symbolises such purposes as well as any. Its essence is the 'removal' of the bride from her father's custody into that of her husband's. The ceremony 'consecrates', or consigns, the woman to her husband against all the world; the wedding contract, which formally ratifies the relationship, is read to the congregation. The core of most Judaeo-Christian legal systems, until they began to be reformed, rested precisely on such a reduction of women's powers to disturb men's public dominion. The contract was struck both with an individual man and with the wider society which men commanded. In China, foot-binding achieved the same ends by somewhat different methods: women were persuaded, and persuaded themselves, to the beauty of being thus hobbled. In the Jewish wedding ceremony, which takes place under a canopy – one of the symbols of monarchy in Jewish historical tradition – a woman is persuaded to feel, on her wedding day, that she is royal.

A sense of ancient pieties, and aesthetics too, may invite approval for such a ceremonial, in a world where piety of any kind has been so scorned, and beauty itself is under pressure. But the frightened male binding of women's powers is a different matter. In the Islamic tradition, women are enjoined (by men) to cover their faces as well as their bodies, in order not to disturb male equanimity in the public domain; in the most orthodox Jewish tradition, married women have their hair shorn and replaced by wigs, in order to make them less attractive to other men. In the Proverbs of Solomon, as in the injunctions of St Paul, the contracted wife is a protection against male 'temptation' by random lusts, a temptation which is both desired and feared. In the former text, the temptress is the 'strange woman' whose 'lips drop as an honeycomb' and whose mouth is 'smoother than oil'. Excitable male fear of 'enticement' – a matter of simultaneous attraction and anxious recoil – is older than the mutant violences against women to which it now increasingly turns. The 'end' of the 'strange woman', even Solomon warns, is 'as bitter as wormwood, sharp as a two-edged sword. Her feet go down to death; her steps take hold of hell.' Solomon left such a fate to God or natural causes; the 'provoked' modern brute takes matters into his own hands.

Only modern Islam rationalises women's physical self-concealment as a means to greater freedom. It offers, so Muslim women themselves argue, the freedom from unwelcome male attention, freedom from anxiety about the appearance of the body, and freedom from the pressure to compete with other women in attracting male notice. Such arguments may be thought (by some) to address plausibly at least part of women's predicament in face of male predation. However, the Koranic injunctions to women that they not only 'cast down their eyes' and 'guard their private parts', but that they also do not 'reveal their adornment' save to their husbands and close family members, are fully in that male tradition which seeks to deny female sexuality because it fears its own. The sense of women as potential disturbers of male peace of mind – together with noble condemnations of female oppression, and professions of an egalitarian ethic – is strong in the Islamic code. But such ambivalence about women, the classic ambivalence of latent male hostility and sexual preoccupation, is not so much Islamic as male. 'Those [women] you fear may be rebellious, admonish,' the (male) faithful are advised; 'banish them to their couches, and beat them.'

In December 1990, Iran's President Rafsanjani, in a public speech, recommended that male sexual desire and religious scruple could be satisfied together by 'short-term, or temporary, marriage': the one-night stand made holy. In June 1989, the United Arab Emirates, in the name of upholding Islamic values, banned male tailors and sales clerks from measuring women clients; six months' earlier a similar ban had prevented male hairdressers from touching women's hair. In May 1990, a senior Iranian cleric urged the authorities to 'take steps against' women who wore make-up; six months later, the Saudi Arabian government banned women, described as 'infidels' and 'fallen', from driving cars. In July 1990, the former (English) wife of a British Muslim complained not only of beatings meted out in the community to 'immodestly dressed women', but also of child abuse, domestic violence and sexual abuse. (A year later, a young Jewish *hasid* was being tried on charges of indecency with children.) In May 1991, Jordan's education minister, Abdullah Akaileh, issued a ban on male parents watching girls in gym-slips at school sports' days. Plato, at least, did not share such sexual obsessions, which have served in many Islamic countries to limit the scope of educational provision for girls. Girls in Plato's model republic, as described in the *Laws*, were not only to be subject to the same educational objectives as boys but the content of their education was to be the same. 'I have no hesitation in saying that riding and gymnastics are just as proper for women as men. There is no sense', the philosopher declares, 'in the ordinary practice of assigning different pursuits to the two sexes.'

Even-handedness is not possible for the obsessed. Obsession magnifies the significance of whatever is its object; sexual obsession torments itself over the enlarged focus of its desires. Beating back such obsession then becomes the task, or necessity, of moral and other injunction; obedience to such injunction in turn becomes the criterion of virtue. The whole is a moral (or immoral) whirligig, in which self-laceration lacerates others, and vice chases its own tumescent tail. It is a labyrinth, too, in which good and evil lose themselves together; or a masque, in which the greatest wickedness may wear the best moral disguise.

In the exploded utopia of socialism, theory had proposed to restore a harmonious balance between the sexes. The force of reason, vanquishing obscurantism in every field, would free the body, male and female alike, from the coils of obsession. Plato's moral ideal was the ideal of modern socialism also. Women were to be emancipated 'comrades', not feudal chattels or market sex-objects. In practice, Leninist sex as a refreshing 'drink of water' – objective and insipid – contained its own pruderies and proletarian inhibitions. Female 'comrades' were also 'less equal' than male; the Platonic ideal quickly gave way to Stalinism's heroic housewife. Women might have the freedom, a blissful freedom by Western standards, to walk the streets at night without fear; they might have, as in East Germany, one year's paid maternity leave, free day-care centres for children and abortion on demand; they might be spared pornography and prostitution. But, together with such exemption and provision, there were also (often) demeaning forms of drudgery, an absence of basic necessities, high rates – much higher than in some Western countries – of divorce and family breakdown, and little genuine role in the exercise of political power. Nor was women's circumstance improved by the overthrow of bourgeois manners, and their replacement by the domestic and sexual habits of the proletarian. There might (officially) be no brothels, but there was a shortage of adornments; no beauty contests, but a lost sense of grace; cultural curbs on male predation, but much suffocation of sexuality also.

At the first moment of release, socialist puritanism began to give way, with early relief, to the exercise of many tabooed sexual freedoms. Some forms of it were banal and relatively harmless; others were more threatening, especially to women's well-being. 'Wherever you look there are pictures of young sexy women,' declared the manageress of an employment advice centre in the former East German city of Schwerin. 'In the old communist magazines the women in the pictures had a more solid, committed look,' she said. 'Now everything is sexy.' Although sales were to slump later, Leipzig's first porn shop, so it was said in January 1991, earned enough in its first one and a half minutes of business to pay its rent for a month. Life-size inflatable dolls appeared in Warsaw; violent pornographic videos, imported from Thailand and Hong Kong, were on sale even in Hanoi by 1989. *Komsomolskaya Pravda*, once the puritanical paper of the Soviet communist youth movement, sought new subscribers with advertisements of naked women; *Tema*, a paedophile magazine, was being sold at the entrances to Moscow metro stations by November 1990. A Committee for Public Morals, set up by Gorbachev, began work the following month to 'devise criteria for the regulation of pornographic publications'. Prostitution, too, spread rapidly with the coming of the free market. The old life of the brothel could again be found from Southern China to the Saxon village. Escape from sexual inhibition was less than joyous; it brought with it, at once, not only the sexual exploitation of the vulnerable, but the immediate expression of a taste (in some) for the forms of sexual violence familiar in the West.

It had been innocently thought that decades of cultural enclosure would have made post-communist man relatively immune, at least for a while, from choosing Western plebeian ways of exhibiting his sexual aggression. Instead, when the doors to the West were opened, male instincts flourished on the West's imported sexual diet as if the socialist interregnum had never been. Sexual crime, like every other kind of

crime, began straightaway to soar in the collapsing Soviet Union, as in
the rest of Eastern Europe. Women's fears rose with it. In Tirana, for
example, fourteen teenage girls were 'kidnapped in the street or seized
from school' – and some of them raped – in a single month, March
1992, as a wave of crimes against women followed the fall of the
Albanian communist regime. Under communism, domestic violence
against women at the hands of latter-day Russian *muzhiks* or drunken
Polish peasants was common; the hard-working woman with a drunkard
and several children to feed was as familiar a figure in communist as in
pre-communist peasant culture. Western forms of sexual violence and
offence were rarer. But post-communism, rapidly sinking into slough
and depression, was as good a recruiting-sergeant as any to the armies
of the 'universal plebeian'. Indeed, between the disillusioned proletarian
in the East and the Western plebeian there were already many cultural
bonds in common, and others still in the making. In shared experience
of work, of insecurity, of ugly industrial environment, of loss of skill, of
loss of faith, of sexual taboo, and of domestic breakdown, they were
already brothers and sisters under the skin, nurtured to similar forms of
male anger and female dejection. They would also seek their requitals
in similar fashion, from hedonism to violence, male sexual violence
among them.

It was soon plain that non-communist and post-communist societies
lived in one sexual world in other respects too. A new sexual anxiety,
which knew no boundary of class or culture, had arrived to threaten the
body, sexuality, taboo, and even (some thought) the human future
together. Everywhere, those given to averting, or pretending to avert,
their gaze from the sexual, found the sexual – or worse, the homosexual
– at the heart of public concern. Questions of ethics, law and behaviour,
historical analogies and statistical projections revolved around the Aids
visitation. Sufferers were seen, as in a mediaeval tableau of the Dance
of Death, as wasted embodiments of sin, error and folly; much less
commonly, as subjects for medical treatment of a disease 'like any
other'. Even here, right and left had their distinguishable positions. The
former were inclined to identify Aids as a 'new plague' and to blame
the 'victim', the latter to resist both moral judgment and comparison
with earlier pandemic affliction.

A seaman who died in Manchester Royal Infirmary in 1959 had
puzzled his doctors with his unusual symptoms; they described his
condition in the *Lancet* in 1960. Tissue taken from his body, and stored,
was found in July 1990 – when Aids had become familiar – to have

been 'HIV-positive', that is a carrier of the virus known as HIV. The virus, which destroys the body's system of defences against disease, was first identified in the United States in 1981, and the surmise offered that its 'extensive spread' had probably begun in the 'late 1970s'. Other research theories, some exotic, placed its first outbreak as long as '140 to 160' years ago, when a 'divergent monkey virus' similar to HIV (such as is found in the chimpanzee and sooty mangabey) was transmitted from monkeys to humans; or seventy years ago, when malaria-infected blood from chimpanzees was first experimentally injected into humans in the search for a malaria vaccine. Whatever its first origins, about which both scientific and popular speculation was intense, by 1992 it was being estimated by the World Health Organisation (WHO) and other research bodies that between 1.5 and 2.6 million people had developed the 'full-blown' disease of Aids since it had first been identified and records had begun to be kept in the early 1980s. It was also estimated that, worldwide, 5,000 people – perhaps more – were being newly infected each day by the virus, and joining some 11 to 13 million people who were already carriers of the disease.

The forms of the disease and the pattern of morbidity were complex and varied. In malnourished and debilitated regions of the Third World, the time-span between becoming infected, becoming ill, and dying of the disorder was quicker than in prosperous conditions. In general, a sufferer from 'full-blown' Aids in Britain could be expected to survive between ten and twenty months; New York blacks with Aids died in nineteen to twenty-three weeks. There were also at least two different strains of the virus, one more 'aggressive' than the other. But the virus itself was *sui generis*, posing an unprecedented and, some pessimists intermittently thought, 'unanswerable' challenge to medical science.

Among the many problems which the virus set, and which suggested (to some) that it would be 'rampant for years', was that it was able to place copies of its own genetic material in the genes of the infected person, making the disease heritable and the removal of such genes from the human cell an inordinately difficult task. In addition, because of the long latency period – ten years and longer – during which the virus could be carried in a seemingly healthy body without the individual becoming ill with Aids, an infected person could remain unaware of the infection while infecting others for a decade and more. More bewildering, the virus seemed to be capable of making variations and mutations of itself, and thus of ultimately eluding whatever drug therapies might be found. Finally, the 'aim' of the virus was to attack the heart of the body's immune system, invading or attaching itself to the very cells which would normally have kept the virus in check. By 1992, it had come to be believed by some scientists that the Aids virus carried molecules on its surface which 'mimicked' those in healthy T-cells, responsible for guarding the body's immune system, and 'tricked' the T-cells into destroying themselves. Whatever the process, it made the infected person vulnerable – and the more malnourished, the more vulnerable – to other micro-organisms, and therefore to other infections, including those which give rise to pneumonia and tuberculosis.

In face of the scientific difficulties of finding a 'cure' for such a disease, some projections (which themselves tended to fluctuate wildly) of its future course were apocalyptic; a minority of optimists thought medical science would 'solve the problem' within five years. A WHO official declared that the 'existence of entire races' was threatened. By the year 2000, the WHO estimated there would be 30 million or 40 million people infected by the virus with 12 million to 18 million suffering from 'full-blown' Aids and dying at the rate of one million a year; Harvard Aids Centre's much higher projections for the year 2000 were for up to 120 million infected and 25 million with Aids.

Perhaps 80 per cent, or even 90 per cent, of these infections and deaths would be in the Third World, where the disease's spread had been most extensive and most rapid. By the year 2000, the WHO estimated, 6 million Africans would have died of Aids, and there would be 10 million African children, many themselves sufferers, orphaned by the disease. Some African countries could have lost up to a quarter of their workforces, while in Asia, where the disease was now spreading most rapidly of all, the rate of HIV-infection would be 'heading straight off the graph'. The pessimists, who assumed a doubling of the infection rate in young adults every five years if no cure was found – the proportion was said to stand at 'one in 250' of young adults infected worldwide in 1990 – pointed to a rate of 'one in 63' by the year 2000, but 'one in 16' a decade later. The US Bureau of the Census predicted, in February 1991, that there would be 70 million infected by 2015 in sub-Saharan Africa alone, again assuming that no cure was found. The epidemic might last 'another 150 years', warned a professor at Imperial College, London in November 1987, more apocalyptically still.

Some of the statistics of prediction seemed feverish, as if there were a will, on the part of some, to believe the worst. But this was a response which could itself be counted as one of the historic symptoms of pandemic. Terrified flights of fancy are an inseparable part of every record of past plague-visitation; 'the Report of these things lost nothing in the Carriage,' declared Daniel Defoe in his *Journal of the Plague Year*, which gives an account of the London Plague of 1665. Boccaccio, in his description of the 1348 Plague in Florence, says that 100,000 of Florence's population of 130,000 died. The true figure is thought to have been half this. Similarly, foreign observers excitedly reported that 20,000 people died in a day in London in 1665. The true figure, at its worst, seems to have been one-third of this.

In 1987, it had been predicted by some that there would be 50 to 100 million infected worldwide by the Aids virus in 1991, but this was between four and nine times the actual estimated totals announced by the WHO for that year. In January 1987, an 'expert' also predicted that there would be '2 million dead or dying' in Britain by the year 2000; by 1992, actual deaths were reported to be around 4,000. Nevertheless, it was also clear that the effect of the spread of Aids in some societies was, by 1992, becoming increasingly serious. In some Ugandan cities and towns, up to half of the 'sexually active' were said to be infected. In the Ivory Coast, approaching half of all male deaths, and a third of all female, were reported to be from Aids. Sixty per cent of soldiers in the Zimbabwean army were said to have tested HIV-positive; it was 'cutting a swathe' through the population of the Central African Republic, claiming policemen, politicians, judges and academics among its victims. In the United States, where an estimated 200,000 Americans have died of Aids in the last decade, over one million were said to be infected, with 40,000 to 50,000 new infections each year and a death from Aids 'every twelve minutes'. The estimated ratio of infection in 'sexually active' males, aged fifteen to fifty, was already one in fifteen in New York and as many as one in nine in San Francisco. By 1991, over 700 doctors, 1,300 nurses, 1,100 medical aides and 170 dentists were said to be among its American victims. (In the London Plague, too, 'the very Physicians were seized with it,' wrote Defoe.) The disease was also now to be found in Iran, Vietnam and China, Mexico and Poland, Switzerland and the former Soviet Union, where the first known Aids death occurred in October 1988.

Diagnosis and reporting of infection being a patchy and uncertain thing, there has throughout been a lack of precise knowledge as to how many were infected; and further confusion as to how many of these had developed Aids. Some thought that the 'real' figures were running at many times, even 'seven times', the totals declared. There could be no final proof, either, of how many Aids victims had already died. But there was not much doubt that the scale of the disease had begun to justify comparison – despite some objections to such comparison – with past scourges. This might not be the Great Plague of 1345 to 1350, which carried off 'nine-tenths' of the city of London, 'half' the population of Italy (including 'three-quarters' of Venice and 'two-thirds' of Bologna), and reduced Smolensk to 'five persons', but its gravity could not be concealed by squeamishness, unconcern or wishful thinking.

In fact, many responses to Aids, whether on the part of the authorities, victims, doctors, moral critics or other observers were strikingly similar to past responses to epidemic visitations. Again despite some protestations to the contrary, it was as if Aids was being recognised as the successor to past fates which had befallen the human population. On earlier occasions, not least because of the speed at which the infected died, there was more panic over the scythings of the Grim Reaper. 'The Imagination of the people was really turn'd wayward and possess'd,' reported Defoe; they were 'turn'd out of their Wits by Prognostications . . . crying the Destruction of the City'. One such testamentary prophet 'ran about Naked, except for a pair of Drawers about his Waist, crying Day and Night, "O, the Great and Dreadful God!" with a Voice and Countenance full of Horror'. The spirit of this age is more phlegmatic, or passive. Nor did this prophet stop to converse with those who tried to detain him, but 'held on to his Dismal Cries continually' and kept on running.

But if there is less panic today, there is more prudishness and similar superstition. Some popular assertions as to the 'original source' of the Aids virus have been little advance upon the quality of mediaeval and post-mediaeval explanations of the plague, which was blamed on the 'air', comets, locusts, Saturn in Aquarius, witches, Levantine merchandise, including cloth – a close guess, for the plague-carrying fleas it might contain – 'noxious and pestiferous Effluvia', and so forth. Today's choices for Aids have included an 'escaped bug' from a US army laboratory in Maryland, African insects, vampire bats and (perhaps nearer) the use of monkey blood as an aphrodisiac in the Great Lakes area of Central Africa. Conversely, Kampala bar-girls blamed the Aids virus on *mazungu* (white men), the Japanese blamed it on *gaijin* (foreigners) and Chinese politburo conservatives blamed it on 'bourgeois worship of the West' by political reformers. Such ascriptions were of a kind with those of earlier, ostensibly less scientific, ages.

Moreover, the appearance of the notion that Aids was a moral 'sign' was itself one of the historic signals in human behaviour of anxiety that a new Plague might have come upon mankind. Cardinal Siri of Genoa called Aids a 'holy plague to punish sinners'; a leader of Uganda's Muslims, Sheikh Hussein Kakooza, similarly described it as 'God's punishment to sinners'; the 1987 General Synod of the Church of England was told by a cleric that Aids was attributable to the use of the 'anal passages' of women by Africans (again) 'in a way which God had not intended'. Even a British policeman, provoked by the association of Aids with infection from intravenous drug-taking and homosexual relations, found the disease to be a 'judgment on promiscuous society' and 'evidence of people swirling about in a human cess-pit of their own making'. In post-communist Poland, a deputy health minister believed that the only people in danger from Aids were 'perverts'. When such declarations were made, it was as if a revived desire, eagerly seized upon, to chastise sin with 'whips and scorpions' had come to the assistance of the moral censor of sexuality as such, as well as of drug-taking. In the mediaeval past, though sin was similarly excoriated in times of plague, it was less the use and abuse of the body than religious heresy, the backsliding of the faithful, and moral frivolity which caught the eye of a Savonarola.

The search for a 'cure' for Aids also raised echoes of past efforts to combat plague. The modern attempt to trick the body's immune system into hyperactivity with a false virus is not very different in principle from the old Paracelsian magic of trying to stimulate the 'vital magnetic force' in the body to expel the plague. But today's research struggles to detect the Aids virus more quickly, to slow down cell infection by therapy of diverse kinds, and to stop the replication of the Aids virus by means of the genetic engineering of a human protein designed for the purpose – among other lines of inquiry – represent some of the most advanced aspects of modern medical effort.

Ancient forms of pure quackery have been quick to emerge also. In infected San Francisco (and elsewhere), Aids victims tried *shiitake* mushrooms, transcendental meditation, Chinese cucumbers, Ayur-Vedic medicine, herbal therapies and acupuncture; in sixteenth- and seventeen-century plagues, patients were treated with powder of vipers, 'washing the head in vinegar' and the placing of baked onions on plague boils. The mountebanks who were selling a counterfeit of the Aids-retarding drug AZT in the red-light district of Seoul in February 1989, or the two British doctors struck from the medical register in October

1991 for peddling plant extract and faeces in tablet form to Aids patients, had their plague forebears. In previous visitations, instead of condoms, men were instructed to wear talismans and amulets – often inscribed with the magical word 'abracadabra' – or 'wrapped their nostrils in fumigated kerchiefs'. Pope Clement the Sixth's choice was to sit between two fires with a large emerald on his fingers which he turned variously south and east, according to the prescription of his physicians. Defoe called such things 'Whymsies' and their authors 'Wizards quacking and tampering in Physick', with whose 'Pills, Potions and Preservatives' men 'poisoned themselves beforehand'. There were some compensations. The aroma inside London churches during the 1665 Plague, Defoe writes, was of 'an Apothecary's Shop' or 'like a smelling Bottle. In one corner it was all Perfumes, in another Aroma-ticks, Balsamicks and Herbs; in another Salts and Spirits.'

The Aids victim has also suffered from an old recoil. Even Aids doctors and nurses (with some justification, as the American statistics reveal) fear being 'splashed by body fluids', or accidentally pricking their fingers, or having abraded skin when treating Aids patients. In past pandemics, as in today's, many physicians and medical helpers gave their lives in carrying out their duties. Others fled the scene. In the Vienna Plague of 1679, doctors had to be 'led in chains' to the city's hospital. In Marseilles in 1720, 'the Physicians and Chirurgeons deserted the City'; they returned only when their salaries were prodi-giously raised to 2,000 livres per month. In the early stages of the London Plague, Defoe reports, some doctors 'ventur'd their Lives so far as to give them'. Later, at the Plague's height, there were 'very few Physicians which car'd to stir abroad to sick houses;' those who left the city entirely were called 'Deserters' when they returned at the waning of the Plague. If today's doctors and nurses have been more stalwart, and governments have borne the rapidly mounting costs of treating Aids – 10 billion dollars in the United States in 1992 – other plague-like fears have been succumbed to, in historically reminiscent fashion.

They have been expressed, above all, in the desire to remove the infected, or merely those who might be infected, not only from the immediate neighbourhood, but from the national territory itself. The former Soviet Union and the United States, Bulgaria, China, South Africa, Sri Lanka and the Yemen, among other countries, deported foreigners suffering from Aids. Germany's interior ministry instructed border police to 'turn back all foreigners suspected of carrying the Aids virus'; 'justified suspicion' was declared, mediaevally, to be a sufficient ground for exclusion in the name of 'protecting the German population'. Incoming long-stay visitors, especially students, were tested for Aids in many countries, including Belgium, China, Costa Rica, Czechoslovakia, Germany, India, Iraq, the Philippines and the former Soviet Union. In Florence, in 1348, 'all sickly persons' were likewise forbidden entry into the city. In Marseilles, during the Plague of 1720, the authorities ordered 'all strangers to go out of Town, on pain of being whipped . . . The dread of that horrible Distemper', wrote a contemporary observer, 'stifled all Sentiments of Charity and even of Humanity itself.' Today, there is more mercy; but 'only those who go looking for it, get Aids', declared an Italian health minister, continuing the older tradition.

The leader of South Staffordshire district council in England expressed a harsher view still in December 1986: the only way to 'stamp out' Aids was to 'put 90 per cent of homosexuals in the gas chamber.' Two Mexican congressmen in May 1989 proposed compulsory euthanasia for Aids victims and a 'round up' of homosexuals; the English *Daily Star* called in December 1988 for 'leper-like colonies of promiscuous homosexuals'. In San Francisco and elsewhere, 'gay-bashing' (and worse) became increasingly common. One victim, who had his eye knocked out, was told by his attackers that they would 'cure Aids' by 'getting rid of your type'. To put an Aids hospice anywhere, as was the case with pest-houses in earlier times, was to arouse hostile and sometimes violent emotions. There were reports from many countries of arson and other attacks on the homes of victims, and innumerable cases in which the HIV-positive were sacked from their employments. A six-year-old haemophiliac girl with Aids, contracted by blood transfusion, was admitted to school only on the condition, imposed by a Florida court in August 1988, that she remained 'isolated in a glass booth, 6 feet by 8 feet, with air conditioning and a sound-system'. Cuba put its Aids sufferers behind barbed wire and under armed guard in 'sanatoria'. In a British Gallup poll, conducted in September 1989, six out of ten respondents were in favour of the HIV-positive carrying identity cards. In June 1990, Bucharest gravediggers refused to bury children who had died of Aids; in Padua, a special cemetery plot was set apart for Aids victims, as happened in the Plague. Public figures might make a point of visiting and shaking hands with Aids patients in their hospices, and some terminally ill prisoners had their sentences reduced – as in Norway and Britain – but active sympathy was in short supply.

This was not least because the disease was closely associated in the public mind with moral misconduct; it was almost as if infection were not an illness but a crime. Research carried out by the universities of York and Hull, and published in April 1991, showed that more than half of those with Aids or HIV-infection were not getting moral support even from their parents. One in four had not told or had not dared to tell them, and in another 28 per cent of cases, parents were 'actively unsupportive' or 'too severely disturbed to respond to their needs'. In the Florentine Plague of 1348, too, Boccaccio reports how 'Fathers and Mothers fled away from their owne Children, the wife forsooke the Husband, the Sister the Brother'. Indeed, reports in 1991, almost 650 years later, of how HIV-infected inmates of Stafford Jail were attached by their handcuffs to a chain between six and eight feet long when being escorted to the local hospital – because of warders' fears of contamination – could have come from the pages of Boccaccio. So, too, could accounts of prisoner-patients being tethered to their hospital beds with leather-covered chains in Buenos Aires.

In Holland, exceptionally, there were 'Aids cafés' in many major towns where sufferers could go for company, tolerance and welcome; in Britain, there were many examples of employees' infection being kept secret – including in jobs involving food-handling and preparation – in the name of 'non-discrimination'. But, as in the case of plague, fear of contagion was a stronger emotion than all others. At an international Aids conference in Florence in June 1991, even the traffic police were equipped with rubber gloves. Orthopaedic surgeons feared the fine mist, or aerosol, of tissue and blood generated by the use of power tools in the operating theatre; sportsmen feared blood; hotel chambermaids quaked at a bedroom's detritus.

For sufferers, the long drawn-out sense of isolation was reported to be the disease's particular burden. Plague victims had died quickly; its pneumonic form could catch and kill in hours. 'Many died frequently in the Streets suddainly,' wrote Defoe of the Great Plague of London, 'without any warning . . . Others perhaps had time to go to any Door, or Porch, and just sit down and die.' In other less precipitate deaths, the victims of plague infection, Defoe reported, 'did not feel the Effects of it for several Days after'; not feeling the effects of HIV-infection a decade or more after becoming infected is of another order. But, even with such a short latency period as in plague, Defoe's contemplation of what he described as 'this infecting and being infected, without so much as its being known to either Person' aroused in him something close to modern journalistic relish. 'Such as had received the Contagion and had it really upon them and in their Blood,' Defoe elaborates, '. . . did not show the Consequences of it in their Countenances, nay even were not sensible of it themselves . . . Neither the Person giving the Infection, nor the Persons receiving it, knew anything of it.' In the case of Aids, as was reported to a London conference on the subject in April 1991, the first that some parents knew of having been HIV-positive for several years was when their children sickened.

Aids' long latency period is among its most lethal and tragic aspects, setting problems for the identification and isolation of the infected which are beyond solution in the Cuban fashion. 'If anyone is infected,' wrote Martin Luther in 1527, of plague, 'he should isolate himself or let himself be isolated from all others, and immediately seek medical assistance. He should not be forsaken in his need, so that the infection may be curbed in time, not only for the benefit of the one person, but of the whole community.' To Defoe, as to today's medical workers, the matter was not so simple. 'Removing the sick will not do it,' he wrote, 'unless they [the authorities] can go back and shut up all those that the Sick had convers'd with, even before they knew themselves to be sick, and none knows how far to carry that back or where to stop. For none knows when, or where, or how they may have receiv'd the Infection, or from whom.' Today, precisely such problems are newly compounded, with civil liberty pitted against compulsory testing, and medical ethics entering the lists against the disclosure of confidential information even to the spouses of the infected. Routine screening with the full consent of the individual – let alone compulsory testing of, say, marriage licence applicants or prison inmates – has aroused uproar in one place or another. Civil libertarians have also objected to the demands of life insurance companies to know about applicants' 'lifestyles', code for their sexual and other habits.

The human body, protected by taboo, itself stands in the way of the struggle against the disease. That Aids is sexually transmitted, among other modes of transmission, is arguably the greatest of its misfortunes. Efforts to control its spread demand, as plague did not, a candour about sex and sexual proclivity, as well as about past sexual conduct, which is impossible for many people, in many cultures, and for many reasons. The question of government-issue condoms for prisoners or drug-addicts (or, in New York, for high school children) is, for some, a moral nightmare, despite their routine issue to soldiers in wartime. For some, a taboo against the very discussion of condoms, let alone their use, appears to be more powerful even than the fear of universal annihilation by the virus and its mutations – free syringe 'swap-shops' for drug addicts create much less upset. Modest proposals, such as the call by bold American Catholic bishops for the use of condoms to be 'explained in Catholic schools and youth programmes', have touched on the most potent of ethical scruples. Calvinist Afrikaaners mounted protests against the introduction, prompted by Aids, of condom-vending machines in the land of the Boers; in Israel, orthodox rabbis pronounced against Aids posters featuring condoms with smiling faces; President Museveni of Uganda, among the worst afflicted of countries, was opposed to the use of condoms at all. In Australia, several state governments objected to the placing of six-foot long pink condom advertisements on the sides of buses.

Nevertheless, public discussion of such matters became (intermittently) more open. Gothenburg's female council members, dressed in mini-skirts and fishnet stockings, posed as prostitutes in order to 'inform would-be clients about the dangers of Aids'. 'Extra strong' condoms appeared on the market for the purposes of anal intercourse. Official Danish information videos on Aids showed a close-up of a woman placing a condom on a man's erect penis. But much of this earnest prophylaxis fell, so to speak, on deaf ears. Prostitutes in Glasgow – there were similar reports from around the world – charged their clients £10 for sex with a condom, and £30 without. 'They are risking their lives for £20,' as a Scottish doctor grimly put it. An Ivory Coast prostitute in Abidjan described in July 1991 how 'most men' would not use condoms at all, 'particularly the Muslims. They say their religion won't let them.' In this, too, there were plague echoes. Defoe refers to the 'supine negligence of the People themselves, as thoughtless for tomorrow as ever', who, in addition, 'would by no means believe the Afliction to be the Plague, alleging a Hundred false Excuses'. In the Marseilles Plague of 1720, 'the Publick were so Foolhardy that they began to condemn all the Precautions as wholly Useless and Unnecessary.' An East Prussian surgeon sent to Szabin during an outbreak of plague in 1710 asked to be recalled, because his work was futile. 'The incredible lack of obedience,' he wrote back (in Prussian despair) to his superiors, 'prevents all benefit to those who are still living.' The 'Labouring Poor', Defoe writes of the 1665 Plague, were 'madly careless of themselves'.

In Britain there were some initial signs of changed forms of sexual practice, including among homosexuals. It soon appeared, however, that such changes were confined to a minority, or were temporary only.

Thus, a fall in the incidence of male rectal gonorrhoea, a symptom of perilous conduct, was brief, as the first wave of fear about Aids passed; many drug-addicts similarly continued the lethal habit of sharing needles. Or, as Defoe put it, 'many People, being harden'd to the Danger, grew less concern'd at it, and less cautious . . . than they were at first.' 'I'm fed up with hearing about Aids' was its modern variant. Increases in condom sales were reported, but many surveys indicated that 'safe sex' was not being generally practised. In 1991, of all sixteen- to twenty-five-year-olds in Europe, only '20 per cent' were estimated to use condoms. In Britain, it was thought that perhaps 15 per cent or 20 per cent of 'sexually active' males used them; no research put the estimated figure as high as one-third. Moreover, there was some evidence that the 'most sexually active' – those with four or more partners per annum – used condoms least. A small-scale inquiry into young British women's holiday behaviour, published in July 1991, found that as many as 45 per cent had had sex on holiday with men not previously known, and that 60 per cent of them did so without protection. (Almost one in five claimed to have had sex 'within two hours' of meeting their new holiday-partners, and 40 per cent 'within two days'). Similarly, nearly half of British sixteen- to twenty-year-old males were estimated in April 1990 not to be limiting their sexual partners; 40 per cent of them claimed to have had two to six partners in the previous year. In May 1992, psychologists at St Mary's hospital in London found that one in four women attending its clinic for sexually transmitted diseases had also never practised 'safe sex', and that one in seven, having begun to do so at the time of the first wave of anxiety about Aids, had reverted to 'risky behaviour'.

Many appeared to believe that a cure for Aids would be found, and all would be saved. Some, as in times of past affliction, were convinced that they were singled out to be secure; some refused to use a condom for fear that their partners might think they had Aids; some thought that they could tell 'merely by looking' whether a person had the virus. There was little doubt that many, perhaps a great majority, regarded Aids as a risk run only by others: Exeter University's 1991 research among young people in the south-west of England found that '89 per cent' considered they had 'no chance', or only a 'slight chance', of becoming HIV-infected in the next two years. Another report, in April 1992, suggested that most Asians in Britain believed themselves to be entirely immune from the Aids virus. (In the 1665 Plague, Defoe remarks, 'many Persons were infected . . . to their unspeakable Surprize'.) But that there was less unconcern than might appear was evident from the surfacing, exactly as in past pandemic, of cases of 'phantom Aids' and acute 'Aids phobia'. In the former, doctors found swollen lymph glands, weight loss and mouth infections – as in Aids – in anxious patients who did not have the disease. In the latter, as in times past, the fear of having contracted Aids drove some individuals to kill themselves. In August 1989, for example, a Greek policeman shot himself while waiting for the result of an Aids test which proved negative. Others, out of similar fear, murdered their partners and even their children. In Brescia, in February 1987 – there were many such examples – a man shot his wife and himself thinking (wrongly) that they both had Aids.

Suicide on being told of real infection was not uncommon. On Christmas Eve, 1990, a London clergyman who worked as a counsellor to Aids victims, learning that he was HIV-positive, ran naked from a hospital bathroom, through a ward, and up a flight of stairs to the fourth floor, where he jumped to his death from a window. 'When the Plague boils grew hard,' Defoe records, the victims 'threw themselves out at Windows, or shot themselves, or otherwise made themselves away.' In Marseilles, in 1720, 'they cut their own Throats, or threw themselves out of the Windows of their Houses, or into the Sea'.

Other forms of Aids-related violence have echoed, and sometimes gone beyond, past responses to plague. In February 1990, the Old Bailey heard how a Soho club manager was 'stamped to death' (again) when he confessed to his homosexual lover, just after they had 'had sex together on the club's dance-floor', that he was HIV-infected. (There were similar cases in the United States.) His attacker 'jumped up and down on his body', crushing his chest wall and rupturing his heart; robbed him of his gold watch and ring; and then set fire to his body, using alcohol from the bar. In the same month, and in the same court, a jury was told how a 'masochistic homosexual', suffering from Aids, was kicked and punched to death by three men – one of whom also had Aids – on Hampstead Heath in London, where he used to go in order to find partners to beat him. Evidence was given by one of the accused that the victim 'pleaded for more' as he was kicked, crying out 'Is that all you can do?', and 'Do you call yourselves men?'

If there is nothing in Defoe to match modern body torments such as these, other crimes committed by a small minority of Aids victims have trodden closely in plague's footsteps. They have included knowingly giving infected blood for transfusion, deliberately trying to pass on the disease by sexual assault, and with the same motive spitting at or biting others, in particular policemen and warders. Indeed, the question of whether it should be a specific criminal offence for one person 'wilfully to infect another' became a new, or old, subject for legal debate, including in the British Home Office. In May 1992, Southwark Crown Court heard how an HIV-positive man of twenty-two attempted suicide by slashing his wrists; when police went to his aid he 'sprayed his infected blood at them', shouting 'Have some HIV blood, you bastards' and 'Catch it, catch it'. 'I spat on him,' declared an HIV-carrying Harlem prostitute, of a police officer whom she had also bitten, 'and he said, "Oh my God, now I have Aids."'

The resonances in her vengeful sense of triumph were historic, or human. In Magdeburg, in 1625, a plague attendant, himself ill with the disease, was reported to have 'thrown his cloak over a woman's head, breathed in her face, and said, "Ha, wench, that will do for you."' Similarly, in 1665, as Defoe recounts, a man in London's Aldersgate Street 'with the Plague upon him' – 'just as a mad Dog runs on and bites at everyone he meets' – 'caught hold of a Gentlewoman and kissed her ... When he had done, [he] told her he had the Plague', as the Soho club manager told his lover he had Aids more than 300 years later, 'and why should she not have it as well as he?' In July 1990, a prisoner in Sydney's Long Bay jail stabbed a warder in the buttocks with a syringe containing HIV-positive blood, and went off shouting 'Aids!' The woman kissed in Aldersgate Street 'fell down in a Swoon, or in a Fit'; the Australian warder, who tested HIV-positive five weeks later, was said to have been more composed. But he might survive years; the woman of Aldersgate, in a plague-ridden city, days.

Fear of such events may magnify and embellish their telling; the same fear may suppress the desire to hear of them. Anxiety can stop the imagination as often as feed it, and in half-consciousness of risk imprudence can flourish. Moreover, in plague-like afflictions the border between wilfulness and negligence has always been a fine one. Today's examples include resistance to being tested for Aids out of fear of the outcome; knowledge of infection which, as in the past, is concealed from others; and, further along the scale from thoughtlessness to crime, there are those who do not 'take the least Care or make any Scruple of infecting others', as Defoe puts it. He found his own explanation in 'human nature', which, he gloomily speculated, 'cannot bear to see itself more miserable than others of its own Specie, and has a kind of involuntary wish that all Men were as unhappy or in as bad a Condition as itself.' Luther, writing of similar phenomena in the Wittenberg

Plague of 1527, denounced such conduct as that of the 'most wicked people.'

But, however well-established the precedents for delinquency of this kind, the more ordinary desire not to believe that Aids is as serious a matter as it is, together with the instinct to conceal its incidence, are also part of a long tradition. Indeed, the instinct to concealment, which has reappeared in the Aids epidemic, is one of the factors leading medical statisticians to believe that the true death rate from Aids might be double or more than the officially reported figures. In 1665, plague deaths were recorded (and concealed) as 'Consumptions, Imposthumes, Gripes and the Like', since, Defoe tells us, 'it was of the utmost Consequence to families not to be known to be infected.' In Britain, from the outset of Aids mortality, some doctors – and obituarists – have been similarly disposed to give, as proximate causes of death in Aids cases, not HIV-infection but 'pneumonia', 'broncho-pneumonia', 'chronic airways obstruction' and so on, in order to spare relatives embarrassment or knowledge of the truth, or both.

Knowledge of the body's truths, especially for the squeamish, can be an awkward or delicate business. (Violence against women is sexual fear's quickest and most brutal route to such knowledge.) But Aids had brought back to an age of empty fashion, and of pretensions to eternal youth, a gaunt *memento mori*. The black blotches on the skin from sub-cutaneous haemorrhage in Aids-related Kaposi's cancer were little different in their impact, emotional and aesthetic, from the 'black or blew spottes which would appear on the armes of many, others on their thighes' in Boccaccio's account of the most feared symptoms of plague in Florence, in 1348; the spots were an 'assured Sign of neere approaching Death'. And just as it is now seen in a suffering Aids patient, so Defoe saw 'Death in his Face' in a plague victim.

Ancient reflex has also reappeared in the ascription of 'blame' for Aids to 'others'; foreigners, strangers, the morally aberrant. Yet, in no pandemic – in this Aids is typical – has it been known where to place the first appearance of the homicidal virus, or precisely whose conduct, if any, was 'responsible' for its dissemination. In the fourteenth-century plagues, Jews were popularly accused of 'poisoning the wells', and killed by the thousands for it. In Lyons in 1564, it was heretics who were blamed for 'smearing the houses' of Catholics with 'ointment received from Hell' and 'plague pus'. Today, homosexuals and drug addicts have attracted the kind of attention that witches, lepers, gipsies, vagabonds and other outcasts once attracted.

Looking to Africa, and to blacks in general, for the root of epidemic evil is also part of an old story. In mediaeval children's games, a 'Black Man' represented plague-death; and, though its meaning is contested by historians, the 'Black Death' contains, and in turn suggests, a familiar association. In the case of Aids, it has similarly been asserted that 'Africans are genetically more susceptible to the Aids virus'. Moreover, since blacks constitute less than 13 per cent of the population of the United States but account for more than 30 per cent of its Aids cases, it has been inferred (by some) that they have succumbed in such numbers because they are black, and not because drug-addiction, sexual promiscuity, inner city overcrowding, failures of hygiene, and immune-systems undermined by poverty invite infection. To one mediaeval reflex, some blacks in New York have themselves added another: in a 1991 poll carried out by the *New York Times* and the Columbia Broadcasting System, no less than 29 per cent of blacks said they believed it to be 'possible' that the United States government had 'created the Aids virus in a laboratory' in order to 'infect black people'. In April 1988, a black Chicagoan and community liaison officer, Steve Cokeley, expressed the view, centuries-old in its impulse, that the Aids epidemic was a 'result of white doctors, especially Jewish ones, who inject the Aids virus into blacks'.

During the post-war decades, the body, so it has been conventionally argued, was gradually 'liberated' (in the West) from trammels placed upon it by the moral and sexual inhibitions of a previous generation, or generations. But this 'liberation' also made the body a more open battlefield of hostilities and desires. Now, a pandemic associated – retributively, for some – with the abuse of this same 'freed' body was forcing old moralities and fears back to the centre of ethical and physical attention. On all sides there were moral dilemmas, each likely to become more pressing if a 'cure for Aids' were not found. Some were faced with acknowledging and talking about anal sex, others with giving fertility treatment to HIV-infected couples; some, with conducting tests for Aids on unknowing patients, others with weighing religious scruples about condoms against the need for protection from Aids. A British philosopher advocated that Aids sufferers should be offered counselling on how to commit suicide, as an 'escape route'. Some doctors agreed, but more argued that patients should not be encouraged to take their own lives.

Other moral conundrums only a Solomon might resolve. Was it morally right or wrong to segregate and confine those who could infect others? If wrong, how could the healthy be protected? Were drugs

which helped the infected to remain well for longer not also extending
the individual's potentiality to spread infection? Was the question of
whether an individual was infected, or had sought testing in order to
ascertain it, a fit question for the state to ask of a citizen, or for private
individuals to ask of one another? If it was a fit subject, might it not
deter some from taking the tests at all? What rights did the infected
require to have defended, if any? The right to protection from job
dismissal on grounds of infection? The right to mix freely with others
in any circumstances whatever? Or what rights should the infected lose,
if any? To marry? To bear children?

In the meantime, while such questions were being increasingly fitfully
debated, or not debated at all, Aids was at its work in many different
populations. The poor and the anonymous were falling by the tens of
thousands in Africa, and the spread of Aids was becoming rapid in Asia;
in the United States and Europe, hopeful statisticians thought they
detected a 'levelling off' in its rate of increase. But many hundreds of
thousands had already died, and many millions more carried the virus
in their bodies. The rich, the prominent and the gifted had been struck
down (most often without the fact of Aids-infection being made known),
just as plague had once claimed Petrarch's Laura, Ghirlandaio and
Perugino, Holbein the Younger and Titian.

Yet, a manifest public sense of what could be afoot should a 'cure for
Aids' not be found seemed largely to be absent. Only in unconscious,
reflex behaviour was there unwitting testimony of such knowledge.
Intellectuals, in general, kept away from the subject entirely. 'We know
so little about ourselves,' wrote Pascal in his *Pensées* at some time in the
1650s, 'that many people think they are going to die when they are
quite well, while many think they are quite well not sensing the abscess
ready to form, and the approach of fever.' Today, such philosophical
sensibility as to what might have struck mankind, with Aids, is lacking.
Imaginative response is also slight. It is as if intense sexual preoccupation, sometimes violent, and equally intense consciousness of fashion
have exhausted most interests, artistic and non-artistic alike, in the
circumstances of the body, and made Pascal's ethical awareness a
remote one.

And if a 'cure' were to be found, what then? After the Plague, Defoe
tells us, people behaved 'like Sea-men after a storm is over'. They were
'more bold and harden'd in their Vices and Immoralities than they were
before'. That, too, if a magical vaccine were to be discovered, is surely
coming, with other violences against the body.

TEN

Killing Time

The historic continuities of crime or the clinician's knowledge of mental aberration explain little enough of the pathology of today's violence. It is not so much the frequency as the types of killing and brutal conduct – including gratuitous cruelty – which (fleetingly, now) draw the jaded attention. Before the Flood, the earth was 'filled with violence', but not, surely, more than it is now. Nor could it have been so inured to it as it is now, when savage crime often merits only a bottom-of-column newspaper filler, and is instantly forgotten. Today, routine violence and a casual habituation to killing make for deaths without solemnity, and wounds which no longer bleed. The jesting grave-digger in *Hamlet* is one thing, murder reduced to triviality another. For some, morally iller, violence is fascinating, and report of it entertainment.

Impassivity towards violence committed against others is equally troubling, even if such a response is a compensation for fear. When, in May 1987, a gang taunted a disabled man of thirty-three and 'beat him to the ground' (in broad daylight) in an Oxford shopping centre, he 'lay bleeding and crying for help as shoppers walked past him'. In December 1987, according to report, a girl who had been stabbed on a London underground train staggered through carriages past passengers who 'did not stir', and lay bleeding to death from a five-inch deep wound. In the same month, police in Newcastle criticised the 'hundreds of shoppers' in the city centre who, they said, had ignored a woman's cries for help as she was being robbed. In November 1988, on the motorway at Quincy-Voisin, south east of Paris, a twelve-year-old girl was run over by 'at least twenty cars', none of which stopped, after she had attempted to wave down passing traffic to save her dying father injured in an earlier accident. Eventually, one driver, a thirty-year-old woman – whose car was found to be 'badly damaged and covered in blood' – went to the police; she had not stopped at the time, she explained, since she had her own children in the car whom she 'did not want to frighten'.

In July 1990, the Old Bailey heard how a raped and weeping twenty-four-year-old nurse, cut and bruised, banged in vain on doors as she 'staggered round a housing estate' in south London. She told the court how, earlier, while she was being raped in a car-park, she had called out 'Please help me!' when a car had drawn up nearby, only to hear voices saying 'Oh dear, I think it's a rape', as the occupants walked away. In August 1991, a woman described to Southwark Crown Court her struggles with a man who was pushing her towards the platform edge as a train entered the underground station where she was waiting, loaded with shopping, in the evening rush-hour; 'other commuters did nothing to help', the court was told. Such accounts, in which fear and moral unconcern are sometimes hard to distinguish, are becoming common. They can be replicated by similar accounts from other countries; the accounts themselves attract only perfunctory concern. Not all 'impassivity', however, is what it seems. For example, in Britain, fear of retaliation by council estate neighbours and local gangs, a factor increasingly noted by police, plays its own part in deterring intervention and stifling a civic response to violence.

In Britain, between 1940 and 1990, there was a tenfold increase in the number of crimes committed per 100,000 people: in 1991, in England and Wales, there were 5.3 million recorded crimes in total. Moreover, it is estimated that less than half of all criminal offences – especially of vandalism, thefts from vehicles and wounding – are reported to the police. Worse still, and depending on both the statistical source and annual variations in the rate of commission of different kinds of offence, only from 'one in four' to 'one in sixteen' recorded crimes are 'cleared up', which represents an even smaller proportion of the actual crimes committed, from murder to minor harm. Habituation to crime, fear of crime and, as one can see, the relative impunity of crime constitute a vicious circle. In particular, propensity to violence of all kinds (in Britain, to go no further) seems plainly to be increasing year by year, even if the actual rate of increase fluctuates. The carrying of weapons is also increasing; in Britain, a knife is now used in about a third of all street robberies. Pub disturbances were also reported by an Oxford research group in August 1990 to be becoming more violent, with more than one in five fights now involving weapons, with women participating in 18 per cent of violent pub confrontations, and with 'working-class young men the worst offenders'. In August

1991, the Bristol Royal Infirmary reported in the *British Journal of Oral Surgery* that facial injuries for street assaults and bar brawls had risen by nearly a half in ten years. Between 3,400 and 5,400 violent offences involving the use of glass – bottles and drinking glasses – are now recorded in England and Wales each year. The head and neck are usually the target. Indeed, by the mid 1980s no less than 'one in three' British men, despite the low rate of 'clear-up', were being found guilty by the age of twenty-eight of a 'serious crime': that is, of an indictable offence or of certain summary offences such as aggravated assault or cruelty to a child.

In addition, a rising proportion, now approaching 40 per cent, of the male victims of murder in Britain are killed by strangers, for most criminologists a more ominous index of increasing violence than would be a similar increase in the rate of killing by familiars. In the United States, too, murders by strangers have increased since the 1960s at double the rate of murders by acquaintances. Similarly, a quarter of a century ago roughly half of all reported rapes in the United States involved people who knew each other; now, over two-thirds of American rapes are carried out by strangers.

Like assaults on other public servants in Britain, assaults on the police – in whom trust is at the same time said to be falling – are increasing, and stand at around 20,000 per annum. Public insecurity in the street, on public transport and even at home, especially in the largest conurbations, must now deter, as it has not done before in modern times, a significant amount of social movement. Fear of being attacked or robbed was the reason most cited by people over 60 for not attending theatres and concerts, according to research carried out for the Arts Council of Great Britain, and published in January 1989. Yet Britain, compared with the United States, is law-abiding. Although 600 crimes are now registered in England and Wales every hour, and the chances of an individual becoming a victim of crime have risen seven-fold since the 1950s, there are 'only' some 750 homicides in England and Wales a year, compared with over 24,000 American (and over 15,000 in the former Soviet Union), a seven-fold higher rate in the United States per 100,000 of population. Nevertheless, some of the forms of violence committed, even if not their frequencies nor the weapons used in them, have been converging. Aggressive physicality has become a shared language, and resigned habituation to it a common feature, of many plebeianised Western cultures, the British included.

As with types of crime, so the gestures of violence have become increasingly standard. Thus, kicking a victim – including, in extremes, to death – has entered the everyday vernacular of crime. 'Bovver boots' were an early symbol of it; 'getting your head kicked in' an increasing commonplace, both of threat and deed. How far such reflex reaches into the cultural subconscious can be measured by the frequency of calls to 'stamp out violence', itself a violent (and contradictory) image; it now passes, like much other violence, without notice or comment. Such reflexes may appear in 'normal' educated jocularities, too. 'The Young Conservatives,' a *Guardian* reporter wrote in February 1988, 'gather in Eastbourne tonight to celebrate their 40th anniversary by kicking the hell out of each other.' 'Don't Kick the Tories Out, Just Kick 'Em!' declared a similar slogan, that of the boot-boy 'anarchist' movement Class War, in the February 1987 Greenwich by-election. The *Sun* made the violent plebeian impulse to kick out at others even clearer in May 1990, when stating its (violent) position on the proposed desegregation in prison of previously segregated 'child molesters' and rapists: 'Good. Then they will all get the kicking they so richly deserve,' the paper declared.

'Stamping' and 'kicking – like the equally plebeian head-butting – are now too commonly employed as methods of dealing out actual bodily harm to take such references lightly. In 1984, a fifteen-year-old from Croydon in South London even had his skull fractured in what was called a 'kicking game' on the school playground. In September 1987, the Old Bailey was told how an off-duty tube-train driver was 'kicked to death' outside a pub after he had remonstrated with two teenage youths, sentenced to life imprisonment, for eating a local darts team's sandwiches. In February 1989, in Birmingham, a Catholic priest was 'kicked unconscious' by two youths and two girls when he came upon them trying to steal his car. In September 1989, in West London, a man was jailed for four months for kicking another man in the testicles – one of which had to be removed thereafter by surgeons – during an altercation over a minor traffic incident. In May 1990, a gay actor, aged forty-nine, was 'kicked and stamped to death' in a public lavatory in West London. Before he died, he was able to say that 'about seven' men had taken part in the attack on him, described by the police as a 'severe beating of a merciless and savage nature'.

Some of this brutality, as has been noted in relation to attacks on women, is now both opportunistic and almost casual. It may also be provoked by a glance, a gesture or a word. In such cases, where violence is poised on a knife-edge and wildly triggered at an instant, accounts often suggest not merely an extravagantly aggressive predisposition looking for an excuse to harm, but mental illness. In March 1992, the Old Bailey heard how an Islington building worker, aged thirty-four, threw corrosive acid in the face of a complete stranger – who later died – in the course of a pub argument; in May 1992, in Whiteville, North Carolina, a youth league baseball coach, aged forty-five, cut the throat of the coach of an opposing team in front of the teams' eight- and nine-year-old players, during an argument about the rules. ('Unsporting' was the *Guardian*'s cynical headline.) Yet, as frequently and more alarmingly, mental illness will be denied in the evidence of experts. Nevertheless, many murders and serious assaults in Britain, as well as in the United States, begin their course, especially in pubs, clubs, restaurants and discos, with the assailant (or his wife, or other female companion) claiming that the victim-to-be was looking at him (or her) 'in a funny way'; in many such cases, generally of violence committed by young males, there is what appears to be a paranoid obsession with the 'staring' of others. It is not exclusively young men who manifest this type of phobia, nor only the 'starers' who suffer. In May 1991, the Old Bailey heard how a man of forty-eight, eating with his wife in a Blackheath pizza restaurant, abused two youths, aged fourteen and sixteen, whom he believed – according to his wife's evidence – to be 'staring at him' while they waited for a take-away. The youths in turn goaded him into following them outside, where, in a nearby alley, they 'battered him to death'; he was said to have died from 'terrible injuries' and 'in a matter of seconds'.

Nor is it only 'staring' which can lead to violence upon an instant of 'provocation', real or imagined. A mere request for a courtesy, if the moment is ripe, can set off the swiftest aggression. In a cinema in Baltimore, Maryland in December 1987, a man asked by a woman's companions to move because he was blocking her view, shot the woman in both legs. In Birmingham, also in December 1987, a company director whose wife had got out of their car to ask a girl to move from a pedestrian crossing – where the latter was drunkenly stripping off her clothes – was stabbed by the girl's companion after a brief altercation. A reminder of duty, a refusal of a request, a moral reproach, a complaint about behaviour, can all lead to a knifing or killing. Thus, in November 1987, a schoolboy of sixteen came before Manchester Crown Court for stabbing an eighty-year-old woman a dozen times after she had refused to lend him money. In May 1988, a (white) man dining with his wife and son in an Indian restaurant in Essex asked five men at a nearby table to stop using racist language, and was knifed to death. At a west London underground station in November 1988, a ticket-collector who challenged a young 'fare dodger' was slashed across his head, face and arms and needed fifty stitches in his wounds. In November 1990, a youth of eighteen was jailed for life at Winchester Assizes for stabbing his father more than fifty times after the latter had complained about the volume of the music which the former was playing. ('Music Killing', ran the flippant *Independent* headline.) In July 1991, a Southwark lorry driver, aged fifty-three, murdered his neighbour – by plunging a knife seven-and-a-half inches into the latter's chest – after a row over the smell of smoke from a barbecue which the victim had refused to douse.

Cross latent violence's path, and catch it on the raw with a wrong word, a request out of time, a refusal on the nerve, and a physical attack can follow. A British youth of twenty, seeking access to his girlfriend in a Dubai housing compound, but refused entry late at night by an Indian watchman, beat the watchman to death and was sentenced to ten years' imprisonment for it in June 1987. In December 1987, at the Old Bailey, a youth of nineteen was convicted of stabbing to death a student from the Maghreb after the latter had irritated the former in a pub by patting his dog. ('My dog don't speak to foreigners, especially if they are Arabs or blacks,' said the aggressor, who had run home to get a kitchen knife for the killing.) In August 1988, a man of thirty-two was jailed for life at the Old Bailey for 'bludgeoning to death' a friend who had mocked his pool-playing; in July 1989, Nottingham Crown Court also passed a life sentence on a youth of twenty who had stabbed another man to death for accidentally spilling coffee on him in a café. The following month in Central Park, New York, a man who, with others, had been told by a lifeguard to leave the park's crowded swimming pool because the water had become murky, opened fire. He shot the lifeguard in the back several times, also hitting other bathers, including a thirteen-year-old child whose eye was pierced by a bullet.

In the United States, violence and killing are mainly carried out with guns, and less frequently with knives and other implements; in Britain, mainly with knives, boots and cudgels, and less often with firearms, even though their use is increasing. But the hair-trigger impulses, or readiness for recourse to violent action, no longer differ as greatly as once they might have done. In Washington DC, where murder is now the capital's leading cause of death among young black males – and nine times the rate of Chicago in Al Capone's day – the majority of violent homicides are a by-product of petty thefts, street arguments and domestic quarrels. In both societies, resort to violence, whether with fists, bottles and boots, or knives and guns, can come more swiftly than ever on the heels of private irritation or public anger. When racial tensions flare, as in Los Angeles in April 1992, the demon of the lynch mob can on the instant reappear; in certain social circumstances, a child which cries once too often, in Britain or in America, is in increasing danger of being seriously harmed, or even killed, by its parents; merely when the inner city's lights fail, as in Chicago in July 1990 and Handsworth, Birmingham in August 1991, looters in both countries can seize their moment to ransack local stores. In Britain, the violently touchy reactions of the opportunist aggressor or the chronically aggrieved have also spilled over increasingly into worlds which were once benign, often with the tabloid media in excited attendance. The 'tension' before a 'big match' between the England and Scotland rugby teams in October 1991 was such, the *Daily Star* predicted, that it would 'spark into open warfare at the first sign of ill-temper'. It did not. But it was not for lack of that base media enjoyment of 'trouble' – or violence as entertainment – which whets the appetite (of some) for aggression. Even American TV networks and newspapers refused to carry advertisements for the viciously titled British film, *The Pope Must Die*.

It was as if, in the last decade, the spirit of foolish emulation were pushing the managers of less overtly violent cultures, such as the British, in the direction of the more violent, such as the American; as if to be unaggressive in thought and action, taste and conduct, were itself a symptom of inertia or a sign of weakness. The American murder rate is over five times that of average European levels, and some twelve times that of the average rate in the world's twenty-one most developed nations; and within the American statistics the homicide rate among young black males aged from fifteen to twenty-four is as much as seven times higher than that among white Americans in the same age group. But to baulk at such figures is no longer (if it ever was) *manly*. More than six murders a day in New York, 70 per cent carried out with handguns – and 275 daily robberies – become, under the rules of such bizarre competition, statistics without moral resonance. At worst they come to seem the data of a modern, vibrant city a-glitter with event, cinematic derring-do, and heady attraction. Thirty years ago, there was only one murder a day. Now, New York is six times more 'colourful', with American losses in the Gulf War equivalent to less than an average fortnight of New York murder. In three decades, over half a million

Americans have been killed by guns in their own country, over 2 million wounded by gunfire, and over 3 million robbed at gunpoint. These are statistics which have become grist to the mill of an entire culture, a culture also made available to voyeurs the world over. Americans, who number some 250 millions, are now said by the US Bureau of Firearms to own 201, 837,000 guns between them, including handguns, shotguns, semi-automatic weapons and even modified submachine guns. At the present rate of increase, there will be a gun for every citizen – man, woman and child – by the mid-1990s.

The logic of it is bewildering. In cities like Atlanta, over 200 serious crimes per 1,000 residents are already being reported each year. A significant proportion of the crimes, including rape and murder (and not only in the United States), are now being committed by the young and very young. Nearly half the suspects arrested for murder in Washington in 1991 were under twenty, and one in five were seventeen or under; in Britain, one third of all convicted burglars were of school age. At Belleville, Illinois in July 1987 a fourteen-year-old boy was sentenced to '120' years in jail for shooting five other children and cutting the throat of a sixth, all of whom survived their injuries. Five months later at the Old Bailey, a seventeen-year-old girl and her fifteen-year-old lover were found guilty of luring the former's thirteen-year-old sister into woods and killing her, after she had threatened to tell her parents about her elder sister's affair. As the fifteen-year-old strangled the thirteen-year-old, the Old Bailey was told, the seventeen-year-old said 'Do it, do it!' in the fifteen-year-old's ear, pulling a plastic bag over her younger sister's face until she stopped breathing.

But the capacity for indignation is lost. The case passed, as such brutality now passes, with little notice. In April 1988, near Northampton, two girls of twelve and fourteen were alleged to have been involved in the murder (by a seventeen-year-old youth) of a thirteen-year-old schoolmate. In July 1990, a boy of sixteen was sentenced to life imprisonment by Birmingham Crown Court for murdering an eleven-year-old girl by beating her head repeatedly with a brick, the prosecution alleging that the assailant had earlier expressed 'the intention to commit a rape or a murder'. In October 1990, in Birmingham, four youths aged sixteen and seventeen stripped a fifteen-year-old girl on the school playground, scrawled obscene graffiti on her body, and inflicted stab wounds on her; in the same month, Sheffield Crown Court heard how a boy of sixteen had used a hammer to batter a schoolfriend to death while 'acting out a scene from an Arnold Schwarzenegger video,

Commando'. In Wolverhampton, in March 1991, a fourteen-year-old boy was charged with the murder of a seventy-eight-year-old woman; in the same month, a thirteen-year-old boy in Washington DC was being sentenced to six years' detention for the rape of a three-year-old, a severe blow to whose head had also left the child partially paralysed; in Solihull, in February 1992, two sisters, aged fourteen and fifteen, were charged with stabbing to death a fourteen-year-old girl.

Quick recourse to aggression and opportunist violence for trivial motives have begun to make their marks even upon the youngest of teenagers. From the late 1980s, the phenomenon of one child attacking another for desired fashion-clothes and footwear began to be reported from several American cities, including New York, Los Angeles, Detroit and Chicago. By February 1990, such assaults were said by police authorities to be 'increasing in frequency'; expensive training shoes and bomber-jackets bearing football team logos were capable in the United States of provoking murder. In Reading, in England, in January 1991, three youths, not to be culturally outdone, were reported to have assaulted a thirteen-year-old boy, pinned him to the ground, and stolen his new trainers; in April 1992, in Walsall, a man of twenty-four was attacked 'for his leather jacket' by a gang of ten youths and stabbed to death. Common cultures follow, at a distance, in each other's footsteps. Research findings on the incidence of 'street robbery and snatch' in Islington in north London, published in April 1991, reported that schoolchildren were 'increasingly robbing each other in order to acquire "status" goods like mountain bikes, skateboards and sports wear'; crime, too, has its passing youth fashions. The most common victims in the United States were black teenagers. 'The individual wants to hang on to his coat because he paid so much for it, so they just blow him up,' a Los Angeles police spokesman declared.

By the end of the 1980s, such youth violences had brought the New York school authorities to introduce an automatic one-year expulsion rule for pupils 'caught carrying guns or other weapons' in school – one in five high school students in the US was said to take a weapon to school for self-protection – and for 'beating up teachers and pupils'. In 1991, there were forty-five incidents in New York schools involving guns, eleven children were shot, and one died; sixteen New York high schools had doorway metal detectors; no fewer than 2,000 guns (and many more knives) were confiscated. At one school alone, Thomas Jefferson High in Brooklyn, over seventy students have been shot, stabbed or otherwise wounded since 1988, and three have died.

The 'hacking to death' of a London policeman at Broadwater Farm estate in October 1985, by youth in riot, suggested the spread of further new degrees of capacity for brutality in common. When a man with a knife stabbed three policewomen and a male sergeant in a north London shopping centre in December 1991, so the Old Bailey heard in March 1992, one of the policewomen, 'pouring with blood', was told by an onlooker, 'You've got what you deserved'; a man giving the wounded sergeant first aid was pulled away by another who said, 'Let's have a look. He has done him good.'

Among the callous worst of it was the gratuitous violence, most often committed by the young, against the victims of robbery, often old, or very old. In January 1987, a Stockport dress-shop owner was left critically ill by robbers who blinded her in one eye, inflicted skull and facial fractures and severed her right ring-finger, before escaping with the day's takings. In August 1987, at the Old Bailey, a part-time home-help of twenty-two was charged with involvement in the murder, by her accomplices, of a frail eighty-two-year-old woman for whom she had worked. The old woman, who weighed six stone, was robbed, tied up, gagged with sticky tape round her nose and mouth, and left to die. In January 1988, a gang of four young people, including a girl of fifteen, was tried for the murder in the course of robbery of a seventy-eight-year-old Camberwell woman, 4 feet 6 inches tall, who walked with the assistance of a walking-frame. Thirteen of her ribs, her right arm and her spine were fractured, and her breasts and the inside of her mouth bruised: sadistically-inflicted injuries which distinguish certain types of today's violent crime, and criminal, from the footpad robberies of an earlier age. A month later, a court in Bolton was told of the robbery and similar battery to death of an old man of seventy-seven, who had been 'tortured before being killed by being repeatedly stabbed in the neck with garden shears'. In Redhill, in July 1988, a retired ninety-year-old dentist was beaten to death in the course of robbery; a Manchester widow of eighty-eight was beaten to death as she made a 999 call, her cries of 'Why are you doing this to me?' automatically recorded.

In June 1989, a Croydon woman, who disturbed a gang of three men when she got home, was tortured for refusing to disclose where money and valuables were kept; she was handcuffed to a chair with a carrier bag placed over her head, and beaten with a hammer and an air-gun. She suffered a fractured skull and temple, a broken nose and upper jaw, fractured collar-bones and broken bones in her hand; her left eye was dislodged from its socket; and the air-gun was fired into her nostril.

(No arrests were made.) Even this catalogue of injuries turned public attention cold for mere moments, before the crime was lost from view in the everyday, or in media events more arresting still. In January 1991, in South Tyneside, a woman of eighty-five was even attacked in a rest-home by a man in his late teens, his motive robbery, and her skull fractured; in Leeds, the following month, a ninety-eight-year-old woman was kicked, robbed (of a small amount of money) and left tied to her walking-frame; in Swindon, in March 1992, a widow of ninety-one was attacked in her home and robbed of £60, suffering serious injuries which required the subsequent removal of her left eye. In many such cases, no arrests are made; the type of violence can occur in any part of the country. The San Francisco policeman who retired in January 1991 after twenty-eight years' work as a plainclothes' 'decoy', disguised as a frail, elderly man carrying a stick, reported that he had been 'choked, kicked, beaten and robbed' on 'more than 200 occasions': an index, like the cases in Britain of violence against the old, not only of 'crime' but of moral disorder.

The muffled response to it – sometimes, now, a matter of resignation or a swift turning of the page – matches the often-reported indifference of the violent at the consequences of their actions. A teenage stepfather, accused of battering his seven-month-old stepson, watched cartoons on television, so the child's sister told the Old Bailey in November 1989, after the child had been taken, dying, to hospital. But the sardonic *Independent* headline, 'Too Cruel', over a six-line news item in January 1989 describing how a teenage girl in Ohio robbed an 'octogenarian cripple' before throwing his artificial legs out of reach as she made her escape, was no less cool, if in a more 'sophisticated' fashion. Yet, when killing and assaulting the most vulnerable and unguarded 'for fun' – for kicks, as well as for cash – has entered the standard repertoire of modern crime, it is unsurprising if judgment is dislocated.

Killing for fun, killing at random, and killing at a sudden whim are often hard to distinguish. In September 1990, eight members of a New York gang called FTS (Fuck That Shit), with cries of 'It's killing time, let's go!', set upon a family of Utah tourists on their way to dinner. The father was robbed of 200 dollars, the son received a fatal knife-wound; with the money for a night out obtained, the gang went on to Roseland dance hall. Other types of random killing, such as in 'drive-by' shootings of pedestrians by teenage gangs in New York and Los Angeles, have been reported in the United States since 1990. In January 1990, at the Old Bailey, three young men received life sentences for sadistic crimes similarly committed during a night's otherwise motiveless violence as they drove, masked, from place to place in Surrey choosing their victims at random. One, a fifty-seven-year-old man with a weak heart, was bound with electric cable, repeatedly kicked (suffering a fractured sternum and five broken ribs), soaked with petrol, and left lying in a field to die. His injuries, the post-mortem report declared, were 'consistent with being stamped on'; as he fought for his breath, one of the attackers was said to have remarked that the victim 'made a good actor'. Two young men, aged twenty-four and eighteen, who had built a cardboard shelter for a mentally ill tramp, then set it on fire and burned him to death, received a life sentence for it at the Old Bailey in June 1987; they claimed they had done it 'for a laugh'.

Gratuitous assault by able-bodied youth on the handicapped, often in the course of minor robbery, is becoming common. After a spate of such attacks in the mid-1980s, blind students at Queen Alexandra College in Birmingham had to have their white sticks fitted with sonic alarms. In February 1987, a wheelchair-bound paraplegic student at Liverpool University was robbed in her wheelchair; in March 1987, a disabled woman of seventy-one wearing calipers and her wheelchair-bound husband of eighty-two were beaten 'black and blue' for a few pounds. In August 1989, a twenty-two-year-old blind man was seriously injured after being attacked on a Surrey train by three men who punched and kicked him, robbed him of £17, and took his white stick also. Four months later, at the Old Bailey, a girl of twenty-two was jailed for blackmailing a blind man by threatening to 'poison his guide-dog'; in May 1990, a judge at Oxford Crown Court sentenced a man of twenty-four to twelve years' imprisonment for raping and robbing a young deaf-and-dumb woman; in October 1991, a Middlesborough man, aged nineteen, received a life-sentence at Teesside Crown Court for beating to death a one-legged Dunkirk veteran, aged seventy, in the course of burgling his home; in September 1992, in a car park in Reading, a man was robbed of twenty pounds at knife point while suffering an epileptic fit. In all such cases, court verdicts and custodial sentences do not touch the transgression of the moral order. Justice itself cannot be done, and, knowing it, passes to other business.

But, at the next turn, today's spate (in Britain) of violent cruelty to children, much of it committed by parents, also challenges judgment with wickedness beyond measure. Increasingly frequent are cases of punching, deliberate scalding with boiling water, burning with ciga-rettes, and striking the victim against walls or furniture, often in a crescendo of repeated violence until death. Deaths from malnutrition as the result of starving, deaths from head injuries, deaths from the rupture of internal organs – most often from kicks and punches – increasingly catch the eye. A child may be locked away in a room and subsequently be found, dead or alive, covered in filth and sores; another, a few weeks or months old, may be killed for keeping its parents awake or 'interrupting the television'; a third may be 'smacked too hard' and die of a violently ruptured bowel.

Analysis of the ages of the victims of homicide has shown that in Britain babies aged less than one year are at the greatest risk of murder, the risk now being some three times greater than that for any other age group, child or adult. Three-quarters of the serious head-injuries inflicted on young children occur between infancy and the age of four; most of the assailants are young parents (married or unmarried) between the ages of eighteen and twenty-five, mothers included, and young male cohabitees of women who have children of other fathers. The battering violence that kills and injures the very young – as the result of which a small child may typically be brought to hospital with multiple fractures, old and new, and sometimes extensive internal injury – has been variously dignified as a 'syndrome' of its own, the ill-doing of the 'immature', or an aspect of the violence of the age.

Others have pointed to the high rate in general in Britain of 'smacking and striking' children. Research carried out at Nottingham University, and published in October 1989, claimed that three-quarters of all children were 'smacked at least once a week' at the age of four; that domestic violence against children was commonest in 'unskilled work-ing-class homes'; that in the latter, at eleven-years-old, 36 per cent of children were being intermittently beaten with an implement by their fathers, mothers, or both. Study of the cases that have led to court prosecution for grievous injury or murder discloses a now familiar pattern: of violent, and often unemployed, aggressions, and of the depressions and life-styles of the 'universal plebeian', under the rule of which a child can be reduced to a disregarded object among others. Idly cruel whim, quickly triggered response to 'provocation', harm for fun, and extremes of physical brutality also afflict children. Age, whether of the very old or the very young, is no deterrent.

In March 1988, a Nottingham court heard how a young mother had dipped her two-year-old son's penis in hot tea and spun him around inside a spin-dryer. In March 1989, similarly, an Ealing woman of twenty-six was found guilty of having put the feet of her screaming

eighteen-months-old child into boiling water, leaving the child severely
scarred and needing to be 'taught to walk again'. In June 1990, at
Ipswich, a young father aged twenty was sent to jail for three years for
having poured boiling water over his six-week-old son's leg for ten
seconds – described by the judge as a 'distasteful' act – leaving the
infant with burns to the muscle, requiring skin grafts, the amputation of
two toes, and finally the amputation of the entire leg. In June 1988, the
mother and stepfather of a young teenage boy from north-east London
were accused of 'six years of cruelty' against him, including kicking him,
burning him with cigarettes, forcing him to record pornographic videos,
and on one occasion 'throwing him from a moving van at thirty miles an
hour'.

In the same month, at the Old Bailey, a security guard and his
partner, a former shop assistant, were accused of having starved their
two young children to death. One of them, aged two, was reduced
before death to being 'unable to walk or smile'. When found by
ambulancemen the child was 'covered in vomit and blood'; the court
heard that the couple's dog had throughout been well fed. At Bristol, in
December 1988, a father aged twenty-five was found guilty of having
beaten his five-year-old daughter to death (turning up the stereo so that
the neighbours would not hear) with tubing and a kettle-flex, for
'annoying' him by refusing to spell her name for him; she had suffered
'fifty blows' to her face, hands and body. In a case heard at the Old
Bailey in November 1989, a seven-month-old child was shaken so
violently by its mother and stepfather – aged eighteen and seventeen
respectively – that blood vessels in its eye were ruptured; fingers had
also been pressed into its eyes, its skull fractured with a 'rounders bat'
and its wrists broken. In another case, which came before the Old
Bailey in April 1991, a twenty-three-month-old child's injuries were so
severe that photographs of them were declared to be 'too distressing' to
be shown to the jury; in another, an unemployed former security guard,
aged twenty-three, repeatedly punched the fourteen-month-old child
of his partner in the face, chest and stomach, fracturing the child's skull
and splitting its liver, for crying while he was watching a World Cup
football match on television.

In defence, the aggressor will typically say, 'He would not stop
screaming,' or even, 'I never touched him;' or claim that the assaulted
or killed child had 'had fits', or was 'accidentally burned', or had 'fallen
down the stairs'. A mother may say helplessly to police or hospital staff,
'I think he has killed my baby;' a male defendant, admitting guilt, may

declare that he 'went berserk' or 'lost control'. In the grimmest cases, there appears to be no moral concern. Domestic life may continue with a malnourished or injured child locked away in a room, or dying before its parents' eyes. In October 1991, Peterborough Crown Court heard how an eleven-month-old child with 'terrible injuries' – including eleven fractured ribs, four of which had been broken more than once, and a ruptured bowel 'from a punch or kick in the stomach' on Christmas Eve – 'slowly died in her cot' while her twenty-year-old parents, each of whom was later to blame the other, celebrated Christmas in the next room. By the time an ambulance was called, on Boxing Day, the child was dead.

In the scale of things, it could be said, such domestic killings of children in Britain, however pitiful, are a kind of humdrum. Incidents of plebeian daily life which momentarily break the surface of public notice, their very mention is considered by some to be 'distasteful', and by others to bear a meaning too difficult to fathom. And since behind every delinquency, past or present, stands another and another, this or that horror may even be considered to be, at worst, like any other. In any case, thinks Giant Disregard, briefly contemplating the children kicked or punched to death, Britain is not Brazil, where an average of three homeless and slum-dwelling children are said to be murdered daily, including by gangs allegedly paid by tradesmen to 'clean up' the streets of the city.

Nor, in turn, are these the killings of Mafia and Camorra extortion – there were more than 700 such murders in Italy in 1991 – or of American inner city gangs, which claim thousands of lives each year. The turnover of the drug trade, its profits defended with increasing violence, has been estimated at £300 billion dollars annually, more even than the value of a year's sales on the world oil market; other estimates put the figure higher. In New York alone, racketeering and extortion, with their attendant bloodshed, were alleged in August 1991 to be worth as much as '600 billion dollars' a year; nearly 16 per cent of Italy's public sector contract spending is estimated to go directly to Mafia criminal enterprises, and more than half of Italy's 227,000 restaurants and bars were said by the president of their trade association in June 1991 to pay extortion money. In the Greater Washington area, whose population is some 3 million, it is estimated that 24 million dollars is spent each day on cocaine, or over 8 billion dollars a year. Crack-gang warfare in some American cities is ever more violent; 85 per cent of killings in Washington are said to be drugs-related. Fighting for 'turf control', and defending a market, costs lives. Its toll, like the toll of killings in certain areas of southern Italy and Sicily, is that of civil war in microcosm. The intermittent 'teenage curfews', such as that of March 1989 ordering all under-eighteens off the streets of Washington by 11 p.m. on weekdays and by midnight at weekends, are decrees akin to those of martial law. But democratic insouciance takes even this in its stride; the more than one thousand heroin deaths a year in New York are, or have become, the 'acceptable casualties' of battle. In Los Angeles, there are estimated to be perhaps 50,000 feuding blacks, whites, hispanics and others in some 450 different street gangs, some armed with automatic weapons; their organised violence, added to that of the Los Angeles police department, helped to ignite the city in the April-May 1992 riots. In New York, no less than forty people, including ten children, died in 1990 after being struck by stray bullets from gang cross-fire.

Even mass murder may become a jaded subject, the moral price of familiarity satiated with a surfeit of violence of all kinds. Indeed, in these times, fear itself may be stupefied or dulled from the assault upon the senses of reports of outlandish forms of crime, and anxiety turn to laughter at its excesses. Multiple or (now) 'serial' murders have a long enough history – there have been numerous 'Bluebeards' and 'Rippers' – but killings committed with relish and diminishing notice dim, as the Holocaust dimmed, every comprehension. When one human quarry after another is pursued by an aggressor capable of cunning forethought and careful reason, reason itself withdraws, not least because it knows that no punishment could fit the crime, and that no court is fit to judge it. In March 1987, when the Philadelphian Gary Heidnik was brought to trial, evidence was presented of his having kept the dismembered body-parts of women in his refrigerator; 'I hope to hell they hang him. I'll even pull the rope,' said his own father, not less brutal. Ed Gein, the Wisconsin farmer, used the body-parts, skin and tissues of his victims (fifteen neighbours) as chair-seats, lampshades – reminiscent crime – and bracelets; Jeffrey Dahmer, the Milwaukee factory-worker, had human hands in his kettle and severed heads in a filing cabinet; the Ukrainian, Andrei Chikatilo, who in April 1992 admitted to more than fifty murders, ate the genitalia of some of his victims.

Explanation also staggers at the mass killing in October 1991, by a malcontent 'loner' and 'heavy metal' fan armed with a semi-automatic weapon, of twenty-three café customers, most of them women, in a small town in Texas. He was said to have constantly played a tape called

'Bitch Ain't Nothing but a Word to Me'; 'hiding from me, bitch?' he inquired of a cowering victim before he shot her. Donald Harvey, the Cincinnati murderer, pleaded guilty in August 1987 to twenty-four murders, and admitted thirty other killings, of elderly hospital patients by poison and suffocation. Diagnosed by a psychiatrist as having a 'personality deformity' but as 'not psychotic', Harvey was described in court as 'someone who must satisfy an inner need, a tension' – or a mutant form of De Tocqueville's 'feverish wants' – 'by killing'. Other psychiatrists have described 'serial' killers as frequently driven by the belief that they are 'doing good for society by killing certain types': a morality turned, half a century ago, into a reason of state, and its moralists into the butchers of millions. Today's small town lusts for similar ends are satisfied with a dozen, or two dozen, corpses.

Killing, whether on film or in fact, in make-believe or in earnest, of a few individuals or of whole hosts of humans, has become easier as time has passed. It has become technically more simple, and morally less of a burden. To do away with scruple, and dispatch man, woman or child, is a labour of seconds, whether on the battlefield or on the screen; hands can be washed and dinner served thereafter with barely the batting of a moral eyelid. The daily bill of killing fare is drawn from all parts of the world and brought on the instant to the table. Cruelties, easy to cook up, are as easily digested; and the appetite, however jaded, has been trained to expect more. In March 1989, at Liverpool Crown Court, the thirty-seven-year-old deputy matron of a Southport rest-home was jailed for ten years for attempting to murder an elderly resident, while her partner stole his savings. She struck the old man over the head with a bottle, kicked him, and shouted 'Die, you bastard!', leaving him naked all night in a pool of blood. It was a case, like all the others, whose life – both as 'news' and as a moral issue – lasted a moment, and vanished. Regimes of cruelty may be those of states, institutions or private persons, and their actions may afflict millions, one hundred, or only one other individual. But the visibility of all of them is increasingly short-lived, their differences of scale quickly reduced to one-dimension (whether in black-and-white or colour), and with another channel always at hand. Moreover, if moral objection makes too loud a sound, its volume can be turned down and nothing be heard at all.

Nonetheless, the life of passionate ethical judgment, of goodness and beauty, and of 'ordinary civil society' continues. Killing a policeman may bring stardom and leadership in a Los Angeles gang, but still the foundation of order remains. Two Liverpool boys, aged fourteen and fifteen, may have attacked with a hammer and 'almost killed' their assistant headmaster in March 1987, but other Liverpool schoolchildren continued with their studies. Seemingly disastrous challenges to the moral order, the moral order itself withstands. When an East London 'knife gang' murdered a randomly chosen Asian immigrant in the street, holding his arms behind his back and plunging a ratchet-knife up to the hilt into his stomach, the accused 'jeered and laughed' at the judge as he passed sentence on them at the Old Bailey in November 1987; but the rule of law trembled only briefly. And if killing has become easy for some, or arouses the most perfunctory of feelings, for others both life and death remain sacred.

Such venerations, however, are increasingly hard to sustain, as temptations to cast them aside grow stronger. The awe-stricken who sees God's hand everywhere may always have been both saint and fool; but the man on his knees today cannot see his adversary coming. Moreover, habituation to violence – state violence and police violence included – takes a large moral toll on both saint and sinner. And when familiarity with killing and aggression are combined with an angry fear that violence by others will go unpunished, the moral outcome may be still darker. When an armed 'subway vigilante' in New York took the law into his own hands in December 1984, and shot four black teenagers whom he thought were about to rob him, leaving one of them paralysed below the waist, he became a popular hero and was released from jail after less than a year. In May 1987, in Los Angeles, a group of youths took turns in 'beating and stamping to death' a man who had snatched an elderly woman's bag; in New York, in March 1988, a drug-addicted 'mugger' was himself beaten to death by an 'angry mob' after he had robbed a woman of twenty dollars; in Paris, in August 1989, a woman driver chased two youths who had snatched her handbag and 'mowed them down', killing one and seriously injuring another; in August 1990, again in New York, a group of Bronx residents cornered a tenement robber and, without bothering to call the police, stabbed him to death. Bodyguards, armed chauffeurs, privately organised and armed street patrols, bullet-proof clothes for schoolchildren – including denim jackets, raincoats and satchels – and even armed child-minders have arrived in New York City. And in August 1991, *Final Exit*, a book of precise and energetic instructions on different methods of committing suicide, reached the top of the New York non-fiction bestseller list: a last salute, the salute of De Tocqueville's impatience, to killing.

ELEVEN

Citizens and Strangers

The right and left dream different dreams about the ideal society. The right generally dreams of a peaceful and orderly community, ethnically homogeneous, in which prosperous, law-abiding and god-fearing citizens know their places and duties. They practice reciprocal good neighbourliness, value family loyalty, respect national and local tradition, and suffer only those intrusions upon the realm of the private as are necessary for peace and order. The left generally dreams of a happy and contented community, generous in its embrace of others, in which good-natured individuals combine their efforts in order to promote harmonious and mutually beneficial relations between themselves. They practice the morality of sharing, value camaraderie and cooperation, respect community tradition, and aspire towards egalitarianism as a *sine qua non* of a just and peaceful order. Actual individuals, unless they are out-and-out bigots, veer between (and can see the virtues, in turn, of) each utopia. Actual individuals, whether of right or left, also know their respective utopias to be equally threatened, and threatened in the same ways, by the insensate flux of the world, its predations and violences, its impatiences and unreasons.

For purposes of party, or from ideological habit, the left might once have blamed the right, and the right the left, for many of the world's problems, social, economic, political, moral. Each, especially in the heyday of the Cold War, would accuse the other of obstructing the path – on left or right – to the solution of such problems; each identify the values and interests of the other as antipathetic to good government, morality, or public well-being. But when communism fell and socialism was humbled with it, such orthodoxies had already lost much of their hold, even if political reflex continued to sustain them. Wider preoccupations with the unmanageability of many of the world's travails had superseded hitherto fixed ideological positions. They had led the traditional right to discard much of its conservatism, and the traditional

left to ditch most of its socialist nostrums. Only diehards for the old
pieties on the one hand, and for the old class loyalties on the other,
remained, and remain. The most ardent advocates of the former are
now to be found in societies which suffered the communist experience;
the most ardent advocates of the latter are to be found in societies
which escaped it.

These have been abandonments, right and left, of the familiar and
the known. The 'radical new right' (but not so new) has espoused the
very interests, economic and cultural, which least respect the traditional,
or conservative, established order. The ex-socialist left (not new either)
has embraced the very interests, market interests above all, which most
disdain the egalitarian ethic. In the confusion, a large moral vacuum
yawns, and the scope for anxiety grows larger. The established order,
faute de mieux, comes to be defended by 'extremists' in the name of race
and nation; socialist aspiration, plebeianised, falls into the hands of
lumpens ready to fight the 'class war' with fists and knives. Between
them there is a fine line, and a common cause to be found. Gang
loyalties and the urge to harm are made for them. Nor can 'socialist
virtue', with millions of deaths meted out in fraternity's name, take a
convincing moral distance from political street thuggery waiting for its
next affray. As for 'modern capitalist freedoms', they have turned to
hedonisms so gross that moral outrage against delinquencies thought to
be even grosser can hardly be expressed in such freedoms' name; or
not without a blush of shame. When 'leisure' is proclaimed the 'life-
style of the Nineties', a flick-knife and a fly-reel acquire equal moral
status.

However, the greatest loser in these times is not the ideologies and
expectations of old right-and-left but the sense of civic society itself.
What its moral purposes are has largely ceased to be a subject of debate.
Even the existence of civic society is, for many, a lost hope. Some have
retreated entirely from identification with the civic order, just as they
have retreated from the inner city, whether because they can no longer
make their emotional way amid its heterogeneity of population, or out
of fear of violence, or from some other cause. Others, from absence of
a civic education, or lacking any sense of citizen obligation, have no
notion of what the term 'civic society' might mean. Others, again,
preoccupied with self and its tribulations, or separated from community
by community's disintegrations, have neither time nor energy for their
neighbour. Aggression in words, gestures and demeanours, in social
response and political reflex, repels many, driving them homewards;

inner cities, deserted after nightfall, cease to be places of social concourse. Social and economic inequalities – as when tens of thousands in a single city, from Liverpool to St Louis, are on relief or welfare, excluded from many of the pleasures of living – turn the civic bond to mutual reproaches and resentments. In the United States, more than 10 million single-family heads are receiving welfare; in Britain, around 100,000 children 'go missing' annually, many eventually returning home, and many not. More than half of black American teenagers are being brought up fatherless; in Britain, where over 8 million people receive the 'supplementary benefit' of the poor, 10 per cent of the unemployed have never had a job. 'Civic society' in such circumstances becomes a shadow of itself, or loses all meaning.

Today, the metropolis contains millions of citizens who know nothing of its history and traditions. The gods of place, their altars overturned, have fled. (In May 1990, a man was arrested at the Arc de Triomphe in Paris for urinating on the tomb of the Unknown Soldier.) Whole nations have lost, or are in the process of losing, their sense of particularity, while to argue so is to be accused of the most benighted form of reaction. In once-communities, the next man has become a stranger, the passer-by an atom with neither local habitation nor name. In New York, where, under the criminal law, 'depraved indifference' to the fate of another can attract a charge of 'second degree murder', there are said to be over 150 separate ethnic groups; in Los Angeles, eighty-five languages are spoken by the children in its school system. Demands that ethnicity should have its own institutions – in New York only 43 per cent and in Detroit only 25 per cent of the population is white – multiply to the disaggregation of the whole. In New York, a city 'full of stirs', a 'tumultuous city', the pattern of racial exodus and influx has left ethnic embattlement and increasing inter-ethnic violence to their anti-civic devices. But lamentation over civic breakdown is an ancient tradition: Judaic judgment found many a 'faithful city' turned 'harlot' or 'full of murderers', as Jerusalem was found to be by Isaiah. There was 'depraved indifference' in the London of the Plague, too; Defoe reports how drunken carousers, when they heard the 'Dead Cart' passing, would open the tavern windows to 'mock and jeer at the Mourners' as they proceeded to the grave.

Moreover, the 'anomie' of the citizen in modern sociological theory was long ago anticipated by De Tocqueville. 'In certain countries of Europe,' he wrote in 1838, 'the natives consider themselves as a kind of settlers, indifferent to the fate of the spot on which they live ... This want of interest ... goes so far that if his own safety or that of his children is endangered, instead of trying to avert the peril, he [the 'settler'] will fold his arms and wait till the nation comes to his assistance ... When a nation has arrived at this state, it must either change its customs and its laws or perish: the source of public virtue is dry; and though it may contain subjects, the race of citizens is extinct'. De Tocqueville's obituary was premature. The nation did not 'perish', but was driven to heights of aspiration (and wickedness) hitherto unknown. There was also sufficient 'public virtue' to revive and sustain the body politic despite the worst that wars and revolutions could do. And if, under benign welfare regimes, 'folding the arms' and waiting till the nation came to the individual's assistance became commoner than even a De Tocqueville could have foreseen – so that the very word 'citizen' fell into disuse – the civic bond was maintained even in the most unpromising of conditions. But, at the same time, the Aristotelian premise that the individual can find his true self only in the community, or *polis*, has become for many human beings a dead letter in a social limbo. On the move, lost in the city crowd, overwhelmed by state power, the 'true self' of the individual now requires as much to be protected from others, as discovered through association with them.

The price the individual pays for slipping the bonds of social order, or for finding no rewarding place in it, is a high one. It has effects on private life, as well as on public. Retreat into the 'privacy' of the home may well be thought to arouse expectations of, and place pressures upon, personal relations which they cannot bear. According to the fragmentary evidences of British poll and research findings, more than 50 per cent of forty- to fifty-year-olds in Britain claim to have 'no close friends'; watching television is said to be the 'favoured pursuit' of seven people in ten; the British are claimed to own the highest number of home videos *per capita* in the world. An increasing percentage – over 50 per cent not only of the old but even of young adults between the ages of twenty-five and thirty-five – say they prefer to 'stay at home' rather than to 'go out'. Yet, at the same time, less than half of British families whose members live at home are now said to sit down to an evening meal together, and even the family Sunday lunch is asserted to be 'gradually disappearing'. Research by the Institute of Environmental Studies found that over half of its sample of British house-owners would not have moved to their present homes if they had 'known about the neighbours'. In the United States, a poll survey published in May

1991 found that 72 per cent did not know their next-door neighbours at all.

If some of these findings must be treated with reserve, other data – such as those relating to accelerating divorce rates, among which Britain's is the highest in Western Europe – point to a complex but decipherable web of civic and domestic failure. It has brought common solitudes, severance from community, moral doubt and family break-down to many millions of individuals. In a recent American poll, 47 per cent were 'not certain' that they would marry their present partners if the choice was again before them, and 33 per cent of the HIV-positive had not informed their partners. Once, the faltering of religious faith was counted as the profoundest of personal moral crises; the combi-nation of domestic unhappiness, moral confusion and loss of community are heavier burdens still. In general, the forms of urban life – as in Britain – do little to alleviate them. Even the opportunities for idly pleasurable 'people-watching', as a report funded by the Gulbenkian Foundation pointed out in June 1991, have diminished in the harassing British city, when parks become 'dangerous', pubs the only places of resort, and the townscape gradually more forbidding.

The consequences of all such shrinking in the scope of life are not only political, but moral. In the final reduction of civic culture to a fleeting street-exchange, and in the atrophying of citizenship to the recording of a vote or the collection of benefit from a local post office, the scale of individual deprivation is severe. Today's lost sense of belonging – to place, to community, to family – represents as much a crisis of faith as did yesterday's loss of faith in God. Indeed, lack of interest in the continuing public effort of others, and a closing of the door upon the world, are not greatly distinct from the moral sloth which the pulpit once belaboured. Neither pleasure-seeking nor the urge to violence can make such frustrations of social purpose good: civic society can be reanimated neither by the market-search for novelty nor at the point of a gun. Moreover, a condition of moral doubt as to 'right and wrong' is exactly the situation which De Tocqueville feared might be the outcome of a democratic order. It would be a situation in which the 'very elements of the moral world' became, as he put it, 'indeterminate'; in which religion failed and, with little to replace it, the 'moral tie' was undone. Americans, according to one observer, have now lost, along with the substance, even 'the vocabulary for collective moral discourse'. (Part of this vocabulary, it might also be argued, has been carried away for good by socialist failure.) Yet, it is precisely in non-despotic societies, where personal liberty holds a high status and force cannot serve to maintain order, that government most requires to be conducted on the basis of a shared faith and common values.

The term 'citizen', both on traditional right and left, has always been considered to be more than a narrowly political or constitutional term. Even Marx, in his essay *On The Jewish Question*, made 'citizen' and 'moral person' (meaning a person vested with civic rights and obligations) into synonyms. The traditional right, and much of the non-communist and nonconformist traditional left also, conflated duty to God and civic obligation in the belief that both were grounded in the same, or similar, moral impulse. But the right and much of the left parted company, at least until the recent socialist debacle, on the issue of the social and moral effects of the secular eclipse of religious feeling.

On the traditional right, deep bonds of community, and even the civic sense itself – the sense of belonging to a citizen body with common rights and duties – are held to depend upon the maintenance of a shared system of belief. Without the latter, it is insisted or implied, the former cannot be sustained. Socialists, however, have traditionally been suspicious of all faiths but their own, or recognisable versions of it. The Marxist kingdom of heaven was closed to the religious believer. Even for the more tolerant non-Marxist socialist, a professing Christian needed to be more a socialist than a Christian (and a Jew a non-believer) before, in general, his morality and faith could pass muster. Moreover, the idea of moral teaching, the teaching of distinctions between 'right and wrong', fell foul of socialism's moral relativism and class reflexes. Indeed, absolute distinctions of right and wrong, unless ratified by socialist scripture, were always suspected of being 'bourgeois', and not only among Marxists. The right's sense, or intuition – shared by the young Marx himself until Marxism got the better of him – that 'civic society' is a moral as well as a political construct, and that civic morality must be taught, was only acceptable to most socialists if a moral order meant an egalitarian or classless order. It also had to be one in which fully paid-up socialists had charge both of the polity and its system of moral education.

Even in non-socialist societies, this combination of moral relativism and moral authoritarianism was, and still is, one of the distinguishing features of the socialist teacher. On the surface better adapted to the competing demands of a plural, multi-faith (and non-faith) immigrant society, the very limitations of this moral relativism can be re-presented in the classroom as 'non-doctrinaire' virtues. To proclaim the 'equal educational value' of all religions, for example, itself became, and still is for the left, a democratic badge of faith. Theology became sociology; 'God' a varying totem of tribe in multiple incarnations. On the one hand, this was, and is, an antidote to that religious exclusivism which would make Muslim, Hindu or Jew incorrigible aliens. On the other, it was, and is, a solvent of known and coherent moralities in favour of a shifting left ethic, whose substance has always depended upon the choices of often faithless teachers. (Their belief in socialism has often been skin-deep too.) The generally absolute values which the immigrant of faith had brought with him encountered – in Britain in the 1960s, for instance – relative values frequently frail, arbitrary and uncertain.

When admission to a new civic society is accompanied, as in most countries in the West, neither with ceremony nor obligation such defects appear the greater. In Britain the morally half-educated, to whom the inculcation of such obligation has been surrendered, have led the offspring of the morally certain into an ethical no-man's-land, yet in the name of education. The demand for 'separate schools' for 'ethnic minorities', and pressure towards the further disaggregation of civic society, have been among the logical outcomes. The 'old-fashioned' insistence of some embattled British teachers that all their charges, regardless of origin, faith or preference, should receive a 'Christian education in a Christian country' has been regarded by some as 'racist'. But pluralist sympathy, insisting in its turn on the egalitarian treatment of all faiths and cultures, has only the 'principle' of a (free market) choice of moralities – a paradox, since most of its advocates are on the left – to offer in 'racism's place.

The scale of immigration, relatively small in Britain's case, has not in itself created this moral confusion. It has revealed and aggravated it. Nor has it been confined to Britain. In addition to plain recoil from the immigrant, it is moral doubt, and unhappy anxiety about moral doubt, which has gnawed everywhere in the West at the 'immigrant issue'. Nor is it surprising; in California, for example, in consequence of Asian and Hispanic immigration, 'Anglos' may themselves be an 'ethnic minority' by the year 2000. At the same time, it has been one more morally sapping conundrum among many, in which civic society has disclosed its ethical disarray in the face of multiple challenges which it has been unable to master, and from which the majority has preferred to look away.

Thus, when the British government introduced proposals in 1991 to make parents legally and morally responsible for the crimes of their children – including by imposing a duty on magistrates to punish the parents of young offenders – the proposals were swiftly swept away in an ethically incoherent hubbub of disapproval. To one objector, the family would be 'put under great stress' if the sins of the children were visited upon their fathers; to another, it was 'dangerous' (that is, set a dangerous legal precedent) to punish one person for the crime or delinquency of another. To others again, the proposals were 'silly', 'unworkable', 'crazy' and so on. But the central ethical question as to how any moral order whatever can sustain itself without the assumption of moral responsibility by parents for the conduct of their own children in the community – or, as a last resort, by the imposition of responsibility upon them by legal measures – was lost from view. The bill was withdrawn; and the lifeless body of the citizen as a 'moral person' had yet another shovel of plebeian earth thrown down upon it.

In the muddled political flight not merely from the conception of citizen obligation but from many other questions of ethics, the churches have made fitful attempts at moral intervention. The Papal Encyclical of May 1991, *Centesimus Annus*, was an example, with its pious declaration that the 'purpose of a business firm' is 'not simply to make a profit' but is to be found in its 'very existence as a community of persons'; the pale ghost of civic society is here fleetingly present. The Church, the Encyclical declared, 'has always refused, and continues to refuse, to make the market the supreme regulator and almost the model or synthesis of social life. Something exists that is owed to man just because he is man.' But this elusive 'something', more important (according to the Encyclical, and justly so) than an 'appeal to the appetites' or 'purely utilitarian values', no longer has any agreed meaning, nor a shared vocabulary with which to express it. A Solzhenitsyn might declare that 'spiritual qualities and the purity of social relations are more important than abundance', while those who seek to articulate such thoughts are still attended to by the adherents of all faiths, and of none. Yet, the belief that there are moral purposes unserved by the freedoms of the market on the one hand, and the tyrannies of the socialist schema on the other, remains on the defensive, despite the excesses of both. The voices of such belief remain barely audible, drowned in a whirlpool of human movement and competitive desire. Moreover, in a world being shaped and reshaped to the purposes of such movement and desire, the language of 'civic morality' is the language of a lost age.

To this debacle the left has made a large contribution. As early as 1940, George Orwell – risking, and earning, left denunciation for it –

dared to write of the 'spiritual need for patriotism and the military virtues', for which, as he put it, 'no substitute has yet been found, however little the boiled rabbits of the left may like them'. Half a century ago, when such virtues were called upon to withstand a greater 'Satan' than any that today's militant Islam knows of, the left's scorn for the Orwellian appeal knew no bounds. The virtues to which he addressed himself in 1940 were – in the eyes of the left – the virtues of the 'reactionary', the bloodthirsty, and the most narrowly nationalistic. (Only in the service of 'struggle' with 'imperialism' did such qualities take on a reflected lustre.) The idea of fidelity to place, too, has always been suspect to the left. For such fidelity fatally suggests not the kind of allegiance which gives the individual an identity and a home, and which therefore establishes the ground of civic society itself, but the instincts of a belonging which meanly excludes others. (Indeed, notions of fidelity and allegiance, even to many not on the left, now have associations only with the bent knee and forelock.) Specifically socialist fidelity, however, provided that it was renamed 'fraternity', 'solidarity' or 'comradeship', was considered by the left to be a cardinal virtue. Yet, without the kind of moral stamina upon which *every* form of fidelity depends – whether to place, to person, or to an ideal – no healthy civic order could be sustained.

Today, such arguments have less authority than they had in 1940. Allegiance, runs the blind counter-syllogism, is a quality of political reaction; allegiance to tradition is an obstacle to progress; allegiance to place is sentimental doting; allegiance to nation is mere chauvinism, or crypto-fascism; allegiance to tribe, for some the most sinister allegiance of all, is racism. The only exception to such anathemata, allowed by some left feminists, concerns allegiance to person, which is inconsistently permitted to be *prima facie* a virtue. But even if 'dying for your country' is regarded by the left cynic as a folly, it is plain from research into 'football hooliganism' that, in the absence of a taught sense of civic virtue, football fans will 'fight for things like honour, reputation and pride' with lump hammers, stanley knives and broken bottles. Without a more elevated sense of common interest, a baser sense will be found; without an educated sense of history or nation, blood-ties and boxer-shorts in the colours of the flag will serve; without a rational sense of collective pride, the irrational will savagely make do. This is a high price to pay, as the past has shown, for neglect of the human impulse (and the need) to belong. It is also the price paid for the scoffing detraction, or spoiling, of the familiar, or of that which reminds the human animal of 'home'. It is the high price, above all, which is paid for failure to train the individual to be a citizen, and the citizen to be his synonym, the 'moral person'.

Between the right and the left there has always stood another overshadowing issue. Are nation and race the only coherent and lasting principles upon which must rest a sense of the citizen's self, and of the civic society of which he is a member, or are there others which can make a like appeal to obligation and ardour? The old ethics of liberal democracy and socialist aspiration once answered together, although with different arguments, that the individual could, and must, be brought to citizenship by a sense of where his true interests lay. In the former case, the member of a well-ordered but free civil society, who was to be respected and protected as of right, would be continuously prompted to reciprocal obligation: this was the liberal democrat's very heaven. In the latter, a socially just and egalitarian class-order demanded of all its beneficiaries, real and imagined, cooperation in a work of common and elevating endeavour: this was the socialist utopia. Both sets of ethics shared, at least in intention, Plato's distinction between 'the city', or civic society, on the one hand and the 'mere conglomeration of people' – the conglomeration which mass urban community has become – on the other. The former was a work of political art and moral education, the latter an accidental aggregation of bodies, whose inchoate energies threatened rather than enhanced individual well-being. But liberal democratic institutions were not built to resist the retreat of civic obligation, nor socialist ones to withstand the advance of moral corruption and economic failure.

Indeed, the defence of a civic society against the threat of its becoming a 'mere conglomeration of people' is harder to sustain than once might have appeared, not least because its vulnerabilities are essentially moral. Civic values are precariously based, and are not guaranteed to flourish merely because men 'obey the same head and the same laws', if and when they do. A civic society, like any other coherent social body, depends upon the prevalence of common assumptions, especially ethical assumptions, widely shared. It also requires, whatever the internal conflicts of its members, sufficient mutual familiarity among them to sustain the civic bond. It is plain that, in general, no such moral conditions now exist in the mass metropolis, taken as a whole, let alone in teeming nations of tens and hundreds of millions. A civic society – a society of citizens vested with civic rights and duties –

cannot be founded upon relations between myriads of people who are
'entire strangers to each other', who have come randomly into association with different (and even diametrically opposed) moral purposes, or
who have little or no sense of the nature of the national body to which
they belong.

Such an arrangement, and it is no more than an arrangement, may
be kept stable by the energies of efficient administration, the selective
use of force, or the inertia induced by mass depresssion of spirit. But it
ceases to be a moral body which depends upon, or will seek to enhance,
the sense of the civic. On the contrary, the passivity of millions, rather
than their engagement in the civic order, itself becomes a species of
civic virtue. Political art comes to be directed, now, to the exclusion of
the majority from interference with, or more-than-token involvement
in, the political process, however ostensibly democratic. And provided
that they do not turn to civil war or insurrection, even a high level of
'anomie', personal violence, and heterogeneity of population can be
tolerated and managed.

In such circumstances, a sense of 'national identity' gradually
becomes more vestigial, is confined to a minority – some of whom may
be driven to violence to express it, against a tide of indifference – and is
increasingly regarded as 'out of date', or aberrant. To compensate for
its loss, concepts of 'citizenship' (together with 'charters of citizenship')
may come to be promoted, as they have been in Britain, in the name of
constitutional reform and in order to safeguard the individual's rights
against the state. But what is also being sought, sometimes uncon-
sciously, is a new badge, or token, of belonging – that is, a semblance
of the civic – which might in part fill the place where mutuality of rights
and duties in a coherent social body would otherwise stand. Absent
from such artifice is the 'social contract' of classical liberal democratic
theory, under which the insecure and asocial individual was rescued by
the state from the law of nature, and, in return for the new-found
security and enlargement of his rights, lost much of his licence to act
asocially in pursuit of his own interest and self-protection. That is, he
became 'a citizen, a moral person', not a mere bundle of rights which
might be asserted against the body of which he was a member. Today,
to make civic matters worse, (largely invisible) managerial interests
prefer asocial public apathy to active citizen participation in the *polis*,
while compensatory reforming zeal prefers the enhancement of individual rights to the placing of restraints upon individual freedom. This is
the pursuit of 'citizenship' in a civic void.

Insofar as a civic context is lacking, the enhancement of rights in this fashion, if such enhancement can be secured, becomes merely an act of welfare, important as may be. Without the possession of a civic consciousness – the lack of it is one of the defining characteristics of the 'universal plebeian' – the mere enhancement of the individual's rights against the civic order is, whatever the short-term benefit, another act of dissolution of the sense of the civic itself. Moreover, anomic uncertainty, whether in the individual or the wider 'conglomeration of people', is not met by the enhancement of rights alone. A sense of boundary, or obligation, is required for the moral health of the citizen as of the private individual. Much of this sense is derived not from the letter of the law, but from the moral education which knowledge of history – history of family, history of place, history of nation – provides. Such knowledge itself creates a sense of obligation, and of obligation which elevates as well as constrains. In the absence of such knowledge and the obligation which flows from it, sense of identity and purpose are themselves diminished. An American survey, published in May 1991, found that 68 per cent of a sample of 2,000 people believed that there were 'no American heroes'. Such a finding, however small-scale, points not so much to an egalitarian refusal of hero-worship as to a civically-debilitating lack of historical knowledge.

A citizen is an individual who, among other things, knows enough of his own society to act the citizen's part. Certainly, he should know more of it than the stranger, who is, or once was, recognised as a stranger precisely because of his lack of knowledge of the community to which he came. When the nominal citizen, or ostensible belonger, himself lacks such knowledge he becomes as strange as a true stranger; at worst, more alien in his own society than the knowledgeable outsider. In April 1989, at the Guildhall, Mikhail Gorbachev expressed his 'respect for the nation that has given the world great authors, scientists, artists, historians and philosophers, without whom European culture would be inconceivable; the nation of famous seafarers, inventors, workers and engineers, without whom modern civilisation would be inconceivable; the nation whose political experience has enriched the history of the world'. There are few British 'citizens' with sufficient knowledge to give substance to this description – its very tone has become alien – and few, too, who would think the defect a moral handicap in a citizen as a citizen. But there are many who, by reflex, would consider even the broaching of this issue to be a matter of reaction, or worse. There have also been few leaders of the British left who would have dared to show such 'respect' in public for their own nation; the *Guardian* dismissed Gorbachev's speech as part of a 'charm offensive'.

Indeed, the citizen as 'moral person' could not survive at all if he were to succumb to the even more cynical efforts of those in whom historic legacy – a building, an institution, a value system – arouses an urge, or instinct, to vandalise and destroy. The intelligentsia has its own plebeians. 'All that has been built up on seventeenth-century foundations, the "English ideology", must die,' the journalist Neal Ascherson wrote in November 1990. The 'Druid camp', as he sneeringly described those resistant to the call of 'Europe' and to the limiting of the sovereignty of the British parliament, 'see this very clearly. They see that, in the ways that move them most, England will no longer be allowed to remain England . . . My difference with them is only this: they weep, but I rejoice.'

Such 'rejoicing' is a strange business. The 'death' of the 'English ideology' is something to be celebrated with more caution, and less relish, not least because the 'English ideology' (with its 'seventeenth-century foundations') also contains whatever remains of a civic culture. It may, and does, require reform. But dancing on its grave is a serious matter, from which not only 'Druids' – non-Druidical Jews included – have good moral reason to recoil. Once more, it is not 'history' or 'tradition' as empty abstractions which are in this fashion put to the reforming sword, at least in swashbuckling fancy, but the very elements of which a civic sense is composed. The notion, advanced with an anticipatory savour, that England will 'no longer be allowed to remain England' plays with more than the (authoritarian) attractions of radical reform. It also shows an intrusive and dangerous disrespect, in the name of the citizen, for the citizen-identities – such as they are – of others.

In attitudinising arguments of this kind it is common for 'the past' to be held up to be a 'burden' upon 'the present', as if the former could in some sense be disowned in the name of the latter. During the campaign, in June 1989, to save the traces of Shakespeare's Rose Theatre in London, a callow young objector to the campaign took exception to 'the extent to which we have collectively been brainwashed by a heavily retrospective culture', as if 'culture' were not both by definition and necessity 'heavily retrospective'. In October 1989, a young Oxford University student, writing in the *Independent*, similarly found it 'sad' that the 'hallowed institution' of Oxford was 'a place where students who are talented and clever have to seek to "establish themselves" to fit into a pre-established system', as if a university were not, also by definition and necessity, a 'pre-established system' into which in-comers must be 'fitted'. Once again, it was not so much 'history' or 'tradition' in the abstract which were being questioned as a loss of historic memory, itself part of a civic culture, which was being revealed. The varieties of forgetfulness, unconcern, destructiveness and absence of knowledge of the past, hastened by (and further hastening) the dissolution of the civic bond, are numerous and complex; they also now pass with little correction or notice. Thus, an American journalist, William Pfaff, writing in the *International Herald Tribune* in October 1991, could blandly describe the wartime sufferings of the Poles and Jews, in authoritative tones, as 'unimaginably distant from anything that has ever happened in North America', as if there had been no extirpation of the indigenous Indians of the continent, and no unending columns of black slaves. A British journalist, Derek Brown, writing in the *Guardian* in September 1989, could similarly call the Victoria Memorial in Calcutta a 'huge pile of white marble commemorating an irrelevant past which has never quite died'.

Here, disorientatingly, not only relation to the past but sense of the present too, and of the place of the living individual within it, flounders. Under a host of unrooted influences such as these, the citizen need prove, and need be, nothing in particular, or anything which he chooses, and whether with or without information as to his choices. That Britain, for example, is not an Islamic state, not a Vatican fiefdom, nor a second Zion – even if there are substantial numbers of Muslims, Catholics and Jews in the country – becomes all one in the careless discarding of a nation's sense of identity, and the citizen confusion which attends it. Moreover, in the failure of the majority's civic sense, or sense of itself, the minorities are increasingly left to their own exclusive devices amid the prevailing disorder. In this disorder, the absence, as in Britain, of an indigenous or domestic clerisy with a coherent sense of moral purpose and direction must be made good by the imam, the rabbi and other intercessors. More important, in the collapse of a sense of place and time, the uninstructed, simultaneously losing knowledge of themselves, must invent their own. And in the noble name of the toleration of diverse opinion, the centre cannot hold; precious rights to difference (of speech, thought, worship) become, on all hands, rights to reject – or, worse, ignore – the very idea of a national culture.

Migration, the migrant, and the impact of migration have in such a context necessarily changed. Now, the migrant sues for (or illicitly gains) entry to his new land, and, as ever, gratefully kisses the adoptive soil. The gratitude, however, is now in general shorter-lived. More swiftly with each passing year, he has found the local mores distasteful, often with good reason; more boldly than in the past, he seeks to protect himself from harm by them. Yet, at the same time, with gradually diminishing regard for what he finds, the migrant must make his way, aware of, but also contributing to, the civic disarray around him. Indeed, he will have already lost much of his readiness to respect his adopted civic order just as its best representatives seek to embrace him. He is finally assisted to the inner rejection of it by the combined efforts of the racist, who seeks to drive him away, and of the opportunist politician who fastens (for his own ends) upon, and encourages, the migrant's sense of grievance. In March 1989, in the heat of the Rushdie controversy, Gerald Kaufman, Labour's then shadow foreign secretary, described government injunctions to the Muslim community to 'observe British laws and customs' as 'authoritarian'; Roy Hattersley, Labour's then shadow home secretary, declared it to be 'racist' to assert that Muslims were 'welcome in Britain if, and only if, they stop behaving like Muslims'. Muslims, announced another Labour member of parliament, were right to 'demand respect from British institutions'. In its turn, the *Guardian*, in February 1989, declared it to be the 'inalienable right' of immigrant minorities to 'isolate themselves from the larger society (as long as they observe its laws) without being penalised for it'.

These were, in themselves, taken singly and outside their context, unexceptionable expressions of the sentiment of toleration, a sentiment as much part of what remains of the civic culture as any. Taken together, cumulatively, and in their context, their significance was different. They were evidence of the extensive dissolution of citizen-feeling, and spoke eloquently to the absence of Muslim participation in the civic order. They also indicated how far the ostensible citizen, any ostensible citizen, could retreat, if he chose, from the duties of the 'moral person', as well as providing further rationalisations for it. Remote from such opinion was the notion, common among Jewish migrants of an earlier generation – however particular their sense of themselves – that the immigrant could be no true citizen, nor consider himself to be a citizen, without at least a will to share the values, and not merely the benefits, of his adoptive society. Even at his most hesitant, the migrant of the past felt morally bound to acknowledge the host society's values, in whole or in part, as a desirable and appreciated feature of his new existence. But, today, such values are scoffed at by some, unknown to many, and in question for most of the long-standing indigenous population themselves. Hence, the expectation that the immigrant alone should play the citizen part, when the native plebeian does not, is plainly unjust. When most are strangers to each other in an increasingly strange land, the true stranger is no longer as strange as he was. This is a plural society to some, but no society at all to others, native and migrant alike.

Nevertheless, a 'multi-cultural', multi-ethnic and over-populated society is not as wholly distinguishable from past circumstance as the extreme atavist (or racist) would make out. In his time, the Norman baron was as much an alien to the native world – itself a multiple hybrid – of the 'Anglo-Saxon' peasant as the god-fearing Bangladeshi shop-keeper is, in his time, to the heathen East London plebeian. A Bradford imam at Friday prayers might even have had more in common with a Merlin than would an English country parson, past or present. And just as not every Jew is a banker, nor every Irishman a navvy, so not every Englishman is a Knight of the Round Table. The ethnic stereotype, in real life, is a relatively rare bird. Moreover, cultural heterogeneity is often more apparent than real, tends to diminish with time, and may be considered to have its own virtues. But with few shared memories and a reduced feeling for the civic, with national values scorned and the city community embattled, mutual estrangement gradually becomes com-moner than the sense of belonging, and civic society itself must begin to fail.

In such circumstances, divided loyalties, as in the British Muslim community during the Gulf War, come to appear better than no loyalties at all. And better too, so it may seem, that loyalty be a matter of contention than a matter of indifference to others. Complaint, based on loyalty to faith and to the Islamic social bond, that British war policy had 'taken no account of Muslim feelings' in Britain was as legitimate a representation of interest – indeed part of the public interest – as any. Pleas, such as those addressed to government by a Bradford conference of 200 Muslim leaders in 1991, that the war 'stop immediately in order to end further destruction of Muslims' (not loss of life in general) and of 'their resources and land' at least made seething passions known. But at the point when expression of particular interest and feeling turned to approval of the foe, as in October 1990 in Bradford when 400 Muslim representatives 'endorsed' Saddam Hussein's call for a 'holy war' against all Western forces in the Gulf, the obligations of the citizen as 'moral person' were being roundly set aside. Not only that. They were set aside without public reproach, and on the ambivalent citizen's – or ostensible citizen's – own private terms. There were similar offences to the civic bond in France, where some French citizens openly espoused calls for the striking down by a foreign enemy of fellow-French citizens. But they did so with impunity; and in the land of Dreyfus.

In their different ways, these were assertive acts of civic estrangement, but in already-estranged orders which were no longer able, or willing, to take account of them. Likewise, the religious injunction that a Muslim girl wear a scarf of modesty at all times in public was claimed by Muslims – for instance, in France in 1989 and 1990 – to give rise not merely to a Muslim duty but to a 'fundamental right' in France. Against some local objection, as in Paris in October 1989, the slogan 'the Koran is our Constitution' could be seen in the streets of the French capital. Racists made political hay with it; and the French Conseil d'État, the highest administrative court in the land, decreed that, in the name of freedom, symbols of religious affiliation 'could not be forbidden', but that 'disciplinary measures' could be taken wherever there were 'pressures on others, propaganda, proselytism and provocation' in the matter of the wearing of the scarf. This was perceived, by some, to be Solomonic in its wisdom, combining official respect, in a multi-ethnic and multi-religious society, for the religious scruples of a minority with the avoidance of too open a breach with France's secular constitution and secular civic values.

The Muslim argument, however, was outlandish, in every sense. It was as if the devout Jew had declared the custom of wearing a skull-cap to be not merely a personal moral duty or a private choice, but a juridical right, which – as it must do in a civic order – imposed countervailing legal obligations on all others to accept. The Muslim stance insisted upon, rather than merely chose, estrangement; condemned morally, and even sought to condemn by law, those who were estranged by the estranging insistence; and, above all, acted out the role, in public, not of the citizen but of the stranger. The Jews are more knowledgeable about the risks of such conduct. They have also known better than to sack the pork-seller's shop, as happened in Valence in March 1991 (at the hands of some one hundred Muslim youths), or refuse to attend biology lessons on the grounds that they are 'immoral', as eighteen Muslim girls declared them to be at Neuilly in November 1989. 'We cannot live in this country together with *The Satanic Verses* and Salman Rushdie,' the British Muslim, Kalim Siddiqui, announced in July 1989, 'they will have to go.' But the civic order, on its knees, could not respond.

The serious moral dilemmas which such (now deliberate) challenges pose cannot be met by those whose own moral ground has been turned into a quagmire, and even less by those for whom moral issues have not much remaining significance, or no significance at all. That the realm of the civic is part of the moral realm is, for many, a declaration without discoverable meaning. In such circumstances, 'to live and let live' becomes the *summum bonum* not merely of the morally apathetic but of the (seemingly) engaged also. Toleration is then elevated into something which it is not: a moral virtue for all seasons, and a means of resolving – or turning the back upon – all dilemmas. Where 'ethnic chauvinists' constitute a large and sufficiently awkward minority, harassed authority, in the name of such 'toleration', now takes the line of least resistance, whatever the general will, law or custom might dictate. Social peace is purchased at the price of ignoring civic duty; toleration makes concessions which principle would abjure. The outcome is, in general, neither morally nor socially coherent. Incitement to murder is tolerated, but the *muezzin* is forbidden to call the faithful to prayer in British towns. The imbalance is itself amoral.

It is the product of a cultural upheaval – being experienced in many Western nations – and of mutual incomprehensions between the races which might have tested any social order to near breakdown, especially one in which a general violence was increasing. Resilience and passivity between them continue to do what they can to heal communal wounds; liberal-minded shoulder-shrugging tries to counter the bigot; simple decencies resolve complex differences which neither law nor bloodshed could settle. But when heightened ethnic awareness is combined with a reduced sense of nation, and the trigger-happy aggressions of the minority are united with the moral inertia of the many, such benign devices can no longer be relied upon.

At the same time, 'twenty-three million' Hispanics in the United States (the unofficial figure is much higher), or three million Muslims in France, or a million Chinese in New York, or half-a-million Japanese in Los Angeles – the composition of the American population has changed more rapidly during the last decade than in any other period this century – raise issues which are beyond the reach of the simple-minded racist. Job recruitment and promotion, housing policy, policing practice, educational judgment, judicial sentencing, political representation and many other civic matters have become battlefields of reform and resistance. Difficult issues of mother-tongue teaching, religious taboo, ethnic quota, ghetto confinement, equal opportunity, welfare entitlement, separate schooling, ethnic minority crime-rates and racial discrimination require practical administrative solution. While 'separatism' and 'integration', 'pluralism' and 'assimilation', argue their respective corners, problems of setting a limit to immigrant entry, or of establishing a qualification for citizenship, or of maintaining statistics by race provoke and divide emotions; politicians and hooligans alike stir controversy, or incite hatred. When Lech Walesa declared himself to be '100 per cent Pole' in the 1990 presidential campaign, his message was clear to Poles, but the feelings to which he was appealing were universal.

The question of who is and should be a citizen, and who is and deserves to be a stranger, is at the heart of the matter in every country. Nor is it always the case that the more 'civilised' the political and social order, the steadier the judgment on this issue. Even where settled law and written constitution, further sanctioned by custom and convention, have much to say on the subject, and citizenship amounts to something more than the mere obtaining of a passport, the established citizen may still find himself, as Jews know, transformed once more into the unwelcome stranger by arbitrary fiat, by reason of state, or by wave of popular unreason. Nevertheless, without some distinction of substance between citizen and stranger there can be no true civic order. Without some discrimination between values, when those values are incompatible with each other, there can be no coherent body of values at all. Each state, and each civic society, defines itself by the principles, whatever they may be, by which it chooses to live; and even though such principles will be transformed by time, adapted to circumstance and undermined by neglect, each viable society must at least attempt to live by them as they currently stand.

But, today, many states and societies are bending under the cultural and administrative strain of assault, both violent and non-violent, on their remaining integrities and traditions. To defend such integrities is to invite further conflict and strain; to abandon them to their fate is, at least in the short term, to avoid such stresses. Indeed, to surrender to cultural *force majeure* when the decision-maker's own sense of cultural direction is lost, is often the easiest and most obvious option. Given the scale of today's migratory pressures, it may even seem to be the only option. Moreover, the anxieties and practical problems which such pressures create turn most certitudes and fixed positions – such as they now are – in the direction of administrative compromise, and turn compromise to moral equivocation, as in the Rushdie case. In the West, the stranger, or ostensible citizen, with his own value-system generally more secure than the native's, here encounters the 'liberal tradition' at its most vacillating and doubtful. Emboldened by the tremors of the morally confused (who mistakenly wish to be thought well of, or are over-anxious not to cause offence), the migrant *arriviste* presses social claims and moral demands which he himself would not allow if the positions were reversed. In a further irony, the latter not only mounts these pressures against a civic order from the broken heart of which he remains excluded, but to which he does not himself wish to belong except on terms of his own selection.

This is a false civic relation without precedent. It robs the term 'fellow-citizen' of its last shards of meaning, meets none of the community ideals of left or right as I have set them out, and satisfies neither citizen nor stranger. Nor is the confusion it causes that of the host community alone. In July 1990, delegates to a Muslim conference in Britain voted, for example, to 'uphold' the death sentence against Salman Rushdie, while at the same time professing to be 'loyal British citizens' with an 'overriding duty to obey the law'. More agonising, generations and families (as was the case with the Jews) are divided by conflicts over the appeal of, and resistance to, assimilation. And if the host community pays a price for its loss of moral bearings, the immigrant community begins to do so also as it comes under disintegrating pressures in the name of integration. It may find itself simultaneously wishing, and not wishing, to be left alone in order to promote its interests. It may simultaneously see itself as part of a world community and of the community it has uneasily joined.

In the Muslim community's case, it may also privately – and not so privately – disdain the society to which it partially belongs. On the one hand, there is a greater percentage of home-owners *per capita* among the Asian population in Britain than there is among the 'indigenous white population'; on the other, one of the Asian community's writers, Hanif Kureishi, could describe England in 1988 as a 'squalid, ugly, uncomfortable place, an intolerant, racist, homophobic, narrow-minded, authoritarian rat-hole, run by vicious, suburban-minded, materialistic philistines'. (Yet he, and more than two million other Asians, have made this 'rat-hole' their home.) Such description of England is that of a stranger, not a citizen, but a stranger who insists both upon his citizenship and his estrangement, and who confidently demands of a civic order in disarray that both be respected. And should they not be, those who (justly) refuse such respect will be termed 'racist'.

In conditions of moral debacle, the charge of 'racism' is easily made and can now rarely be coherently met. There could be no answer, or none which was morally fitting, to the allegation made by the defence in the 1990 case of the raped and beaten Central Park jogger that the prosecution of the accused was informed by 'racist bias'. In wild charge and counter-charge on this ground – when the ostensible citizen becomes merely black or white (or Jew) – the civic order falls into a moral abyss, and ethnicity becomes an instrument with which to assault the body politic still further. Indeed, the term 'racist' is now resorted to, for purposes of reproach or abuse, in ways which are no more rational than some of the behaviour to which objection is being made. As a badge of belonging, the epithet is that of the tribe, not the nation. Used, sometimes with justice, to reduce its target's moral status, it as frequently debases the embattled user. Injured feelings, and frightened defence of self or culture, may denote the 'other' a 'racist', as Jews may denote the hostile 'other' an 'anti-semite'. But when the accuser is himself at moral fault, and the charge of 'racism' is a last resort, such accusation becomes doubly amoral. At the trial of the mayor of Washington in June 1990 for drugs offences, the counter-charge by his defenders that elected black officials were being systematically 'targeted' expressed such a reflex; employed in this context it struck a blow against civic order itself.

Use, abuse and misuse of the 'ethnic' are *prima facie* symptoms of civic breakdown, and now appear in many guises. False objection in New York to an allegedly 'Eurocentric' (that is, 'white') educational curriculum promoted a counter-curriculum which had less to do with an alternative knowledge than with pride of tribe. Yet, real discrimination, grounded in prejudice, may in fact seek to deny, disqualify or marginalise one race's truths which it is inconvenient for another race to teach, or embarrassing to have known. There are many complexities here. Racial bias may be intertwined with objective judgment, arrant prejudice with genuine moral scruple, fact with fiction, truth-telling with lies. With the confidence which numbers bring, the migrant, sustained by tribe, may confusingly seek and at the same time despise the rights he gains, contemning both gift and giver as to the 'universal plebeian' manner born.

In reaction against it, nation itself can turn back to tribe, and cry 'Germany for the Germans', 'Vienna for the Viennese', or 'Keep Sweden

Swedish'. Such reaction can demand the 'mass expulsion' or 'forcible repatriation' even of ostensible citizens, born and bred in the country. And in a further derogation from the civic, the immigrant and immigrant family must then keep their heads down, seeking the shadows from the instinct for self-preservation. Real citizens, too, after generations of settlement and acculturation, can come to the same pass and respond in the same fashion; the Jew traditionally lies low when his cemeteries and synagogues are being desecrated. Today, however, the ostensible citizen, more emboldened, is as likely to turn himself back into a stranger whenever he feels most threatened, openly asserting his difference, deepening others' sense of it, and increasing his own problems.

But the civic and moral order which reaction seeks to defend by harassment or expulsion of the alien, or by the closure of borders, can no longer be reconstituted as it was. The old integrities, fondly – and often falsely – recollected, cannot be restored. Traditionalism's reveries for lost hearth and home are for worlds which, in most Western countries, are dead and buried. The post-war immigrant stranger, far from being the source of all evil, intruded upon a scale of private griefs and long-evolving social ills already beyond repair; he made only a relatively small, even if significant, contribution of his own.

In the inter-war years, reaction, already in despair, had preached a return to 'children, church and kitchen'. Now, in Britain for example, almost four in ten marriages end in divorce, a nearly six-fold rise in thirty years. Approaching 30 per cent of all live births – and just over 50 per cent in Manchester – occur outside marriage; it was less than 12 per cent in 1980. Almost one in five of all British families are single-parent, the highest proportion in Europe, with two million children being raised in them, a number which has doubled in two decades. In Britain, the average life-span of a marriage is now less than ten years; by the end of the century, on present trends, almost one half of all British marriages could end in divorce. (This proportion has already been reached in Moscow.) Millions of British children have experienced the divorce of their parents in the last two decades; many millions more will experience it in future. In the United States, the figures are direr, with more than half of black families headed by single women and two-thirds of black children born out of wedlock, a three and a half-fold increase in forty years. The nuclear family may be a prison, as feminists and others have averred. It is also, for good and ill, a microcosm of the social order. By the year 2000, it is possible that in Britain the proportion of children in a 'conventional household' – that is, one in which the parents are married to each other and have stayed together in order to bring up their children together – could have fallen to as low as half of the total child population.

The statistics of such developments are not merely those of demography. Their implications are civic. In America, it has been estimated that 70 to 90 per cent of all children born out of wedlock become dependent on welfare. In Britain, a long-term study based on two sets of national survey data of children going back to 1946 and 1958 respectively, and reported to the British Psychological Society in September 1991, showed that the children of divorced parents were more likely than the children of undivorced parents to leave school early and with fewer qualifications, less likely to go to university, more likely to be unemployed, and more prone to a variety of emotional and psychological problems. Other research findings both in the United States and Britain suggest that the children of single-parent families are 'more prone to deviancy and crime', as well as more likely than other children to repeat the 'cycle of unstable parenting'. It is an instability whose consequences, like other such consequences, are passed on from the failed family to the failing civic order. At least a quarter of the children now being born in Britain can expect, before they are sixteen years old, to see their parents' relationship break up; nearly half of the current generation of American children will spend at least some of their childhood lives in a single-parent home.

In both countries, the marriages of the most socially deprived are the least stable. They are also the most productive of further disability and are becoming less stable than ever. Further complex social correlations within correlations can be made out, which plausibly link the failure of private relationships to phenomena of much wider public concern. They include the circle of correlations between divorce and unemployment, between unemployment and educational attainment, and between levels of skill and divorce rates, which both in the United States and Britain are highest among the unskilled and the unemployed. And within this intricate matrix of harmed lives and collapsed relations, violence, both private and public, finds its most fertile ground. Parental divorce dissolves the unhappy tie, and is the means of release for many – men, women and children – who have been caught up in it. But it also has a shaping role (in largely unknown ways) upon the future emotional lives of the dissolved family's members, and even upon their social prospects. Vast and increasing numbers are now touched by it. Moreover, to the other forms of human unsettlement and upheaval, it adds the stresses of private migration from family to family, and from home to home. In its own fashion it also serves to turn familiars into strangers, by the tens of million.

No less striking is that in Britain, for example, at the heart of civic society, one-quarter of all households is composed of a single person – whatever the cause of this singleness – who lives alone. It is a figure which has doubled in thirty years. In twenty years' time, by present trends, no less than 31 per cent of British households will contain a solitary person: that is, 7.6 million separate units, or civic atoms, of whom the great majority will be old. Today, as it is, some one million of the individuals in Britain who live alone are said to have 'no regular visitors'. Over half of all Americans with elderly parents are, with related effect, estimated to be unable or unwilling to look after them. Even the social pressure for, and moral acceptability of, euthanasia for the elderly sick appears to be growing.

Many old people, whether or not they live alone, and many of those who live alone whatever their age, have joined the ranks of the community's ostensible citizens and actual strangers. But civic estrangement – lack, or loss, of sense of place and of identification with communal purpose – may express itself in many different ways. It may also stem from many different causes, race, age, domestic circumstances and varieties of disillusion among them. Accident of origin, the passage of time, or the effects of personal misfortune may become, or be made by others, into the ground of social isolation. But there are arguably no greater present obstacles, particularly in Britain and America, to the remaking of strangers into citizens than those caused by lost vision, and lost control, in the education of children.

'Man', Plato chillingly declares in Book Six of the *Laws*, 'can become the most savage beast on earth if he lacks training, or is badly educated'. In Book Four of the *Republic*, the duty is therefore prescribed to rulers of 'keeping close watch on education and training to prevent them deteriorating unnoticed'. Among the 'chief offices of state', control of the content and standard of education is described in the *Laws* as 'much the most important'. Today, the quality of the education of increasing numbers of future citizens, especially in Britain and America, is 'deteriorating' in many of the ways that Plato feared, even if it is not deteriorating unnoticed. In a pedagogical muddle of dogmatism and innovation, lost disciplines and bureaucratic interference, shortage of resources and inadequate training of teachers – many turning out to be themselves half-educated – increasing millions of young people are being effectively disenfranchised by educational failure. De Tocqueville's optimistic civic assumption that a 'democratic government' would 'always presuppose' what he called a 'high degree of enlightenment in society' is being roundly defeated.

Furthermore, the difficulties are growing. Schools and school systems are being increasingly overwhelmed by logistical problems, funding shortages, always more desperate policy changes and, above all, the transfer by parents of their own civic duties in relation to their children on to the shoulders of teachers who are unable to meet the strain. The consequences in reading difficulties, in numeracy difficulties, in 'underachievement', in insufficient training of the mind, and in low levels of factual knowledge are civic. If an estimated '23 to 27 million' adult Americans are 'functionally illiterate' or have 'serious reading difficulties', if 'three-quarters' of American seventeen-year-olds 'cannot write adequate imaginative prose', or if 'one in three' teenagers in Rochdale – as researchers at Lancaster University revealed in 1987 – do not know what 50 per cent of 180 is, the matter does not merely concern, or sometimes fail to concern, the subjects of these findings themselves. For educational disability of this degree is one more disability which makes citizens into strangers, not least in their own eyes. Moreover, elementary puzzlements as to the way the world is, in afflicting individual self-regard, may turn to angers which, as Plato knew, have the capacity to do great harm to others. 'Happy is the man,' declares a proverb of Solomon, 'that findeth wisdom, and the man that getteth understanding'; unhappy the man who does not.

Now, as matters deteriorate, even those receiving educational certification, including to graduate levels, are frequently being discovered to lack the most basic of skills. Those already most disadvantaged show an increasing tendency, particularly in the United States, to 'drop out' of education early – 35 per cent of all Hispanic children in the United States, or some 4 million children in total, do so – leaving school for uneducated lives which invite further hardship. But the falling quality of education and of educational attainment does not only threaten individuals. It threatens the prospects of entire nations. However, the mere statistics of it, and the expostulations or strenuous denials which generally greet them, cannot reach the heart of the issues.

One of them, and perhaps the most puzzling, concerns the recoil from 'didacticism', or formal teaching itself, in the pedagogical theory and practice of many of today's teachers. Instead, it seems, 'classroom management' has (for some) become as important as, or even more important than, instruction. The learning of 'rules', whether of grammar or number, has been re-perceived, under the rule of a no less authoritarian counter-dogma, as authoritarian 'drilling' or mere 'rote learning'. Moreover, 'thinking for oneself' has been given philosophical primacy over the transmission of received knowledge. Solomon, at least, held a different view of the wisdom of ages. 'Fools,' bluntly declared the son of David, 'despise instruction.' But that some teachers themselves should have come to despise, or at least disavow, instruction (and the instructor's civic task) as 'drilling', does not have, and could not have, many precedents in the history of education. Nor do the statistics of failure appear to deter the pursuit of failing method. Moreover, it is one thing to share Aristotle's sentiment, expressed in his *Art of Poetry*, that 'to be learning something is the greatest of pleasures'; the attempt, however well-intentioned, to turn into 'fun' the acquisition in childhood of basic intellectual skills, the precondition of all learning, is another.

The (to a Jew) strange recoil from education's rigours has made the teaching of grammar a 'sterile' matter for the first time in the history of the pedagogy of language. It has also perversely made the regular testing of young children's intellectual progress into a threat to their well-being. But it is more than merely perverse. In industrial societies beset by civic collapse, unshared memory, unmanageable demographic change and lost bearings, the ideal notion of a body of received knowledge being passed on by sage teachers to dutiful pupils, in preparation for a community life in which few or none are strangers to one another, has plainly become unreal. To 'teach the people knowledge', having first given such knowledge 'good heed' and 'set [it] in order', is now an impossibily antiquated task, even if it is the best, or only, way to Solomon's wisdom. There are also some features of today's educational catastrophe which were known long ago, but as perils to be utterly avoided. Even Plato, in the Athens of four centuries before Christ, had observed the 'extraordinary situation', as he called it in the *Republic*, in which 'teachers flatter their pupils', and 'old men ape the young, joking with them as equals to avoid giving the impression of being domineering'; it did not, however, prevent them from teaching their charges to read and write.

The ancient observation, made tantalisingly on the wing, occurs in the course of a discussion of 'lawlessness' and its symptoms. Yet, if it speaks to perennial concerns, it also does not meet the scale of contemporary fears about the ultimate civic effects of today's forms of lack of training and bad education. Now, it is not the fate of a few hundred or thousand young Athenians let loose on the city state 'unprepared for citizenship' which wrinkles the philosopher's brow. It is of millions of the callow and the ill-educated taking their adult places in modern metropolises where the idea of the citizen has become unfamiliar, and where most are already strangers to one another. In every age, and now as never before, the energy and application, talent and invention of youth galvanise the spirits of the entire social order. But in no age save this could a twenty-two-year-old unemployed English father name his newborn daughter after a hit record and his favourite car – Sudio Porsche Carrera – and six weeks later, in November 1990, 'unable to stand the sound of her crying any more', kill her by 'smashing her head against a wall'.

A moral bulwark against unreason, and against the citizen's fear of suffering harm at unreason's hands, might once be found, in part at least, in the reassurance of community and the constraints of belonging. Individual reputation and self-esteem depended, for the humblest and the grandest alike, upon the esteem of fellow citizens, family members and neighbours. It was an esteem which could be swiftly lost by the asocial, and by those who otherwise offended community or civic feeling. In the atrophying and absence of such feeling, many old forms both of moral restraint and of moral compulsion – including the compulsion to self-improvement by education – are eased or lifted entirely. Fear of punishment is further lost in the torrents of unjusticiable crime; the individual becomes, in every sense, a law unto himself. The wayward parent of the wayward child, passing on his own social estrangement from generation to generation, surrenders the obligation to repair the moral harm to teachers and social workers. They, in turn, as I have argued, are unable to bear it; and the child, 'failed' by family, school and wider social order takes his due, or allotted, place in the statistics of social disadvantage. In this mockery of the process of socialisation – or asocialisation – the citizen-bond is transformed into a new archetypal relation: that between the state and the social victim. This mutant civic-bond may become a lifetime's civic bondage, the potential citizens held in its grip further recruits to the standing army of strangers.

Such a fate is the mark of the social distresses and failures of the plebeian 'under-class'. But the more privileged are not immune from the effects of civic dissolution and citizen estrangement. Moral certitude and sense of belonging, reassurance of continuity and knowledge of the past, are no more guaranteed to the educated than to others. In the American Congress as in the British parliament, legislators debate the causes of the day with diminishing reference, or no reference at all, to the history of their nations. A lost historical sense, and even the lack of elementary historical information, has become a commonplace feature – across the social spectrum – of a wider loss of civic identity, and of a steadily enlarging failure of education.

On the occasion of the bicentenary in 1989 of the French Revolution, Margaret Thatcher, the then British prime minister, told the French that the British had 'managed things much more quietly'. A mid-seventeenth-century regicide in public, the abolition of the House of Lords, the declaration of a republic, a decade of civil war, rule by a military dictatorship and a monarchic restoration had all been forgotten, or cancelled. In a survey by the National Endowment for Humanities, published in October 1989, one in four American *university students* gave the wrong century for the arrival of Columbus in the New World; two in five could not place the American Civil War to within fifty years of its correct date; one in four thought that the Marxist 'from each according to his ability, to each according to his needs' was a principle of the American Constitution; one in three even believed Magna Carta to have been signed by the Mayflower pilgrims. Loss of bearings may be geographical as well as historical. In a Gallup survey of 1988, 50 per cent of adult Americans were unable to locate South Africa on a map, and only one in three could find Vietnam, despite the scale of media coverage of the Vietnam War, in which 57,000 Americans died. Fifteen per cent, or between one in six and seven adults, could not even locate the USA.

In panic, particularly (again) in Britain and the United States, national achievement tests, curricular reforms, changes in teacher training, 'crash programmes' of one kind and another, educational commissions, increases in funding and new pedagogical theories seek to make good the civic failure and, once more, to 'take fast hold of instruction'. But the failure is a cultural one in the widest sense, and beyond the reach of merely bureaucratic reform. It rests, not least, in the flouting of the Judaic tradition that 'wisdom is the principal thing'. Knowledge and skill are the true princes of the civic order, and require to be exalted to its highest places of honour. Once dethroned by teacher frailty, false theory, parental neglect and pupil unconcern, they do not easily recover their positions. A thin awareness has begun to dawn, at a time when tens of millions of the increasingly poorly educated already compose so large and confident a part of the civic societies they inhabit, that the democratic notion of a 'right to education', or (even) of a 'right to learn', is nothing without an Hebraic duty to study. Too late, the British Labour Party in 1991 proposed a 'school contract' of mutual obligation, under which parents, in exchange for being 'fully informed about their children's educational progress', would undertake – voluntarily – to 'encourage their children to read, check their homework, discourage the watching of television and see that they have a good night's sleep'.

The very need to set out, and spell out, parental obligation in such basic terms pointed to the rootedness and reach of the 'universal plebeian' style, and of the civic, as well as domestic, dissolution to which it has contributed. Moreover, objection to Labour's proposals was immediate, including from teachers themselves, on the grounds that such expectations of the (voluntary) fulfilment by parents of their most elementary moral and civic obligations were 'impractical' or 'unnecessary', or both. It was even declared, again by teachers, that such a 'contract' would 'make some people feel even worse parents'. Plainest of all was the confirmation that the language of civic obligation, let alone its enforcement, no longer had any real moral status.

Duties without rights make slaves, but rights without duties make strangers. Only rights and duties in balance make citizens of randomly associated individuals. And while bureaucratic imposition and Kafkaesque state regulation estrange citizens from the state, and make citizens strangers to each other, the plebeian reflex of helplessly blaming 'them', the anonymous servants of the state apparatus, also makes for civic disenfranchisement. That 'the state' *is* the citizen body, acting on the citizens' behalf and in the citizens' interest, and has contractual obligations of its own towards the citizenry which it must fulfil, becomes (under conditions of increasing civic disintegration) opaque and even unknown. It is then that 'the state' becomes the ultimate stranger among a host of strangers, and crowns the process of a general and mutual recoil.

To 'privatise' the state's principal obligations to its citizens, or ostensible citizens, is another means by which the legal and moral contract between the state and the citizen may be comprehensively broken. It is the duty (among other duties) of the citizen to obey the state and its rules, in return for the assumption by the state of the duty (among other duties) to protect the citizen from his fellows, and to administer an impartial system of justice on their behalfs. In the isolation and violence of many modern cities, the ostensible citizen – armed to the teeth in the United States – is already increasingly unprotected, or must find the means to protect himself; when the individual finds himself continuously under such constraints, the state can be said to have broken its contract with him. But when the 'privatising' state goes further, and begins to 'contract out' its legal and moral duty of protecting the citizen to a handful of other citizens acting for their own profit – as, most notoriously, when even prisons are placed in private hands – the breach is more serious still. (In the United States, as many as half of its prisons are now 'in the private sector'.) Here, the civic bond, already under multiple forms of assault at the hands of the citizens themselves, as well as of hosts of strangers, is attacked from a new direction: by action of the state itself. And if the state neglects, refuses, or surrenders its obligations, then why should not the citizen too?

In the collapse of socialism and the generalisation of market relations, the 'individual' – another term for the 'universal stranger' – has acquired the moral dominion which the 'citizen' once possessed, even if only in name. Moreover, if 'individualism' has its limits, and it does not now seem to have many, they are set less by the duties of the citizen than by the whims of the individual himself. Indeed, his actions are less curbed by the fear of the law or moral disesteem, than by the unaffordability or exhaustion of his choices. Even action in and for the community, despite every philanthropic exception, comes to be governed less by the shared values of the citizen than by the arbitrary (and often selfish) caprices of the *de facto* stranger. In this non-civic world, individual plutocrat and individual plebeian are at one, while remaining strangers to each other. Indeed, one law of common estrangement comes gradually to link all 'individuals', whatever their condition. 'Individual rights', even when termed 'civic rights', remain the rights of the individual as stranger. They are rights which are shared, in a phantom social order, by all individuals, but between whom no citizen-bond has been established.

This parody of civic society, in which belonging becomes a tenuous matter for all, now increasingly stands for society itself. Socialism's failure, moreover, has (for some) ratified the parody as the only possible model of the social order. Moral speculation as to how civic society might be otherwise constituted is more than ever utopian. Moreover, memory of how it once was, in the recent as well as in the more distant past, is gradually annulled by the uneducated passage of time. In the name of the 'individual', community is weakened; 'tradition' is turned into a saleable market option, or abandoned; freedom of choice becomes the moral imperative which stands above all others. The 'individual' in an ordered civic society who possesses a live sense of communal and moral obligation is one thing, and still survives. The 'individual' with few moral scruples, and taking his chances in a jungle of competing strangers, is another. More complex still, these two 'individuals' now occupy the same asocial space. Indeed, the moral (and sometimes physical) assaults of the latter on the former are becoming, with the diminution of the struggle of the classes, the principal form of social combat of the age. And if Plato's 'savage beast' has always rubbed shoulders on the streets of the city with common decency and cultivation, it was never before in such conditions of mass mutual estrangement, when no single moral system – and perhaps no moral system at all – could command authority over the millions.

In consequence, the main task of intellectuals and politicians concerned with the health of civic society is today no longer to refine and extend 'individual rights', a task which was the moral legacy of the French Revolution. Instead, it is to redefine and help enforce civic obligation, so that a true citizenship might begin to be restored to myriads of strangers. The demise of socialism, with its false collectivities and uprooting of civic tradition, has helped to clear the way for it. The giant metropolis, in which violent impulse comes increasingly to dictate the responses of half-educated strangers towards each other, cannot be the model of civic society. Once, the promotion and defence of the rights of the citizen against a prevailing system of arbitrary or tyrannical power justly took moral precedence in the struggle to create, and to maintain, a civic order. Although vigilance in these matters will always be required, the moral priorities are changing. Without the compensating enhancement of civic obligation, the reduction of the former body politic to a condition of adminstratively managed mass-estrangement points into greater civic darkness. In such darkness, there can only be increasing resort to violence, whether by the ostensible citizen or by those in authority over him. And where even ethical choices come to be governed by quirks of passing fancy, there is neither rhyme nor reason in the *polis*.

In such a political and moral quicksand, it is not rights – their increase in number, their enlargement in scope, their devolution in practice, and so on – to which attention needs to be primarily paid, but obligations, for which civic rights should properly be both a political and ethical *quid pro quo*. When moral disorder increases, citizen obligation must be the first, not the second, term of the political equation, if society's duties to the individual are to be fulfilled in a balanced, reciprocal relation. Such enhancement of individual obligation would be a mark of civic progress, not a mark of reaction; a *duty* to participate in the civic order, whatever managerial problems it poses, is as essential a feature of a progressive order as a *right* to do so. But duty to self and family – 'self-management' has many dimensions – is a civic duty, too, and one which, in matters of health care, educational provision and criminal responsibility, can alone give an ethical balance to the state's presently unrequited moral and legal obligations to the individual. The mere payment to the state of taxes for services is not a citizen relation. 'To be free', as the French historian Guizot put it, 'men must be informed of their duties'. These must now include civic duties which will require gradually more authoritarian means of enforcement if they are flouted – to respect nature, to restrain the licence of wasteful consumption, and to reduce the rate of population increase. As ethical voluntarism fails, and the degree of civic estrangement worsens, the need to sustain civic order will increasingly dictate such measures as loss of civic rights for certain forms of anti-civic conduct; just as in sixteenth-century Florence the individual adjudged to be a *bandito* was deprived of civil rights, prevented from carrying out legal transactions, and excluded from other benefits of the social order which he had outraged. Compulsory community service, less easily gained divorce, parental and community liability for young people's crime, the repetition of the school year for educational failure, work-sharing, and rationed access to place are also unlikely to be avoided.

To the left, hostile to all notion of citizen obligation except under socialist rule, 'duty' has been seen amorally as a 'right-wing' word and a 'right-wing' virtue. It suggests to the left, as I have pointed out, the forelock and the flag, the parade-ground salute and the bent knee of the servant. But the discomfiture of socialism has opened the way for the dutiful citizen's return in a non-socialist and post-socialist world. Indeed, the very word 'citizen' is derived from the Latin *ciere*, to 'summon': in Roman times, and in all ages save our own, 'citizen' signified a member of a civic society with both determinate rights and known duties, protected by the former but ready to be summoned to the latter.

Randomly surviving social instinct, mutual fear, bureaucratic rule, and stoical public spirit are insufficient to compose the civic order. They are not equal to the task of preserving civic life in the megalopolis of these times, nor in smaller centres of like estrangement. The welfare state, by assuming responsibility for wide areas of traditional personal obligation – in matters of familial caring, for example – lifted heavy burdens from many shoulders, burdens which they could not bear. But when the moral duty of the 'individual', or universal stranger, is delegated to, or shrugged off upon, the state's professional servants, such relief from personal obligation is frequently gained at an ethical price, ranging from further familial estrangement to abandonment of all duty to self and others. If the principle of the welfare state is an embodiment of many aspects of civic morality, it also serves as one of the solvents of the citizen's moral obligations. In public provision, the citizen gains the *ethical prize* of citizenship, and – provided he fulfils his duties as a citizen – justly so. But when the state's servants (its nurses, its social workers, its home visitors) begin to live the absolved 'individual's own moral life for him, the citizen is made even more of a stranger to civic purpose; and with the world of public provision at his disposal, may lose his own soul.

In the failed world of 'real socialism', it had been the moral intention of many to replace the 'illusory community' (Marx) of the market with the 'true' community of the proletariat. Instead, the imposition of socialist illusion gradually turned even the sense of ethical obligation sour, leaving 'socialist man' in a moral limbo of public cynicism and thwarted personal ambition. Civic society, placed under 'the rule of the uncivilised' in Havel's words, had suffered the severest ethical blows; after Romanian miners attacked anti-government protestors with staves and clubs in June 1990, President Iliescu formally thanked them for their 'civic awareness'. Citizen estrangement was no less estrangement for being larded over with the language of the fraternal; even Pol Pot was known as 'Brother Number One' in his murderous prime. Subsequently, it was the hope of restoring civic society and lost civic tradition – 'the life the Bolsheviks stole', as it came to be called – which inspired much of the anti-communist movement. Ironically, many anti-communists, wearied by the communist politicisation even of private virtues, aspired to assume in freedom precisely those forms of personal moral responsibility for the civic order which in the West have been so undermined.

In all societies, the 'individual' has a need of obligations – to family, to community, to class, to nation – as well as a need of rights, if his actions are to be invested in his own estimation with more than narrow personal purpose. Now, in the West's own civic crisis, obligations of public service might reverse the scale of voluntary retreat and private recoil, on the part of privileged 'individuals', from the communities they inhabit. Such obligation, with loss of rights – in preference to loss of freedom – as sanction, might also help to train the 'universal plebeian' to return to the civic order which he now contributes so much to destroy. The assumption of moral and social duty by invitation, or plangent appeal, may evoke a sentimental response when the object of 'charity' is distant. The task of finding a way to the moral (and physical) reconstitution of the life of the city nearer home, and to the transformation of tens of millions of its strangers of every kind into 'moral persons', is a tougher matter. It will, sooner or later, require increasingly authoritarian measures. Without them, the future 'good life' for the citizen will be even harder to secure. But Plato's 'savage beast' is now likely to be unyielding, even with them.

TWELVE

The Spirit of the Age

Pascal's mid seventeenth-century anxiety over the 'abscess ready to form' and modern pessimism's prophetic unease over the world's future are one. Between the old Jansenist and the older Judaic spirit there are fears in common. The optimist celebrates technical invention, love, medical progress, youth's energy, and nature's beauty; the gloomy Elijah, dogging optimism's footsteps, declares, sometimes with perverse satisfaction, that there 'shall not be dew nor rain these years'. Anxiety has the skeleton beneath the skin before its eyes, while hope fastens for preference upon the robust body; faith cheerfully entrusts itself to a wing and a prayer, while doubt questions every conquest made by reason. To those who live in hope, there is a solution to every problem, and a cure for every disease; to the darkest spirits, the death of the world beckons. The spirit of the future, lacking (as never before) a sense of the past, proclaims the 'end of history' at the very moment of atavism's resurgence, gun and ancient text in hand. New technology vanquishes time and space, while old anxiety grows uneasier even with the word 'progress'. Western optimism celebrates 'victory' in the Cold War; pessimism, the eternal stranger at the wedding, finds such 'victory' pyrrhic.

When communism failed, the Western rationalist (or wishful thinker), tired of 'class' and 'ideology', raised his spirits. Briefly, but ahistorically, he gave himself over to speculation about 'new beginnings', a 'new era', a 'new world order'. Old and inconvenient interests, and the truths which such interests had established, were – he wanted to believe – not merely discredited but abolished. Energies too long concentrated upon the ideological foe could now be directed to improving and propagating the only viable social model, the Western liberal-capitalist model, for profitably harnessing the skills and efforts of mankind. Euphoria, albeit guarded and discreet, briefly kept at arm's length the anxious sense that economic and intellectual decline, environmental damage, the hostile imbalances between 'North' and 'South', the advance of disease, the resurgence of nationalist and ethnic hatreds, and the belligerence of Islam promised no 'new dawn'. Sporadic outbreaks of 'old' forms of the conflict of classes, especially in the post-communist world, could now be perceived with more confidence as passing aberration. The free world's freedoms had, after all, proved themselves to be more than a match for socialist unreason. Socialism, so the argument ran (and continues to run), had reaped its bitter harvest and been taught its overdue lesson. Truth, so happy Western delusion was tempted to decide, now lay easier in its bed.

The notion that the 'last word' has been spoken – whether on God or the economy, on the moral order or social organisation, on the past or on the future – is an ancient fallacy. Declarations of triumph, especially in the battle of ideas, have generally turned to ashes. Even the most practical solutions to human problems have their natural span; there are few *idées fixes* which are not overtaken or swept from the record. Moreover, most conceptions of order and reason have their manichean *alter ego*s in attendance upon them. The market-as-panacea cannot drive from the field other notions of public interest and economic virtue, nor the spirit of the collective finally subdue the warring interests of the individual. When capitalism presents itself as democracy's guardian, truth cries out against its rewarding of corruption, exploitation and injustice; when socialism declares itself synonymous with morality, its victims shout from their graves for revenge.

The man of the right rests his case upon law and custom, religion and tradition, as guarantors of a just order; but the man of the left knows that such justice must be fought for. The man of the left in his turn espouses the 'cause of the people', but the man of the right smells humbug and self-deception. When the left declares that capitalism would not have been driven to modify its rigours but for socialist opposition to the unregulated market, it has the past and much of the truth on its side. But when the right argues that socialist regulation stifles endeavour, the left now knows this to be so. Many such acknowledgments of the obvious remain unspoken. Rival dogma does not cease to claim the 'last word'. Yet, this too has its point, however fallacious such absolute claims may be. The opposition of left and right continues, and will continue in every generation, to shape and reshape the truth of things long after those who seek the 'middle path' (also in every generation) have wearied of ideological conflict and retired from the fray. There will not even be an end to the 'class struggle'. A society without class, and without hierarchies and conflicts of class, is as unimaginable as a society without a social structure.

Moreover, between the more worldly and the less, between rival protagonists of race and nation, between the 'citizen of the world' and the keeper of hearth-and-home, between the rationalist and the man of God, between the instinctive 'liberal' and the equally instinctive 'authoritarian', there could be no lasting concord, not even on the Day of Judgment. In the post-communist world, all the interests and values familiar to non-socialist systems, released from artificial containment, have sprung into renewed combat. Restoration of pre-communist tradition now vies with the desire for a 'new' post-communist order; recovery of the spirit of nation confronts the international interests of the market. Catholic social teaching, Protestant individualism, and Judaic fears of Armageddon have resumed their places in the ethical arena. In the judgment of the right, 'neo-communism' – or the ghost of socialism – continues to haunt the ruins of the Soviet Union and Eastern Europe. In the judgment of the left, the amoral privateer stands crowing on the midden which has been made of noble socialist aspiration. The sceptic, in his turn, doubts whether economies prostrated by socialist experiment can be levitated at all by 'market forces'; the 'turn to democracy' seems to him to be a simulated or false dawn, while grim new tsars wait in the wings for reform's 'inevitable' failure. Optimism is now ready to spend money, in billions, on the ravaged economies of the failed communist utopia; pessimism, always more miserly, thinks it a waste of resources.

Belief that the Western model of economic, political and cultural development is the best, or only, model for the world's emulation is in the ascendant. It perceives the presently dark continents and nations, the continents and nations of 'others', as merely mutant versions of the Western ideal. Western self-approbation, forgetful of the grosser defects of what it is promoting, earnestly presses largesse, instruction and condescension upon the 'underdeveloped', or those in political error. It masquerades (to the background sound of domestic gunfire, and the snorting of the cocaine-sniffer) as the fount of universal moral virtue; it simultaneously invites the begging hand and incites the closed fist of its beneficiaries and dependents. 'Backward' societies and individuals are nevertheless conceived to be in a process of 'transition' from darkness towards reason's Western light. Now, foreign investment in the ravaged post-communist countries is held, exactly as it was in the case of the Third World, to be the key to both their economic and their social progress. Yet, capitalist development is being (anarchically) supervised in such countries by Western governments and financial institutions which are at the same time struggling with their own forms of moral and economic crisis. It is as if the rich nations felt driven to beggar themselves in order to prove the superiority of their social systems.

In grotesque outcome, as stock exchanges opened in the immediate aftermath of communism's fall, socialist state firms scrounged for buyers. Hoarders could have been seen in bleak former Soviet and East European cities carrying homewards uncut sides of beef and cartons of Sicilian oranges, while in the new free markets Hogarthian peasants demanded payment in dollars for their carrots and cashiered Party functionaries turned themselves into shopkeepers. In a Bucharest boulevard, within months of Ceausescu's overthrow, a Ranx Xerox copy centre, a ragged begging gypsy, a theatre bill for Goethe's *Torquato Tasso*, a bullet-pocked façade, and a Garucci clothes-shop with modish Italian shoes in its window were rivals, in one spot, for the roving eye. Silk-suited Japanese businessmen, French television technicians, plain-clothes Securitate agents, and working-class American purchasers in the Romanian baby-market jostled one another in crowded hotel lobbies. 'Down with the Nomenklatura! Down with Neo-communism!', shouted the painted street-slogans, while pallid desperation, swaddled against the biting cold, fought, foul-mouthed, for a loaf in shop doorways. Everywhere in the tragi-comic turmoil of the search for the 'normal', ex-Marxists became overnight whole-hoggers in the market, at the same time trying to reject the rest of the market's political and moral prospectus. Others saw 'the Market', in the Party-man's instinctively manipulative fashion, as an institution to be secretly managed in the interests of the Party, now gone 'underground' pending its reconstitution. Others again, torn between the moral demands of self-interest and socialist instinct, veered from one position to another, egalitarian homily on their lips and their elbows in the next man's ribs.

To this new-found or restored 'enterprise-culture' in the post-communist world have been brought fears and guilts, habits and desires, which can at best be only partially known to the naive Western protagonists of 'plural democracy' and the market system. Here, no 'last word' can be spoken; the old Jansenist and the older Elijah know better. Moreover, only in an ideological dumbshow could the abstract 'individualism' of the market ideal be offered as the desirable alternative to the abstract 'collectivism' of the socialist utopia. In an American or Japanese corporation, or under the influence of youth fashion, or in the persona of the 'universal plebeian', the independence and integrity of the 'individual' is more apparent than real. As for the surrender of ego and the 'solidarity' required of 'collective man', they were the virtues of an ideal type, not of an actual human being. Invocations to 'individualism' and 'freedom' on the one hand, or to 'fraternity' and 'class rule' on the other, short-circuit thought about the complexities of real being. Reduced to abstractions, they stand as totems of belief, not practical guides to living.

Moreover, 'individualism' as a creed is no newer-fashioned, including in its specific present reincarnation, than the 'socialism' which it fancies itself to have replaced. In 1914, three years before the Bolshevik Revolution, H. G. Wells termed 'Individualism' a 'key word of contemporary thought'. Describing its then fashionable doctrines as being those of the 'extreme optimistic school', he dismissed it for resting on a simple-minded belief that the 'welfare of man' could be entrusted to the 'spontaneous and planless activities of people of goodwill'; he dismissed it, too, for perceiving state intervention as the only impediment to the attainment of 'individualism's goals.

Indeed, far from being the shining ethical principle of a final struggle with socialism, this 'individualism' is the Protestant ego's old fetish, lately refurbished as a counterfoil to socialism's defeated moral claims. More misleading still, it has been elaborated in some minds into a new secular myth for an ungodly age. Instead, the ideal of an autonomous individual at large in a freely self-determining society offers as illusory, and tragic, a vision of man as any dreamed up by the socialist utopian. Personal interest, unguided exertion and 'common sense' – especially if rooted, as they frequently are, in moral indifference – can no more lead the way to the promised land of peace and well-being, or milk-and-honey, than could tyrannical socialist imposition, armed with what Alexander Herzen called the 'insulting conviction that the individual will endure anything' in the name of socialist dogma.

The Jew, the most ambivalent, or many-sided, of all modern figures, is in general prone to believe successively (or even at the same time) in the virtues both of optimism and pessimism, personal freedom and political order, private enterprise and social justice, tradition and overthrow of tradition. When the die has been cast for one, he thinks, and even works for, the other; on the most tranquil of days, hears the sound of approaching uproar; and in one human debacle will generally detect the source of another. For a Jew, the collapse of empire is a time both of jubilee and fear. Leaving the Soviet Union behind him, he foresees the nation's afflictions as well as his own. Here, his ambivalence serves him and his prophecies well. He might have benefited from post-communism's new intellectual freedoms or its 'enterprise culture', but he was at greater risk, so he feels in his bones, from its anarchic licence, economic failure and need for scapegoats. Hence, too, the idea of 'progress' generally appears to the Jew as a mixed blessing. On the one hand, it promises emancipation of thought and energy. On the other hand, it threatens disturbance to an existing order in which he has found his place, and with which he has become familiar. The Jew is inclined to prophecy, because unforeseeable consequence suggests danger; disposed to caution, for fear of provoking trouble; yet, paradox of paradoxes, often restless for the change which brings it.

Today, a time of great intellectual and political upheaval, the Jew's sense of insecurity – barometer of a wider social crisis – is growing. He fears that the order for which he looks might fail him, and that the human energies he most admires might in some way turn against him. Insofar as socialism promised a Messianic realm of justice, its failure, a form of Jewish failure, deepens his pessimism. Yet, anti-socialism's hollow triumph is nothing for him to celebrate either. But it is the unpredictable outcome of the disillusion and confusion of others which gives him the greatest (and most ancient) cause for troubled speculation. Here, he is mankind's weather-vane, the twists and turns of his consciousness visible in his exoduses and entrances, as well as in his intellectual changes of direction. They reflect the deepest eddies of the spirit of the age. Whether disowning socialism's lies and violences or doubting the very notion of progress, whether flocking from the former Soviet Union or being increasingly caught up in the market's corruptions, whether expressing a fearful distaste for the 'universal plebeian' or searching anew for a lost sense of identity and Messianic purpose, the wandering Jew helps lay bare, in a period of turmoil, the lineaments of wider preoccupation.

At its heart for the Jew, as for others, is an unmet need for reassurance and equilibrium. His intellect is now at work not only upon the task of pessimistically questioning the idea of progress, but of optimistically attempting to give it new meaning. The spontaneous, organic process of revolution which swept communism away may appeal to his sense of the tragic and elemental. But that it was beyond prediction and without coherent programme arouses old fears of the unknown. The recovery of history and tradition, of names and places (even if obliterated by some Jews themselves in the territory of Palestinians), is biblical in its justice. Yet, it also recalls to the Jews that St Petersburg no more than Leningrad can be a finally secure home. Whether as believer or free-thinker, he celebrates the end of the suffocation of citizen minds and spirits; but as a Jew, he fears the loosening of tongues and the freedom from taboos. As the course of each national history, interrupted by socialist ukase, resumes, he may be quick to seize the opportunity to contribute to it; but the more national, the more exclusive. Freed to think and speak his own thoughts, his voice, so he fears, may easily be drowned.

In contemplating a contemporary capitalism increasingly let off the moral hook – particularly if the Jew should find himself being tempted by it – he may well feel a further reason for unease. Socialism's opposition to the market's excesses provided for decades the critique which capitalism, and the wider society, required. Without an ideological alternative on the left to the injustices it inflicts when hard-set to its devices, those who are disadvantaged must turn further rightwards for their emotional and political compensations, at great risk to the safety of Jews, among others. Indeed, the fact that socialism was, or appeared to be, anti-fascist was one of its main sources of attraction for Jews. Its contervailing powers offered, so it seemed, a permanent bulwark – organised, in its communist form, around the brawn of a neutralised proletariat – against the irrationality of those more insecure even than the Jews. But any left confidence that a socialism of the 'working class' is 'bound to reappear' with the 'unleashing of market forces', is more utopian than ever, or feigned. To the Jew, the unleashed plebeian is a more realistic prospect.

It is societies off-balance which the Jew has learned most to fear. Today, socialism's failure has not only dragged down whole polities in its wake, but mired in doubt every former confidence about the nature of the 'public good'. At the same time, adding to the confusion, there are few, even among those most strenuously loyal to the 'values of the market', who would think such values the source of lasting moral virtue. There are also few politicians whose professed admiration for the capitalist system is so strong as to free them from the need to look over their shoulders at the social consequences of the market's operations. And if the malcontent of the future can no longer be a utopian leftist, his options will be dangerously narrowed. (All observers could be brought to see this, so the Jew thinks, if they shared Jewish fears.) Yet, market economies which are based, with little qualm and diminishing scruple, on privatisation, competition and rationing by price are here to stay, East and West. So, too, is knowing anti-socialist objection to the state in any role more interventionist than that of guarantor of the market, sustainer of the entrepreneur, and residual provider of those public goods which are beyond the scope of the market to provide, or unenticing to its motives. In such circumstances, a 'more just' society must be left to fetch for itself from its profits, not its values, while the fig-leaves of 'freedom' and 'democracy' cover its multitude of sins. Here, the Jew-threatening 'universal plebeian' can find his mean nurture; here, old 'class organisation' can mutate into the armed city gang. Nor is this the 'moral vacuum' or 'anarchy' of commonplace diatribe. The organisation of despair requires, as did old Nazism, its own moral order (however amoral by other standards), its own priorities, its own 'principles' of social selection.

New illusions about the market, as utopian as the non-market illusions which preceded them, promise new dangers. 'Without the market', declared Boris Yeltsin in April 1992, 'there will be no entrepreneurship, social protection or recovery;' 'only the market', declared Mikhail Gorbachev in October 1990, could ensure both the satisfaction of people's needs and the 'fair distribution of wealth, social rights, and the strengthening of freedom and democracy.' And if all this were not enough of false hope, the market, promised Gorbachev, would give weary former Soviet citizens 'access to all the achievements of world civilisation'. This was socialist pressure-selling, standing on its head in the citizen's doorway; or a new chimera to replace the old one, worn out and no longer in political fashion. To offer simultaneously to satisfy (unsatisfiable) needs, meet the claims of social justice, and reduce the powers of the state was to offer to square the political circle. It was also to invite the certainty of delusion and anger. 'World civilisation' and the 'achievements of human thought' – also briefly on offer, in April 1990, in the post-communist prospectus of Moscow's Democratic Platform – were even less easily within the gift of the black-market huckster or the reach of the milling throng. Yet, post-communism quickly showed itself as capable as is anti-communism of such democratic, or populist, illusion. It was even intellectually ready, without much further question, to accept the history of the West in the way that the West had written it. 'Russia,' Boris Yeltsin declared in the United States in June 1991, 'wants to enter the civilised world ... in other words, [take] the civilised way that has been travelled by most countries, including the United States.'

But this 'civilised way' has claimed the Jew's life, among others, many million times over, in intermittent outbreaks of the greatest violence. Neither 'civilisation' nor 'barbarism' are mutually exclusive categories to the Jew. (In Europe, especially, it is this consciousness which marks him out intellectually from others; even Spinoza placed the problem of 'the multitude' at the centre of his philosophical concerns.) He can therefore fully trust neither the egoism of the free, not the self-sacrifice of the stoic; in times of moral derangement, the first can take the anti-semitic initiative, and the latter obey it. Whether man sees himself as the pinnacle of creation to whom everything is permitted, or as mere clay in the hand of God, he has been equal prey to the wildest unreason. Both enlightened self-interest and the call of faith have put the scapegoat to the sword. Hence, the secular and the spiritual, the material and the ideal, are equally seen by the wandering Jew as offering no guarantee of safety. His own intellectual espousal of them is almost always conditional, and, in the depths of his feeling, almost always wary. When (the Jewish) André Maurois brashly proclaimed 'recalcitrance to collective thought' to be the 'greatest of virtues', he offered for celebration, instead, the right of 'individual conscience' – the Protestant conscience – to 'form its own opinions on philosophy, economics and politics'. But generally, the Jew sees merit in both; or, if his own circumstances warrant, neither.

In the ambiguous actual world, whose archetypal reflection he is, both 'collective thought' and private conscience shape the perceptions and moralities of the Jew. The dichotomy between them is, in any case, a false one. Moreover, the Jew tends to move from one ideal figment of the moral imagination to another more freely than most. The 'right-wing' Jew's utopia of a 'free market, a strong state, limited government and stable families' – offered for approbation by Sir Keith Joseph in August 1990 – can be readily exchanged, in his heart and head, for the socialist Jew's older dream of a just social order of egalitarian aspiration and open-handed public provision. But neither can satisfy anxiety for long. The very notion of the 'good life' seems precarious and unpersuasive, and the condition to which it points both temporary and elusive, if it exists at all.

'The market', 'economic efficiency', 'social progress' also appear to the Jew as means, not ends. Yet, what these ends might be itself remains contingent and uncertain, until the (equally unlikely) day 'when the Messiah comes'. In the meantime, vigilance-for-self and altruism, individual freedom and the striving for social justice, private property and collective sharing, can seem equally to be virtues, as well as parts (however incompatible) of a virtuous whole. Similarly, to suppress the claims of the poor seems to most Jews as wicked as to deny special reward to intellect, or other manifestation of individual merit. More than that, it is neither just nor even possible to choose ethically between them. And it is precisely in such moral and political dilemmas that there lie the main conundrums of political order. That the ambivalent Jew is usually acutely aware of them derives either from personal experience or from collective tradition, or both. The poor but worthy Jew, whose intellect and true merit remain known only to himself, is every 'successful' Jew's *alter ego*.

Reading history or sacred scripture, attempting to fathom social laws or observe religious scruple, the Jew has always attempted (at least in his head) to master his fate and to give his life, and the life of others, meaning. But his acquisition of knowledge, wealth or position in the pursuit of such self-command can arouse as much suspicion and dislike as his itinerant poverty once provoked in other days. This is a further reason why his identification with secular power is rarely complete. He sees himself, even when riding the purple, as a past or future petitioner at power's door. It is therefore not hard for him, however graced by fortune, and whether a man of good deeds or bad, to imagine himself among the outcast or 'disadvantaged'. But his sense of duty to 'master his fate', generally in his own way, may also serve to establish a distance from others.

Here the Jew, sometimes wilfully, courts danger. He may be accused, even before he has the instinct to feel it, of being 'different'. He may be seen, sometimes most abruptly, no longer as a citizen but as a stranger, and be judged accordingly. If surrounding circumstances worsen, he may find curiosity turn to antipathy and suspicion to hatred. In the worst of all circumstances, the estrangement of 'others' from him has turned to mass murder. In this last experience, the Jewish moral ideal – sometimes honoured in the breach – of advancing ethically through time and place towards the creation of a heaven-on-earth found itself in a charnel-house, where much of the spirit of Jewish socialism also died. Thereafter, in Central Europe, communist regimes were grandiosely founded, in the name of the Hebraic Marx, upon the ruins of an order which had itself been driven by a desire to slay the Jews. Indeed, in much of the history of modern Europe's anxieties and struggles, dreams and nightmares, Jewish preoccupation and preoccupation with the Jews have gone hand-in-hand. Neither abates. In phases of renewal, as well as in phases of crisis, such preoccupations are renewed.

The causes and issues around which these preoccupations revolve – chasing their tails – have always been at, or close to, the heart of the wider revolutions, intellectual and political, of their times. It is not different now, even if a principal focus of Jewish concern, and of concern with Jews, has moved since the Second World War to the narrower battlefield of their nation-state. But the general forms of premonitory Jewish doubt, shaped by historic trial, still derive from intellectual speculation on a larger plane, of which Europe, its culture and its fate, remains the centre. Now, as in the past, the predicament of the Jew stands in the thick of the main contradictions of the age, above all those which counterpose the claims of universality against the claims of race and nation. Moreover, the explosive content, not merely the form, of Jewish moral doubt, as Christ and Marx between them showed, has long had the capacity to set off revolutions in thought and deed. Today, in Europe, the traditional Jewish mistrust of secular power is balanced by a greater fear of headlong social disorder, the instinct for personal freedom checked by an older recoil from the licence of the crowd. In addition, the moral conflict between the spirit of self-seeking competition on the one hand, and guilty preference for an egalitarian order on the other – or between aggression and compromise in Israel – continues to divide the ambivalent Jew, who is simultaneously of one party and another.

In all these (archetypal) moral tensions, universal doubts reside. If the need for authoritarian political control over social aberration grows, as it will, what ethic will inform it? If the expropriation of the poor 'South' in the interests of the rich 'North' is to rage unchecked after communism's fall, who or what will end it? If the 'underdog' is no longer to be sustained by a socialist political creed ostensibly devoted to him, what alternative will organise his aspirations? And is not the very idea of a 'post-socialist era' premature? Socialists may have failed to draw any intelligible conclusions from their failures, but the *ethical* grounds at least for a renewal of socialist messianism are as plain as the ethical grounds for a refusal of it. The redemption of the 'suffering poor' may be pursued by various means – according to the prescriptions of the Jewish Christ or the Jewish Marx, for example – but the cause itself does not recede. Likewise, old scorn continues to scoff at revived Jewish fears, but familiar obsessions about 'international Jewry' stir at capitalism's newest failures; in some of these failures Jews may appear, but to their own greater cost.

Utopian socialism, that false dawn of fraternity which foolishly promised to resolve all doubts and relieve all tensions, squandered its moral capital – much of it invested by Jews – in excess of unreason, and in tyrannies both large and small. Now, for all that its ideals may still be needed, the faded creature can contribute little to the promotion of social and economic development, or of individual self-realisation; and promise nothing that non-socialists and anti-socialists could or would trust. Yet, if socialism's long attempt to confine the individual to the anonymity of class has been a failure, the reduction of the proletarian to membership of an equally anonymous plebeian mass bodes well for no one. If the 'working class' is not to have its multifarious interests shaped to both a governing and a redeeming purpose, disorder, moral as well as physical, beckons; if working conditions and rewards are to be placed increasingly at the mercy of an unstable market, the absence of social ethic declares open season both for rapacity and social reaction against it. The more competitive (and destructive) the social and economic order, the greater the need for the safeguarding of social and other standards against its predations. But of all the risks to the potential scapegoat, a failure of belief in the future must be counted the greatest. When cynicism and a despairing anger take charge of popular opinion, and the rule of law fails, the whetted plebeian knife is sooner or later placed at the scapegoat's throat.

History, however, does not repeat itself; it is historians, as Balfour pointed out, who repeat each other. Nor can Marx's dialectic any longer make sufficient sense of the times. The relatively innocent idea of linear progress has also begun to falter, yet reason shies away from alternative vistas of eternal stasis or final disaster. Here, the main purposes of the intellectual Jew remain. They have to do with the keeping of records and the acquisition of knowledge, just prophecy and careful witness, whether on his own behalf or others'. Although he has committed gross errors of judgment or calculation, to the point of imperilling his own existence, the Jew has also discovered, by trial and error, how to use his faculties for survival. At a time when mankind's resources are being misused on a grand scale, and sense of moral purpose is turned to passivity or confusion, the Jew as survivor, rather than as 'victim', assumes larger dimension; but only to run an increased risk of attracting odium. (Most Jews have no wish to be seen as archetypes of the threatened and battling human species as a whole, even if they are.)

Indeed, it is here that the Jew stands at the centre of yet another of the world's paradoxes.

Jewish materialism shares in, and has helped to create, many of the delusions that surround the near-universal dream of an ever-rising standard of living and comfort. This makes the Jew of the modern world an unconvincing guide to a utopia of shared work, or ascetically reduced consumption. But if the Jew will not lead the way there, it is unlikely that anyone will. Of the three great *fin-du-monde*, or doomsday, theories placed before mankind – the Judaeo-Christian, the Marxist, and the ecological – the Jews initiated two. The first posed a fateful choice between eternal damnation and the redemption of body and soul. The second counterposed to the world-ending anarchy of capitalism the bliss of socialist salvation. The third holds up to our eyes the death of Nature and a last-minute rescue by rigorous self-command. In each case, including the first, an appeal to the light of truth and reason serves as the ground and instrument of persuasion. In each case, knowledge, whether spiritual or worldly, whether religious, historic or scientific, is the pre-condition for illumination. And in each successive case, prophecy pits itself against the foe, whether such foe be idolatry and darkness of soul, 'false consciousness', or the hedonism of the morally blind. In all three, utterance is jealous of its truths and rabbinic in its admonitions. Sententiousness (sometimes presented as the simplicity of pure insight), moral superiority, and disdain for the unenlightened colour their manner and inform their substance. In each case, those who do not believe the prophecy are presumed to be against it. Hebraic moral intolerance, never so intolerant as when professing meekness of spirit, is inscribed upon them all.

But the strengths of these *fin-du-monde* ideas were, and are, too little for the forces arrayed against them. Against the challenges of Islam, or the global power of the market, or the ransacking of the natural order, Judaeo-Christian, socialist and ecological shibboleths, however high-sounding, do not count for much in the struggle for the conquest of minds. Judaeo-Christian moral ardour is too fitful (or absent), socialist – and especially Marxist socialist – certitudes have retreated, and ecological objection to the abuse of nature is no more than that of largely ineffectual protest. Moreover, the authoritarian impulses, often just, which underlie each *fin-du-monde* vision have been variously sapped, deterred, or defeated by ethical scruple, practical failure, and the scale of the interests marshalled against them. In moral argument, doomsday's publicists and spokesmen, priests and gurus, may have commanded the world of words. On the ground, where the labourer gains his hire, the gangster pulls his knife, and forests fall, they have less reach than ever.

The Jews, despite it, have always been disposed to celebrate their own visionary intellectualism, and many go about the world with the names of Heine and Einstein, Freud and Kafka, Marx and Mahler, Proust and Spinoza inscribed on their hearts, or in the phylacteries they place on their foreheads; even St John of the Cross was of Jewish descent – perhaps Cervantes and Columbus too – and Teresa of Avila was a Jewish convert. Moreover, whatever his paternity, the Jews also know Christ to have been a Jew not merely by matrilineal descent, but as itinerant moralist and recognisably anxious sage. Yet, such Jewish pride – for the Jews are secretly proud of as well as irritated by Christ – is a snare, when it suggests either that force of mind is a sufficient title to princely rule, or that the Jewishness of Christ might vanquish anti-Jewish hatred and unreason.

Indeed, when the connection between Judaism and Christian belief, including in the latter's founder, is suppressed emotionally even by most educated Christians, the 'Judaeo-Christian' becomes an empty term. Yet, it is not only that Moses and Isaiah, Jesus and Paul were all equally Jews. Ethical monotheism, the Mosaic code, belief in the rationality of the universe as well as the equality of all before God, the Hebraic content of the Gospels, including the Sermon on the Mount and the Lord's Prayer – in which verse for verse, and phrase for phrase, are taken from the Talmud – and the very forms of worship link the faiths in vain. The Christian 'Do unto thy neighbour as thou would'st be done by' was preceded by 'What is distasteful to thee, do not to thy neighbour' of Jesus' older contemporary, Rabbi Hillel; 'thou shalt love thy neighbour as thyself' can be found in *Leviticus*, Book XIX, Chapter 19. Even 'Amen' is Hebrew.

Once, pious Christians identified with the 'Israelites' of old; today, this is the stoniest of biblical ground. Mere liturgical lip-service is now paid to the 'Zion' of once-common aspiration. Indeed, the stiff-necked refusal of both Jews and Christians to acknowledge and act upon this commonality of inspiration is an ethical disability they share. Not even common foes can unite them. Hostile memory and old rancour take precedence over the moral imperative to defend together a heritage which has given shape to Western belief; a shared provenance of thought has proved less persuasive than a record of misdeeds. The hook-nosed Jew and blue-eyed Christ of bigotry and bad faith bar the way; the ethical pass is sold to the market, or the mullah. Yet, the surrender itself flouts history. Hebraism and Christianity jointly lent their beliefs in the equal dignities of men to the inspiration of the English Revolution of 1640, gave moral strength to the victorious armies in the American War of Independence and Civil War, and helped form the words of the French Revolution's Declaration of the Rights of Man. Judaic disdain for the Christian, and Christian recoil from the Jew, do not weigh heavily in the historic scale, when the very philosophy of Western constitutional government rests on the Hebraic idea of a covenant between God, the people and their ruler.

The 'Holy Family' and the 'incarnation' of God in man may be rank blasphemy to a Jew; to a Christian, the Jewish refusal of Christ's divinity may pronounce the Jews' spiritual doom. The Jew may reject the idea of personal salvation as the reward of virtue; the Christian may reject the Jewish conception of the 'Messianic Kingdom'. But even the lengthy past history of Christian religious violence – in the name of Christ – or present Jewish betrayals of the spirit and letter of Hebraic justice cannot conceal the reciprocal moral influence on Jew and Christian of the Sermon on the Mount and the Ten Commandments. Moreover, at the heart of the West's very imagination the Hebrew Bible stands, translated into the vernacular by the Christian scholars of Europe. In the account of Man's fall from grace in the Garden of Eden to the hope of redemption at the 'end of days', a common civilisation's entire morality, or what remains of it, is contained.

Its consequence is that, despite every difference and every silence, there is a sustained, and sustainable, awareness in both Christian and Jew, which is not shared with others, of an unending mutual relation, including of hostility, between them. Thus, the exodus of Jews from the former Soviet Union, a token of left idealism's collapse, can be instinctively understood by both Christian and Jew as an exodus of biblical resonance and proportion. A common sensibility and a common imagination, even where they arouse different emotions, instruct them both. For the Christian and the Jew – perhaps for the apostate, the agnostic and the non-believer too – the sharing of a (now faded) culture still gives the possibility of a shared understanding of the Jewish and Christian sense of moral duty, even when it fails. Both Jew and Christian can imagine themselves, with whatever reserve, at each other's altars, where many of the same prayers from the same, or similar, texts are spoken. The Jew understands, even when he disapproves, the Christian mission; the Christian recognises, even when he dislikes, Jewish invocations to Zion. Likewise, the Jew's demand that persecution atone for its many crimes is known by the Christian – from a shared sense of justice – to be a just demand, even when it is refused. And when the Jew, for his part, refuses to turn the other cheek, he himself knows the moral force of Christian acts of forgiveness. Indeed, what is moral offence to the one is moral offence to the other; moral strength, also.

But even were such true 'common sense', the common sense of a shared ethical system, to be miraculously restored to the ordering of our affairs, it would have come too late. The secular legacy of Judaeo-Christian values – the legacy of a shared belief in free will, in the dignity of human life, in the rule of law, in the right of moral dissent, together with a shared fear of unreason – has shown itself to be unequal to the task of protecting the civic order from the asocial, and those who are otherwise strangers to its values. In the battle with violence, with the abandonment of social duty, and with the exploitation of the liberal spirit of toleration, aggressive moral unconcern has everywhere ridden roughshod over pleas for greater scruple. Feverish wants, idle fun, pressing need and unholy zeal easily brush the liberal plea aside. Indeed, the very heart of that body of Judaeo-Christian values which is so easily flouted – the moral belief in free will and its political correlate, the freedom of the individual – is also the heart of Western civic society's weakness. In the name of freedom, and using its rights, freedom may be debased and overthrown.

In the aftermath of socialism's failure, it is precisely here that moral anxiety finds its universal home. In the restless Jew, who is again intellectually and physically on the move, such anxiety will in due course provoke a new round of moral and political dissent against that species of freedom, including the freedom of the market, which merely destroys itself. Moreover, in conditions in which socialism, the politics of ethnicity, and demagogic populism can none of them meet the demands of reason, it is an anxiety which will find its temporary relief in increasingly authoritarian moral speculation, directed to the minimum and most urgent requirements for the salvation of the civic order. The 'good society' can be constructed from liberal democratic nostrums, trans-national aspirations, and secular tender-heartedness only on paper. Belief in Providence is ethically beguiling, but insufficient in practice. The moral disarmament of the city gunman or drug-dealer, if it is now to be achieved at all, is a task beyond the reach of the liberal (or the socialist) mind.

In principle, Jew, Christian, Muslim and rationalist alike might be inspired in common to repair their damaged mutual relations, now that socialism's grosser delusions have been set to rest. If reciprocal odium and collisions of zeal were to abate, so a recovered idealism might dictate, then shared ethical interests could together bend their efforts to the keeping of the peace, both within the social order and between the nations. Instead, the prospect is receding; hope of it is the familiar fruit of liberal wishful thinking.

'Believers!', declares the Koran, in Chapter Five ('The Table'), 'take neither Jews nor Christians for your friends. They are friends with one another. Whoever of you seeks their friendship shall become one of their number.' Against this judgment, an anathema pronounced by the faith of one billion persons – but posited upon awareness of the ideal Judaeo-Christian relation – moral ecumenism has no real chance. The asocial injunction knifes the civic bond. On the one hand, Islam proclaims itself a respecter of the faiths of others. It pronounces itself not only at one in its monotheism with the Hebraic and Christian, but also at one with Judaism in its acceptance of Abraham, and at one with Christianity in its acceptance of Christ, seeing both as God's prophets. On the other hand, for all that its own provenance is Judaic, it stands on the far side of an ethical and emotional chasm where neither Jew nor Christian can reach it. In Islam's growingly anti-secular world-view, Satan and the Infidel become real, and fear is openly pronounced to be as worthy an emotion as love. Killing – and not merely self-sacrifice – for faith is holy. Moreover, both Caesar and the Graces must bow to God. In denial of its ancient tradition of scholarship and inquiry, Islam has come to represent, for many, the culture of the closed and even the lost mind; no Jewish or Christian Rushdie could have been hounded by modern rabbinical or priestly conclave into hiding, and the fear of death. Moreover, as its political confidence and military strengths have grown, as well as its perception of being under Western crusader attack, Islam's proud, or aggressive, sense of itself as the 'decisive religion' has grown also. Particularly since the Iranian revolution, it has appeared to the West to become morally more assured and more belligerent both in word and deed, its youth increasingly won over to militancy of holy purpose.

Despite the debacle in the Gulf, Islam plainly sees itself as an ascendant faith. It also sees itself as having gained ground over and even humbled the Infidel in combat, physical and moral, during the last decades. It considers itself to have worsted his interests at Suez, in French Algeria, in the Shah's Iran and the former Soviet Afghanistan, fighting him to a standstill in the Lebanon, and challenging him morally, not only in the Maghreb and the Palestinian *intifada* but, now, in the Muslim diaspora as a whole. In the heat of ethical and military battle (against a physically superior but morally decadent foe) it has re-found its old sense of purpose. It counts its legions, including in former-Soviet Central Asia, in hundreds of millions; with 'compassion' and 'mercy' inscribed on its standards, it seeks to set the world alight with the passion of faith and fire. Moreover, both its strategic and its moral perspectives are increasingly global. When Gorbachev appeared to have been ousted in the August 1991 coup, much of Islam cheered; he was seen by many Muslims as the 'liberator' of the Soviet Union's Jews in the interests of Israel. Algeria, Iran, Iraq and Libya – each offering its blandishments to former Soviet nuclear scientists and dealers in enriched uranium – hanker for an 'Islamic bomb'; Pakistan has achieved it. And since there is as little likelihood of lasting peace between Jew and Arab in the Middle East as in the times of the Old Testament's warring tribes, conflict between Islam and the West must grow.

The West regards such a prospect with trepidation, not least for its economic interests in the Arab world. But the more radical chiefs of Islam see in a 'global storm' only their advancing cause, the cause of the self-defence of faith against the unholy and imperialist foe. Indeed, fundamentalist Islam at its most extreme considers itself to be at war with a universal Satan bent upon the destruction of all religion. Even democracy was described as 'pure atheism' by the thwarted fundamentalist victors of the December 1991 Algerian election, while those who had voted for non-Islamic parties would, they said, 'go to hell'. It is a 'war' which knows no frontier and in which no quarter can in the end be given, since at stake, so militant Islam thinks, is the whole world's soul. Even the most pacific of Muslims, the overwhelming majority, are combatants for their faith and must mount their chargers – as did the Iraqis and Iranians in mutual slaughter – if called upon to do so; and new Saladins, doubtless, wait to be born to the 'Arab nation.'

In the thick of this world-historical combat of mind and body (which the West has barely joined, and thinks falsely can be settled by mere force of arms), the Jew, now himself armed, again stands. Relatively few in numbers, he is, and is accused of being, at the eye of the storm. In the war of moralities, his affinities – with Muslim as well as Christian – are lost from view. In the heat of battle for what he in turn perceives as self-defence for survival, the Jew may lose his own sense of justice, in particular when his opponent's moral cause is entirely discounted. At the same time, in recoil from the bloody arena, anti-Muslim and anti-Jew may make common cause, accusing the Muslim of 'fanaticism' and the Jew of being an eternal source of conflict.

Indeed, it is Western distaste for the dark underworld (as it is seen) of alien ethnicity and belief that helps explain the volatile *furor europeus*, or counter-passion for the rediscovery and defence of the 'European idea'. In its openly racist form it has decried, for example, the growing 'Africanisation and Islamicisation of Europe's population'. In more statesmanlike and labyrinthine fashion it could declare, in the words of the Italian industrialist Giovanni Agnelli, speaking in Oxford in June 1991, that 'Europeans' with their 'collective and common understanding' were 'certainly united in those differences which separate us, for instance, from the Asian or Islamic worlds'. In this, there is an early sense of the girding of Western Christian loins for a future fight with the alien foe on behalf of 'European values', in which the spectre of Muslim ardour to prove the truth of Islam in the field seems gradually to be taking hold of the 'European mind'. The sense of an embattled and equally foreign 'international Jewry', caught on the wrong side of 'Europe' and ready (with nuclear weapons) to fend off a last Masada, has also begun a new, or old, germination.

For a Jewish intellectual, the most serious immediate implication of being pointed to, once more, as a 'stranger', is the prospect it brings of cultural estrangement from the civic society to which he belongs. Moreover, the risk is increased by his own increasing self-preoccupation. In addition, the values he shares with Christian ethics are values which are themselves being subjected to disintegrating pressures. In such a context, a compensatory (and short-term) Eurocentrism, when 'Europe' is itself riven by heterogeneity of every kind, offers a poor alternative intellectual home. Better, because less illusory, a confederation of sovereign European states, preserving their own distinctive political wills and attempting to maintain what remains of their civic orders in their own ways, than a sharing of their disaggregation in a false unification of purposes, bureaucratically managed. Nor have the Jews much to gain from a resurgent sense of 'Europe's Christian values'. Better the nation state with its own notions of citizenship and rule – notions good, bad, very bad and indifferent, according to political choice – than a further loss of national identity and purpose in the fictitious name of a 'new Europe'. This 'new Europe' will be the old, but on a larger scale. Its virtues will be ostensibly pooled, its faults and fissures enlarged. Separate identities, national and sub-national, will be required to battle even more strenuously for survival; together with wealth (unevenly) increased, its periodic economic crises will become more comprehensive. The Jews, supposedly and sometimes actually cosmopolitan citizens of the world, are only so by historic *force majeure*. By instinct and choice they are – even when revolutionaries – generally conservatives of place, their restlessness a restlessness of mind. To a Jew, 'Europe' is a continent, not a true habitation.

The protection of the civic order from whatever threatens it cannot be carried out in the abstract, nor upon a broad and unfocussed plane, 'European' or any other. When the civic bond begins to fail, in dereliction, mutual estrangement and violence, it fails in its own fashion in a specific community and a particular location. Neither moral energy nor political authoritarianism can be marshalled at a continental distance. Bureaucracy and bureaucratic methods move, generally, in a moral vacuum and are often synonyms for it. The citizen as 'moral person' is so, and proves himself to be so, in his own setting and no other. In addition, the legislator is himself a citizen of a particular civic society, or is nothing. The rule of law, too, is more than an administrative abstraction; disembodied fiat itself destroys the sense of the civic. For authority to be judged neither arbitrary nor provisional it must be at hand. That is, it must preside visibly and accountably over the particular citizen's affairs and on the citizen's behalf. If it does not, law becomes (for some) the more quickly a dead letter, and civic morality a more precarious or passing matter. At a time when the citizen, struggling with the moral vacancy of much of his daily endeavour, has a growing need for human tasks and social duties, invisible rule is more disabling to civic societies than ever.

In the dispersal of power – or 'surrender of sovereignty' – there is also one of the grounds of that irrationalism which can respond to fear of national and civic dissolution with apocalyptic schemes for the 'purification' of the citizen (and ostensible citizen) body; schemes which derive from the belief that racial heterogeneity is the root of political weakness and moral evil. Expulsion or exclusion of the ethnic stranger, so it is fancied, will help restore the body politic to itself; greater homegeneity of citizen origin will ensure the restoration of the civic bond. The vanishing of the Jew, the black and other 'aliens' – but not those citizens who are *moral* strangers to their neighbours – will permit the social order to regroup its forces in the name of the long-lost but authentic nation. The time of this old idea is once more returning. The scale of social crisis, both imaginary and real, and especially in the most harmed cities of the industrial world, has ensured it.

To its aid has come the historially recurring sense, boosted in this period by the sudden sweeping away of the communist empire as if it had never existed, that there are no moral bounds to what may be contemplated and done. The Jew, who fears 'fascist' racism above all things, is no longer inclined, as he was in the 1930s, to disbelieve in the capacity of 'others', even if they are virtuous-seeming, to do their worst to him. (He also knows that his worst could never be as bad as theirs.) Nor could he any more permit a flimsy confidence in the future to disarm him. The trend of things is a better guide. There is, as Burke argued, a 'mighty current in human affairs'; the fevered ransacking of the world to meet mankind's growing needs and greeds is its rising tide, which not even the most authoritarian measures could bring under control. Certainly, to attempt again to destroy the Jews, or any other scapegoats for such disorders, would avail nothing. New utopian illusion, moreover, cannot reach the heart (and type) of metropolitan crime, for example, while any moral absolutist's vision of the just society, whether that vision be religious or lay, is a world away from the tawdry aspirations of the 'universal plebeian'.

Above all, a modest, or timidly self-confining, accommodation with the constraints, both economic and moral, of a finite human existence and a fragile natural order is not a sufficient life-programme for the world's billions. Ambition, individual and national, is rarely checked by the miseries it may cause. Both nations and individuals have always fought tigerishly, and will continue to fight tigerishly, for their ends. Abandonment of the continuous 'expansion of desire' – a voracious compulsion – in favour of a more humane, because more limited, understanding of human purpose on earth would be to undermine impulse itself. The old rationalist illusion that possession-of-mind, correctly informed and unobstructed by superstitious fancy, can carry *homo sapiens* to the heights of wise self-control is as fanciful as any. Since man's nature, physical and social, animal and intellectual, is as it is, there is a finite number of possible ways in which his appetites and predispositions, needs and habits, can be accommodated and politically organised. With one way exhausted or found wanting, the social order historically turns – each time believing itself to be engaged in an unprecedented enterprise or adventure – to another, or another. But the gamut is soon run.

The Jew has often been in the forefront of this turning to and fro. In the latter part of the nineteenth century and the earlier part of this century, moving westwards from Russia and Poland across the face of Europe, he arrived in numbers in the capitalist United States (and other countries, including Britain) in search of the promised land; in the communist era, his brother sought another way; in the overthrow of communism and its further migrations – back to the capitalist United States, Western Europe and Israel – he retraced his steps. These movements, however, have been those of duress as well as of choice. The tide was a tide which he joined as well as one which he formed. In Germany and other countries of Central Europe in the 1930s he found himself, annihilatingly, in the wrong place; in the United States and other Western countries he generally prospered; in the Soviet Union, he found an increasingly uneasy home; in Israel, a doubtful and a disputed refuge. But in Western Europe and the United States, where for decades the Jew has justly seen himself as a citizen among citizens, the ground he stands upon has also begun to shift.

This has less to do, and even nothing to do, with his own qualities and defects, or numbers, which are small. It is the outcome, rather, of the scale of the gathering moral, social and economic crisis of which he is willy-nilly a part. Absolute population decline in many European countries, with growing unease in the United States about the sustaining of its world position as standards of education fall, as well as rises in personal and national indebtedness coupled with manufacturing and technological failures, arouse complex varieties of public and private fear, many of them subterranean. Whether it be from informed doubt about the national future, suppressed anxiety for familial and personal well-being, revulsion at the city and its spiritually bruising conditions of existence, or unemployed despair, changes of individual mood gradually coalesce into a collective, or public, temper which sets alarm bells ringing. The neurosis of the anxious Jew may be over-receptive to indices of malaise, and the apocalyptic may tempt his imagination. But a sense in 'others' of siege and failure, however their own fantasies exaggerate it, historically bodes ill for him.

Moreover, many of the symptoms of Western discomfort are those of real decline, as it is conventionally measured. The European birth-rate (in an overpopulated planet) has fallen steadily in the last three decades, and in many countries – France, for example – is below the death-rate; by the year 2030, on current demographic trends, the population of Germany could be 20 million less than it is today. The proportions of the old in the American and European populations, assisted to greater

longevity by science, are consequently increasing. By the end of the
century, if present trends continue, a third and more of the citizens of
some European countries, Germany for example, will be over sixty. Or,
looked at from another (conventional) standpoint, the American share
of world output has halved in the last fifty years. Only 5 per cent of
American school students are up to the Japanese average in mathemat-
ics. In many fields the Japanese, falter as they may, are now technologically more developed than the United States – over half of the world's
advanced robots are in Japan – while the European Community's
combined domestic product is only some 70 per cent larger than
(protectionist) Japan's. Less profligate also, the Japanese produce their
goods and services with half the energy consumption *pro rata* of the
United States; the expectation of life of the Japanese, as well as their
standards of education, excel those of the British; the murder-rate
among young adult men between the ages of fifteen and twenty-four is
more than seventy times higher in the United States than in Japan. And
by the next century, other Asian Pacific countries, but not the United
States nor 'Europe', are expected to challenge the primacy of Japan,
whose own birthrate is low and falling, in high technology production.

Here, speculation about the 'good life' and the model social order
meets another impasse, perhaps the last. Japanese hierarchy, moral
taboo and sense of shame, literacy, prosperity and level of public order,
social conformism and intensity of labour, are inaccessible to Western
emulation. They are also undesired. (Even less than other possible
worlds, the Japanese is not the Jew's; its morbid sense of the alien
makes every non-Japanese a stranger, and not just the Jew.) Yet, the
West has long had fears of what has come to pass. More than three-
quarters of a century ago, the prescient Wells thought that by the end
of this century American development might have been 'arrested
altogether', while an 'awakened Asia' would be 'reorganising its social
and political conceptions in the light of modern knowledge and modern
ideas'. It was 'quite possible', he wrote before the outbreak of the First
World War, 'that the American John Smiths [or 'the average man'] may
have little to brag about in the way of national predominance by AD
2000. It is quite possible that the United States may be sitting meekly
at the feet of at present unanticipated teachers.'

During this American century, some of its 'teachers', and its John
Smiths, have been Jews. The 'American Dream' was, in part, a Jewish
utopian confection, both kitsch and true. Indeed, the Jew as American
capitalist – merely one of his modern incarnations – became, for some,

the archetype of the Jew himself, a parodic or even sinister figure who held the whole world in his grasp. And if not the planet's banker, paranoia could equally make him the universal revolutionary plotter, prejudice's *ego* and *alter ego* within one cartoon persona. That the Jew became a capitalist, or a communist, or neither, was as any man may: in pursuit of his own and others' ends, moral and less moral. But what the Jew became – American capitalist, Russian communist, English liberal and so on – was also not in the way of others. He remained, and remains, a Jew, open or covert, whether *in propria persona* or in partial disguise. That is, 'he is a Jew that is one inwardly', as St Paul's Epistle to the Romans correctly declares.

The partially disguised Jew, of whom I am one, has been responsible for many awesome half-truths both about himself and the world, Freud's, Marx's and Christ's half-truths among them. Yet, truth-telling ('I am that I am' is the Judaic God's self-description) is for the Jews a holy passion. The paradox is only a seeming one. In the *golem* stories a clay man comes alive when the Hebrew word *emeth*, or Truth, is written on its forehead; 'the Hebrew god is the god of Truth,' as the Italian Jewish historian, Arnaldo Momigliano, put it. In the confusion and hubbub of his migrations, from Mosaic times to these, the Jew strives constantly to hear his own true voice and to make himself known to himself, and sometimes fails. How 'others' know him, and what voice they hear, has always been less important to him. Nevertheless, at the same time, the struggle to reveal general truths about the world – whether by means of scientific inquiry, imaginative prophecy, artistic insight, or moral speculation – has always occupied the Jews; the progress of truth is to most Jews, of whatever secular persuasion, progress *per se*. 'Silence is the real crime,' said Nadezhda Mandelstam of the suppressions of the Stalinist era, but speaking for all Jews, for whom silence about, and denial of, the Holocaust is the crime of crimes.

In the further passage of events which has swept aside the communist farrago, the coming to light of the truth about it consoles even for the defeat of the world's greatest utopian fancy, a fancy promoted and adopted by many Jews. The setting free of language from its socialist embrace, the recovery of a true (or truer) record of national and individual pasts after decades of Party-inspired falsehood, the calling of things and people by their right names, the rehabilitation of the victims of past lies, and the admission as truth of what everybody knew in secret to be so – all represent the 'progress of truth', progress's highest form. The invention of history by its own protagonists, the air-brushing of its pictures and the rigging of its record so that such history might accord with what its protagonists themselves wished to have occurred, was history written (and therefore made) by false faith's zeal. It was not experienced in truth, nor inscribed by reason. In a moral environment steeped in falsehood, 'we became used to saying something different from what we thought,' wrote Vaclav Havel in January 1990. Seven months later, hunger strikers in Sofia who were demanding the removal from its mausoleum of the embalmed body of Georgi Dimitrov – Bulgarian communism's avatar – called their tented camp-site not merely a 'communism-free zone' but a 'city of truth'.

There is truth and truth, half-truth and half-truth, each pitted against the other, trying for the other's fall. Release from intellectual thraldom revealed, in Eastern Europe and the Soviet Union, that some truths (and half-truths) are superior to others; that a myth which oppresses can make men physically and mentally ill; that advances in knowledge of self, past and place may help to restore citizens to themselves. Ex-communists, like pallid but recovering victims of a contagious disease, queued for final absolution from moral taint by the Great Lie. The 'public perception' of communism had been of 'something entirely abhorrent', declared the last general secretary of the Communist Party of Great Britain in September 1990. Polish communism, said Jan Krzysztof Bielecki, the then Polish prime minister, in May 1991, was a 'short-lived insane experiment' and a 'forty-year aberration in the thousand-year history of Poland'. Communism was 'just a temporary episode in our history', said Milovan Djilas, Tito's former comrade-in-arms, in July 1991; a 'myth', declared Yuri Afanaseyev, the Soviet historian; a 'terrible illness', said Thomas Siraku, one of Albania's leading composers. Its depredations had 'enslaved' Soviet society, announced Eduard Shevardnadze, also in July 1991. The 'political experiment of 1917' had 'ended in disaster', declared the British Communist Party, as it disappeared into the political night. Gustav Husak, responsible for purging tens of thousands of dissident Czech intellectuals from public life and employment after the failure of the Prague Spring – confessing Christians among them – requested the last rites of the Catholic Church on his death-bed.

Valediction for communism was usually brief. 'One day', wrote Joseph Brodsky, the Russian Jewish novelist and Nobel laureate, of the 1917 Revolution and Lenin's role in it, 'a train arrived at the Finland Station [in St Petersburg], and a little man emerged from the carriage and climbed on to the top of an armoured car. This arrival was a disaster for the nation.' In this ending, other fleeting Jewish voices, vanishing into darkness, could be heard. 'We were not keen to be informed,' declared Bert Ramelson, the former industrial organiser of the British Communist Party, in January 1990, speaking of the 'serious mistakes' made by the Party; 'if I had tried harder,' he added, 'I could have found out more.' 'For people of my generation,' said the historian Eric Hobsbawm in the same month, 'it is back to the drawing-board, or very nearly.' With mumbled explanation and the vaguest of gestures to the sorry past, the leaders of the communist enterprise – the Honeckers, the Zhivkovs, the Husaks – backed off the stage. Moral and physical exhumation began to find various types of cadaver and relic, including 30,000 bodies of Buddhist monks executed in Mongolia on Stalin's orders and 30,000 microscopic sections of Lenin's brain kept in a Moscow institute since 1924. The United States, it was calculated, had spent some 5 trillion dollars on 'meeting the military challenge of the Soviet Union'. But the regime which such prodigious expense had sought to contain was bankrupt.

Communism, wearied of its burden, was glad to lay it down. It had had two lives: that of its own private world, where the truth was always known, and that of its dissembling relations with others, including its own citizens. The communist system, the then Polish president General Jaruzelski declared in May 1990, had 'for about a dozen years' served as a 'useful vehicle for post-war reconstruction. But it soon exhausted its locomotive powers. We tried economic reforms time and again, but they always met with public resistance.' It was a brisk obituary for a political order which, under Kremlin pressure, he had defended a decade earlier with fierce rhetoric and the stiff-backed imposition of martial law. 'The end, however lofty it may be,' announced Vadim Medvedev, the last ideology chief of the Soviet Communist Party, in London in February 1990, 'cannot justify any means to achieve it.'

Attempts to falsify the truth continued to the last. Petar Mladenov, Zhivkov's 'reform communist' successor as president of Bulgaria, was overheard declaring, during an anti-government demonstration by the democratic opposition in Sofia in December 1989, that 'the tanks had better move in.' A video with sound-track, which caught these words, he at first described by reflex as a 'primitive and slanderous montage', before admitting its authenticity and resigning in July 1990. His resignation was described as a 'victory for the truth' by the opposition. As the air-brushed 'blank spots' in Soviet and East European history began to be filled in, and the Soviet imperium's labour camps and mass graves – at Katyn, at Kharkov, at Schmachtenhagen, twenty miles north of Berlin, and other places – began to be opened, not even 'glasnost' could admit the scale of what had occurred. 'Thousands of people', declared Gorbachev, in August 1990, of the millions of victims of Stalinism, 'were subject to moral and physical torture. Many of them' – that is, many of the 'thousands' – 'were annihilated'.

But as the truth began to prevail, it was recalled how, at the height of the 900-day wartime siege of Leningrad by the Germans, the city authorities had restored the pre-revolutionary names of many streets and squares in order to raise the citizens' morale. Todor Zhivkov, at his trial in Sofia in February 1991, jocularly admitted that he had 'never read' large swathes of his bogus thirty-nine-volume *Collected Works*. 'Now that I am a pensioner,' he said, laughing out loud in court, 'maybe I'll read all my books.' For decades, he had hectored the frightened Bulgarian intelligentsia on the virtues of 'scientific materialism' and its methods; he was revealed to have been himself under the daily influence of astrologers and clairvoyants. In the 'workers' republics', it was also plain, statistics of herculean productive achievement had been sedulously falsified for years. Romanian cereal production, for instance, was discovered to have been only 'one quarter' of what it had been said to be, while 'Comrade-Academician Doctor-Engineer' Elena Ceausescu was found to have had only four years of primary education, her scientific papers on polymer chemistry written for her by others.

With the dawning of the light, the true facts of the Chernobyl disaster were disclosed. Similarly, Eduard Shevardnadze revealed (in Moscow's *Literary Gazette* in April 1991) something of the pressure brought to bear on the Kremlin to use force in order to try to halt the anti-communist revolutions in Eastern Europe. Disclosure came, too, of East Germany's funding and training in 'intelligence and military matters' – for instance, at Bad Duben near Leipzig – of Iraqi, Libyan, Palestinian and Syrian agents, among others. Members of West Germany's Red Army Fraction were also trained and given sanctuary in the then German Democratic Republic, under the supervision of the ministry of state security. Czechoslovakia and Hungary were similarly involved. Straining credulity, and often swiftly concealed, there were fleeting glimpses, too, of West German firms trafficking in arms with South Africa through East German state officials; of Ceausescu's brothers selling Soviet military secrets and equipment, including mobile rocket-launchers and radar equipment, to the United States. Conversely, from 1983, the American government-funded National Endowment for Democracy, always described as a 'private foundation', was shown to have aided Polish Solidarity, the Czech Charter 77, nationalist groups in the Baltic states, and Lech Walesa's 1990 presidential campaign.

The 'last word' on none of these matters has been, or ever could be, spoken, and every species of Pascalian anxiety about the ways in which the world is governed remains. But in a political darkness teeming with falsehood, half-truth and truth, a brief light – the light of reason – shone, as communism, mutant heir of the Enlightenment, fell. Imposition upon hand and brain was lifted, and there was light. Freely expressed wishes, however perversely expressed (for some), displaced 'revolutionary truth' and Party falsehood. In this new light of 'normality' every kind of Pascalian 'abscess' could be seen forming, and no one might know what the next day would bring. Some felt Abraham's horror of further 'great darkness' to come, others that justice and truth had been vindicated and a great work done. Jews, the universal citizen-strangers, belonged to one camp and the other; but most, as ever, to both together.

INDEX